The Somme Campaign

The Somme Campaign

Andrew Rawson

Pen & Sword
MILITARY

First published in Great Britain by
PEN AND SWORD MILITARY
an imprint of
Pen and Sword Books Ltd
47 Church Street
Barnsley
South Yorkshire S70 2AS

Copyright © Andrew Rawson 2014

ISBN 978 1 78303 051 4

Printed and bound in England by
CPI Group (UK) Ltd, Croydon, CR0 4YY

Typeset in Times by CHIC GRAPHICS

Pen & Sword Books Ltd incorporates the imprints of
Pen & Sword Books Ltd incorporates the imprints of Pen & Sword
Archaeology, Atlas, Aviation, Battleground, Discovery,
Family History, History, Maritime, Military, Naval, Politics,
Railways, Select, Social History, Transport, True Crime, and
Claymore Press, Frontline Books, Leo Cooper, Praetorian Press,
Remember When, Seaforth Publishing and Wharncliffe.

For a complete list of Pen and Sword titles please contact
Pen and Sword Books Limited
47 Church Street, Barnsley, South Yorkshire, S70 2AS, England
E-mail: enquiries@pen-and-sword.co.uk
Website: www.pen-and-sword.co.uk

Contents

Regimental Abbreviations

Regiments in Alphabetical Order	Abbreviations Used
Argyll & Sutherland Highlanders Regiment	Argylls
Bedfordshire Regiment	Bedfords
Black Watch Regiment	Black Watch
Border Regiment	Borders
Buffs (East Kent) Regiment	Buffs
Cambridgeshire Regiment	Cambridge or Cambridgeshires
Cameron Highlanders Regiment	Camerons
Cameronians (Scottish Rifles) Regiment	Scottish Rifles
Cheshire Regiment	Cheshires
Coldstream Guards	Coldstreamers
Connaught Rangers	Connaughts
Devonshire Regiment	Devons
Dorsetshire Regiment	Dorsets
Duke of Cornwall's Light Infantry	DCLI
Duke of Wellington's (West Riding) Regiment	Duke's
Durham Light Infantry	Durhams
East Lancashire Regiment	East Lancashires
East Surrey Regiment	East Surreys
East Yorkshire Regiment	East Yorkshires
Essex Regiment	Essex
Green Howards (Yorkshire) Regiment	Green Howards
Gloucestershire Regiment	Gloucesters
Gordon Highlanders	Gordons
Grenadier Guards	Grenadiers
Hampshire Regiment	Hampshires
Herefordshire Regiment	Herefords
Hertfordshire Regiment	Hertfords
Highland Light Infantry	HLI
Honourable Artillery Company	HAC
Irish Guards	Irish Guards
King's (Liverpool) Regiment	King's
King's Own (Royal Lancaster) Regiment	King's Own
King's Own Scottish Borderers	KOSBs
King's (Shropshire Light Infantry) Regiment	KSLIs
King's Own (Yorkshire Light Infantry) Regiment	KOYLIs
King's Royal Rifle Corps	KRRC

Lancashire Fusiliers	Lancashire Fusiliers
Leicestershire Regiment	Leicesters
Lincolnshire Regiment	Lincolns
London Regiment	Londoners
Loyal North Lancashire Regiment	Loyals
Leinster Regiment	Leinsters
Manchester Regiment	Manchesters
Middlesex Regiment	Middlesex
Monmouthshire Regiment	Monmouths
Norfolk Regiment	Norfolks
Northamptonshire Regiment	Northants
North Staffordshire Regiment	North Staffords
Northumberland Fusiliers	Northumberland Fusiliers
Oxford and Buckinghamshire Light Infantry	Ox and Bucks
Queen's (Royal West Surrey) Regiment	Queen's
Queen's Own (Royal West Kent) Regiment	Queen's Own
Rifle Brigade	Rifle Brigade
Royal Berkshire Regiment	Berkshires
Royal Dublin Fusiliers	Dublin Fusiliers
Royal Fusiliers	Royal Fusiliers
Royal Inniskilling Fusiliers	Inniskilling Fusiliers
Royal Irish Fusiliers	Irish Fusiliers
Royal Irish Regiment	Irish Regiment
Royal Irish Rifles	Irish Rifles
Royal Munster Fusiliers	Munster Fusiliers
Royal Newfoundland Regiment	Newfoundlanders
Royal Scots Regiment	Royal Scots
Royal Scots Fusiliers	Scots Fusiliers
Royal Sussex Regiment	Sussex
Royal Warwickshire Regiment	Warwicks
Royal Welsh Fusiliers	Welsh Fusiliers
Scots Guards	Scots Guards
Seaforth Highlanders	Seaforths
Sherwood Foresters (Notts and Derbyshire)	Sherwoods
Somerset Light Infantry	Somersets
South Lancashire Regiment	South Lancashires
South Staffordshire Regiment	South Staffords
South Wales Borderers	Borderers
Suffolk Regiment	Suffolks
Welsh Regiment	Welsh
Welsh Guards	Welsh Guards
West Yorkshire Regiment	West Yorkshires
Wiltshire Regiment	Wiltshires
Worcestershire Regiment	Worcesters
York and Lancaster Regiment	York and Lancasters

Introduction

Another book on the 1916 Somme campaign I hear you say as you pick a copy off the shelf or browse the internet. Surely there are enough out there already? What does this one tell me that the others do not? Well, some concentrate on the politics, some on just the opening day, some on the German view and some on the personal experiences of the men who fought and died. This one concentrates on the British Army's experience during the five and a half month long campaign.

In my experience books on the Somme campaign follow a similar structure. The first third of the narrative concentrates on the build up to the campaign, covering the politics and raising of the divisions, particularly the New Army divisions. The second third focuses on the disastrous first day on 1 July when the British Army suffered over 57,000 casualties; the highest number in one day in the Army's history. The final third of the book covers the remaining 141 days of the campaign and a fair amount of that is devoted to the arrival of the tank on the battlefield on 15 September. So the narratives have an unequal balance which focuses on gallant failures rather than some of the heroic successes which came later.

This book does have large sections on 1 July and 15 September because they were major battles. But it also has large sections on the other significant battles, such as the 14 July, 25 September and 13 November. It also covers all the medium-sized actions to clear tactical points such as woods and villages down to the small actions to capture individual trenches. They all get the same treatment.

One omission is the Battle of Fromelles on 19/20 July. While First Army's unsuccessful attack falls within the timeframe and was supposed to divert attention from the Somme, it did not. So it did not influence Fourth Army's attacks against High Wood, Delville Wood and Guillemont. There are books dedicated to the battle if you have an interest in it and they are listed in the suggested reading list.

The information came from many sources. The backbone of the narrative was created from the Official History, the two Somme volumes forming part of the twenty-eight volume series complied by Brigadier General Sir James Edmonds. The first volume was printed in 1932 and it covers the background the battle, including the politics, planning and preparations. It also narrates the fateful first day of the campaign. The second volume was printed six months later and it covers the rest of the campaign, ending on 19 November. It also includes a series of controversial conclusions on the conduct of the campaign and the casualties.

The Pen and Sword Battleground series of books, which are part narrative and part travel guide, has over a dozen volumes dedicated to the 1916 Somme campaign. The quality of information inside the books varies from the minimum to an overwhelming amount of detail, but they all contribute something. They also helped to confirm, or in some cases contradict, the Official History. I say contradict because the official version often smoothed over the reasons why attacks failed by omitting the mistakes, problems or pure bad luck which prevented success.

The same goes for the divisional histories and regimental histories, the majority of which were printed on behalf of the units before the Official History was published. Their quality varies enormously with some giving the bare details of a unit's accomplishments while others are virtually a copy of the daily unit War Diary. But most provided more interesting detail than the Official History. They usually gave explanations of what went right and what went wrong although, naturally, units tend to blame the actions of others, rather than their own.

Virtually all the regimental and divisional histories can be accessed for an annual or individual fee at the http://www.militaryarchive.co.uk/. You can also access medal rolls, army orders, army lists and get assistance with the location of biographical details, awards and photographs of individuals. Joining the archive gave me prolonged access to all this for the same cost of a day visiting the London archives. If you are interesting in printed histories and medal rolls this is the website for you.

Having checked the Official History and the printed histories, you are right to ask why did I not consult the war diaries in the National Archives held at Kew, London. In my experience they often do not tell you much about a battalion's experience on the day of battle but they tell you plenty about what happened in the quiet times in between. The reason is the war diarist is fully occupied on the day of battle, both physically and emotionally. But sometimes material you would expect to find is missing because it has been removed or lost.

The main reasons I did not consult the war diaries were time and the word count. It would have taken weeks to go through several hundred battalion war diaries. Then there would be the brigade and division diaries because they often provide more information about the planning, execution and aftermath of a battle than the battalion diaries. The word count had also risen above the acceptable limit by the time I had worked through the printed books and I was facing having to reduce it rather than increase it. I did consider splitting the book into two halves, the first covering from 1 July to 14 September and the second from the 15 September tank battle through to the end of the campaign on 19 November. However, I was assured a double volume set would not appeal to readers; it would be too big.

As an author you often have to judge at what level of detail to pitch your narrative. Too shallow and the reader will not learn anything new; too deep and the reader will become overwhelmed with details. So I admit that this book is not an exhaustive account of the Somme campaign, but it is a comprehensive one which goes further than others across the whole campaign. Maybe one day someone will do an exhaustive account; I wish them luck because it is a huge subject.

Another decision I took was to buck the Army trend of describing deployments and events from right to left. We read text and look at maps from left to right. So I chose to write the narrative from left to right unless the sequence of events dictated otherwise.

One thing I hope will help you understand the campaign is the inclusion of many maps, nearly ninety of them. The line goes 'a picture is worth a thousand words' and I believe the same goes for maps. Time after time in military books we read page after page of battle accounts with only a single small-scale map to help; and it does not help. My inspiration was Noah Trudeau's book *A Testing of Courage* about Gettysburg in the American Civil War. I had read several books and watched numerous documentaries on this huge three-day battle but I was still confused as to what went on. Trudeau's book changed that because it had a clear large-scale map every few pages, illustrating the development of the day-by-day actions, often over the same ground. It helped me understand the unfolding battle when I visited Gettysburg.

I wanted to do the same for the Somme. While the Official History maps are sometimes cited as good examples, the level of detail and clarity diminishes rapidly over the course of the campaign. Some maps are small scale, some cover many days' fighting and some are devoid of all but the main terrain features. The overriding theme with the maps seemed to be inconsistency, leading to confusion as you read the text.

I chose to create a map for each corps on each occasion there was an attack with a gain or loss of ground. Only a few which did not work geographically use two maps to cover a corps action. A section of trench map was used as the topographical background because they are well known to anyone with an interest in the First World War. Their grid system is a standard size of 1,000 yards (914 metres) for each large square and 100 yards (91 metres) for each minor graduation. The main advantage of using a trench map is that the terrain is virtually the same today as it was a century ago. Contours, roads, watercourses and woods have not altered while villages have changed little; only the trenches have gone. It means the maps can be used to help visitors to the Somme battlefield locate the places they want to find.

The symbols have been kept as simple as possible. Front lines before the battle commences are marked in solid lines while ground captured is marked by a line of dots. When only the front line trench was taken a dotted line replaces the solid line but there should be no confusion because no man's land is always easy to identify. Occasionally a deployment line is marked by a line of small diamond shaped dots. Occasionally ground temporarily taken, particularly on 1 July, is marked by a dashed line.

The position of each division is marked and the positions of the brigades are marked, either at zero hour or at the conclusion of the attack, sometimes both; whichever I felt appropriate. Why did I not plot the position of the battalions at zero hour like some maps do? Because battalion labels would clutter the maps and obscure important topographical information. Battalions usually leapfrogged each other every few hundred yards and it would be impossible to chart their progress on maps of this scale. You only have to look at the Official History maps covering 1 July to experience the sort of confusion I wanted to avoid. So while a compromise has been made, I hope you will find it an agreeable one. By reading the text and checking the maps together, it is quite easy to estimate a battalion's position.

As stated earlier this is not a comprehensive study of the campaign. So what is not included? There is no talk of politics and little opinion on the relationship between the War Office and GHQ. The same goes for the relationship between General Haig, Field Marshal Joffre and General Foch. But there are explanations about the meetings between the British and the French and their objectives, and discussion about compromises over the dates and zero hours of attack and the problems affecting them. There is also little information on the German units involved in the battles but there is information on their defensive arrangements and their impact on the British attacks.

Accounts on the Somme campaign usually study the qualities of the New Army divisions which were raised by cities and towns following the outbreak of war. They make out that it was their baptism of fire and that they were very different from other divisions. But were they? For a start the first batch of New Army Divisions had participated in the Battle of Loos nine months earlier, some successfully, others not so.

The Regular Army divisions had been in action for nearly two years and they had all experienced heavy casualties. Their replacements, many of who joined during the 1914 campaign, were reservists recalled from civilian life. They had little refresher training and were often older men than the volunteers for the New Army divisions. The Territorial Force divisions were also raised in towns and cities and the original 'Terriers' had trained together for years before heading to France and Belgium. Only a few had seen action and they too had been reinforced by replacements.

For these reasons I did not include a background to the New Army divisions; after 1 July they were handled the same as the Regular Army and Territorial Force divisions. After all, this is a study of the entire campaign.

You will not find narratives from personal diaries, letters or printed histories in the narrative either. The ones you often read have a similarly depressing theme of mud, blood and a desire to be somewhere else and the ones with the bleakest outlook are usually chosen to set the soberest tone as the norm. The few quotes given were chosen for their eloquence in writing, their pride in the men's determination and their dark humour.

There are few mentions of casualties unless they were disproportionately high or low. I felt it served little purpose to keep reeling off the numbers after each action. Records are also incomplete so it would be inappropriate to mention some units and not others. Casualties were always high and both sides suffered.

I did consider listing the grave locations of those named in the text, however, a sample study illustrated it was not practical in a way I had hoped. Many of those named survived the war while equally as many survived the Somme only to die later on, maybe at Arras, Ypres, or during the huge 1918 campaigns. Around one third of the casualties have no known grave and their names are on the Thiepval Memorial. A large number of those who have known graves are not buried in their original location. Their remains were moved during the post-war clear up in which many small cemeteries were closed and the graves moved to the large concentration cemeteries. Finally, we have those who died of their wounds. They were either buried behind the lines by the dressing stations and casualty clearing stations, near the coast at one of the base hospitals, or in the United Kingdom having been sent home to. The bottom line was very few casualties were buried close to their place of death.

So what will you find in the text? You will find plenty of information on the reasoning behind each battle and the objectives. There is discussion on artillery bombardments, tactics, zero hours, the terrain and an attempt to understand the successes and failures of each attack. Where possible the men who made a difference are mentioned, the men who led the assault companies and bombing teams, those who cut the wire and led the survivors into the German trenches, those who stopped the counter-attacks and those awarded the Victoria Cross.

The British Army faced many tactical problems, some natural, some man-made, and they had to devise ways to solve them. The only way to overcome them was to try and learn from their mistakes and the narrative illustrates how. Then try again and again until the attack succeeded or the Germans withdrew. The staff, the artillery, the infantry, the engineers and Royal Flying Corps all had a part to play in learning their own lessons and then co-ordinating new ideas.

The problem was it took casualties, thousands of them, to discover the errors and solve the problems and the next division in line did not always appreciate the solutions, despite efforts from the corps headquarters. But the cadre of survivors kept trying and they kept teaching the replacements. One thing that became clear was that all commanders from company up to divisional and corps did not blindly follow orders. They suggested ideas and questioned orders and sometimes their superior officers took note and amended their instructions.

Two important things become apparent as you read the narrative. The first is that it was extremely difficult to organise the successful assault and consolidation of a position during 1916, far more difficult than defending one. The second is that everyone, from the company commanders to the corps commanders, strived to get it right with success and lives at stake. They also made changes and tried new techniques and tactics to improve their chances of success. One thing is sure: mistakes were recognised and learnt from throughout the campaign.

So much had to be arranged and done and so much could go wrong or, in some cases, pure bad luck intervened. The co-ordination of the infantry advance and the artillery bombardment had to be carried out with precision if the attack was to stand any chance of success. Very often there were problems, but lessons were learned and solutions tried.

It had been a few years since I had last visited the Somme and while there have been developments to accommodate visitors at the main sites, like Beaumont Hamel and Thiepval, the area has hardly changed. It is still peaceful and still thought provoking, whether you are there on a sunny day like 1 July 1916 or a wet autumn night like the later battles. If you have not been, I recommend you do; you will not regret the experience.

I would like to thank David and Julie Thomson for looking after me while I stayed at 'Number 56' in La Boisselle, a 'bed and breakfast oasis on the Somme' during my Western Front research trips – a great place to base yourself and great people to spend time with.

It is seven years since I wrote about the First World War and I enjoyed the return to this fascinating period of history. Researching the events of the summer and autumn of 1916 has fulfilled a long-standing ambition: to increase my understanding of the campaign. I was fascinated writing about the Battles of the Somme and I hope you enjoy reading about them.

Chapter 1

Planning the Offensive

Background

Fourth Army's General Sir Henry Rawlinson met General Ferdinand Foch, commander of the French Northern Army Group, and Sixth Army's General Émile Fayolle on 30 April and 8 May and they agreed the boundary between the two armies would be a mile north of the River Somme. On 16 May the British General Headquarters[1] confirmed the decision to attack on the Somme had been made and the front would be twice as wide the Loos offensive had been the previous September. But this time Fourth Army would have double the reserves, twice as many guns and a huge reserve of ammunition. GHQ's only doubt was that the French would be unable to take part due to their commitments at Verdun.

The following day Rawlinson outlined the objectives to his corps commanders. They would advance to a line stretching from Serre in the north, through Pozières to Montauban. The three left-hand corps would then form a defensive flank while General Hubert Gough would take over the two right-hand corps and advance to Ginchy and Guillemont.

On 27 May the commander-in-chief of the British Army, General Sir Douglas Haig warned Rawlinson that Second Army was preparing to attack seventy-five miles north of the Somme, at Messines Ridge, south of Ypres, and he was not sure which army would attack first. First Army and Third Army would also create a diversion by digging trenches and gun emplacements; they would then fire artillery barrages three days before the main attack, finally releasing gas and smoke while making raids.

On 29 May Haig warned the Chief of the Imperial General Staff, General Sir William Robertson, and Rawlinson that the campaign would have to be a wearing-out battle rather than a breakthrough battle if the French could not take part. He also told them the forthcoming battle would leave the Allies in a good position for a campaign the following spring.

While the date for the Somme offensive was set for 1 July, only two days later instructions were drafted for Gough's transfer, complete with

---

1 General Sir Douglas Haig's General Headquarters (GHQ).

Fourth Army's front, north of the River Somme.

divisions and heavy batteries to Second Army, if Fourth Army met 'very considerable opposition before it captured the first objectives'. Haig also warned Fourth Army that GHQ's reserve might have to be sent north to Second Army.

On 11 June the commander-in-chief of the French Army, General Joseph Joffre asked Haig if the offensive could be brought forward to 25 June. Rawlinson and his corps commanders thought it was achievable but the timings would be tight. The last battery would be in position on 16 June and the wire-cutting started four days later; the last division would arrive on the 19th. However, speeding up the delivery of the ammunition upset the transport timetable and labour arrangements. It meant the bombardment had to start on 24 June with the assault starting five days later. Foch later asked for a two-day postponement but Haig refused.

There were also compromises over the time for zero hour. Rawlinson wanted 7am but Foch wanted 9am, so their spotters could observe the final part of the barrage. It was set at 7.30am and although the French later asked for it to be put back another hour, Haig refused.

On 12 June Rawlinson discussed the final details of the plan. It had become more ambitious with all five corps advancing together with the army's left on Miraumont and Martinpuich and the right on Ginchy and Flers. Fourth Army issued its artillery programme and operation order two days later.

On 16 June Haig explained his plan. He wanted the attack to be 'pressed eastwards far enough to enable our cavalry to push through into the open country beyond the enemy's prepared lines of defence. Our object then will be to turn northwards, taking the enemy's lines in flank and reverse, the bulk of the cavalry operating on the outer flank of this movement, whilst detachments should be detailed to cover the movement from any offensive of the enemy from the east.'

The 1st and 3rd Cavalry Divisions would advance to Bapaume under Gough and then head north behind the German lines, once the infantry had relieved them. While Rawlinson discussed the cavalry's role at the final corps commanders' conference on 22 June, Haig still had the Messines area in mind. He believed the cavalry could be transferred to Second Army if they could not be used on the Somme.

Rawlinson also discussed the likely German reaction to the Somme attack. GHQ intelligence believed there were thirty German battalions[2] facing Fourth Army while another sixty-five could reach the battlefield in six days. Rawlinson finally made it clear that the New Army troops were not as disciplined or well trained as regular troops and steps would have to be taken to make them reorganise after capturing each position.

The Royal Flying Corps (RFC)

The RFC had to dominate the skies over the battlefield so observation planes could spot targets for the artillery and chart the infantry's progress. GHQ had 9th Wing and 21st, 27th and 60th Squadrons and two flights of 70th Squadron would attack German planes. Fourth Army had two of 14th Wing's squadrons while 3rd, 4th, 9th and 15th Squadrons from 3rd Wing were split between the five corps.

2 Or two divisions and eight battalions.

Each corps had two contact aeroplanes and one would drop messages and marked up maps at corps headquarters while the other transmitted wireless messages. Each corps had one aeroplane spotting targets for the heavy howitzers while two more searched for German batteries. Sixteen planes worked on close reconnaissance and destructive bombardment missions while nine worked on the destruction of kite balloons and photography. Number 1 Kite Balloon Squadron was split between the five corps while an extra balloon section was allotted to VIII, X and XV Corps.

Third Army had eighteen of 8th Squadron's aeroplanes and a Kite Balloon Section to cover the Gommecourt salient. In total the RFC's 185 aeroplanes outnumbered the German air service. Bombers would bomb troop billets, transport, ammunition dumps and headquarters and hit the railways to delay reinforcements.

Preparations

Fourth Army's preparations followed the memorandum written by the Chief of the General Staff, General Sir Launcelot Kiggell, called 'Preparatory Measures to be taken in Armies and Corps before undertaking Offensive Operations on a Large Scale'. It was split into three categories:

Front Line Measures
• Reconnaissance and intelligence
• Artillery preparations, battery positions and observation posts
• Organising and improving trenches and command posts
• Front line communications and signalling
• Training and deployment of the infantry, cavalry, machine-guns,
   engineers
• Reinforcements and deployment of reserves

Rear Area Measures
• Aircraft and anti-aircraft arrangements
• Rear area communications
• Ammunition dumps, water, depots and stores
• Road control, transport, railways, police arrangements
• Medical, veterinary, remounts, collection of stores, casualties, billeting

Post Battle Measures
• Clearing the battlefield and re-equipping

The Medical Arrangements

Heavy casualties were anticipated and the injured would be divided into five categories; the dead, those unlikely to survive, those to be discharged, those needing a long convalescence and those needing a short rest.

The battalion stretcher-bearers picked up the injured from the battlefield and carried them to the regimental aid posts where the Royal Army Medical Corps took over. The divisional field ambulances set up thirty-nine advanced dressing stations, nineteen main dressing stations and nine walking wounded centres to administer emergency first aid and assess the wounded. They also set up rest centres where men could have a short break before returning to their unit.

There were eight pairs of casualty clearing stations (CCSs), one for serious injuries and one for light injuries, as well as two advanced operating centres behind the Somme front. Motor ambulances carried the severely wounded, while lorries and buses carried the lightly wounded. The CCSs carried out emergency treatment and all but one camped next to a railway siding so ambulance trains could carry patients to the coast. Those who needed a short rest were taken to convalescent centres and, when ready, put though a physical exercise programme. Those who were going to be discharged or needed prolonged treatment were taken to England on hospital ships on the Le Havre to Southampton route. They were then taken by train to a hospital, usually one near their home.

Tactical Preparations

Rawlinson wanted assembly trenches digging 200 metres from the enemy front line, to reduce the width of no man's land, but some corps commanders objected because it would warn the Germans.[3] The commanders were allowed to decide and while some divisions dug new trenches, many were not as close as Rawlinson desired. The majority of assault troops would instead move into no man's land during the final stage of the bombardment, ready to advance at zero hour.

The Infantry

On 8 May GHQ issued a memorandum on 'Training of Divisions for Offensive Action' and it raised concerns about the New Army divisions.

> 'The officers and troops generally do not now possess that military knowledge arising from a long and high state of training which enables them to act promptly on sound lines in unexpected situations. They have become accustomed to deliberate action based on precise and detailed orders. Officers and men in action will usually do what they have been practised to do, or have been told to do in certain situations, and it is therefore the more necessary to

---

3 As if the prolonged barrage was not enough warning.

ensure that a close understanding should exist among all ranks as to what action is to be taken in different situations that may arise in battle.'

While GHQ wanted the infantry to practise, they did not have time to practise and there were insufficient instructors to teach them, so they were issued definite instructions instead. The accepted rule of thumb in the attack was that a single line failed, two lines generally failed, three lines generally succeeded and four lines succeeded. The attack orders called for an advance 'in successive lines, each line adding fresh impetus to the preceding one when this is checked, and carrying the whole forward to the objective'. While Haig raised the question of advancing in small detachments during a conference on 15 June, Allenby,[4] Rawlinson and Gough wanted a uniform advance in waves so the German machine-guns could not concentrate on isolated groups.

The memorandum reminded divisions to practise passing waves through each other so fresh troops could continue the advance, a practice known as 'leap frogging'. They had to guard against crowding the assault columns and to consider how they could provide mutual support. It also warned divisions to allocate enough troops for 'the clearing up and consolidation of a position passed over by the assaulting columns', a process known as 'mopping up'. Emphasis was put on officers to pass back information and conserve reserves. Finally, the memorandum stated: 'troops must push on at all costs till the final objective is reached and all must be prepared for heavy casualties'.

While GHQ did not have a training section, Fourth Army issued a booklet of tactical notes to all officers down to captain level on 17 May. The infantry would advance in lines 100 metres apart with men at two or three pace intervals while 'the ideal [was] for the artillery to keep their fire immediately in front of the infantry... battering down all opposition with a hurricane of projectiles'. The artillery set the pace as 'experience has shown the only safe method of artillery support during an advance is a fixed time-table of lifts to which both the infantry and artillery must rigidly conform'.

But there were no special instructions for the inexperienced New Army soldiers; there was no mention of crossing no man's land at a good pace; there was no mention of co-operating with or helping other units; there was no mention made of bypassing strongpoints and exploiting breakthroughs. While the corps commanders were left to decide how to achieve their objectives, Haig and Rawlinson visited units to discuss training and preparations.

---

4 Lieutenant General Edmund Allenby, Third Army.

The Artillery
There had been a few changes in artillery tactics since the offensive at Loos in September 1915. The artillery had to deal with the German artillery before it could concentrate on the targets facing the infantry. Fourth Army prepared the artillery plan (the first issued in the British Army) and then the corps developed their own programmes from it. Each corps allotted batteries to Heavy Artillery Groups, creating mixed groups ready to deal with all types of targets. Fourth Army issued a daily 'Active Hostile Battery List' during the bombardment and each corps filed a progress report so it could be updated.

Flash-spotting and sound-ranging were in their infancy during the summer of 1916. Flash-spotting involved observers noting the time and direction to a gun flash. The results were compared and the gun battery position was estimated by trigonometry. Sound-ranging used low frequency microphones to estimate the range to batteries. While there were daily supplies of RFC photographs, the art of reading them was in its infancy. Estimating adjustments for wind and atmospheric conditions was also in its early days. But the best way was for the spotter planes to find targets and then adjust a battery's fire for maximum effect.

The Bombardment
The preliminary bombardment was planned for five days, U, V, W, X and Y-Day, with the infantry assault on Z-Day. The first two days were dedicated to registration while the destructive bombardment would last three days. On 20 and 21 June Haig asked Rawlinson about shortening the preliminary bombardment to three days, to reduce the wear and tear to the guns and to conserve ammunition, but there was no change.

The heavy guns and howitzers targeted trenches, strongpoints, machine-gun posts and observation posts by day and billets, roads and tracks at night. There was also plenty of counter-battery work. Heavy trench mortars hit villages and strongpoints while 2-inch mortars and Stokes mortars targeted the front trenches. Wire cutting operations by the field guns and 2-inch mortars covered all five days. The 18-pounders targeted villages and woods while the 4.5-inch howitzers hit communication trenches and machine-gun emplacements; in many cases their shells were not heavy enough to silence them.

The bombardment programme was carried out in two-hour periods with eighty minutes of shelling and forty minutes standing down time to rest the crews and let the guns cool. The bombardment on Z-Day was only going to be sixty-five minutes long in the hope of fooling the Germans. The culmination of the bombardment would be signalled by an intense barrage on the enemy front trenches while the infantry crept into no man's land. At zero hour the guns would lengthen their range to the next trench and the infantry would advance.

Both Haig and Rawlinson made it clear the artillery set the speed of the advance and Rawlinson told his corps commanders 'nothing could exist at the conclusion of the bombardment in the area covered by it'. While the barrage would provide protection for the infantry, it was a very rigid affair with each battery working to a timetable, firing on a definite lane from zero hour through to the final objective. Artillery commanders could not change targets, even if the infantry commander asked them to do so. Forward observing officers (FOOs) would go forward with the assault troops to report progress and artillery liaison officers and infantry brigadiers could then discuss changes. But while each battery had its own observation posts (OPs), they were a long way from the front line. Any order to shorten the barrage range had to come from corps headquarters and even then, new bombardments would only be thirty minutes long.

Fourth Army had one field gun every twenty-one metres and one heavy gun every fifty-seven metres along the 25,000 metre front:

- Field artillery (1010): 808 18-pounders and 202 4-5-inch howitzers
- Heavy guns (182): 32 4.7-inch, 128 60-pounders, 20 6-inch, 1 9.2-inch and 1 12-inch
- Heavy howitzers (245): 104 6-inch, 64 8-inch, 60 9.2-inch, 11 12-inch and 6 15-inch
- French guns (40): 16 220mm howitzers and 24 French 120 mm guns[5]

But many of the 4.7-inch guns and 6-inch howitzers were obsolete while only a few of the 6-inch howitzers could fire 10,000 metres.[6] The 8-inch howitzers were re-bored coastal guns with shortened barrels and they had a range of 10,000 metres. Fourth Army also had 288 medium and 28 heavy trench mortars supplied with 800,000 rounds of ammunition and 35,000 smoke bombs.

The ammunition began arriving on 8 June and deliveries increased when it was believed Z-Day might be moved forward. After a herculean effort, the forward dumps and railhead stocks were ready by 20 June. Fourth Army's main ammunition allotments were:

18-pounders, 2,600,000	4-5-inch howitzers, 260,000
6-inch howitzers, 100,000	15-inch howitzers, 3,000

---

5 Sixty 75mm guns were also used to fire gas shell.
6 The old pattern 6-inch guns only had a range of 6,500 metres.

Fourth Army fired 1,732,873 rounds in eight days, and while that was nearly seventy rounds for every metre of front, the figure is not so impressive when you consider the final objective was sometimes 1,500 metres away. It is even less impressive when you consider only 600,000 shells were larger than 4.5-inch; only twenty-four heavy shells for every metre of front. The daily allocation of rounds was:

- Target Registration: 138,118 rounds on 24 June and 188,881 rounds on 25 June
- Initial Bombardment: 211,886 rounds on 26 June and 235,887 rounds on 27 June
- Extended Bombardment:[7] 168,363 rounds on 28 June and 189,757 rounds on 29 June
- Final Bombardment: 375,760 rounds on 30 June and 224,221 rounds on 1 July

The Day by Day Bombardment
There were heavy rainstorms on 24 June and while the wire-cutting and shelling of the trenches began, the counter-battery work could not start until evening. After dusk the bombardment of billets, roads and tracks began but gas releases were cancelled due to a lack of wind. When 25 June dawned clear the registration began in earnest, with over 100 German batteries engaged, and several ammunition dumps were hit.

June 26 was showery and the destructive bombardment began with the heaviest period between 9am and 10.20am. A cease-fire was called at 3.30pm so observation planes could assess the damage. The wire cutting was going badly so the 18-pounders were allowed to fire an extra 400-500 rounds per day but shrapnel was still not the ideal ordnance. June 27 was misty and then heavy showers stopped aerial observation. While the number of rounds were increased, they could not compensate for observed fire.

The weather did not improve and a two-day postponement was agreed on the morning of 28 June; the extra days would be called Y1 and Y2 while the new Z-Day would be 1 July. But the extension meant Fourth Army had to economize on heavy gun and howitzer ammunition. Future bombardments would be weaker and part of Fourth Army's ammunition reserve would be used.

The weather brightened up on 29 June and the observer planes resumed their work. Clear skies prevailed the following day and 171 enemy batteries were spotted. The final barrages were doubled in intensity in the hope of breaking the Germans' morale.[8]

---

7 Extended due to bad weather.
8 There were premature bursts while many failed to explode; many shells fell short of their target.

The Infantry Preparations

The infantry carried out raids to test the German reaction, take prisoners and check the bombardment's damage at first hand. Four raids on the night of 25 June had mixed results; 8th Division and 34th Division reported the trenches at Ovillers and La Boisselle were full of men while 18th Division and 30th Division found few in the trenches they entered.

Three gas-cylinder companies and three smoke companies released gas and smoke at random intervals on 26 June; they discharged a lot more the following day. The German artillery responded each time and the British observers noted their locations. There were ten raids overnight and they reported on the state of the trenches and the wire; two groups of prisoners were also taken.

On 27 June Haig moved to his advanced headquarters at Chateau Valvion, Beauquesne, close to Rawlinson's at Querrieu and Gough's at Toutencourt. His first task was to order the two-day delay but while the infantry were soaked by the rain, the raids and patrols still went out during the night. Yet again some reported more activity while others reported abandoned trenches; wire damage also varied.

At noon on 28 June Fourth Army issued an order for the infantry to exploit any breakthrough and push forward while 49th and 19th Divisions would join Gough's cavalry advance. But raiding parties were finding more Germans in the trenches and they were alert, as if expecting an attack. Tensions were mounting and the Germans stood to each time smoke or gas was released. A prisoner taken near Mametz reported his comrades expected an attack although there had been no formal warnings.

More patrols were sent out the following night so as not to arouse suspicion but the Germans were on full alert. Parties also inspected the wire and cleared gaps but their reports were varied. The wire opposite XV Corps and XIII Corps had been virtually destroyed. Large gaps had been torn in other places but the troops would have to bunch up to get through. In some places, particularly on the steep slopes of the Ancre, the wire had hardly been touched.

On the morning of 30 June battalions paraded and heard messages of encouragement before the first companies marched off. The rest of the men fell in at nightfall in fighting order,[9] with their steel helmet, entrenching tool, groundsheet, water-bottle, two gas helmets and tear gas goggles, a field dressing and haversack filled with personal items. Officers and NCOs carried four flares so they could signal the contact planes.

The columns of men moved forward past dumps, picking up 220 rounds, two Mills grenades for the bombers and two sandbags. The assault

---

9 They left their packs and greatcoats behind.

companies also collected picks, shovels and wire cutters, and the consolidating companies took additional tools and sandbags. In total each man carried around sixty-six pounds (thirty kilograms), stopping him from running; it would also be difficult to climb in and out of trenches, lie down and get up.

Hundreds of columns of men marched forward guided by tapes, posts and lanterns under a moonless sky. There was little enemy artillery fire so a lot of movement was out in the open and only the final stretch was through the trenches. The first troops reached their assembly positions by 2am and the last troops were in place by 5.15am. Gaps in the wire were cleared and the jumping off tapes laid, all there was left to do was wait for zero hour.

The bombardment had smashed the wire in places, battered some trenches and destroyed various strongpoints, but by no means all of them. There was also a belief that the bombardment had seriously undermined the German infantry's resolve, but the majority were still in their deep dug-outs, uncomfortable and weary but alive. They were just waiting for the attack to begin.

At 6.25am on 1 July, the final bombardment began. At 7.25 thousands of men clambered out of their trenches, walked to their jumping off tapes in no man's land and lay down. Thousands of others waited to climb over the parapet. At 7.30 the guns lifted their range and then the waves of infantry stood up or clambered over the parapet and began the long walk towards the German front line.

Chapter 2

One Disastrous Day –
1 July

The Artillery Barrage

At zero hour the artillery's focus turned to protecting the infantry advancing across no man's land. The heavy artillery lengthened its range, lifting from trench to trench to cause last minute destruction. The 18-pounders reverted to divisional control and fired a curtain of shrapnel in front of the infantry, lengthening their range at regular intervals as they advanced. They fired on a trench, to suppress the garrison, and then lifted a short distance beyond, to catch anyone retiring. Sometimes the barrage remained stationary while the assault troops cleared the trench and sometimes it kept moving, while the assault troops kept advancing and moppers-up cleared the trench.

VII Corps was a poor relation when it came to the number and types of artillery pieces allocated to the Gommecourt salient. Each division had an open flank and two minutes before zero half of the heavy guns lifted to the next trench line while half hit the inside flanks of the first objective. The divisional 18-pounders moved forward in short lifts at zero hour and continued to the final objective. On the north side of the salient, Major General The Hon. Edward Montagu-Stuart-Wortley had made the mistake of asking the heavy artillery not to shell the first trench in front of his 46th Division because he wanted his own troops to occupy it.

VIII Corps field artillery was timed in six lifts while the heavy artillery jumped to the next objective five minutes before zero. The corps instructions show how the barrage was expected to move:

'the divisional artillery will lift 100 metres and continue lifting at the rate of 50 metres a minute to the objective, firing three rounds per gun at each step. The rate of advance of the infantry has been calculated at 50 metres a minute. Infantry must not arrive before the times shown on the map, as the artillery will still be firing on these points… The success or otherwise of the assault largely depends on the infantry thoroughly understanding the "creeping" method of the artillery.'

One big question at VIII Corps headquarters was the timing of the detonation of 40,000lbs of ammonal[10] under Hawthorn Redoubt on 29th Division's front. Lieutenant General Sir Aylmer Hunter-Weston wanted to blow the mine four hours early so his men could capture the crater before zero hour. But the Inspector of Mines reported British troops rarely won a crater battle and recommended blowing the mine at zero hour. He calculated the debris would land within 20 seconds of firing, having little effect on the advancing troops. Rawlinson disagreed and on 15 June he issued orders for all mines to be detonated in the eight minutes before zero hour. General Hunter-Weston suggested blowing the Hawthorn Ridge mine at zero minus ten minutes and Rawlinson agreed.

But the timing created a problem for the artillery. The artillery had to lift from the Hawthorn Redoubt area because British troops would be running forward to occupy it. However, VIII Corps' orders called for all of its heavy artillery to lift to the reserve trenches at 7.20am. Five minutes later all the howitzers shelling the support trench would lift to the reserve trenches. Half of 29th Division's artillery was also ordered to lift to the support line three minutes early 'to avoid a pause at zero'. The order would give the German infantry time to man their parapet.

X Corps' heavy artillery was detailed to lift in six jumps while the super-heavy guns lifted seven minutes before the others. The field artillery would make ten lifts between the trenches while the 4.5-inch howitzers hit the strongpoints. Batteries were not allowed to switch targets unless the order came from on high until after midday, while artillery officers were not allowed to accompany the infantry. The communication wires were cut early and only the observers across the Ancre remained in contact with the guns. Thiepval's machine-gun nests were a concern but two 9.2-inch howitzers detailed to destroy them were knocked out when a shell detonated prematurely inside one.

III Corps' infantry commanders were unhappy about the artillery bombardment of Ovillers and La Boisselle and a Stokes mortar battery was detailed to target the latter. The barrage would advance in eight lifts with the sixth landing north of Pozières and Contalmaison 85 minutes after zero. The plan was for the barrage to move forward two miles in 107 minutes. While the heavy artillery jumped from trench to trench, the divisional artillery moved in short lifts between them, as 34th Division's artillery officer explained: 'divisional artillery will rake back gradually to the next line'.

---

10 Nearly 17.9 tons of explosive in a tunnel under the German front trench.

XV Corps artillery orders suggested a crude creeping barrage for the attacks around Fricourt and Mametz. 'When lifting, 18-pounders should search back by increasing their range, but howitzers and heavy guns must lift directly on to the next objectives.'

The 7th Division orders made it clear the artillery barrage dictated the speed of the advance:

> 'a barrage of artillery fire will be formed in front of the infantry according to the timings shown on the tracings issued to those concerned. The lines shown on the tracings indicate the nearest points on which guns will fire up to the hour indicated. At the times shown heavy guns will lift their fire direct to the next barrage line. The divisional artillery will move their fire progressively at the rate of 50 metres a minute. Should the infantry arrive at any point before the time fixed for the barrage to lift, they will wait under the best cover available and be prepared to assault directly the lift takes place.'

Brigadier General Deverell of 20 Brigade explained how the infantry would hug the barrage:

> 'At the hour named for the barrage to lift, the leading line will be as close to the hostile position as possible, and on the barrage lifting will at once move forward steadily and only halt or lie down when next compelled to do so by awaiting the lift of the artillery barrage.'

It was the same in 21st Division's orders. 'Batteries will search back to the next barrage in order that the whole ground may be covered by fire immediately before our infantry advance over it.' Lieutenant Colonel Fitzgerald explained the creeping barrage to the 15th Durham Light Infantry as follows:

> 'The barrages will not exactly lift from one point and be put onto another; they will gradually drift forward, leaving certain lines at certain hours. The line of the barrage must be constantly watched by the infantry, whose front lines must keep close up to it.'

XIII Corps' shrapnel barrage would move 'in front of the infantry by increments of range until the final barrage is established... beyond the objective for the day'. The artillery plan also stated:

> 'The heavy artillery barrage will lift direct from one line on to the next. The field artillery barrage will creep back by short lifts... The lifts have been timed so as to allow the infantry plenty of time for the advance from one objective to the next, on the principle it is

preferable the infantry should wait for the barrage to lift than the latter should lift prematurely, and allow the enemy to man his parapets. The infantry will follow as close behind the barrage as safety permits.'

The only question was had the bombardment done its work? The infantry did not have to wait long to find out: the German machine-guns and artillery were soon opening fire.

VII Corps

Lieutenant General Sir Thomas D'Oyly Snow's corps held the trenches facing the Gommecourt Salient. Major General The Hon Edward Montagu-Stuart-Wortley's 46th Division faced the north-west side of Gommecourt while Major General Charles Hull's 56th Division would attack south-east of Gommecourt Park. They had to consolidate their outer flanks, meet in the First Switch Line and then turn back to clear Gommecourt village.

46th Division, North of Gommecourt

After ten days of hard work digging assembly trenches 139 Brigade were exhausted; it was a mistake that would be rarely repeated. The first two waves of the 1/7th and 1/5th Sherwood Foresters lost cohesion as they advanced through smoke, emerging from it half way across no man's land. They then lost heavily as they bunched up to get through the gaps in the wire. The rest of the Foresters struggled to get out of the muddy trenches and were virtually wiped out by machine-gun fire, particularly from Z and Little Z Trenches on their left flank. Parts of the fifth and sixth waves mistook their own trenches for German ones in the smoke and took shelter in them.

Rain had flooded 137 Brigade's assembly trenches and many could not be used. The 1/6th South Staffords and 1/6th North Staffords became disorientated in the smoke and then had to negotiate the gaps in the wire beyond. The first two waves were cut down by machine-gun fire while artillery fire forced the third and fourth waves to take cover in their own trenches. Only a few Staffords reached the German front trench and they were either killed or forced to retire.

The attack by 46th Division had been a disaster and only a handful of men entered the enemy trenches. The Germans emerged from their dug-outs behind the Sherwood Foresters, stopping reinforcements crossing no man's land. The Foresters ran out of bombs while the mud jammed their rifles, leaving them defenceless.

By 9am Brigadier General Williams was sure 137 Brigade's attack had failed. He was determined to renew the attack with the help of the 1/5th

Leicesters but it was impossible to get the men forward through the crowded trenches. Brigadier General Shipley wanted to reinforce 139 Brigade's foothold in the German trenches but he needed more smoke bombs to create a new screen in no man's land.

General Snow approved General Montagu-Stuart-Wortley's plan to attack again at 12.15pm but 137 Brigade was not ready. The advance was delayed until 3.30pm but the smoke screen was useless and General Shipley called off 139 Brigade's attack. In 137 Brigade's sector the 1/5th South Stafford's commander was wounded and no one else gave the signal to advance. The 1/5th North Stafford's commander reported no one else was advancing so General Williams told him to sit tight. All 46th Division could do was spend the rest of the afternoon reorganising.

Captain John Green was the medical officer with the 1/5th Sherwoods and despite being wounded, he rescued a fellow officer from the barbed wire, pulled him into a shell-hole and dressed his wounds. Green was killed while dragging the wounded officer to safety; he was awarded the Victoria Cross.

During the evening 138 Brigade took over 46th Division's front and Brigadier General Kemp incorrectly believed men were still in the German lines. Shortly after midnight the 1/5th Lincolns advanced into no man's land while the 1/5th Leicesters covered their right flank. They discovered the wire had been repaired while the Germans used flares to light up no man's land. The men lay down and waited, hoping that the Germans would settle down; they did not. Lieutenant Colonel Sandall's men suffered many casualties as they withdrew to their trenches.

56th Division, South of Gommecourt
Major Hull had 169 Brigade on the left, 168 Brigade on the right and 167 Brigade in reserve. While smoke had been released on previous days, the smoke released to cover the left flank on 1 July was much thicker and it alerted the Germans. As the leading companies formed up in no man's land, the German artillery targeted the assembly trenches.

The assault troops advanced at 7.30am and although Bangalore torpedoes[11] had blown gaps through the wire during the night, the Germans had repaired many with concertina wire. The smoke obscured the wire and many men were shot down as they searched for gaps; the survivors charged the final few metres with the cry 'London Leads!'

The 1/5th London Regiment crossed the German front trench and passed over the trenches east of Gommecourt Wood. But some Germans had been missed and they emerged from their dug-outs to shoot into the backs of Colonel Dickins' men.

---

11 Thin metal tubes were packed with explosives and pushed through the wire, several could be screwed together to get through thicker wire entanglements.

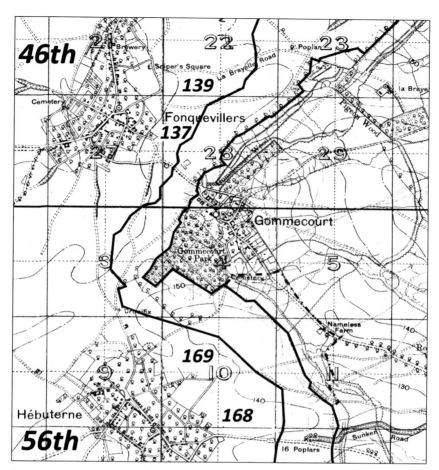

1 July, VII Corps: While 46th Division could not breach the German lines north-west of Gommecourt, 56th Division held a temporary foothold to the south-east.

    The 1/9th London Regiment were delayed by the wire but they crossed the front trench before the German machine-guns were ready. There was no news for two hours and then Captains Cox and Houghton reported three trench lines had been captured. Nearly 300 prisoners were sent back but eighty were killed by German shell-fire in no man's land; many more were held in dug-outs. Most of the bombers sent forward to capture the Quadrilateral were shot down in no man's land.

    The 1/12th London Regiment were also pinned down in no man's land in front of the wire for several hours; some were there all day. Some entered the German trenches on the right and a few advanced past Nameless Farm, never to be seen again.

The 1/14th London Regiment's left went beyond the third trench as a group of Germans emerged from dug-outs to engage the second wave but it found no trenches to take cover in and withdrew. The right of the battalion swerved right and ran into intact wire; half were shot down before the rest realized their mistake and found a gap. By 8am the German barrage had stopped all movement in no man's land and an hour later Major Lindsay withdrew the survivors to the second trench.

The failure by 46th Division on the north side of the Gommecourt salient meant the Germans could concentrate all their efforts on 56th Division and their bombers closed in while the artillery stopped reinforcements getting forward. By 1pm parties of wounded men could be seen crawling back across no man's land, while the Germans manned their parapet either side of 56th Division's foothold. Two 1/2nd London companies were ordered forward around 2pm; none made it across no man's land.

By 4pm the Germans had recaptured the second trench and by dusk only one group was left in the front trench. While the wounded were evacuated, the survivors fought on, first in the trench and then in shell-holes in no man's land. They withdrew when it was dark.

The VII Corps had suffered nearly 7,000 casualties during the attack on Gommecourt and many of the wounded were still in no man's land. The stretcher-bearers worked all night, but many injured were still waiting to be found at first light. Both sides sent out parties to collect the wounded and a large red-cross flag appeared above the trenches opposite 46th Division to signify a truce. A couple of days later a German aeroplane dropped a list of the prisoners taken; soon afterwards a British aeroplane did the same.

VIII Corps

General Hunter-Weston's VIII Corps held Fourth Army's left flank, between Serre in the north and Beaumont Hamel in the south. It had three divisions in the line. Major General Robert Wanless O'Gowan's 31st Division faced Serre, Major General the Hon William Lambton's 4th Division faced Redan Ridge and Major General Henry de Beauvoir de Lisle's 29th Division faced Hawthorn Ridge and Beaumont Hamel.

31st Division, Serre

Four copses called Matthew, Mark, Luke and John, marked 31st Division's front. On the left was 94 Brigade, 93 Brigade was on the right and 92

Brigade was in reserve. Between them they had to form a defensive flank facing north-east.

The day started badly with the German artillery causing casualties in the crowded assembly trenches. Order was restored by dawn and the first two waves formed up while Stokes mortars opened fire from saps in no man's land.

As smoke drifted across the left flank, the British heavy artillery lifted its range while half the field artillery lifted to the second line. At 7.30am the leading waves advanced while the third and fourth waves climbed out of their trenches. Machine-gun fire increased and casualties mounted as lines of men were shot down in no man's land.

The smoke screen failed to cover 94 Brigade's open flank and the 12th York and Lancasters and 11th East Lancashires were shot down as they searched for gaps in the wire. While some of the 12th York and Lancaster's left company consolidated a Russian sap across no man's land, the right company crossed the German front trench and kept advancing towards Serre. A few men from the East Lancashire's right company were seen crossing the German front line and around 100 were seen entering Serre; they were never seen again.

The Germans emerged from their dug-outs and stopped anyone else crossing no man's land. They cut off the men heading for Serre and they were all killed or captured. The 13th and 14th York and Lancasters were pinned down by German artillery in no man's land and Brigadier General Rees stopped the support companies leaving their trenches.

In 93 Brigade's sector Major Neill's 15th West Yorkshires were almost annihilated advancing into a re-entrant while Major Guyon's 16th West Yorkshires were pinned down in no man's land. Captain Ince's company of the 18th Durhams were shot down as they crossed the British trenches and only a few men crossed the German trench while fewer Durhams reached Pendant Copse. The 18th West Yorkshires followed in support but they did not get far either. General Ingles held the rest of the Durhams back to hold the line.

Around 9am Brigadier General Ingles thought the Germans were counter-attacking and he asked the artillery to reduce its range to the German front line. He was also given the 12th KOYLIs[12] to help hold 93 Brigade's trenches.[13]

By noon 31st Division's battle was over and hundreds of men, many of them wounded, were lying out in no man's land. The Germans sniped at anyone seen moving and the collection of the wounded began after dusk; it would take four nights to collect them all.

---

12 Divisional pioneer battalion.
13 92 Brigade was still in reserve with its four Hull Pals battalions.

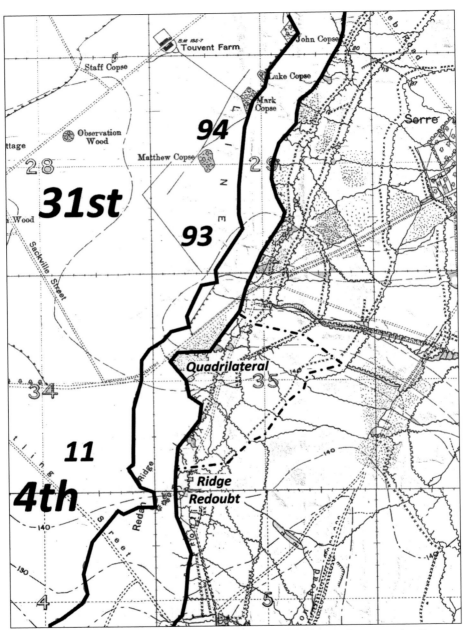

1 July, VIII Corps: 31st Division was cut down in front of the trenches protecting Serre while 4th Division held a foothold around the Quadrilateral.

4th Division, Redan Ridge

Brigadier General Prowse's 11 Brigade held all the division front with three battalions in front and three in support. Once Redan Ridge and Munich Trench had been taken, 10 and 12 Brigades would advance to the third objective. The troops were jammed in the assembly trenches which were nothing more than narrow slits dug off the communication trenches. The situation deteriorated when a burst water main flooded many trenches during the night.

At 7.20am the troops formed up in no man's land while the German machine-gun and artillery fire increased. Ten minutes later the assault waves advanced but while the wire had been cut and the trenches had been damaged, the German dug-outs were intact.

The 1/8th Royal Warwicks suffered from enfilade fire from the left and only the battalion right kept up with the 1st Rifle Brigade. The Germans planned to blow a mine if the British overran Quadrilateral Redoubt[14] but it was accidently detonated early, killing a machine-gun crew, demolishing trenches and blocking dug-outs. The Rifle Brigade advanced beyond the support trench, despite enfilade fire from Ridge Redoubt to the south. But the machine-guns south-west of Serre, where 31st Division's attack had failed, stopped the rear waves crossing no man's land.

The 1st Rifle Brigade's right and the 1st East Lancashires suffered heavy casualties from two machine-guns in Ridge Redoubt. Lieutenant Glover led some of the Rifle Brigade as far as Beaumont Trench but only two men returned. Captain Browne led a few of the East Lancashires into the German front trench south of Ridge Redoubt but the rest were pinned down in no man's land.

The three support battalions entered no man's land at 7.40am. The 1/6th Royal Warwicks were hit by the machine-guns south-east of Serre but the right-hand company carried some of the 1/8th Warwicks forward to Beaumont Trench. The 1st Somerset Light Infantry drifted left into the Quadrilateral, because Redan Ridge was swept by machine-gun fire. Lieutenant Colonel The Hon Lawrence Palk led the 1st Hampshires carrying only his stick until they were pinned down amongst the 1st East Lancashires.

While a mixed group of Warwick, Rifle Brigade and Somerset men advanced to the first objective, the rest of 11 Brigade were pinned down in no man's land. Some troops fired a single white flare to indicate they were stopped by the wire but others were firing three white flares to report they were at the first objective and observers could not distinguish between the signals. The only thing General Lambton knew for sure was that both 31st

---

14 Also known as the Heidenkopf Redoubt.

Division's attack to the north and 29th Division's attack to the south had failed.

Brigadier General Wilding's 10 Brigade and Brigadier General Crosbie's 12 Brigade were supposed to leave the reserve trenches and cross the British front line in artillery formation[15] at 9.30am. Although General Lambton sent an order forward at 8.35am to wait at the front line until the situation was clear, the leading battalions had set off early and only the rear battalions were stopped. At 9.30am four-and-a-half battalions advanced. The commanders of the rear companies held their men in the front trenches when they saw the carnage in no man's land.

In 12 Brigade's sector, the 1st King's Own, the 2nd Essex and half of the 2nd Lancashire Fusiliers were hit by artillery fire. Two small mines were fired under the King's Own as they crossed the German line, but the survivors pushed on towards the first objective. Redan Ridge's machine-guns forced the Lancashire Fusiliers north and they joined the rest of 12 Brigade.

In 10 Brigade's sector, the 2nd Seaforths faltered so Drummer Walter Ritchie climbed onto the parapet and sounded the 'Charge' to rally them. They too swerved north away from Redan Ridge and crossed the German front line south of the Quadrilateral. The Fusiliers and Seaforths kept going until they reinforced 11 Brigade on the first objective. Drummer Ritchie would later carry messages back across no man's land; he was awarded the Victoria Cross. A few of the 2nd Royal Dublin Fusiliers also made it across no man's land on the right. Some advanced as far as Munich Trench and a few may have reached Pendant Copse to the east or Serre to the north but smoke and dust made it difficult for observers to confirm anything.

The 4th Division had taken a large part of the German front position but machine-guns on the flanks were stopping reinforcements crossing no man's land. Only Regimental Sergeant Major Paul and a party of the Somersets managed to carry bombs across. Meanwhile, the Germans were bombing towards the Quadrilateral, threatening to cut off General Lambton's troops.

29th Division, Beaumont Hamel and Y Ravine

The 29th Division's front line ran in an arc around Beaumont Hamel and a deep gulley called Y Ravine. One shallow tunnel would be turned into a communication trench connecting to a sunken lane in no man's land while two more would be opened close to the German front trench for Stokes mortars batteries.

The 29th Division field batteries were given extra orders relating to the Hawthorn Ridge mine: 'at minus three minutes half the sections in each

---

15 In small columns which were much easier to control than waves of men. They were spaced out to avoid casualties from artillery fire.

field battery will lift onto the support line, where they will remain for two minutes'. So for three minutes the German front trench would only be shelled by half of the field batteries. The error would cost General de Lisle's men dearly.

The mine was blown at 7.20am, destroying Hawthorn Ridge Redoubt. Then the Stokes mortars in no man's land opened fire while the heavy barrage lifted. Two 2nd Royal Fusiliers platoons, four machine-gun teams and four Stokes mortar teams rushed the crater but they were pinned down on the near side lip.

As the rest of the leading companies formed up in no man's land, the German artillery and machine-guns opened fire which increased as the British artillery lifted. The assault troops were decimated as they moved

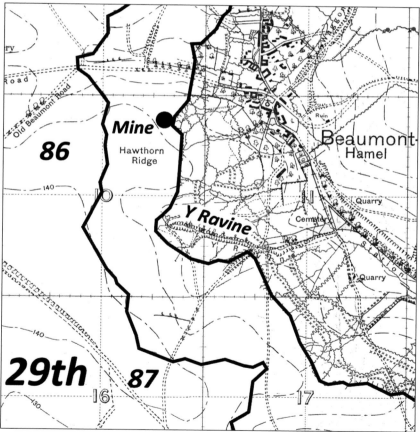

1 July, VIII Corps: The Hawthorn Ridge mine and the alteration to the artillery barrage compromised 29th Division's attack on Beaumont Hamel.

through gaps in the British wire or crossed bridges over their trenches.

Meanwhile 86 Brigade faced east towards Beaumont Hamel which lay hidden in a valley. Captains Nunneley's and Wells's 1st Lancashire Fusilier companies were shot down moving out of a sunken lane in no man's land. A 100-strong bombing party was also shot down leaving the sunken lane. The 2nd Royal Fusiliers suffered heavy casualties too and only thirty-five men reached the mine crater; the number eventually increased to 120 as other men sought cover. The few men who made it to the German front trench were killed or taken prisoner.

The German artillery hit the 1st Royal Dublin Fusiliers and 16th Middlesex as they moved forward through the congested trenches and they did not enter no man's land until 8am. The machine-guns in the Bergwerk strongpoint on Beaucourt ridge joined in and many men were hit passing through the gaps in the British wire. No one else made it to the German trench and the brigade major and a staff captain had to reorganise 86 Brigade's survivors in case there was a counter-attack.

The Germans holding Y Ravine could fire into 87 Brigade's flank as it attacked the line to the south-east. The convex slope also meant the German wire had been difficult to hit and there were few gaps. The 2nd South Wales Borderers were shot down by three machine-guns on the edge of the ravine and only a few men under Captain Hughes made it to the wire on the left. The German artillery then hit the rear companies as they left their trenches. Lieutenant Colonel Pearce's 1st Royal Inniskilling Fusiliers were hit by cross-fire which increased as they cut through the wire. Only a few made it across the front trench and into the valley beyond and they were all killed or taken prisoner.

The commanding officers of the 1st King's Own Scottish Borderers and 1st Border Regiment had asked for a new bombardment but the request was denied because white flares had been seen. Although this was taken to mean British troops were on the first objective, they were German flares reporting something different. The two battalions advanced at 8.05am but the German machine-guns soon stopped them.

However, reports about 87 Brigade's progress were being exaggerated and Brigadier General Lucas thought his troops were on the first objective. So General de Lisle ordered Brigadier General Cayley to move two of 88 Brigade's battalions forward to reinforce the imaginary breakthrough while the brigade machine-guns fired in support.

Lieutenant Colonel Hadow's 1st Newfoundland Battalion left the congested trenches and moved forward alone at 9.05am. Most were shot down before the British wire and only a handful reached the German trench;

none returned. The 1st Essex pushed through the congested trenches and advanced late. The result was the same and only Second Lieutenant Chawner's platoon made it half way across no man's land. After three companies had been shot down, Lieutenant Colonel Halahan held the final company back.

General de Lisle called off further attacks when he heard news of the failure an hour later. He also instructed the artillery barrage to shorten its range but only to the fourth objective because no one was sure how far 29th Division's had advanced; most of his men were dead or injured in no man's land.

VIII Corps' Afternoon Situation

The first reports to reach VIII Corps headquarters were encouraging, but they were few and far between. They were also over optimistic and often inaccurate. While there were reports of breakthroughs, there were few prisoners.

31st Division, Serre

There were rumours of troops holding out in Serre and although 94 Brigade received orders to advance at 12.15pm, General Rees postponed the advance until he had definite news; none ever came. The only report around 4pm was from an aeroplane observer who had spotted a few troops in the German front trenches but had seen none in Serre, Munich Trench or Pendant Trench. General Wanless O'Gowan wanted to advance but neither 93 nor 94 Brigades were able to. When General Hunter-Weston heard the news at 6pm, he ordered two 92 Brigade battalions to attack at 2am. But after dusk hundreds of men, many of them wounded, made their way back to the British trenches, leaving many more wounded lying out in no man's land. As no one had seen any British troops in the German trenches, the attack was called off.

4th Division and 29th Division, Munich Trench

General Hunter-Weston had cancelled 4th Division's and 29th Division's advance to Puisieux Trench at 10.25am and he ordered them to capture Munich Trench, north-east of Beaumont Hamel instead. There would be co-operation from 4th Division's right and 29th Division's left while two of 88 Brigade's battalions were ordered forward to help.

General Hunter-Weston also considered using 48th Division to reinforce the attack. The plan was for a thirty-minute barrage with zero hour at

12.30pm, but the situation was changing rapidly; 4th Division's foothold was under pressure while there were many Germans in the front trench. Munich Trench was evacuated around 11am allowing the German bombers to threaten 4th Division's position. Meanwhile, 12 Brigade had sent forward two 2nd Lancashire Fusiliers companies and a 2nd Duke's company to reinforce the Quadrilateral, but the trenches were crowded with wounded men. On 29th Division's front Lieutenant Colonel Magniac's 1st Lancashire Fusiliers were pinned down in the sunken lane in no man's land while the Hawthorn Redoubt crater group had withdrawn by noon.

The battalions of 88 Brigade eventually heard about the 12.30pm attack at 1.30pm, so it was postponed and then cancelled. The message never reached the Highlanders in 4th Division's sector while the Dublin Fusiliers were not fit to advance. The 1st Royal Warwicks[16] replaced the Fusiliers but they were unable to cross no man's land. While Captain Wilson's 1st Royal Irish Fusiliers company failed to reach the Quadrilateral during the afternoon, Captain Barefoot's company made it across after dark.

Around 3pm General Lambton reported 4th Division was unfit for further offensive action and while 12 Brigade consolidated the Quadrilateral, 11 Brigade gathered in reserve. The Quadrilateral was abandoned the following morning.

While 29th Division held its front with the survivors from 88 Brigade and 86 Brigade, 87 Brigade moved into reserve; it would take over 36th Division's sector on the west bank of the Ancre the following night.

It had been a disastrous day for VIII Corps. It had suffered over 14,000 casualties and both the trenches and no man's land were crowded with dead and wounded. A truce began at midday and stretcher bearers worked in no man's land until the British guns resumed firing at 4pm. Work continued through the night and there was another informal truce the following morning; it would take until 4 July to rescue all the wounded.

X Corps

Lieutenant General Sir Thomas Morland's corps had Major General Oliver Nugent's 36th Division astride the steep-sided Ancre valley, with its right flank facing Schwaben Redoubt.[17] Major General William Rycroft's 32nd Division held the lower slopes of the Thiepval spur between Thiepval Wood and Authuille Wood. Major-General Edward Perceval's 49th Division was in reserve in Aveluy Wood.

36th Division, Schwaben Redoubt

Astride the River Ancre was 108 Brigade, while 109 Brigade was on the

---

16 From 10 Brigade.
17 36th Division referred to the redoubt as the Parallelogram.

east bank and 107 Brigade was in reserve. As zero hour approached, there was consternation in a 14th Royal Irish Rifles' trench when Private Billy McFadzean saw a box of grenades fall from the parapet. Two grenades had lost their safety pins so he lay on top of the grenades and was killed by the explosion, saving his comrades' lives. Private McFadzean was posthumously awarded the Victoria Cross.

The assault troops left their trenches before zero hour, passed through the gaps in the British wire and moved close to the German trench. Then at 7.30am buglers in the front trench sounded the advance and set in motion:

'lines of men moving forward, with rifles sloped and the sun glistening upon their fixed bayonets, keeping their alignment and distance well as if on ceremonial parade, unfaltering, unwavering'.[18]

The 108 Brigade had two battalions on each bank of the River Ancre; it had no battalions in support. The 12th Royal Irish Rifles and 9th Royal Irish Fusiliers climbed out of their trenches on the left bank only two minutes before zero hour and came under fire as they passed through their own wire. It intensified as they moved across no man's land in short rushes and an artillery officer asked his major 'why do they stop there, why don't they move?' The reply was: 'They will never move no more'.

Only a handful of the Rifles led by Lieutenant McCluggage and Second Lieutenant MacNaghten made it across the deep gully in no man's land and into the German trenches. The Fusiliers found the Germans had filled the gully with rolls of barbed wire but Major Atkinson's men cut through and reached Beaucourt station; few returned. Men from the Rifles detailed to advance along the railway did not manage to capture the Mound and they fell back after Lieutenant Lemon was killed.

The survivors of 108 Brigade gathered in the gully, dumped their spare equipment and made their way back along the river bank towards Hamel. Permission to bring the barrage back to the German front trench for a second attempt was refused but a few batteries did so on their own initiative. Major Cole-Hamilton led about 100 of the 12th Royal Irish forward at 10.12am but they did not get far. A third attack by about fifty survivors was called off.

A Stokes mortar smoke screen on the west bank stopped the Germans firing across the river but the machine-guns in St Pierre Divion cut down Lieutenant Colonel Savage's 13th Royal Irish Rifles as they advanced along the east bank. Only a few joined the 11th Royal Irish Rifles in the Hansa Line.

As 109 Brigade advanced onto the high ground north of Thiepval the 10th and 9th Royal Inniskilling Fusiliers overran the front and support

---

18 Some wore orange sashes to commemorate the anniversary of the Battle of the Boyne. It was on 1 July in the old Julian calendar.

trenches before the Germans emerged from their dug-outs. The machine-guns around Thiepval had already stopped 32nd Division's attack and they turned on 109 Brigade, particularly the 9th Royal Inniskilling Fusiliers, as the Ulstermen advanced towards the reserve trench.

Despite rising casualties, the two Inniskilling battalions had cleared the forward trench of Schwaben Redoubt by 8am.[19] Second Lieutenant McKinley led 9th Battalion across the east side of the redoubt, heading for the Hansa Line, but more machine-guns turned on them the further they went.

Captain Eric Bell[20] dealt with one machine-gun team, allowing the advance to continue. He also used trench mortar bombs and a rifle to help out the bombers on three occasions. Captain Bell was killed while rallying groups of men; he was posthumously awarded the Victoria Cross.

Meanwhile, 109th Brigade continued to advance north-east of Thiepval but they were ahead of schedule and the Ulstermen had to lie down in the open while the British barrage continued firing on the Grandcourt Line. The Germans holding the trench initially did not know if the soldiers lying in the grass were their comrades retiring or their enemy advancing; but they were sure by the time the British barrage lifted ten minutes later. As Lieutenant Colonel Crozier's war diary explained: 'if it had not been for the barrage we [the 9th Royal Irish Rifles] could have taken the D Line sitting'.

There were not many Ulstermen left standing when the artillery lifted at 10.10am and while some occupied a battery position on the left, others entered the Grandcourt Line and Stuff Redoubt. They had advanced 2,000 metres into enemy territory and were now under fire from three sides.

As nothing had been heard from the front, the commanders of the 11th and 9th Inniskillings sent their second-in-commands forward to find out what they could. Major Oliphant and Major Peacocke sent back bad news. There was no way 109 Brigade could hold on without reinforcements. Major Peacocke helped Lieutenant McKinley and Sergeant Major Bulloch reorganise their men, but they needed ammunition and they also needed Thiepval's machine-guns silenced.

By 8.30am General Morland was aware of 36th Division's situation. Most of 108 Brigade had been stopped astride the Ancre while 109 Brigade was on its way to the Grandcourt Line. He was also aware 32nd Division only had two small footholds in the German trenches west and south of Thiepval.

When General Nugent asked if he should send Brigadier General Withycombe's 107 Brigade forward as planned, General Morland delayed

---

19 Over 400 prisoners were taken and many ran back to the safety of the British trenches.
20 The commander of the 9th Inniskilling's Trench Mortar Battery.

his reply because VIII and III Corps were reporting little or no progress. Forty minutes later General Morland told General Nugent to hold his men back but it was too late; 107 Brigade had already crossed no man's land. By 9.15am three of Withycombe's battalions were already passing through 109 Brigade.

32nd Division, Thiepval

While 96 Brigade faced Thiepval, 97 Brigade faced Leipzig Redoubt; 14 Brigade was in reserve. As well as having Thiepval to its front, the division's

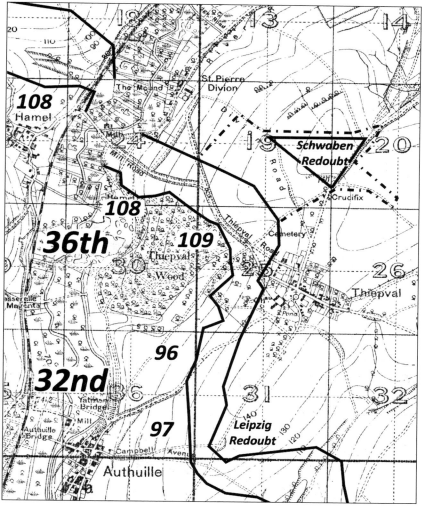

1 July, X Corps: While 36th Division advanced north of Thiepval, 32nd Division could not take the village.

flanks were exposed to enfilade fire from Schwaben Redoubt on the left and the Nordwerk on the right flank. As III Corps was not attacking the south side of Nab Valley this left 32nd Division's right flank exposed.[21] It did not help that General Rycroft's men were tired after days of digging trenches and carrying stores forward.

In 96 Brigade's sector, the 15th Lancashire Fusiliers' first waves crossed no man's land and reached the front trench before the Germans could react. Around 100 men of Captains Heald's and Wood's companies kept advancing alongside 36th Division and a few entered Thiepval. The Germans had manned their front trench by the time Lieutenant Colonel Lloyd's support waves were moving and no more Fusiliers made it across no man's land.

The 16th Northumberland Fusiliers followed a football kicked by an eminent North Country player into no man's land. But the Germans were ready and first Captain Young's and Graham's companies and then Captain Thompson's company were pinned down near their own trench. The Germans then taunted them into advancing further so they could shoot them. Lieutenant Worthington's platoon was the last to go over the top and then the rest were ordered to man the parapet and return fire. One report said only 'bulletproof soldiers could have taken Thiepval'.

The 97 Brigade faced Leipzig Salient and while two battalions faced east, two 2nd Manchesters' companies held the trench south of the salient.[22] Lieutenant Colonel Laidlaw's 16th Highland Light Infantry came under fire as they crept forward before zero hour and it intensified the moment they advanced. Only a few men under Lieutenant McClaren made it across, the rest were shot down passing through the gaps in the wire.

The 17th Highland Light Infantry had also crept close to the German line and they rushed Leipzig Salient when the barrage lifted but the machine-guns in the Wonder Work strongpoint stopped them advancing further. Brigadier General Jardine and Lieutenant Colonel Cotton,[23] the local artillery commander, agreed two batteries should fire on Hindenburg Trench, at the base of the salient, allowing the Highlanders to withdraw to the redoubt where they were joined by some of the 17th HLI and 2nd KOYLIs. While they consolidated the redoubt, bombing detachments tried in vain to enter Hindenburg Trench and Lemberg Trench.

Sergeant James Turnbull fought to hold an important post all day for the 17th HLI although his party was wiped out and replaced several times. He held his position virtually single-handed until he was killed. Turnbull was posthumously awarded the Victoria Cross.

---

21 The corps boundary ran up Nab Valley and there was little co-ordination between X Corps and III Corps about how to deal with the re-entrant.
22 From 14 Brigade.
23 Of 161 Brigade, Royal Field Artillery, supporting 97 Brigade's advance.

Meanwhile, no one had told the 11th Borders[24] in Authuille Wood that the attack had stalled while Lieutenant Colonel Machell could not see through the smoke and dust. At 8.30am they moved into no man's land only to be shot at from the front and from the Nordwerk to the right. Only a few made it to the Leipzig Redoubt; the rest withdrew back into the wood.

Despite the widespread failure, a contact aeroplane message reported British troops in Thiepval, confirming a written message received at 32nd Division's headquarters. Generals Morland and Rycroft believed there were troops in Thiepval and the artillery was ordered to stop firing on the village. At 9.10am General Rycroft ordered Brigadier General Yatman to send the rest of 96 Brigade through the gap created by 36th Division so it could form a link between the Ulstermen in Schwaben Redoubt and the 15th Lancashire Fusiliers in Thiepval. Five minutes later Captain Knott's and Lieutenant Allen's companies of the 16th Lancashire Fusiliers left Johnson's Post at the east corner of Thiepval Wood; no one made it across no man's land.

Meanwhile, 14 Brigade had moved from reserve through Authuille Wood in two columns, unaware of the disaster in front of Thiepval. At 8.45am the 1st Dorsets began leaving the wood in artillery formation while Major Kerr played the regimental march on his flute. They came under fire from the Nordwerk and less than seventy men reached Leipzig Redoubt; the support companies stayed in the wood. Lieutenant Colonel Graham of the 19th Lancashire Fusiliers asked the brigade's Stokes mortars to create a smoke screen after seeing Lieutenant Huxley's company shot to pieces. Then Captain Hibbert's company crossed into no man's land by platoon rushes; only forty men reached Leipzig Redoubt. The hand right column stayed in Authuille Wood having seen what had happened to the Dorsets and the Fusiliers.

Captain Hibbert of the Fusiliers took command of the men in the Leipzig Redoubt and General Compton stopped any further advances after receiving his assessment of the situation. Instead efforts turned to turning two Russian saps into communication trenches.[25]

At 11.40am Generals Morland and Rycroft decided to make a pincer movement against Thiepval. The 2nd Inniskilling Fusiliers,[26] reinforced by battalions from 49th Division, would move around the north side while 14 Brigade would reinforce Leipzig Redoubt to the south.

General Morland organised a bombardment for 12.05pm but the artillery was not to shell the village. The hastily conceived barrage was spread too wide and when two Inniskilling companies and some men of 96 Brigade left Thiepval Wood at 1.30pm they could not reach Thiepval.

To the south, two 2nd Manchester[27] companies stayed to the left, out of

---

24 Known as the Lonsdales.
25 Russian saps were shallow tunnels which were opened into trenches by collapsing the roof.
26 From 96 Brigade.
27 From 14 Brigade.

sight of the Nordwerk. While they advanced beyond the Leipzig Salient, they could not capture Hindenburg Trench and had to fall back into the crowded salient.

36th Division, Later Fighting in Schwaben Redoubt

The fighting was over on the west bank of the Ancre and the survivors crept back to safety under cover of darkness after a long day trapped in no man's land. The stretcher-bearers then began collecting the wounded. Robert Quigg of the 12th Royal Irish Rifles went out seven times to locate his platoon commander, Lieutenant Harry MacNaghten,[28] returning with a wounded man each time when he could not find him. Private Quigg was awarded the Victoria Cross.

Lieutenant Geoffrey Cather of the 9th Royal Irish Fusiliers spent the night and following morning searching no man's land on the west bank of the Ancre. He rescued wounded men and took water to those who were too injured to move. Lieutenant Cather was eventually killed and he was posthumously awarded the Victoria Cross.

There was still plenty of fighting east of the Ancre and Captain Davidson of 108th Machine-gun Company was forced to conduct a fighting withdrawal with the brigade's survivors after all his guns were silenced. On Thiepval plateau 107 Brigade's ammunition was dwindling and casualties were mounting while the machine-guns in Thiepval made it impossible to cross no man's land.[29] It did not help that General Morland was concentrating on trying to capture Thiepval.

Patrols from 107 Brigade encountered Germans in Thiepval, although Mouquet Switch was unoccupied and it could have been used to outflank the village. But brigade and battalion officers had been banned from going forward with the assault troops[30] and the information could not be acted on. By mid-afternoon the Germans had retaken Battery Valley, part of the Hansa Line and Stuff Redoubt, forcing the Ulstermen to retire into Schwaben Redoubt.

While 36th Division fought on, what had General Morland done with his reserve? General Rycroft and General Percival suggested sending 49th Division round the north side of Thiepval, exploiting 36th Division's breakthrough, but General Morland insisted on making a new attack against the village to widen the breach in the German line.

Both 146 and 147 Brigades had been ordered to attack but it was 11.30am before they were ready. Meanwhile 32nd Division sent the 2nd Inniskillings into 36th Division's area to attack Thiepval's north side while 146 Brigade attacked the west side. But the 2nd Inniskillings were too late and 146

---

28 Lieutenant MacNaghten was the son of The Honourable Sir Charles MacNaghten of Dundarave, Antrim. He had been taken prisoner and died of his wounds in captivity.

29 The road to Hamel would become known as Bloody Road due to the number of casualties.

30 To prevent them from becoming early casualties.

Brigade was only just ready in time. Lieutenant Colonel Wade's 1/6th West Yorkshires and a 1/8th West Yorkshire company were shot to pieces when they advanced and Brigadier General Goring-Jones ordered the rest of the brigade to man the trenches in Thiepval Wood. The attack had failed.

By late afternoon General Yatman understood what was going on. There were no British troops in Thiepval while the 2nd Inniskillings were back in the British trenches. At 6.15pm General Rycroft knew a frontal attack on Thiepval could not succeed while it was impossible for troops to reach 36th Division's right flank.

Soon afterwards General Goring-Jones was ordered to send two of 146 Brigade's battalions to 36th Division. But the order was outdated because half the brigade had already been shot up so only two 1/7th West Yorkshire companies were sent. They eventually occupied a trench north-west of Schwaben Redoubt. The rest of 146 Brigade was ordered to join 36th Division four hours later and although two battalions[31] crossed no man's land, they soon joined the general withdrawal to the British trenches.

A 1/7th West Yorkshire company, including Corporal George Sanders and thirty men, was left behind. Sanders refused to give up and his men held a trench north-west of Schwaben Redoubt for another thirty-six hours before they finally withdrew; Corporal Sanders was awarded the Victoria Cross.

Morland had wanted to attack Thiepval with two of 148 Brigade's battalions at midnight but it was called off. Meanwhile, 147 Brigade had still been not given any orders; 49th Division's piecemeal deployment had achieved nothing.

Summary
The withdrawal from Schwaben Redoubt ended General Morland's hopes of taking Thiepval. Orders issued at 11.30pm calling for 49th Division to retake Schwaben Redoubt were cancelled. While 32nd Division's survivors crept back from no man's land, Lieutenant Colonel Luxmoore's 2nd Manchesters[32] and two 2nd KOYLI companies[33] took over the Leipzig Salient. X Corps casualties had been over 9,000 and it would take until 3 July to retrieve all the wounded from no man's land.

III Corps

Lieutenant General William Pulteney's III Corps was astride the Albert to Bapaume road. Major General Havelock Hudson's 8th Division faced Ovillers while Major General Edward Ingouville-Williams's 34th Division faced La Boisselle and the two valleys known as Sausage and Mash.

---

31 1/5th West Yorkshire and two companies each from the 1/7th and 1/8th West Yorkshire.
32 From 14 Brigade.
33 From 97 Brigade.

8th Division, Ovillers

The 8th Division had all three brigades poised to attack the Ovillers spur: 70 Brigade had to advance across Nab Valley, 25 Brigade had to capture Ovillers and 23 Brigade had to advance across Mash Valley. They would be under fire from the valley slopes, from the Leipzig Salient to the north and from La Boisselle to the south. Hudson had wanted the high ground either side of his objective captured before his men left their trenches but Rawlinson rejected his proposal.

As the barrage intensified, the leading waves moved into the wider parts of no man's land and immediately came under machine-gun fire. At 7.30am the barrage lifted, the assault battalions moved forward and while the fire from the German trenches increased, the German batteries shelled no man's land and the British trenches. Casualties mounted and only a few groups of men reached the German trenches.

The attack by 32nd Division held the attention of the German machine-guns on 70 Brigade's left so the leading waves of the 8th KOYLIs and part of the 8th York and Lancasters crossed three German trenches. The third and fourth waves were shot down in no man's land, leaving their comrades isolated. All was going well until the 2nd Lincolns fell back on their right and the KOYLIs and the York and Lancasters followed.

The machine-guns on Thiepval spur turned their attentions on the 9th York and Lancasters as they crossed no man's land and few made it to the German trenches. Brigadier General Gordon mistakenly believed his neighbouring brigades were advancing, so he ordered Colonel Watson's 11th Sherwood Foresters forward; the first wave was shot down at the German wire, the second wave did not make it that far. A group of fifty bombers was also stopped from advancing along a sunken lane from the Nab.

In 25 Brigade's sector Lieutenant Colonel Holdworth's 2nd Berkshires were pinned down in no man's land. Second Lieutenant Mollet led a few into the German trenches but they were stopped by enfilade fire from the communication trenches and then forced to withdraw by bombing attacks; they gathered in the front trench under Lieutenant Colonel Bastard of the 2nd Lincolns. Unfortunately, the British bombardment had virtually destroyed the trench, so Bastard's men had little cover.

Meanwhile, the 1st Royal Irish Rifles and 2nd Rifle Brigade were delayed in the congested trenches. The Irish Rifles were stopped by the German barrage while the Rifle Brigade were ordered to wait. A second attempt to cross no man's land only increased the casualty count.

In 23 Brigade's sector the 2nd Middlesex and 2nd Devons were hit as they crossed no man's land and while a few reached the German trenches, cross fire from the communication trenches stopped them going far. Major Savile of the Middlesex gathered around 100 survivors and they watched as Captain Harkness led the first two 2nd West Yorkshire companies into no man's land at 8.25am; only a few reached the German front trench. While General Pollard stopped the 2nd Scottish Rifles going over the top, Bastard went back to collect reinforcements only to be told no more men would be sent forward; he returned to organise a withdrawal.

The three brigade commanders were ordered to organise their men for a second attack, but they all reported the barrage would hit the groups of men in the German trenches. They also reported they had barely enough men to hold their front line so the attack was called off. Later that night the survivors crept back from no man's land.

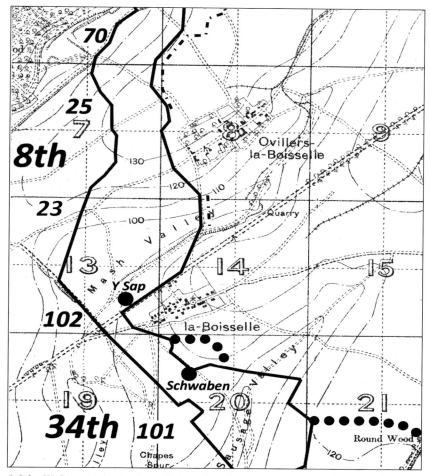

1 July, III Corps: 8th Division failed to clear the trenches covering Ovillers while 34th Division gained footholds either side of Sausage Valley.

34th Division, La Boisselle

The line held by 34th Division ran north-west to south-east across the Albert to Bapaume road, along the foot of a low ridge, known as Tara and Usna Hills. The German line skirted La Boisselle at the Glory Hole, curving back along the upper slopes of two shallow valleys. Here 102 Brigade had to advance up Mash Valley to the north-west while 101 Brigade moved up Sausage Valley to the south-east.

General Ingouville-Williams' plan was for two brigades to advance in four columns of three battalions while bombing parties attacked La Boisselle. But there were complications. Two mines would be detonated at 7.28am and the two flanking columns would be crossing no man's land while the centre columns waited five minutes for the debris to stop falling.

The brigade and battalion commanders were sceptical but Ingouville-Williams reminded them that General Rawlinson had promised the artillery bombardment and mines would stun the German garrison. The patrols clearing gaps in the British wire disagreed. To make matters worse a German listening post intercepted an order concerning the assault around 2.45am.

A 40,000lb mine detonated under Y Sap and two minutes later Column 1, with the 20th, 23rd and 25th Northumberland Fusiliers, advanced up Mash Valley.[34] German machine-guns to the front and right cut the Tynesiders down, while artillery fire hit the assembly trenches. Lieutenant Colonels Lyle and Sillery were two of the few men who reached the German trenches and Lyle was last seen walking with stick in hand; both were killed.

The second mine destroyed Schwaben Hohe[35] to the right of Column 2 and the 21st, 22nd and 26th Northumberland Fusiliers[36] moved off while the debris was still falling. They overran Schwaben Hohe, Kaufmanngraben and Alte Jagerstrasse trenches while under crossfire from La Boisselle and from across Sausage Valley. Some men reached Quergraben III and while a few reached Bailiff Wood; most were killed or taken prisoner. The Germans soon forced the 200 surviving Tynesiders back to Kaufmanngraben Trench.

Meanwhile 101 Brigade advanced up Sausage Valley in two columns. Column 3 advanced at 7.35 am 'as [if] on parade and never flinched'. Lieutenant Colonel Cordeaux's 10th Lincolns were hit by fire from Bloater Trench and Sausage Redoubt while artillery fire hit the 11th Suffolks and 'men were soon spun round and dropping everywhere'. Only a few men made it across no man's land and while some sought cover at the mine crater, a few climbed Fricourt spur to the right. A dozen men tried to capture Sausage Redoubt only to be burnt to death by flame-throwers. The 24th

---

34 1st and 4th Tyneside Scottish, then the 2nd Tyneside Irish.
35 Creating what is now known as Lochnagar Crater.
36 2nd and 3rd Tyneside Scottish, then the 3rd Tyneside Irish.

Northumberland Fusiliers were ordered to wait in the front trenches but some had already moved out; most were cut down in no man's land but a few reached Acid Drop Copse and the outskirts of Contalmaison.

Column 4 started well on the right at 7.30am, with the 15th Royal Scots overrunning Kipper Trench on the west slope of Fricourt spur 'with great heart and in grand form'. But Column 3's late start meant every machine-gun in range cut the 16th Royal Scots to pieces. The survivors drifted right, moving straight up the slope rather than across it. The Royal Scots continued over the crest, meeting 21st Division troops at Birch Tree Wood; a handful of 16th Royal Scots reached Contalmaison but none returned. Despite a deep advance, Column 4 had not cleared Sausage or Scots Redoubt, leaving the 27th Northumberland Fusiliers and Column 3 pinned down in no man's land.

Realising their error, Lieutenant Lodge made the 16th Royal Scots wait along the Fricourt – Pozières road while Captain Stocks led the 15th Royal Scots north along Birch Tree Trench towards Peake Wood. A German counter-attack drove the 15th back to Birch Tree Wood and Shelter Wood while the 16th withdrew to Round Wood. Attention then turned to the original objective and a wounded Captain Brown of the 11th Suffolks and Lieutenant Robson of the Royal Scots led successful attacks against Scots Redoubt and Wood Alley.

By 10am 34th Division's attack was spent. Most of Column 1 were back in their own trenches; only a few men from Column 2 were around the Schwaben Hohe crater; Column 3 was pinned down in no man's land; Column 4 was on the wrong side of the Fricourt spur around Round Wood and Birch Tree Wood.

The Afternoon
In 8th Division's sector, orders were issued for a 5pm attack past the north side of Ovillers by 19th Division's 56 Brigade. But zero hour was delayed because Thiepval spur was still in German hands and then cancelled because the lodgement in the German trenches was lost.

Meanwhile, 34th Division was spent and only a single battalion of 19th Division was sent forward when General Ingouville-Williams asked for reinforcements. An attempt to clear Sausage Redoubt by bombing failed at 3.20pm.

At 5.30pm Pulteney issued instructions for 19th Division's 57 and 58 Brigades to attack La Boisselle at 10.30pm but it was later postponed to the following morning. By nightfall two communication trenches had been dug across no man's land and 34th Division handed over its meagre gains to

19th Division. By now III Corps had suffered over 11,000 casualties and both Ovillers and La Boisselle were still in German hands. The only success had been on its right flank, alongside XV Corps.

XV Corps

Lieutenant General Henry Horne's XV Corps faced a large salient curving around Fricourt and Mametz. Major General David Campbell's 21st Division faced the west side of Fricourt and the Tambour, an area scarred by mining activity. Major General Herbert Watts's 7th Division faced the south side of Mametz. The outer wings of the two divisions would advance at 7.30am and meet north-east of Fricourt Wood, cutting off Fricourt village. The inner flanks would advance at 2.30pm, passing through the village and wood.

21st Division, North of Fricourt

The 64 and 63 Brigades faced the area north of Fricourt while 17th Division's 50 Brigade was on the division's right flank. While the 10th West Yorkshire would form a flank facing Fricourt, the rest of 50 Brigade would attack the west side of Fricourt later.

Engineers had dug a Russian sap in front of 64 Brigade, turning it into a trench the night before the attack for the first wave. The 10th and 9th KOYLIs advanced across no man's land as the Germans fired from South Sausage Trench and the opposite side of Sausage Valley. They reached the support trench, taking 200 prisoners, while the 1st East Yorkshires and 15th Durham Light Infantry followed in support. It had only taken ten minutes but the brigade had suffered fifty per cent casualties. The survivors pushed on and by 8am they had reached the Sunken Road, running north from Fricourt.

While most of the troops reorganised in Lonely Trench and along the road, some captured 100 prisoners in Crucifix Trench. But machine-gun teams in Shelter Wood and Birch Tree Wood on the left and Fricourt Wood on the right were waiting for them.

When Brigadier General Headlam reached the Sunken Road, he positioned men on his exposed left flank, where 34th Division should have been. He then deployed Lewis guns ready to give the advance covering fire. But most of Headlam's party were shot down investigating Round Wood. After instructing Lieutenant Colonel Fitzgerald to hold on, Headlam went back to report the situation. When General Campbell heard both his flanks were in the air, he ordered Brigadier General Rawling to send the 1st Lincolns[37] and the 10th Green Howards forward to reinforce the front line.

---

37 Accompanied by the Bermuda Volunteer Company.

The troops of 63 Brigade came under fire when they climbed out of their trenches five minutes before zero. Only three officers of the 8th Somerset Light Infantry made it to Empress Trench but the survivors advanced past the northern outskirts of Fricourt while the bombers moved up the communication trenches.

The 4th Middlesex's first wave was hit by six machine-guns as they formed up in no man's land and they fell back before zero hour. The officers leading the second wave urged the battalion forward in one line but less than 150 men crossed the German support trench and headed for the Sunken Road. Lieutenant Colonel Bicknell held back some troops in the front trench and they stopped three bombing attacks. These counter-attacks upset the momentum of the assault and Brigadier General Headlam delayed the two support battalions for ten minutes while he assessed the situation. At 8.40am the 8th Lincolns and the 10th York and Lancasters crossed no man's land under heavy fire and reached the rest of the brigade.

Lieutenant Colonel Johnston's Lincolns reinforced the Somersets on the left, while the bombers fought along the communication trenches. Second Lieutenant Kellet's group secured Lozenge Alley on the right flank and while Second Lieutenant Hall's group reached Crucifix Trench, a third group was unable to reach Fricourt Farm. Lieutenant Preston's group then stopped the German bombers reaching the Sunken Road. Although the York and Lancasters advanced beyond the Sunken Road, machine-guns in Fricourt village and wood stopped them going far.

Three mines[38] exploded in the Tambour area on 21st Division's right at 7.28am. Two minutes later the 10th West Yorkshires advanced on 50 Brigade's front. The leading companies crossed Koenig Trench and headed for the Red Cottage at the north-west corner of Fricourt. But by the time Lieutenant Colonel Dickson and Major Knott led the rear companies into no man's land, the Germans in Fricourt and the Tambour craters were ready to shoot them down. When one company hesitated, Major Stewart Loudoun-Shand helped his men over the parapet and cheered them on until he was mortally wounded. He insisted on being propped up in the trench and encouraged his men until he died. Major Loudoun-Shand was posthumously awarded the Victoria Cross.

A message was sent back asking for the artillery to target the Tambour area but it was too late for the West Yorkshires. The survivors pushed on along the communication trenches towards Red Cottage where the majority were surrounded and overrun; only a few joined 63 Brigade in the Sunken Road.

---

38 9,000lbs, 15,000lbs and 25,000lbs.

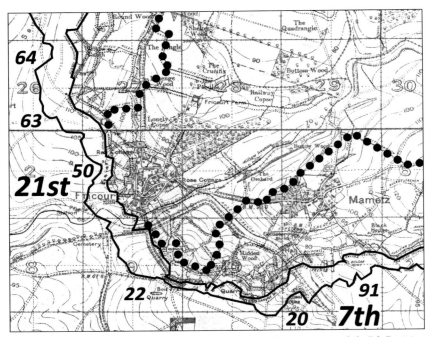

1 July, XV Corps: 21st Division faced a tough fight north of Fricourt while 7th Division eventually cleared the Mametz area.

7th Division, Mametz

The 7th Division's three brigades held a north facing front opposite Mametz: 20 Brigade would wheel left, through the west side of Mametz, to form a flank facing Fricourt; 91 Brigade would advance through the east side of Mametz village onto Mametz spur; 22 Brigade would advance through Fricourt once 7th Division had met 21st Division north of Mametz.

The front trench occupied by 20 Brigade was in a poor state so the assault troops started from the support trenches. Four small mines exploded in a crater field on the left and the 2nd Borders overran the stunned Germans before wheeling left over Quarry Spur into Apple Valley. Although they reached Hidden Lane by 9.30am, they were under machine-gun fire from Mametz and Hidden Wood on their right.

The 9th Devons assembled 250 metres behind the damaged front trenches and they came under machine-gun fire as the clambered down a steep slope, suffering heavy casualties before they reached Mansell Copse; Captain Martin was one of the first to fall.[39] There were machine-guns in the support trench and more in Fricourt Wood beyond. The Devons cleared

---

39 Captain Martin had made a model of the battlefield help train the troops. He predicted a machine-gun in the Shrine would cut them to pieces; he was correct and was one of the first to fall.

the first two trenches but all the officers had fallen and the survivors stopped while the rest of the brigade continued advancing.

The 2nd Gordons' left company was stopped by wire hidden in a dip in the ground. A small 200lb mine destroyed a sap in front of the right company and it cleared the trench across the battalion front. The delay meant the Gordons lost the barrage but they reached Shrine Alley around 8am, despite machine-gun fire from the Shrine and Mametz. The survivors were then stopped by enfilade fire from their left, where the 9th Devons should have been.

While the Borders cleared Hidden Wood on the left, the Devons and Gordons were too weak to do anymore. The final 8th Devons company entered no man's land around 1pm and Lieutenant Savill had to guide his men to the left to avoid fire from the Shrine; they filled the gap between the Gordons and the 9th Devons.

A 2,000lb mine destroyed Bulgar Point sap on 91 Brigade's left. The 1st South Staffords and 22nd Manchesters suffered few casualties crossing a narrow no man's land but they were hit by machine-guns in Mametz and Danzig Alley as they climbed the slope beyond. By 8am the South Staffords had captured Cemetery Trench and entered Mametz while the Manchesters occupied Bucket Trench, only 200 metres short of their objective. Although many Germans surrendered or ran, a few machine-gun teams held on in Mametz and Danzig Alley, allowing their comrades to drive the South Staffords back to Cemetery Trench. As Captains Snape and Hallam reorganised the battalion, Lieutenant Warwick Hall called for reinforcements.

Around 9.30am Brigadier General Minshull-Ford ordered his support battalions forward. The 21st Manchesters reached the South Staffords on the left, but they could not advance beyond Cemetery Trench. Two 2nd Queen's companies reached the Manchesters in Bulgar Alley and Bucket Trench but they could not capture Danzig Alley.

With the advance stalled, General Watts ordered a new thirty-minute bombardment of Bunny Alley, Fritz Trench and Danzig Alley. When 91 Brigade advanced at 10am the few men who reached Danzig Alley were soon driven out. While 7th Division was struggling to hold its own, General Horne planned another attempt to take Fritz Trench and Danzig Alley at 13.05pm after hearing that XIII Corps was pushing ahead on his right. The bombardment broke up a counter-attack and 91 Brigade found the Germans to be disorganized; only a section of field guns fought on, firing over open sights at two 2nd Queen's companies.

By 1pm 91 Brigade had reached Danzig Alley and while one bombing party moved west, another went north up Bright Alley. Meanwhile, Major

Morris organised the 1st South Staffords and three 21st Manchester companies so they could advance from Cemetery Trench. Lieutenant Potter's platoon was the first to enter Mametz while the Queen's cleared Fritz Trench. By mid-afternoon, 7th Division held all but the north edge of the village.

General Horne now faced a dilemma. He knew XIII Corps was clearing its objectives around Pommiers Redoubt and Montauban while the Germans were falling back to Bazentin-le-Grand. Aeroplane observers also reported seeing German guns withdrawing along the Bapaume road while infantry had been observed moving towards Fricourt and Contalmaison. At 11.45am Horne heard troops were advancing towards Contalmaison and Bottom Wood. At 12.50pm 21st and 7th Divisions were ordered to attack at 2.30pm following a thirty-minute bombardment. Unfortunately, 21st Division was not moving on Contalmaison, it was only just holding its own north of Fricourt. The question was would Horne discover the true situation on his front before it was too late?

The Afternoon Attack

General Horne's plan called for the two inner brigades to advance at 2.30pm and while 50 Brigade faced Fricourt, 22 Brigade had to attack the trenches south-east of the village. The convergent advances would clear the space between the morning's attacks.

21st Division's Afternoon Attack

After a long delay, 64 and 63 Brigades were ordered to advance towards Fricourt Farm and Shelter Wood at 2.30pm. The 63 Brigade had to stop Germans escaping from Fricourt village and link up with 7th Division. The problem was the Germans had had several hours to reorganise.

However, 64 Brigade's order did not reach Colonel Fitzgerald until the artillery bombardment had lifted from Shelter Wood and the 15th Durhams and the 10th KOYLIs advanced ten minutes late; neither went far from Crucifix Trench. While 63 Brigade moved on time from Lonely Trench and Lozenge Wood it was stopped by machine-gun fire from Fricourt Farm and Fricourt Wood.

Meanwhile 50 Brigade was also supposed to advance through Fricourt but Major Kent's company of the 7th Green Howards and the 10th West Yorkshires had already been shot down in no man's land. Brigadier General Glasgow's request to cancel the attack was overruled and at 2.30pm Lieutenant Colonel Fife's 7th Green Howards advanced between the Tambour craters and Wing Corner, at the south end of Fricourt; 350 men were hit in three minutes while the few who entered the village were killed or captured. The 7th East Yorkshires also suffered 150 casualties.

Around 4.30pm General Campbell ordered his men to form a flank facing Fricourt, with 64 Brigade in Crucifix Trench and 63 Brigade along Lozenge Alley. An hour later, Brigadier General Rawling received orders to send the 12th and 13th Northumberland Fusiliers forward to relieve 64 Brigade.

Just before 9pm, General Horne ordered 17th Division to move forward from XV Corps reserve, ready to attack the following morning. But Major General Philip Robertson cancelled the attack when 50 Brigade reported the Germans were withdrawing from Fricourt.

After a long and challenging day, 21st Division had a quiet night. It had been a day of mixed fortunes for XV Corps. While General Horne's left flank had advanced 2,000 metres over the Fricourt spur and his right flank had advanced 2,500 metres through Mametz, the centre had failed.[40]

7th Division's Afternoon Attack

The Maricourt spur south of Fricourt was held by 22 Brigade with Lieutenant Colonel Lewis's 20th Manchesters and half of Lieutenant Colonel Stockwell's 1st Royal Welsh Fusiliers. The advance south of Fricourt began at 2.30pm but while the leading companies crossed no man's land, the support companies came under fire from the slope south of Fricourt. Captain Stevens and Captain Williams's Fusilier companies failed to bomb along Copper and Kitchen trenches towards the village. Some men entered the Rectangle in the centre but they were forced to withdraw and join the companies fighting in Bois Français Trench.

Eventually heavy fire from Fricourt stopped any advance over the top but Captain Stevens led the Fusiliers' bombers along Sunken Road Trench and they captured 100 prisoners. They then seized the Rectangle and linked with 20 Brigade in Apple Alley on the right. By nightfall 22 Brigade held the second support trench and the Rectangle.

In 20 Brigade's sector, General Watts ordered two 2nd Warwicks companies to advance through the west side of Mametz while the 1st South Staffords[41] and 21st Manchesters moved through the east side. At 3.30pm Lieutenant Duff led the 8th Devons past the Shrine into Danzig Trench and while 200 Germans surrendered, the rest fell back towards Fricourt Wood. They then entered Hidden Wood and Mametz, allowing the 9th Devons to move forward. Mametz was cleared by 4pm and Bunny Trench was taken soon afterwards.

By late afternoon 91 Brigade had secured its objectives. The 2nd

---

40 Casualties over 8,000; prisoners over 1,600.
41 From 91 Brigade.

Queen's reached Fritz Trench north-east of Mametz by 6.30pm and an hour later they were joined by the 1st South Staffords; Lieutenant de Trafford's men captured 200 prisoners in Bunny Trench. The Mametz area was clear by evening.

XIII Corps

Lieutenant General Walter Congreve's[42] XIII Corps held an east west line on the south facing slope of Montauban ridge.[43] While Major General Ivor Maxse's 18th Division advanced towards Caterpillar Valley, Major General John Shea's 30th Division had to capture Montauban; 9th Division was in corps reserve two miles behind the front.

18th Division, North of Carnoy

The 18th Division had all three brigades in line with a crater field in the centre of the division's front. The front trench had been badly damaged by the British bombardment and the Germans had filled it with barbed wire and withdrawn to their support line, leaving snipers and machine-gun teams behind.

A 500lb mine detonated on 54 Brigade's left flanks at 7.27am. The 11th Royal Fusiliers and 7th Bedfords advanced across no man's land under heavy machine-gun fire but there was little German artillery fire. Both battalions crossed the smashed wire and Lance Corporal Payne led the Fusiliers across a battered Austrian Trench into Emden Trench while parties cleared the German dug-outs.

The Royal Fusiliers moved fast up the slope and then waited in front of Pommiers Trench until the artillery lifted while their bombers cleared Black Alley; Private Nicholson shot six snipers and silenced a machine-gun en route. The Bedford's leading companies were hit by a machine-gun in the Triangle and all of Lieutenant Colonel Price's officers were hit before it was silenced. Sergeant Impey led the Bedfords forward when the artillery lifted at 7.50am and the two battalions captured Pommiers Trench with help from the 10th Essex on their right.[44]

The artillery lifted at 8.28am but the Royal Fusiliers discovered Pommiers Redoubt's[45] machine-guns were protected by belts of wire hidden in long grass. Captain Johnson led the battalion bombers and two Lewis gun teams along Maple Trench on the left, behind the Redoubt. Once Lieutenant Savage's platoon had dealt with snipers in Beetle Alley, Johnson tackled the garrison while Lewis gunners shot down the Germans running from Maple Trench. The Royal Fusiliers and the Bedfords had cleared Pommiers Redoubt by 9.30am and Beetle Alley by 10.15am, with the help of the 6th Northants. They finally occupied White Trench

42 General Walter Congreve had been awarded the Victoria Cross during the Boer War.
43 North of Carnoy and Maricourt.
44 From 53 Brigade.
45 The Germans called it the Jamin Work.

overlooking Caterpillar Valley, having made a 2,000-metre advance. However, both flanks were in the air because the brigades either side had been delayed.

In 53 Brigade's sector, the 6th Royal Berkshires[46] faced Casino Point. A 5,000lb mine was due to detonate beneath the salient at 7.27am but the mining officer hesitated when he saw the Berkshires moving out into no man's land earlier than expected. He hit the plunger when the machine-guns opened fire and while some of the Berkshires were injured by falling debris, the rest advanced past the crater as the Germans surrendered. Two small 500lb charges were also blown in front of the 8th Norfolks on the right while a Livens Flame Projector[47] dealt with any Germans in the Carnoy Road crater field.

The two battalions crossed Bay Trench and Mine Trench and then the support lines, Bund and Bund Support Trench. The Berkshires and the Norfolks' left were delayed by machine-gun teams in Pommiers Trench until bombers advanced up Popoff Lane and knocked one out; the other two then withdrew. By 7.50am Second Lieutenant Courage of the Berkshires and Sergeant Major Raven of the Norfolks had cleared Pommiers Trench. But they then came under enfilade fire from the Loop on the right where the rest of the 8th Norfolks had been delayed. All they could do was protect the exposed flank with the help of a 10th Essex company; while a second company of Essex was sent forward, it could not reach the Loop. Second Lieutenant Miall-Smith and Sergeant West made sure the Norfolks' right cleared the Castle strongpoint but another group of Germans held onto Back Trench in 55 Brigade's sector.

Lieutenant Tatam's group of the 7th Buffs was too weak to clear the Carnoy crater field on 55 Brigade's left flank. Machine-guns continued to enfilade the 7th Queen's and 7th Queen's Own as they crossed no man's land and the casualties and delay gave the Germans time to man their trenches. The 8th East Surreys were on the brigade right and Captain Neville had given a football to each of his platoons and offered a prize to the first man to kick theirs into the German trench. Neville was killed shortly after kicking his ball into no man's land.

An hour after zero, the enfilade fire from the Queen's sector was still stopping the Surreys from advancing beyond the support line and the Warren. Then help came from the right. 30th Division cleared Train Alley by 9am and advanced towards Montauban. The move forced the Germans facing 54 Brigade to withdraw along the communication trenches. While the Queen's reorganised, Major Irwin and Lieutenant Janion led the 8th East Surreys towards Train Alley.[48]

---

46 Supported by two 10th Essex platoons.
47 A huge static flamethrower with an underground fuel store and an above ground nozzle.
48 With two 7th Buffs' companies.

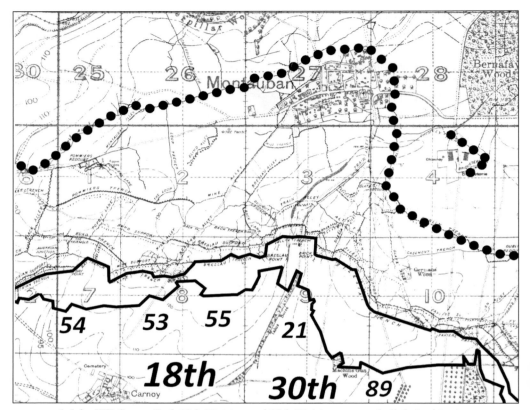

1 July, XIII Corps: Both 18th Division and 30th Division captured all their objectives in the Montauban area.

30th Division, Montauban

The 30th Division held the line north of Maricourt with 21 Brigade on the left and 89 Brigade on the right; 90 Brigade was poised in reserve and 30th Division had dug a new trench across most of its front, narrowing no man's land. Crossing the German front line, 21 Brigade suffered few casualties and the moppers up caught many men in their dug-outs. But the 18th King's and 19th Manchesters moved too fast and had to wait until the British barrage lifted from Alt Trench at 7.45am. The King's then came under enfilade fire from Train Alley, across Railway Valley, where 18th Division was held up. The Warren also caused many casualties during the advance towards Glatz Redoubt; again because 18th Division was delayed.

When German bombers probed the King's flank, Captain Adam sent two parties to deal with them. Second Lieutenants Herdman and Fitzbrown were killed but Lieutenant Watkin's group drove the Germans back along Train Alley. But the Warren still held out in front of the 18th Division.

Meanwhile, the Manchesters had found a weak spot in the German line and the two battalions reached Glatz Redoubt around 8.30am. The problem was German artillery fire had stopped the 2nd Green Howards crossing no man's land in support.

Six Stokes mortar batteries started shelling the German trenches in front of 89 Brigade at 7.22am.[49] Eight minutes later, the 20th King's and 17th King's left their trenches 'as though on parade, in quick time' and the rear companies moved out early to avoid the German barrage. On the right Lieutenant Colonel Fairfax of the 17th King's and Commandant Le Petit of the 3/153rd Regiment, French 39th Division walked forward arm-in-arm to celebrate British and French co-operation.

The two King's battalions overran Faviere Trench and Lieutenant Colonel Poyntz's 2nd Bedfords followed in support, capturing 300 Germans in their dug-outs. Alt Alley and Casement Trench were overrun and then the King's waited for the artillery to lift from Dublin Trench. The trench was abandoned and badly damaged, so many advanced past without noticing it. By 8.30am they were digging in 100 metres beyond.

18th Division Later
Only 54 Brigade was across the crest of Montauban ridge by 10am and the 11th Royal Fusiliers and 7th Bedfords reached White Trench overlooking Caterpillar Valley around 4pm. The centre was pinned down near the German front trench while the right was stuck in front of Train Alley. The 7th Buffs cleared the Carnoy crater field two hours late but the Germans in Breslau Support Trench and the Loop clung on, jeopardising 90 Brigade's advance towards Montauban.

Brigadier General Jackson ordered the 7th Queen's Own[50] to bypass the Loop and keep going to the Pommiers line. All four companies passed through the East Surreys near Train Alley and they reached the Montauban road about noon, signalling to a contact aeroplane overhead. The advance forced the Germans in Breslau Support Trench and the Loop to withdraw, allowing Lieutenant Heaton to lead the 7th Queen's forward around 10am, and they took ninety prisoners. They linked up with the East Surreys and some of the Buffs led by Second Lieutenant Dyson in Train Alley, securing the division's right flank between them.

Meanwhile, Captain Fenner's group of the 6th Berkshires had been closing in on the west side of the Loop and sixty Germans surrendered after Sergeant Major Sayer killed a sniper. Lieutenant Tortiss then led the 8th

---

49 The mortars had been set up at the end of Russian saps opened a few hours earlier.
50 55 Brigade.

Norfolks and 7th Queen's against Back Trench but it took until 2pm to capture the trench along with 150 Germans; Tortiss's men were too weak to do much more.

Second Lieutenant Gundry-White led the 10th Essex bombers from Pommiers Redoubt along Montauban Alley and they reached White Trench around 3.30pm. Two hours later they met Second Lieutenant Attenborough's group of Berkshires and Norfolks which had advanced up Loop Trench. They in turn met a mixed group from 55 Brigade, completing the clearance of Montauban Alley. Lieutenant Attenborough then sent forward parties to establish an advanced line overlooking Caterpillar Wood.

30th Division Later
Once 21 and 89 Brigades had reached Train Alley, Glatz Redoubt and Dublin Trench, it was time for 90 Brigade to capture Montauban. At 8.30am the 16th and 17th Manchesters left the area west of Maricourt with the 2nd Royal Scots Fusiliers following. They filed along Railway Valley while the troops on the first objective screened their advance with smoke candles.

Troops of 90 Brigade reached their jumping off line fifteen minutes early and while the front line waited in Train Alley, the rest had to lie in the open under machine-gun fire. Many casualties were suffered before the 16th Manchesters knocked it out.

There were few officers left when the artillery lifted and the companies soon became mixed together. While Stokes mortars provided a smoke screen, the Manchesters and Scots Fusiliers crossed an unoccupied Southern Trench and entered Montauban just after 10am. An hour later Brigadier General Steavenson's men were in Montauban Alley on the north side of the village. While 100 Germans surrendered, several hundred more were seen running across Caterpillar Valley and signallers made sure the British guns turned on them.

La Briqueterie factory was an ideal observation post overlooking the division's right flank so General Shea ordered the heavy artillery to shoot at the complex. At 12.30pm, Captain Corford's company of the 20th King's went over the top while Second Lieutenant Baker's bombing party followed Nord Alley. While the factory complex held out, they overran a machine-gun team beyond.

The 30th Division had advanced 2,000 metres on a front 1,500 metres wide and it had captured over 500 prisoners and three field guns. The French XX Corps wanted to advance further on the right but 30th Division's left flank was exposed until 18th Division moved up. Although there were reserves at hand, General Shea was aware there had been disasters elsewhere on Fourth Army's front, so he delayed further advances in case his troops had to help 18th Division. Patrols found Bernafay Wood, east of Montauban, was virtually empty while counter-attacks against Montauban never materialised.

Summary

For the cost of 6,000 casualties XIII Corps had cleared Montauban ridge before 6pm. The battle had exhausted both sides and as the single German probe towards Montauban around dusk was stopped, the evening was quiet. The troops at the front were digging in while the rest were carrying supplies forward or carrying the wounded back. It soon became clear the Germans had chosen certain areas to target and observers were letting them know when troops crossed them. Danger areas were noted by using feints to attract artillery fire and then troops were ordered to move quickly across them.

Chapter 3

Clearing the Flanks – 2 to 13 July

Planning 2 to 13 July

By nightfall on 1 July, the catastrophe on Fourth Army's front was becoming clear. There had been over 57,000 casualties, the majority in the first hour, and nothing or little had been achieved on two thirds of the front. In VIII Corps' sector 4th Division was holding the Quadrilateral; it would soon abandon it. In X Corps' sector, 36th Division held Schwaben Redoubt, but not for long, while 32nd Division held the Leipzig Salient. In III Corps' sector 34th Division had two parties in the German trenches south of the Bapaume road. In XV Corps' sector 21st Division held 1,000 metres of the German front north of Fricourt, the situation in the village was uncertain; 7th Division held Mametz. In XIII Corps' sector both divisions had advanced 2,000 metres across Montauban ridge. The French to the south had also had considerable success astride the River Somme.

At 10pm Rawlinson gave orders to attack 'under corps arrangements, as early as possible compatible with adequate previous artillery preparations'. But he was not looking to exploit the success on his right, because it would lengthen XIII Corps' right flank. He wanted his left and centre to widen the breach in the German front.

General Gough took command of VIII Corps and X Corps with orders to capture the German front line and the intermediate line beyond. While III Corps had to clear Ovillers and La Boisselle and advance towards Contalmaison, XV Corps had to secure the Fricourt area before attacking Mametz Wood. Meanwhile, XIII Corps could only advance further if the French covered its right flank.

On the morning of 2 July Haig told Rawlinson there were sufficient replacements but ammunition was limited. But when Rawlinson expressed his concerns over his shortage of heavy ammunition, he was told Haig wanted Fourth Army to shoot what was needed.

Plans for VIII Corps and X Corps to attack astride the Ancre had to be dropped while III Corps' attack on Ovillers was later reduced to two brigades. GHQ wanted XV Corps to advance between Contalmaison and Mametz Wood, to bring it in line with XIII Corps, but it needed time to relieve its divisions. At 8.30pm on 1 July Rawlinson ordered Horne to clear the salient around Bottom Wood and Shelter Wood at 9am the following morning, ready to make the main attack at 3.15am on 3 July. Haig also wanted XIII Corps to advance from Montauban. Although patrols were sent into Bernafay Wood, there was no attempt to occupy it. If there had been, it would have met little resistance. Later that evening Kiggell reiterated Haig's desire to exploit the Montauban position and he planned to visit Foch the following morning to arrange French co-operation.

Both Horne and Congreve believed the Germans were close to breaking point on XV and XIII Corps' fronts. They also thought they could break through, but only if the French protected XIII Corps' flank. But the longer they waited, the longer the Germans had to reorganise and reinforce.

Rawlinson and Foch discussed plans on 3 July and then Foch and Joffre met Haig for the first time since the offensive began. The French made it clear they did not want Fourth Army's right to advance because their fronts would become disjointed. Instead, they wanted the British left to advance between Thiepval and Pozières, widening the breach in the German lines. But Haig said the Thiepval and Pozières defences were still strong and Fourth Army did not have enough ammunition to cover its whole front. When Joffre persisted, Haig said he was willing to follow Joffre's strategy but he refused to follow a tactical plan he disapproved of. He also made it clear as commander-in-chief, he was ultimately responsible to the British Government.

Haig refused to budge and at 9.45pm Rawlinson ordered his three corps to close up to the German Second Line between Bazentin-le-Petit and Longueval; III Corps had to reach a line through La Boisselle and Contalmaison, XV Corps had to capture Mametz Wood and XIII Corps had to take Caterpillar Wood and Bernafay Wood. Fourth Army could then move its artillery forward and prepare the German position for an infantry assault.

On 4 July General Gough's Reserve Army headquarters took over responsibility for VIII Corps and X Corps. Control of the Ovillers sector also passed from III Corps to X Corps. But the shortage of ammunition meant the Reserve Army would initially be relegated to a subsidiary role. Haig told Rawlinson he had to secure his flanks, including Contalmaison and Mametz Wood on the left and Trônes Wood on the right. Foch also wanted Rawlinson to capture Trônes Wood and Maltz Horn Farm so his XX Corps could capture Hardecourt Hill.

FOURTH ARMY, 2 to 6 July

The fighting along the Somme front between 2 and 6 July fell into three separate sectors. The first was around Thiepval in X Corps sector. The second was the combined actions of X Corps, III Corps and XV Corps between Ovillers and Mametz Wood. The third was XIII Corps' capture of Bernafay Wood.

X Corps, Thiepval

36th Division, Schwaben Redoubt

Around midnight on 1 July General Morland learnt a large number of 36th Division's troops were still in Schwaben Redoubt. The artillery fired a box barrage around the area while Major Woods of the 9th Irish Rifles led 360 men across no man's land carrying supplies. But as the hours passed the bombing attacks against Schwaben Redoubt and the Leipzig Salient increased. X Corps handed over the west bank of the Ancre to VIII Corps so it could concentrate on the two lodgements.

Fourth Army wanted the Reserve Army to attack at midday on 2 July but neither VIII Corps nor X Corps would be ready until the following day. Gough had planned to attack with three divisions but Haig reduced it to only two of 32nd Division's brigades because of a shortage of ammunition. X Corps did not learn of the changes until 9.45pm and General Rycroft was surprised to hear only his division would attack on double the original frontage.

32nd Division, Thiepval

The plan was for 25th Division's 75 Brigade to attack Thiepval while 14 Brigade advanced from the Leipzig salient. But 75 Brigade was late and while General Rycroft agreed a three-hour postponement, the artillery did not hear of it in time and the batteries fired as planned. While runners told the batteries of the new zero hour, the guns had already fired some ammunition. So General Rycroft's attack was going to be on double the frontage and with half the ammunition.

Three battalions advanced on 75 Brigade's front but they had not had time to reconnoitre the ground. Lieutenant Colonel Cotton's 2nd South Lancashires were stopped by wire on the left and while Lieutenant Colonel Bond's 8th Borders captured the battered front trench in the centre, they were soon forced to withdraw. Most of Lieutenant Colonel Aspinall's 11th Cheshires were 'mowed down, line after line', in front of the wire but Private Marsden led sixty men in the fight for the Leipzig Salient. The survivors had to wait all day before they could withdraw. On 14 Brigade's front two 15th Highland Light Infantry companies made two unsuccessful attempts to capture Hindenburg Trench, north of Leipzig Salient.

25th Division, Leipzig Salient

The 25th Division relieved 32nd Division in front of Thiepval before dawn on 4 July but the Germans gave Major General Guy Bainbridge's men no respite in the Leipzig Salient. They also attacked 49th Division north of Thiepval. On the evening of 5 July 25th Division made its first move when Captains Russell and Knubley led the 1st Wiltshires[51] into Hindenburg Trench at 7pm, expanding the Leipzig position.

12th Division, Ovillers

X Corps and III Corps planned a co-ordinated attack north of the Bapaume road at 3.15am on 3 July – or rather that was the plan. Twenty minutes before zero Gough told Pulteney that X Corps was not ready and III Corps' half of the barrage would continue firing while two of 19th Division's artillery brigades shelled the Ovillers area. Major General Arthur Scott's 12th Division had to attack Ovillers on its own; X Corps would not advance until 6am.

On the left flank 36 Brigade released smoke but the German artillery opened fire as the four battalions crept forward through the dust and smoke. In 37 Brigade's sector the 6th Queen's Own captured the first two trenches and while the left company of the 6th Queen's joined them, the right company was stopped by wire. In 35 Brigade's sector the 7th Suffolks overran the first trench and became involved in a tough fight for the second one, suffering heavy losses due to the failure on its left. The 5th Berkshires overran two trenches and Captain Wace led them into Shrapnel Trench on the edge of Ovillers but they had overlooked 100 Germans hiding in dug-outs.

As the sun rose, the smoke hid the German trenches but it did not cover no man's land and when two 6th Buffs companies advanced, hardly anyone reached the German trenches. The fight continued for over five hours and casualties mounted as ammunition ran low. The four battalions slowly began to withdraw and by 9am the last footing on the outskirts of Ovillers had been lost.

The only good news was that one of the 9th Essex support companies had lost direction because their assembly trench had been dug at an angle to the direction of advance. Lieutenant Kennifick's men had headed south-east across Mash Valley and captured 220 Germans in the trenches north-east of La Boisselle.

---

51 7 Brigade.

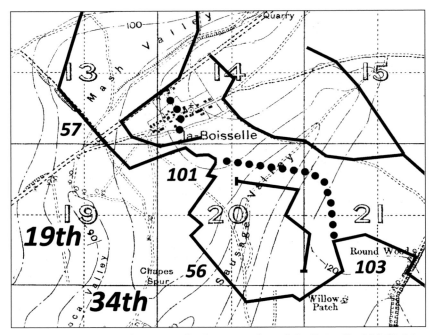

2 July, III Corps: As 19th Division fought its way through La Boisselle, 34th Division cleared Sausage Valley.

III Corps, 2 to 7 July

19th Division, La Boisselle

A night attack against La Boisselle had been planned for 10.30pm on 1 July but 19th Division struggled to take over the front line. By dawn 57 Brigade was still not in position across Mash Valley while only the 9th Cheshires of 58 Brigade were ready around Schwaben Hohe crater, south of the village. They went over the top at 4.30am only to find a deep communications trench blocking their way.

Then 58 Brigade was ordered to attack Sausage Redoubt south of La Boisselle and two 7th South Lancashire[52] companies advanced alone across no man's land at 4pm. Lieutenant Colonel Winser's men captured the redoubt and cleared 1,000 metres of trenches, taking over 50 prisoners; they had advanced the front line by 750 metres and linked up the two footholds south of La Boisselle.

X Corps was unable to attack the north side of La Boisselle on 2 July, but its artillery shelled Ovillers at 3.30pm while 12th Division released a smoke screen thirty minutes later. The Germans fell for the diversion and

---

52 From 56 Brigade.

their artillery shelled the area in front of Ovillers rather than 58 Brigade's actual target, La Boisselle. The 9th Royal Welsh Fusiliers and the 6th Wiltshires scrambled across the Glory Hole crater field and captured the German front trench. Then the 9th Cheshires advanced from Schwaben Hohe into the south side of the village and by dusk they had reached the church.

Major General Tom Bridges planned a pincer attack against La Boisselle early on 3 July and he ordered 57 Brigade to take over the trenches astride the Bapaume road. Lieutenant Colonel Royston-Piggott's 10th Worcesters moved along the south slope of Mash Valley at 2.15am and Lance Corporal Gardner led the final charge, firing his Lewis gun from his hip. The 8th North Staffords simultaneously advanced along the north side of the village assisted by Second Lieutenant Coutlers' and Richards' bombing parties from the 5th South Wales Borderers.[53] The Worcesters' bombers reached the third trench and Private Thomas Turrall took charge when Lieutenant Jennings was seriously wounded. He remained alone and surrounded for three hours until he was able to carry his wounded officer back to safety; Turrall was awarded the Victoria Cross.

An hour later 57 and 58 Brigades advanced through La Boisselle, hauling 150 prisoners from dug-outs and cellars. Captain Symons and Lieutenant Watts of the 9th Cheshires pushed forward along the saps but the Germans fired red flares as they withdrew, to tell their artillery the village had been lost. After a heavy bombardment, the counter-attack drove 57 Brigade out the east end of La Boisselle. The 8th Gloucesters and 10th Warwicks were in danger of losing the west end until the 9th Welsh arrived. Lieutenant Colonel Adrian Carton de Wiart, the Gloucesters' inspirational leader, took control of the all men in the area and made sure they held a line near the church, often exposing himself to fire as he moved along the line to supervise operations. Colonel Carton de Wiart was awarded the Victoria Cross.

At 8.30am on 4 July the 7th King's Own[54] took up the fight and for the next six hours they fought their way to the north-east corner of La Boisselle. Then 19th Division gathered all its bombers but they could not clear the German salient east of the village even though the 1st Sherwood Foresters[55] and the 4th Grenadier Guards[56] joined the fight. During the fighting, Lieutenant Thomas Wilkinson of the 7th Loyal North Lancashires saw a machine-gun team abandon their weapon, so he and two of his men used it to stop a German attack. Then he found some men hiding behind a barricade as the Germans lobbed over grenades so he used his weapon to drive them off. Wilkinson was later killed carrying a wounded man back to safety and was posthumously awarded the Victoria Cross.

---

53 The divisional pioneers.
54 56 Brigade.
55 24 Brigade, 23rd Division.
56 3 Guards Brigade, Guards Division.

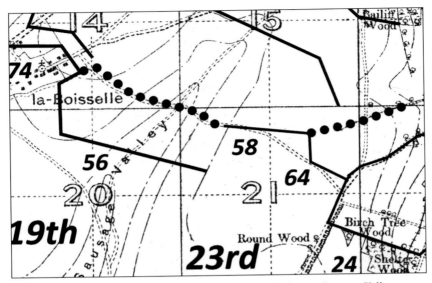

6 July, III Corps: 19th Division struggled to advance further up Sausage Valley.

At 7.30pm on 6 July the 7th East Lancashires[57] attacked the re-entrant east of La Boisselle. While the bombers failed, the attack over the top was successful; the Lancashires then stopped three counter-attacks.

23rd Division, Contalmaison

Major General James Babington was anxious to improve his position in front of Contalmaison as quickly as possible. At 4am on 5 July the 9th Green Howards'[58] bombers advanced towards Lincoln Redoubt on the division's left. The 11th West Yorkshires and 10th Duke's bombers received their orders late and although they captured Horseshoe Trench at 6.45am, the Germans retook the trench by 10am in a fight which involved most of 69 Brigade.

But Brigadier General Lambert was not beaten and the 9th and 8th Green Howards and 10th Duke of Wellingtons were ordered to advance over the top at 6pm. But Lieutenant Gibson first had to knock out a machine-gun on the brigade's left. He was spotted and killed so Second Lieutenant Donald Bell, Corporal Colwill and Private Batey knocked it out and their company reached the objective; Lieutenant Bell was posthumously awarded the Victoria Cross.[59] While Lieutenant Colonel Holmes' 9th Green Howards captured over 100 prisoners in Horseshoe Trench and Lincoln Redoubt, they could not bomb east along Shelter Alley towards 17th Division.

---

57 56 Brigade.
58 69 Brigade.
59 Lieutenant Bell was killed five days later trying to silence another machine-gun in a similar fashion.

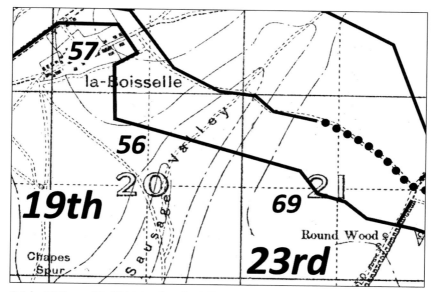

5 July, III Corps: 23rd Division found it difficult to make progress towards Contalmaison.

During the night of 6/7 July 68 Brigade relieved 69 Brigade in 23rd Division's sector and the 12th Durhams occupied Triangle Trench running east from Horseshoe Trench.

XV Corps, 2 July

21st Division, Fricourt Farm
During the night 62 Brigade relieved 64 Brigade in the salient north of Fricourt while patrols captured seventy-five prisoners and two machine-guns in front of Fricourt Farm. The only advance was made around 2pm by the 10th Green Howards, when Lieutenant Gardner's bombers moved to the line of trees called the Poodles, just north of Fricourt Farm, and linked up with 17th Division.

17th Division, Fricourt
Major General Thomas Pilcher had orders to capture Fricourt and link up with 7th Division north of Mametz and the bombardment was set to begin at 11am with zero hour seventy-five minutes later. But a patrol discovered the ruins had been abandoned during the night and early the following morning Lieutenant Turney's patrols from the 8th South Staffords[60] could only find twenty prisoners; it appeared everyone else had left.

---

60 51 Brigade.

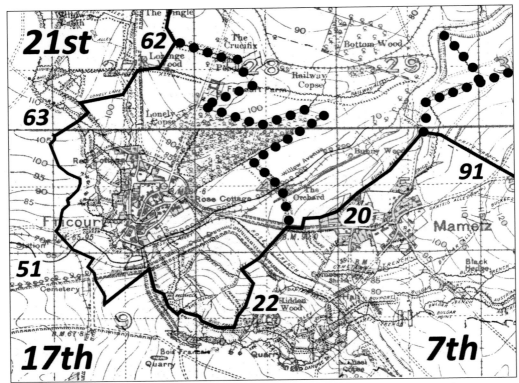

2 July, XV Corps: The German withdrawal from Fricourt village and wood allowed XV Corps to clear the salient.

General Pilcher ordered Brigadier General Fell to advance immediately into Fricourt and the 8th South Staffords and the 7th Lincolns ran across no man's land and found another ninety prisoners. The Lincolns came under machine-gun fire from Fricourt Wood but Major Metcalfe found there was no one on its south side, so his men entered and cleared the wood. At the same time the 10th Sherwood Foresters and the Staffords advanced to the trench connecting the north-east side of Fricourt Wood to Fricourt Farm. By 3pm the link between 21st Division and 7th Division had been made. Later that night, the Sherwoods' bombers cleared 200 metres of Railway Alley on the spur east of Fricourt Farm.

7th Division, North of Mametz
Patrols reported the area north of Mametz was clear before dawn and at 7.30am General Watts ordered his two forward brigades to occupy as much

ground as possible. While 22 Brigade advanced to the railway south of Fricourt, the 8th Devons captured Orchard Trench North in 91 Brigade's sector, meeting 17th Division on the south side of Fricourt Wood. Meanwhile the 2nd Queen's occupied Queens Nullah and White Trench on the brigade's right flank, linking up with 18th Division.

XV Corps, 3 July

XV Corps held an awkward re-entrant east of Fricourt and north of Mametz. Horne's plan was to clear Shelter Wood and Bottom Wood, shortening his line ready to assault Contalmaison and Mametz Wood.

21st Division, Shelter Wood and Birch Tree Wood

The 21st Division faced Shelter Wood and 63 Brigade formed a defensive flank in touch with 34th Division at Round Wood. The 1st Lincolns[61] advanced at 9am and Captain Newbury took command when Lieutenant Colonel Grant was wounded at the head of his men. The 12th Northumberland Fusiliers became involved in the fighting and Shelter Wood and Birch Tree Wood were eventually cleared.

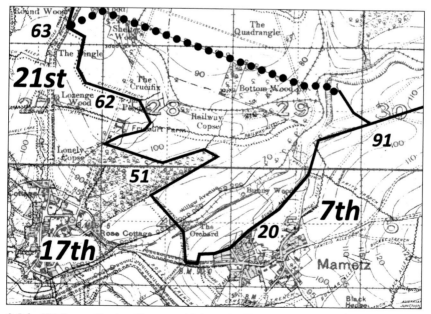

3 July, XV Corps: Further German withdrawals allowed XV Corps to advance towards Contalmaison.

---

61 62 Brigade.

A contact aeroplane spotted a counter-attack developing around 11.30am and the news was quickly relayed to Brigadier General Rawling. He sent the 13th Northumberland Fusiliers forward to finish the fight for Shelter Wood and 600 prisoners were taken. By the time the counter-attack began at 2pm, 62 Brigade was ready for them and it held onto both woods.

17th Division, Railway Alley

The 7th Borders led 51 Brigade's advance across Railway Alley towards Bottom Wood at 9am. Captain Crosse's men were pinned down by machine-guns in the wood and Quadrangle Trench but one company reached the west part of Bottom Wood. It was then cut off and was only relieved after 21st Division cleared Shelter Wood, forcing the Germans in the area to surrender or withdraw.

A planning oversight meant the artillery were not told of the 8th South Staffords' and 7th Lincolns' attack but they still charged at zero hour and they captured dozens of surprised prisoners in Crucifix Trench. Later on the 10th Sherwood Foresters captured Railway Copse. 8th South Staffords were also sent forward along the trenches but it took several hours to clear Railway Alley.[62]

7th Division, Bottom Wood

Bottom Wood had been abandoned by the time Lieutenants Thorniley and Farnsworth led the 21st Manchesters[63] into its east side. General Horne knew the corps line had been shortened by 2pm and he believed the Germans around Contalmaison and Mametz Wood were in disarray. An hour later patrols reported Quadrangle Trench[64] and Mametz Wood were unoccupied but Horne did not want to advance too far yet. He was concerned it might provoke a counter-attack before his men had consolidated a new line.

Night Moves

While 17th Division's 52 Brigade relieved 21st Division, 38th Division moved into XV Corps' reserve. Horne instructed 7th Division to advance to a line from the east end of Quadrangle Trench to the south edge of Mametz Wood but his orders were vague and they presumed Mametz Wood was unoccupied.

The guide for 22 Brigade had little idea which way to go and Lieutenant Colonel Berners refused to move the 1st Royal Welsh Fusiliers until he was sure, by which time it was too late to make the advance. Lieutenant Colonel Dugan decided to send the 2nd Royal Irish Regiment ahead alone but they encountered a large number of Germans in the wood and withdrew. While

---

62 The short advance had also cost around 500 casualties.
63 91 Brigade.
64 Quadrangle Trench ran across the spur west of Mametz Wood.

17th Division's patrols could see no one in Peake Wood, the Royal Irish could only see a few Germans in Quadrangle Trench and Wood Trench.

XV Corps, 5 July

After a wet, stormy night there was a lull in the fighting in the trenches south of Contalmaison on 4 July. Horne planned a surprise night attack and while 17th Division advanced up the spur south of Contalmaison, 7th Division would move to the south edge of Mametz Wood.

17th Division, Shelter Alley and Quadrangle Trench

Zero hour was set for midnight but the heavy rain delayed it for forty-five minutes. The artillery began firing at 12.15am and over the next thirty minutes the assault troops crept close to the enemy trench. In 52 Brigade's sector, Captain's Adcock and Thacker led the 10th Lancashire Fusiliers alongside the 9th Northumberland Fusiliers as they rushed Shelter Alley and Quadrangle Trench, where their 'bayonets were busy and no prisoners were taken'. But while 17th Division had taken their objective, 7th Division had not and it left 52 Brigade in a vulnerable salient.

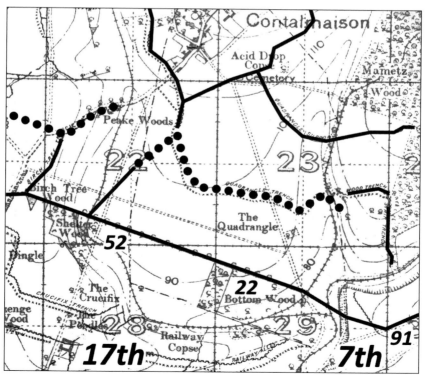

5 July, XV Corps: After a couple of difficult days, 17th Division captured Quadrangle Trench.

7th Division, Wood Trench

In 22 Brigade's sector Captains Stevens and Dadd's companies of the 1st Royal Welsh Fusiliers and Captain Bell's company of the 2nd Royal Irish were hit by enfilade fire as they cut through the wire protecting Wood Trench; Second Lieutenant Siegfried Sassoon[65] also 'did splendidly' during the bombing fight but Captain Gordon-Ralph's bombers found Strip Trench blocked by wire. A dawn counter-attack down Quadrangle Alley forced the two battalions back; machine-gun fire stopped three attempts to take Wood Trench during the night and 38th Division relieved an exhausted 7th Division when the attack was over.

X Corps, 7 July

17th Division, Quadrangle Support Trench and Pearl Alley

Horne needed 17th Division to capture Quadrangle Support Trench and Pearl Alley so the valley west of Mametz Wood could be cleared. While Pilcher argued his troops would be under crossfire from Contalmaison and Mametz Wood, Horne persevered. The 10th Lancashire Fusiliers and 9th Northumberland Fusiliers crept across no man's land during the thirty-five minute bombardment, rising to charge at 2am. By chance the Prussian Guard had chosen the same time to attack and a huge melee ensued as flares lit up the area. A few Lancashire Fusiliers led by Lieutenant Pegrum reached Pearl Alley on the left while others led by Lieutenant Gale and Sergeant Major Harris went as far as Contalmaison. The rest of the brigade regrouped and were reinforced by the 10th Sherwood Foresters[66] but the melee ended in a stalemate and both sides fell back.

Fortunately, XV Corps artillery orders included a 'plan B' if 52 Brigade's attack failed. Zero hour would be delayed for thirty minutes and so would the bombardment. The problem was III Corps did not hear about the delay until 6.15am and 17th Division had been told it would advance at 8am. The late attempt to delay zero hour jeopardised the attack.

The attack by 52 Brigade was delayed because the rain had turned the trenches into muddy ditches and while half of the 9th Duke's and all the 12th Manchesters advanced a few minutes late, two Duke's companies were too late to take part. The machine-guns in Mametz Wood decimated the two battalions and while Captain Benjamin's Duke's could not retake Pearl Alley, the Manchesters were unable to reach Quadrangle Support.

Meanwhile, 50 Brigade did advance on time but it did not get far. The Germans in Strip Trench shot down the 6th Dorsets' company advancing towards the west side of Mametz Wood while the 7th East Yorkshires could not bomb along Quadrangle Alley.

---

65 The war poet Siegfried Sassoon.
66 51 Brigade.

Horne ordered a second attack up the valley west of Mametz Wood at 5pm. But while the artillery was ready, 50 Brigade was not. Zero hour was delayed to 6.30pm but the advance did not start until 8pm and the Dorsets and East Yorkshires were joined by 10th Sherwood Foresters[67] on the left flank. All three battalions were stopped by artillery and machine-gun fire; 17th Division had accomplished nothing and it had cost another 400 casualties.

XIII Corps, 2 to 6 July

XIII Corps held a secure line along the Montauban ridge but the Germans twice tried to drive a wedge between 18th and 30th Divisions during the early hours of 2 July. The field artillery completed their moves before midnight and the heavy artillery was in place before dawn. Then it was time for the infantry to reconnoitre the ground ahead while the artillery registered new targets. The howitzers of 30th Division tried to set Bernafay Wood on fire with thermite shells and patrols later found the wood littered with German dead.

A day of consolidation and reliefs came on 3 July but General Congreve was looking to follow up any German withdrawal. Rawlinson instructed him to take Caterpillar Wood and the 10th Essex[68] occupied it at 4am on 3 July.

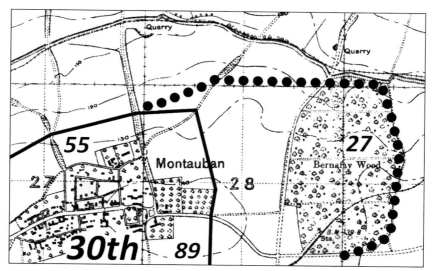

3 July, XIII Corps: 9th Division provided troops so 30th Division could clear Bernafay Wood on Fourth Army's right flank.

---

67 51 Brigade.
68 53 Brigade.

Major General William Furse's 9th Division relieved 30th Division east of Montauban. Congreve believed Bernafay Wood was empty and obtained Fourth Army's permission to occupy it before dusk with 27 Brigade. Following a twenty-minute bombardment, the 12th Royal Scots and the 6th KOSBs advanced towards Bernafay Wood at 9pm, finding only three machine-gun teams and three abandoned field guns inside. Some men dug in on the east and north sides of the wood under Lieutenant Crowden of the Royal Scots, while others occupied Montauban Alley between the village and Bernafay Wood. Patrols also investigated Trônes Wood but the Germans were waiting for them. The final move on XIII Corps front took place on the night of 4 July when 18th Division sent troops into an empty Marlboro' Wood, north of Caterpillar Wood.

7 and 8 July
Planning and Preparations
On 5 July Haig met Gough and Rawlinson to discuss plans for a new assault on 7 July. The Reserve Army would make gas and smoke attacks while Fourth Army captured Contalmaison and Mametz Wood on the left and Trônes Wood and Maltz Horn Farm on the right. Fourth Army reported ammunition stocks were low but Kiggell was optimistic when he spoke to Rawlinson the following day.[69]

Rawlinson and Fayolle also discussed details for a combined attack and while Rawlinson was worried that the French had been driven out of Bois Favière, the French were concerned their flank would be exposed if the British attack failed. They agreed to delay the attack on Trônes Wood to 8 July to give the French time to retake Bois Favière. Foch and Haig were meeting at the same time and they did not learn about the postponement until later.

Heavy showers interfered with the artillery observers' work, flooded trenches and turned tracks into mud but the troops prepared to attack at 8am. The rain also hampered the preliminary night attacks against Ovillers, Contalmaison and Mametz Wood and they all failed to capture ground close to the German Second Position.

X Corps, 7 and 8 July
Leipzig Salient and Schwaben Redoubt
The Germans attacked two locations through the morning mist on 7 July. At 1.15am they attacked 25th Division in the Leipzig Salient. Sergeant Hillings took command of the 1st Wiltshires after all the officers had been killed or injured and his men had the upper hand by dawn, capturing

---

69 Fourth Army only had 56,000 rounds for its 18-pounder field guns and 6-inch howitzers.

sections of the German front line; the 3rd Worcesters helped them consolidate the position. The second attack hit the 1/4th KOYLIs[70] in 49th Division's position in Schwaben Redoubt around 2.30am and the British artillery could only fire SOS barrages on pre-planned map targets. Despite help from the 1/5th KOYLIs and the 1/5th York and Lancasters, 148 Brigade were forced to withdraw to the old front line at 6am.[71]

12th Division, Ovillers

Gough issued new orders to capture Ovillers and while General Scott's 12th Division still held the Ovillers sector, two of 25th Division's brigades had been sent forward to carry out the attack. Brigadier General Armytage's 74 Brigade dug new trenches north of the Bapaume road, reducing no man's land to only 300 metres.

The plan was for 74 Brigade to capture the machine-gun posts covering Mash Valley before 36 Brigade left their trenches. Smoke was released following an hour-long barrage but there was no wind and 74 Brigade's new trench was an easy target for the German artillery. Lieutenant Colonel Messiter's 9th Loyal North Lancashires and Lieutenant Colonel Finch's 13th Cheshires advanced across Mash Valley at 8.05am but they could not silence the machine-guns north of La Boisselle; the 7th Suffolks reinforced them later.

While waiting for zero hour 36 Brigade suffered nearly 300 casualties from artillery fire. But the 9th Royal Fusiliers and Captain May's company of the 7th Royal Sussex captured two trenches, Captain Borlase's company captured the reserve trench and Second Lieutenant Broughall's small group of men went even further.

Only the 9th Royal Fusiliers faltered until Lieutenant Colonel Annesley led them forward, waving his stick in the air as he cheered his men on; Annesley was killed soon afterwards and Captain Beck took over. Although no carrying parties could get across no man's land, the men had been trained to use German rifles and grenades and they made good use of captured supplies. Altogether 36 Brigade captured 1,400 prisoners in front of Ovillers. Lieutenant Colonel Osborn of the Sussex decided there were insufficient men to hold the third trench and he ordered the three battalions to withdraw to the second trench.

Captain Lewis led sixty 11th Middlesex men across no man's land around 3pm; Lewis and twenty men did not make it. Two hours later Captain Crombie led another fifty Middlesex men over and 35 Brigade eventually sent the 9th Essex and 7th Surreys forward to reinforce the position. While bad weather prevented further action, the 8th South Lancashires[72] linked up the two brigades during the night.

---

70 From 148 Brigade.
71 The German bombers were using a new lightweight egg shaped bomb for the first time and they could throw them further than the British Mills bomb.
72 75 Brigade.

At 3.45am the following morning 12th Division's battle for Ovillers resumed. While the 7th East Surreys[73] and the 9th Essex[74] cleared the west end of the ruins, the 8th South Lancashires,[75] 2nd Royal Irish Rifles and 13th Cheshires[76] bombed along trenches south-east of the village. One group eventually turned along the trench towards the church but thick mud still hampered progress.

At 8pm 12th Division made a surprise attack north of Ovillers. Captain Metcalfe's company of the 11th Lancashire Fusiliers[77] captured their objective but they mistakenly advanced another 600 metres before stopping in another trench. When the Fusiliers signalled they had taken the objective, a 2nd Royal Irish Rifles' company moved up to support them. But while the infantry knew where they were, the artillery did not and they shelled the Fusiliers' position. There were difficulties getting the message back to the guns by which time the 13th Cheshires had occupied the original objective, taking 128 prisoners; only a few Fusiliers returned.

During the night 32nd Division relieved 12th Division and 14 Brigade took over a wasteland of shell craters. The troops at the front believed they could cut off Ovillers and maybe enter Pozières. But while the Bapaume road was a weak point in the enemy line, the German commanders appreciated the fact more than their British counterparts.

III Corps, 7 and 8 July

The 19th and 23rd Divisions were supposed to advance towards Pozières at 8am on 7 July but nobody moved at zero hour. Fifteen minutes later 19th Division began advancing north-east of La Boisselle but still 23rd Division

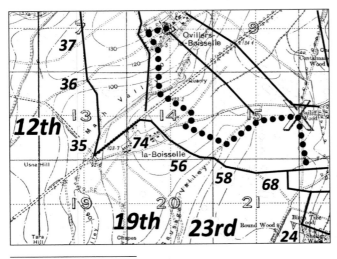

7 July X and III Corps: While 12th Division fought its way into Ovillers, 19th Division and 23rd Division edged towards Pozières.

73 37 Brigade.
74 35 Brigade.
75 75 Brigade.
76 Both from 74 Brigade, 25th Division.
77 74 Brigade.

did not move towards Contalmaison. So what had gone wrong? The 23rd Division had not been able to get into position because 17th Division had lost Pearl Alley, north of Shelter Wood. Thick mud meant the 7th Lincolns could not retake it even though Lieutenant Jones walked along the parapet, tossing bombs into the trench below. It meant 24 Brigade had no jumping-off trench and so 19th Division hesitated; it had not helped that the artillery barrage had not moved forward on time.

19th Division, North-east of La Boisselle
After fifteen minutes, it was clear the 7th King's Own and the 9th Welsh would have to go it alone but the artillery barrage still did not move due to a mix up over the times and the two battalions walked straight into it. It took until 9.15am for the infantry and artillery to co-ordinate the advance.

The advance of 58 Brigade was staggered because the 7th King's Own only had to advance 300 metres on the left while the 9th Welsh had to go 600 metres on the right. By chance, the mix up with the timings took the Germans by surprise and the two battalions captured their objective and over 400 prisoners with the help of the 6th Wiltshires. The 9th Royal Welsh Fusiliers were then sent forward by 58 Brigade to secure the right flank facing Contalmaison.

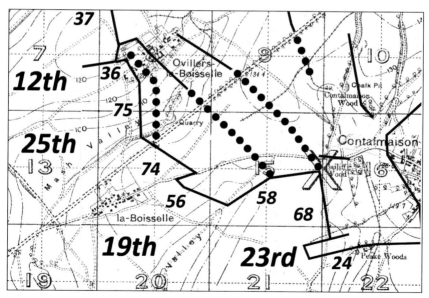

8 July X and III Corps: As 12th Division continued its fight for Ovillers, 19th Division and 23rd Division made good progress towards Pozières.

The Germans bombed throughout 8 July and then a contact aeroplane warned 58 Brigade of a counter-attack heading their way during the evening; it failed to recapture Bailiff Wood. Later on the 13th Royal Fusiliers[78] advanced 1,000 metres along the south-east side of the Bapaume Road, indicating the Germans had fallen back towards Pozières.

23rd Division, Contalmaison

General Babington's revised plan was for 68 Brigade to move as soon as 24 Brigade was ready on its right. But the 12th Durhams advanced early on the left, linking with 19th Division's advanced position. The 11th Northumberland Fusiliers advanced in pouring rain to the south end of Bailiff Wood at 9.15am just as the artillery barrage lifted but the wood was under fire so Lieutenant Colonel Caffin withdrew his men behind the crest. The 12th Durhams then had to cover 19th Division's flank.

Although Brigadier General Oxley revised his orders due to the loss of Pearl Trench, 24 Brigade was late getting to the front line and the advance did not start until 10am. While the 1st East Lancashires were stopped by machine-guns in Bailiff Wood and Contalmaison, the 1st Worcesters advanced into the centre of the village. The 2nd Northants could not reach them and the Worcesters ran out of ammunition after stopping two counter-attacks and had to withdraw.

Pulteney was anxious to make a second attack and 17th Division advanced to the east of Contalmaison at 8pm. But while there were too few men and too little ammunition, there was also too much mud and shelling. Instead General Babington consolidated his line and 68 Brigade dug in west of Contalmaison while 24 Brigade dug in south of the village.

During the night, General Bainbridge gave orders to close the 400 metre gap in the centre of 23rd Division's front but mud stopped the bombers moving along the trenches. Reports that the Germans had abandoned Bailiff Wood and Contalmaison were incorrect and patrols were fired on when they checked them out. An attempt by 24 Brigade to capture Contalmaison was made later that evening but the 1st Worcesters were stopped by machine-gun and artillery fire and the 2nd Northants were shot down as they emerged from Peake Wood.

XV Corps, 7 and 8 July

17th Division, Quadrangle Trench and Wood Trench

The 10th Sherwoods captured part of Quadrangle Trench at 8pm on 7 July but no other progress was made in 51 Brigade's sector. While wire stopped anyone from 50 Brigade entering Wood Trench, the 6th Dorsets bombed along Strip Trench.

---

78 A battalion of 111 Brigade (attached to 34th Division) attached to 56 Brigade.

The following morning, 50 and 51 Brigades' bombers tried in vain for four hours to advance along Quadrangle Trench and Pearl Alley. General Pilcher then learnt his men had to co-operate with III Corps' afternoon attack. But the order was later changed because Pulteney wanted 50 Brigade to attack Quadrangle Support on its own.

After only a twenty-five minute bombardment, the 6th Dorsets, Lieutenant Hare's company of the 7th Green Howards and the 7th East Yorkshires advanced at 5.50pm only to find the damaged trench was knee-deep in mud, leaving the men with little cover. Bombers could not silence the machine-guns on the flanks and they too had to withdraw.

General Pilcher was then asked to capture Wood Trench and at 7pm Captain O'Hanlon's company of the Dorsets rushed the trench and connected it to Quadrangle Trench. And then they waited for the 38th Division to attack Mametz Wood; and they waited and waited.

38th Division, Mametz Wood

The first attack on Mametz Wood was made by 115 Brigade against the Hammerhead. Major General Ivor Phillips wanted smoke to screen the brigade's right flank but the wind was too strong. So at 8.30am on 7 July, the 11th South Wales Borderers and 16th Welsh advanced north-west along Caterpillar Valley. The Borderers were hit by machine-guns in the Hammerhead while the Welsh were pinned down by enfilade machine-gun fire from the Bazentin Woods.

A new bombardment was arranged and Colonel Wilkinson's 10th South Wales Borderers supported a second attack at 10.15am; it ended the same way. A third attack led by Captain Galsworthy at 3.15pm also failed. The Welshmen did not get within 250 metres of the Hammerhead and 115 Brigade withdrew, leaving two 17th Royal Welsh Fusiliers companies to hold the line.

The 38th Division spent 8 July preparing for its next attack. During the afternoon, Horne told Phillips to clear the southern half of Mametz Wood during the night, ready to capture the northern half the following morning. But the order was based on reports that the Germans had abandoned the wood and the Welsh patrols had come under fire from the trees.

Brigadier General Price-Davies was told 113 Brigade would advance into the wood at 2am but a mix up in the orders meant Lieutenant Colonel Gwyther only ordered a single platoon to enter the wood rather than all of the 14th Royal Welsh Fusiliers. The officer returned an hour later saying he could not find a way forward.

9 to 13 July

On 8 July Haig told his army commanders he wanted to extend the attack north across the Bapaume road once X Corps had taken Ovillers and III Corps had taken Pozières. He then spoke to Rawlinson and his corps commanders about their objectives on the Bazentin – Longueval ridge. But Mametz Wood had to be cleared so III Corps could capture Contalmaison and XIII Corps could move into Caterpillar Valley. Rawlinson explained there had been a problem with 38th Division and General Watts of 7th Division had replaced General Phillips.

Again there were three independent battles: X Corps had to clear Ovillers; III Corps and XV Corps had to work together to capture Contalmaison and Mametz Wood; XIII Corps had to seize Trônes Wood.

X Corps, the Battle for Ovillers

The 32nd Division was north-west of Ovillers while 25th Division was to the south-west and south. The front lines were too close together for artillery support so the troops fought with rifles and grenades in the maze of trenches and shell holes. In 14 Brigade's sector the 2nd Manchesters, 1st Dorsets and 15th Highland Light Infantry made little headway on either 9 or 10 July; 75 Brigade was west of the village and a daylight attack by the 11th Cheshires on 10 July also failed. Meanwhile 7 Brigade was on the south side and when the 8th Loyal North Lancashires tried to bomb east of the village, they prompted a German counter-attack; the 3rd Worcesters had to hold the line.

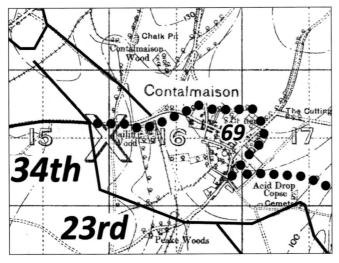

10 July, III Corps: While 34th Division moved into the line, 23rd Division captured Contalmaison.

The first significant progress was made on the night of 10/11 July when the 2nd Royal Inniskilling Fusiliers[79] advanced to trenches north-west of the village. Two nights later 32nd Division's 96 Brigade attacked the west side of the village while 25th Division did the same to the south. In 75 Brigade's sector the 8th Borders captured the German front trench while Lieutenant Powell led the 2nd South Lancashires into the west end of the village.

It had taken X Corps four days to advance a couple of hundred metres and while it was lagging behind III Corps, both corps still had a long way to go to Pozières.

III Corps

23rd Division, Contalmaison

The plan was for 69 Brigade to attack Contalmaison on 10 July but the Germans struck first. Their barrage caused heavy casualties to 68 Brigade but General Page-Croft's men stopped the counter-attack. General Babington was to seize points ahead of 69 Brigade's advance and while the 10th Dukes[80] set up a machine-gun covering the area south of the village, British artillery fire drove the 12th Durhams' patrols out of Bailiff Wood. A second attempt to take Bailiff Wood was interrupted when it looked like the Germans were attacking again.

When the barrage began machine-guns covered the flanks but the Stokes mortars were unable to fire a smoke barrage because there had been

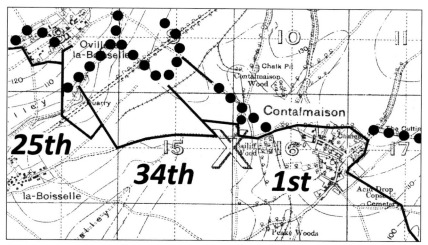

11 July, III Corps: 25th Division increased its grip on Ovillers and 34th Division pushed forward while 1st Division secured Contalmaison.

---

79 From 96 Brigade, attached to 14 Brigade.
80 Attached from 69 Brigade.

insufficient time to bring up the ammunition. To make matters worse, some of the assembly trenches were in a different position to that shown on the map while others had been damaged beyond repair.

Zero hour was 4.30pm and the attack began with machine-guns dispersing 200 Germans moving towards two 11th West Yorkshire companies as they advanced from Bailiff Wood. Lieutenant Colonel Vaughan's 9th Green Howards captured a trench north-west of the village but the 8th Green Howards were shot down as they cut through a hedge woven with netting on the south-west side. The Germans then withdrew as Lieutenant Colonel Holmes' men entered the village. While the West Yorkshires shot any Germans running away, the Green Howards captured nine machine-guns and 280 prisoners, many of them wounded awaiting evacuation.

The 12th Durhams eventually advanced at dusk, taking the Germans around Bailiff Wood by surprise. The rest of the 11th West Yorkshires and the 10th Dukes relieved the Green Howards in Contalmaison but not before Major Western had stopped a counter-attack from Pozières. The village was handed over to 1st Division at noon on 11 July.

17th Division, Quadrangle Support

The 17th Division had to advance up the valley between Contalmaison and Mametz Wood but crossfire made it impossible to move in the open. Horne was anxious to take Quadrangle Support so he ordered General Pilcher to make a surprise attack later that night. At 11.20pm Lieutenant Colonel Barker's 8th South Staffords[81] captured the left half of the trench but the 7th Green Howards[82] advanced four minutes late and Captain Barmby's company was shot down.[83] The 7th East Yorkshires and 6th Dorsets[84] could not take the rest of the trench and the Staffords had withdrawn by 3am.

On the afternoon of 10 July, General Pilcher heard that 23rd Division had captured Contalmaison while 38th Division was advancing through Mametz Wood, so he ordered his bombers forward. The bombers of 51 Brigade followed a sunken road to the west end of Quadrangle Support while 50 Brigade's bombers used Strip Trench and Wood Support to reach its east end. They cleared the trench between them, shortening XV Corps' line. Later that night 21st Division relieved 17th Division.

38th Division, Mametz Wood

Mametz Wood was a large irregular area with an area called the Hammerhead on its east side. General Watts had issued orders for an attack from the south at 4.15am on 10 July. The preliminary bombardment would last forty-five minutes and trench mortars would target the Hammerhead;

---

81 51 Brigade.
82 50 Brigade.
83 The Green Howards believed the Staffords advanced a few minutes early, alerting the Germans.
84 Both from 50 Brigade.

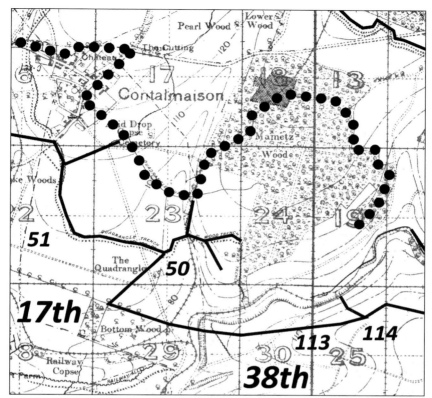

10 July, XV Corps: After a difficult time, 17th Division captured Quadrangle Support while 38th Division established itself inside Mametz Wood.

smoke would also be used. But the orders were issued late and the brigadiers had to visit divisional headquarters to get them. It was nearly midnight before they returned, leaving little time to prepare.

The plan was for 113 Brigade and 114 Brigade to advance from White Trench, clamber down a steep slope and cross open ground to enter the wood, but there was a delay in 113 Brigade's sector. After waiting fifteen minutes for Lieutenant Colonel Ronald Carden to return, Major McLellan gave the signal for the 16th Royal Welsh Fusiliers to advance. However, the barrage had moved on and they were pinned down by heavy fire from across the valley to their left. Carden eventually caught up, tied a handkerchief to his walking stick and rallied his men. The 14th Royal Welsh Fusiliers[85] caught the 16th Battalion up and both battalions advanced into the wood 'without hesitation and without a break'; Carden was killed near

---

85 Two companies did not advance due to a mix up in brigade orders.

the edge of the wood. Although the Fusiliers called for reinforcements, it took time to get the message back and General Price-Davies sent two companies of the 15th Royal Welsh Fusiliers forward.

Although 114 Brigade advanced on time, Captain Godfrey's and Dagge's companies of the 14th Welsh were shot down and disorganised as they advanced. Forty Germans then surrendered to Major Wyther's men and they moved into the wood. The 13th Welsh were pinned down in front of the Hammerhead and they called for reinforcements so General Marden ordered Lieutenant Colonel Rickett's 10th Welsh forward. One company helped the 13th Welsh get into the Hammerhead while the rest of the battalion closed the gap between the two brigades.

The Welshmen soon discovered the wood was a dangerous place to be because the low trajectory shells of the covering barrage were exploding in the tree-tops. However, they had only seen one large group of Germans on the west side of the wood because most had fled. When patrols reported the wood clear, Colonel Hayes of the 14th Welsh and Major Bond of the 13th Welsh asked if they could continue to advance but permission was refused because it was impossible to alter the artillery programme. So they waited for two hours and while the artillery shelled the north part of the wood many Germans crept back inside.

When the barrage finally lifted, it took time for the companies to fan out and move forward through the dense undergrowth. While the machine-guns in Quadrangle Alley stopped 113 Brigade advancing along the west side, the two 15th Welsh companies were driven back through the Hammerhead; Captain Lewis returned with only seven men.

The rest of the advance had stalled but air observers could not see anything and runners were shot down, leaving the brigade headquarters in the dark. So General Price-Davies joined 113 Brigade, while Lieutenant Colonel Hayes of the 14th Welsh took command of 114 Brigade and they arranged to reduce the range of the covering barrage so it was close to the front line.

Seven hours after zero hour General Watts sent two of 115 Brigade's battalions forward and while the 17th Royal Welsh Fusiliers joined 113 Brigade, the 10th South Wales Borderers joined 114 Brigade. The fresh troops renewed the advance and the staff of a German battalion eventually ran from their strongpoint in the centre of the wood while their men surrendered.

Two things happened around 2.30pm. Three companies of the 17th Royal Welsh Fusiliers took over the front line while the rest of the battalions organised inside the wood. The 13th Royal Welsh Fusiliers were also ordered to reinforce their bombers in Wood Support Trench.

The senior divisional staff officer, Lieutenant Colonel Rhys Pryce, found the troops in a 'somewhat confused state' when he entered Mametz Wood but he arranged for a general advance at 4.30pm with Generals Price-Davies and Marden. The two brigades advanced slowly through the wood, reaching the north edge two hours later, while Major Harvey's 10th South Wales Borderers moved north of the Hammerhead. They saw Bazentin-le-Petit Wood ahead and as the machine-guns in the Second Line peppered Mametz Wood, German observers directed artillery fire on the north edge. The 17th Royal Welsh Fusiliers and 14th Welsh were forced to retire 200 metres inside the wood with their flanks thrown back.

A plan to attack Bazentin-le-Petit Wood at 8pm was cancelled and the Welshmen endured a long night under artillery fire with officers sometimes having to force retiring men back into the wood at gun-point. During the night 115 Brigade moved into the wood and the 16th Welsh and 11th South Wales Borderers took over the front line; four other battalions reorganised in the centre of the wood.

On 11 July, General Watts wanted to clear the north edge of the wood but General Evans recommended consolidating inside because the perimeter was under heavy fire. He wanted to make a surprise attack after dusk but Watts disagreed and at 10.40am he gave orders to clear the wood ready for an afternoon attack.

The artillery barrage began at 2.45pm but many shells exploded over 115 Brigade again. It did not lift to the area in front of Bazentin-le-Petit Wood until 3.30pm due to a communications delay but it caught many Germans running from Mametz Wood.

While a machine-gun and a flame-thrower troubled the 16th Welsh on the left, the 10th and 15th Welsh reached the north edge in the centre and the 11th South Wales Borderers advanced on the right. Between them they captured 400 prisoners from five regiments inside the wood. But again they dare not go any further because of the machine-guns in Bazentin-le-Petit Wood.

A heavy overnight bombardment forced the Welshmen to abandon the edge of the wood and they handed it over to 62 Brigade, 21st Division, during the early hours. Patrols from the 13th and 12th Northumberland Fusiliers and 10th Green Howards explored the north end of the wood, finding thirteen artillery pieces and many dead.

Brigadier General Rawling's men endured heavy shelling while they dug in but they eventually established a link with 1st Division on the left and 7th Division on the right. They also prepared assembly trenches for the attack on Bazentin-le-Petit Wood.

XIII Corps

30th Division, Trônes Wood

After several quiet days on Fourth Army's right flank, the plan was for XIII Corps to clear Trônes Wood alongside the French. There was a deep re-entrant at the junction of the British and French Armies but while the French only had to advance 300 metres, the British had to advance 1,300 metres, so the attack would be made in two stages. XIII Corps would clear the south half of Trônes Wood and Maltz Horn Trench at 8am on 8 July; it would push on to Maltz Horn Farm when the French attacked Hardecourt at 9.45am. General Congreve then added more troops to the attack to clear the northern part of the Trônes Wood.

The 2nd Green Howards[86] emerged from Bernafay Wood at 8am only to be pinned down by machine-gun fire and two field guns shooting over open sights from Trônes Wood. A few of Captain Maude's company reached the wood but they were never seen again. Snipers hiding in the trees also stopped Lieutenant Field's bombers advancing along Trônes Alley. After the Green Howards withdrew, the 2nd Wiltshires were told their zero hour had been postponed to 1pm. But the French had captured part of Maltz Horn Trench at 10am and they were under fire from Trônes Wood. So at 12.20pm Congreve told General Shea to secure the wood, even if it took all of 30th Division to do so.

A Wiltshire company crept along a sunken road and charged Maltz Horn Trench, forcing the Germans to withdraw to the farm. After stopping a counter-attack, Captain Ward's men dug in, leaving Maltz Horn Farm in no man's land. A 19th Manchesters company joined them later and they linked up with the French.

A second Wiltshire company advanced from Bernafay Wood at 1pm and this time they entered Trônes Wood. Captain Mumford's men fought their way through the undergrowth only to come under fire from snipers hiding in the long grass beyond the wood. Lieutenant Colonel Gillson was wounded early on but he refused to be evacuated and directed the consolidation of the south end of the wood. The Wiltshires were later joined by two companies of the 18th King's and one of the 19th Manchesters; the 18th Manchesters[87] reinforced the position during the night.

Although 30th Division had a foothold in Trônes Wood it had to take it all and Shea ordered 90 Brigade to clear it before dawn on 9 July. The German artillery hit Bernafay Wood with gas shells during the forty-minute bombardment and it delayed the 17th Manchesters. The 2nd Royal Scots Fusiliers followed the sunken road to Maltz Horn Trench and at 3am they rushed the farm and dug in alongside the French. Captain Macgregor-

---

86 21 Brigade.
87 From 90 Brigade.

Whitton's bombers cleared Maltz Horn Trench by 7am, taking 100 prisoners.

The Manchesters advanced three hours late, gasping for breath in their fogged-up gas masks, but most of the Germans had already withdrawn and Trônes Wood was cleared with hardly a shot being fired; they reached the east side at 8am.

But the Germans were not giving up the wood without a fight. The north end was shelled and when a counter-attack was spotted around 3pm, the Manchesters fell back to Bernafay Wood. Only forty men stayed behind because the runner carrying their retirement order was killed. The 18th Manchesters also fell back to the La Briqueterie, leaving only one company in the south-east corner of the wood. And then the Scots Fusiliers abandoned Maltz Horn Trench. The counter-attack overran the few Manchesters at the north end of the Trônes Wood but the Fusiliers and the Manchesters' company held on at the south end.

General Steavenson immediately ordered the 16th Manchesters to retake Trônes Wood and they charged from the sunken road into the southern edge. They began moving north through the undergrowth at 4am but it was slow and difficult going and some groups got lost, some were hit by snipers, while others discovered the Germans had left. Bombers also occupied Trônes Alley between the north end of Bernafay Wood and Trônes Wood. But while 90 Brigade had cleared most of the wood, there was still fighting around Central Trench in the centre. Then the Germans counter-attacked, driving the Manchesters before them and by 8am they had cleared all but the south-east corner.

As soon as it was dark 89 Brigade moved into line ready to clear Trônes Wood, and 90 Brigade's survivors evacuated the wood during the early hours so the artillery bombardment could start. Meanwhile, the 2nd Bedfords had occupied the sunken road south of Trônes Wood while the 20th King's had taken over Maltz Horn Trench.

The Bedfords advanced at 3.27am and while two companies entered the south-west corner, two companies entered the south-east corner, having swerved right to avoid machine-gun fire. At the same time Lieutenant Small led the 20th King's bombers along Maltz Horn Trench towards the wood. The fighting continued all morning but it was easier for the Germans to reinforce and they had driven the Bedfords from the northern end by midday.

Then there was a worrying development. French soldiers captured orders for a counter-attack against Trônes Wood by two battalions. The news reached XIII Corps at 6pm and Congreve arranged a barrage to hit the area between Trônes Wood and Guillemont which stopped it. After dusk Captain Brinson led two 17th King's companies along the sunken road and into the south-east corner of Trônes Wood. It meant 89 Brigade were back where 90 Brigade had been the day before.

At 8.30am on 12 July British and French artillery worked together to stop another German attack from Guillemont. The rest of the day was spent consolidating and while the Bedfords and King's connected Trônes Wood to Maltz Horn Trench, engineers helped to dig a trench through the centre of the wood. But time was running out because Fourth Army planned to attack the German Second Line early on 14 July. XIII Corps had to secure Fourth Army's right flank so an order was issued to take Trônes Wood 'at all costs' before midnight on 13 July.

18th Division, Trônes Wood

The 18th Division took over XIII Corps' right flank early on 13 July and while Major General Ivor Maxse's men had less than twenty-four hours to capture Trônes Wood, it took them most of the day to prepare. There was a two-hour bombardment and 55 Brigade was due to advance at 7pm but only two of the 7th Queen's platoons advanced from Longueval Alley on time and most were pinned down in front of the wood. Only Lieutenant Haggard's bombers reached the north end of the wood, where they stayed the night. Captain Holland and Sergeant Roffey led the 7th Queen's Own to the tree line but they became disorientated inside the wood and were shot to pieces when they stumbled on Central Trench. Just 150 men reached east edge and while Captain Anstruther believed they had cleared all the wood, he soon discovered they had only secured the south-east corner. Meanwhile, Lieutenant Hayfield's company of the 7th Buffs had only cleared part of Maltz Horn Trench.

A second bombardment at 8.45pm failed to help the 7th Queen's so they withdrew to Longueval Alley when it was dark. The only success in the area was claimed by a bombing party which cleared Longueval Alley as far as the north end of Trônes Wood.

Maxse reported disappointing results at midnight; the attack from Longueval Alley had failed, one battalion was lost in the wood and Maltz Horn Trench was still in German hands. XIII Corps was due to attack the German Second Line in three hours so Maxse prepared to renew the attack with 54 Brigade. At 12.45am Brigadier General Shoubridge was told he had to capture Trônes Wood before dawn; but could his men succeed where others had failed?

Chapter 4

A Different Approach –
14 to 20 July

Planning and Preparation

On 8 July Rawlinson had issued orders to attack the German Second Line on Bazentin Ridge at 8am on 10 July. III Corps would clear the ground north of Contalmaison, XV Corps would advance through Bazentin-le-Petit and Bazentin-le-Grand Wood and XIII Corps would capture Bazentin-le-Grand and Longueval on the right.

The following day Rawlinson met his corps commanders and their chiefs of artillery to discuss the operation and they concluded the date could not be fixed until Contalmaison and Mametz Wood had been taken on the left and Trônes Wood had been cleared on the right. They also needed fine weather so the artillery observers could spot targets. The three corps commanders and their artillery officers wanted zero hour before dawn, before the German machine-gun teams could see properly, but there was a problem. The front lines were over 1,000 metres apart across most of Fourth Army's front, and the troops would have to deploy in darkness in no man's land close to the German trenches. There was the possibly of confusion at least and the potential for disaster if they were spotted.

While Rawlinson was prepared to risk a pre-dawn attack, Haig objected. He did not believe the staff officers had the experience and thought the troops had neither the training nor the discipline to carry out the attack. Instead he wanted XV Corps to capture Bazentin-le-Petit Wood before dusk on 12 July and then turn east along the ridge at dawn on 13 July while XIII Corps attacked Longueval. But Haig's plan had its own problems. The German artillery could concentrate on the initial attack while XV Corps had to present its flank to the enemy in the dark to clear the ridge.

Haig and Rawlinson met on the afternoon of 11 July and while Rawlinson supported the pre-dawn attack, Haig insisted on his own idea and promised extra troops. Fourth Army's bombardment began on 11 July but the shortage of ammunition meant there would be no prolonged barrage. The Reserve Army did what it could to help by shelling Pozières and Courcelette while French batteries hit Ginchy and Guillemont.

While GHQ was still expecting a dusk attack on 13 July, Fourth Army set zero for the early hours of 14 July. Both Horne and Congreve made sure XV and XIII Corps stuck to Rawlinson's plan, hoping Haig would change his mind. Rawlinson eventually wrote to Haig, asking for a night approach and dawn attack and his letter arrived early on the 12th. Rawlinson's Chief of Staff, Major General Archibald Montgomery, also spoke to Kiggell, Haig's Chief of the General Staff about the early attack. GHQ's Chief of Artillery, Major General Noel Birch, further eased Haig's concerns over the bombardment. Haig finally changed his mind and at 5pm on 12 July the order was issued for a 3.25am assault on 14 July.

While Fourth Army asked for the usual thirty minutes intense bombardment before zero hour, 3rd and 9th Divisions' artillery commanders were concerned it would alert the Germans. So it was reduced to five minutes, to cover the infantry as they charged the German front line. High explosive shells armed with delay fuses would also be used in the creeping barrage rather than impact fuses because the larger shell bursts would be easier to follow in the early morning gloom. The plans for 14 July were completely different from those on 1 July and the pressure had come from the army, the corps and the divisional commanders.

III Corps had to secure Contalmaison Villa on the left while the rest of Fourth Army seized the German Second Line on Bazentin Ridge. The first objective ran along the south side of Bazentin-le-Petit Wood, Bazentin-le-Grand Wood and Bazentin-le-Grand hamlet, through the centre of Longueval to the south-west corner of Delville Wood. The second objective included Bazentin-le-Petit village and wood, the north half of Longueval and Delville Wood.

Haig allocated three cavalry divisions to the attack and while 3rd Cavalry Division would move towards Martinpuich, 2nd Indian Cavalry Division would head for High Wood and 1st Cavalry Division would push beyond Guillemont. But while all the plans were being put in place, Rawlinson was disappointed to learn the French would remain on the defensive. They refused to co-operate because they believed the assault would fail.

FOURTH ARMY, MORNING 14 JULY

18th Division, Trônes Wood

While the rest of Fourth Army prepared for the pre-dawn assault, 18th Division only had a few hours left to clear Trônes Wood. Maxse's order reached General Shoubridge at 12.45am and he had no time to reconnoitre the ground. The original plan was for 54 Brigade to attack from the west but Shoubridge decided to attack from the south and sweep north.

On the way along the sunken lane, Lieutenant Colonel Francis Maxwell VC[88] of the 12th Middlesex told a padre: 'I am going this night to instil the spirit of savagery into my battalion.' But while the 6th Northants were ready, only one Middlesex company turned up. So Major Clark's Northants company advanced at 3.40am to the south-west corner of Trônes Wood and began moving slowly through the undergrowth. They were cheered on by a wounded Captain Fleming-Shepherd as they cleared Central Trench. They then pushed deeper into the wood but some became disorientated and thought they had reached the north end when they had only reached the south-east corner.

The Middlesex finally reached the wood at 8am but the Northants were nowhere to be seen. Colonel Maxwell went ahead and found scattered groups all across a quiet wood. While one of his companies attacked the strongpoint on the Guillemont road and the 7th Buffs[89] attacked Maltz Horn Trench, Maxwell gathered everyone he could find. Captain Podmore began by walking on a compass bearing across the southern end of the wood, while his men followed in single file. Maxwell ordered his men to fix bayonets and fire from the hip and they then walked north through the trees.

Although wounded Sergeant William Boulter went forward alone to bomb a machine-gun team holding up part of the advance; he was awarded the Victoria Cross. Then part of the line stopped when they came under fire from a machine-gun team on the west edge of the wood; Maxwell gathered seventy men together and while some gave covering fire, the rest silenced the machine-gun.

By 9.30am the Middlesex were on the north side of Trônes Wood, shooting at the Germans running towards Guillemont. Maxwell's methodical method had succeeded where others had failed and as his men dug in, Maxse was pleased to report XIII Corps' right flank was safe.

Fourth Army's Night Assembly
The Reserve Army made attempts to draw attention away from Fourth Army's front during the early hours of 14 July; 4th Division bombarded the German trenches north of the Ancre before the attack, while 4th and 48th Divisions discharged smoke 20 minutes before zero hour. Meanwhile, Fourth Army's front was busy with movement, all of it in silence.

III Corps

The 1st Black Watch[90] captured Lower Wood and four artillery pieces the

---

88 Maxwell was awarded his Victoria Cross during the Boer War.
89 From 55 Brigade.
90 From 1 Brigade, 1st Division.

evening before the attack. Then twenty minutes after the attack Lieutenants Gunn and Murray Menzies captured Contalmaison Villa, north-east of the village; Lieutenant Gunn captured a dozen prisoners armed only with a knife.

Fourth Army Deployment

Brigadier General Hessey's 110 Brigade was ordered to attack in 21st Division's sector, the 7th Leicesters' leading company deployed fifty metres beyond the north edge of Mametz Wood while the other three deployed inside. The 6th Leicesters deployed 250 metres north of Hammerhead with its rear company in the trees.[91] By 2.30am everyone was in position only 400 metres from the German trenches.

General Watts's 7th Division had relieved 38th Division on the east side of Mametz Wood on the night of 11/12 July. Brigadier General Heyworth's 20 Brigade had been chosen to attack Bazentin-le-Grand wood and by 2am on 14 July the 8th Devons and 2nd Borders were deployed east of Flatiron Copse, only 500 metres from the German trenches.

Deployment arrangements on 3rd and 9th Division's front were similar. Six-inch howitzers had shelled the slopes ahead of the jumping off line and Lewis gun teams occupied the craters the evening before to make sure the Germans did not interfere with the deployment. After nightfall, an infantry officer and an engineering officer used a compass and a field level to lay out 1,000 metres of white tapes on each brigade front. Marker men then took up their positions and at 12.30am the brigades moved forward in single file and deployed along the tapes. Everyone was in place by 1.45am, with the first wave less than 400 metres from the German line. Six brigades, over 22,000 men, had deployed in silence in the darkness close to the German trenches. No one had got lost, no alarms had been raised and casualties had been minimal. It showed what the troops, many of them New Army soldiers, could achieve if they were given the opportunity.

However, there was one major concern: 62 Brigade had discovered its telephone communications in Mametz Wood were being tapped by the Germans, compromising the attack. So a fake message was sent telling the forward companies that operations had been postponed. After a tense wait, it appeared the Germans were no more vigilant than usual and there was no extra machine-gun or artillery fire; the ruse had paid off.

At 3.20am the Fourth Army's barrage intensified, signalling zero hour was close, and the assault troops crept closer to the German front trench, sometimes within fifty metres. Still the alarm was not raised and the only casualties were from a few shells falling short. And then at 3.25am the artillery barrage lifted and the first wave rushed the German lines.

---

91 Each assault battalion had a company of the 8th Leicesters while the rest of the battalion was in support. The 9th Leicesters and 1st East Yorkshires (from 64 Brigade) were in reserve.

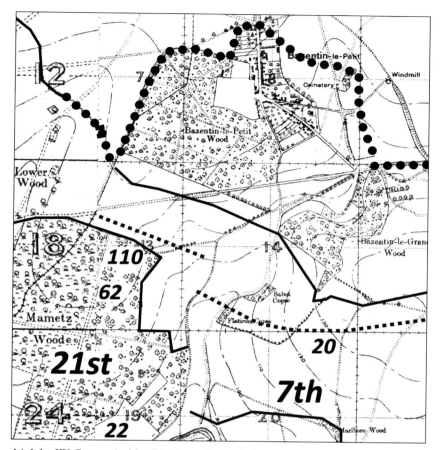

14 July, XV Corps: As 21st Division advanced through Bazentin-le-Petit Wood, 7th Division moved through Bazentin-le-Grand Wood.

XV Corps, 14 July

21st Division, Bazentin-le-Petit

Troops from 110 Brigade charged the German trench in front of Bazentin-le-Petit Wood as soon as the barrage lifted. The 7th Leicesters' centre was stopped by machine-gun fire but bombers on the flanks entered the trench and silenced the teams. The rest of the 7th and all of the 6th Leicesters cleared the second line by 4am and then moved through Bazentin-le-Petit Wood where the only resistance was in the north-west corner; two company commanders were wounded organising attacks against the position. While part of the 6th Leicesters lined the east side of the wood, ready to catch

Germans running across their front, the rest of the battalion advanced into Bazentin-le-Petit, clearing the north part of the village by 6am, with the help of the 2nd Royal Irish from 7th Division. They handed over the village to the Irishmen before digging in to the west.

7th Division, Bazentin-le-Grand Wood

The artillery had destroyed the German wire and battered the trenches around the Snout, a strongpoint which stuck out into no man's land opposite 20 Brigade. The 2nd Borders and 8th Devons overran the first trench and Circus Trench beyond. Captain Bellwood's company of the Devons came under fire from a machine-gun until Private Woods shot the crew. Lieutenant Lewis's company moved fast past the Snout and it was left to Lieutenant Savill's company to clear it. Two companies of Germans ran from Bazentin-le-Grand Wood ahead of the 8th Devons so Corporal Selby and Sergeant Potter shot them down with their Lewis guns.

The barrage lifted again at 4.25am and 22 Brigade advanced through 20 Brigade into Bazentin-le-Grand Wood. While the 2nd Royal Warwicks gave covering fire, Captain Tighe's company of the 2nd Royal Irish entered the south end of Bazentin-le-Petit Wood and they had cleared the village by 7.30am, taking 200 prisoners including a regimental headquarters.

XIII Corps, 14 July

3rd Division, Bazentin-le-Grand

Major General Sir Aylmer Haldane had 9 Brigade west of the Bazentin-le-Grand road while 8 Brigade was to the east and 76 Brigade was in reserve south of Montauban.

The artillery had destroyed the wire in 9 Brigade's sector and the 12th West Yorkshires and 13th King's charged into the German trench. Lieutenant Taylor pushed his company of the 1st Northumberland Fusiliers forward when a gap developed between the two battalions. After a fierce battle the troops advanced over the crest only to find machine-guns waiting for them on the far side. Major Oswald's West Yorkshires pushed forward through Bazentin-le-Grand Wood to seize the next German trench, securing the left flank. However, the King's moved too quickly into Bazentin-le-Grand and ran into the British barrage. They were also hit by enfilade fire from the east side of the hamlet where 8 Brigade had been delayed. The situation was saved when Second Lieutenant Clark arrived with reinforcements carrying a supply of bombs. The rest of the 1st Northumberland Fusiliers then cleared Bazentin-le-Grand and Lieutenant Lynch's bombers cleared the main centre of resistance, a large farm at the east end of the hamlet[92].

---

92 A regimental staff were found in the farm cellars the following morning.

In 8 Brigade's sector, the German wire was on the reverse slope and it had hardly been damaged. After seeing the 7th Shropshires and 8th East Yorkshires pinned down in front of two wide belts of wire, Lieutenant Colonel Forbes of the 1st Royal Scots Fusiliers sent Lieutenants Tinley and Smith with the battalion snipers and bombers through the gap in 9 Brigade's sector. They then bombed along the German trench while Captain Lloyd of the Shropshires cut through the wire. Only then could 8 Brigade enter the trenches east of Bazentin-le-Grand where they captured 350 prisoners and eight machine-guns.[93]

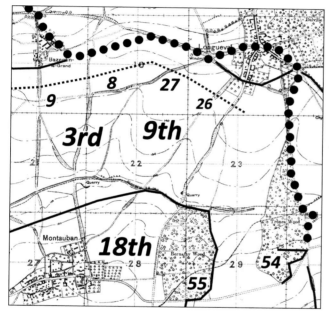

14 July, XIII Corps: 18th Division cleared Trônes Wood just in time but while 3rd Division cleared its objectives early, 9th Division had a prolonged battle for Longueval.

9th Division, Longueval

General Furse had 27 Brigade facing the trenches west of Longueval while 26 Brigade faced the village itself; the South African Brigade was in reserve south of Montauban.

In 27 Brigade's sector, the 9th Scottish Rifles advanced through the mist and cleared their trenches, digging in south of Duke Street, alongside 3rd Division. The 11th Royal Scots faced uncut wire and Lieutenant Winchester's Lewis gun teams silenced snipers while their comrades cut a way through. Captains Henry and Cowan were killed but Lieutenants Turner's and Fleming's men found a gap on the right flank and Winchesters' Lewis guns gave covering fire as they bombed along the trenches.

---

93 Another account says 284 prisoners.

In 26 Brigade's sector the 10th Argylls had trouble with the wire until the left company cut through and helped the rest of the battalion get into the front trench. The first wave then advanced too fast and ran straight into their covering barrage. They lay in shell holes and waited while a piper played the regimental march; he played the charge when the guns lifted. As the Argylls advanced to Clarges Street, the follow up waves cleared the dug-outs while the support battalions consolidated the captured trenches.

The 8th Black Watch advanced into Longueval and around 6.30am General Furse heard the village had been taken. But the information was incorrect; Captain Miles's company had only taken the south half while Captain Butter's company was struggling to clear a strongpoint in the south-east corner of the ruins. Lieutenants Armit and Noble had led the 12th Royal Scots forward but they could not cross the village square, where the Germans were waiting behind a barricade.

FOURTH ARMY, AFTERNOON 14 JULY

III Corps

Artillery observers had seen Germans leaving Pozières but Pulteney did not want 1st Division to advance on its own. It was hoped the Germans might abandon Pozières following the capture of the Bazentin Ridge position and aerial reports seemed to confirm they had. But 34th Division's patrols were fired on when they moved forward after dusk. 1st Division did not move from its Contalmaison position but it did take over the west edge of Bazentin-le-Petit Wood from 21st Division.

XV Corps, Bazentin-le-Petit and High Wood

Following the successes all along the front, the 2nd Indian Cavalry Division received the order to advance at 7.40am but it took time to move forward and the situation on Fourth Army's flanks was deteriorating. Meanwhile 21st Division was still engaged in the north-west corner of Bazentin-le-Petit Wood while the Germans recaptured the northern end of Bazentin-le-Petit around 8.30am. Lieutenant Hegarty's Royal Irish company held onto the cemetery but it would take until the evening until Captain Lowe's Royal Irish company retook the village with the help of the 2nd Gordons.[94] While Trônes Wood had been cleared on the right flank, the fight for Longueval was still in the balance.

But it appeared a breakthrough had been made in the centre of Fourth Army's front and by late morning senior officers were walking up the slope towards an abandoned High Wood. But while 7th Division and 3rd Division could have pushed on, the situation in Bazentin-le-Petit and

---

94 20 Brigade

Longueval made Rawlinson and Horne reluctant to let them. General Watts asked Horne if 91 Brigade could move forward, only to be told the cavalry would be advancing soon. General Haldane also asked if 76 Brigade could advance, only to be told to hold his position in case of counter-attacks.

At 8.50am Horne issued new instructions to advance at 2.30pm by which time he was hoping the cavalry would have seized the area around High Wood ready for 7th Division to occupy it. The problem was the Secunderabad Cavalry Brigade would not reach Montauban until 11.30am. Rawlinson felt the cavalry were taking too long and he told Horne to order 7th Division forward, towards High Wood. But Horne was concerned the fight for Longueval would leave his right flank exposed and wanted to wait until the village was secure. Congreve agreed and he held the Secunderabad Brigade back.

Horne eventually heard that Longueval was secure at 3.10pm and he issued new instructions to 7th Division to move towards High Wood at 6.15pm. He also told Congreve to move the cavalry forward to cover its right flank. But the orders were issued too late to be acted on and while 33rd Division's leading brigade did not receive theirs, 91 Brigade and the Secunderabad Cavalry Brigade received theirs an hour late. The two brigades faced crossing 1,200 metres of open ground to get to High Wood and the Germans had had all day to reoccupy it.

There were tense moments as bursts of machine-gun fire were directed at the troops advancing towards the wood but the 1st South Staffords and 2nd Queen's found few Germans inside. While the Queen's dug in on the west side, the Staffords could not take Switch trench at the northern end, despite the efforts of Lieutenant Seckington and Second Lieutenant Potter. Instead the Staffords dug in across the middle of the wood where they fought all night, with the help of 22nd Manchesters, to stop German attempts to force them out.

XIII Corps, East of High Wood and Longueval

The 20th Deccan Horse and 7th Dragoon Guards came under fire as they crossed the open ground east of the wood. The 7th Dragoon Guards even charged infantry and machine-gun teams hiding in the long grass and crops. But nightfall was approaching, so the troopers dismounted and dug in while the rest of the 2nd Indian Cavalry Division returned to their bivouacs.

Major General Herman Landon never received his orders to deploy 33rd Division but when Brigadier General Baird heard 7th Division was expecting help from 100 Brigade, he sent the 1st Queen's and the 1/9th

Highland Light Infantry forward to fill the gap between Bazentin-le-Petit and High Wood.

In 9th Division's sector, the fight for Longueval lasted well into the afternoon. The 12th Royal Scots tried in vain to capture the barricade blocking the exit from Longueval's square while the 1st South African Regiment fought through the afternoon and night to establish a foothold in the north end of the village.

The 7th Seaforths joined the Black Watch in the fight for the strongpoint at the south-east corner of the village and they eventually captured it around 5pm. The Seaforths and 5th Camerons could not reach Waterlot Farm south-east of the village but they did occupy Longueval Alley, establishing touch with 18th Division on the right.

Summary

Fourth Army had breached 6,000 metres of the German Second Line for the loss of 9,000 casualties. Over 1,400 prisoners had been taken and there were many more dead and wounded. But the success left Rawlinson with a dilemma. While resistance opposite XV Corps was negligible, XIII Corps was in a salient and its artillery was finding it difficult to fire at targets to the north and the east at the same time. Concern over 9th Division's fight in Longueval had made both Rawlinson and Horne hesitate while the desire to use the cavalry had added to the delay.

As a footnote, General Balfourier of French Sixth Army thought Fourth Army's plan for a pre-dawn attack was foolish and sent a message via the British liaison officer, Captain Spears, saying so. Rawlinson's Chief of Staff, Major General Montgomery's reply was: 'Tell General Balfourier, if we are not on Longueval ridge by 8am tomorrow morning I will eat my hat.' When Rawlinson sent a message late on 14 July to Balfourier, Fourth Army's liaison officer, Captain Sérot, said: 'They dared and they were able.' Rawlinson replied: 'So General Montgomery does not eat his hat.'

FOURTH ARMY, 15 JULY

At 9.45pm on 14 July Rawlinson ordered his corps commanders to capture the remainder of their objectives the following morning. While he was concerned about his low ammunition stocks, he hoped to use his cavalry divisions to exploit any confusion in the German lines. But the Germans recovered quicker than expected and reinforcements were rushed forward to recapture the Bazentin Ridge. Bad weather also interfered with both sides' plans. Mist and low cloud prevented aerial observation while two days of rain turned the battlefield into a quagmire.

III Corps, 15 July

34th Division, Contalmaison

The 8th East Lancashires[95] advanced from a line between Contalmaison and Bailiff Wood at 9.20am towards Pozières. Although the Lancashires were expected to clear the village, machine-guns stopped them in front of Pozières Trench, 500 metres short of it. Undeterred, General Ingouville-Williams ordered the Lancashires to try again at 6pm with the 10th Royal Fusiliers but the same machine-guns stopped them going far. The Fusiliers had planned to use flares to signal zero hour but they would not light in the damp conditions. It resulted in platoons advancing at different times, and the machine-guns dealt with them one by one. Overnight 112 Brigade and the Fusiliers deployed alongside the Lancashires, digging a new trench 250 metres in front of Pozières Trench.

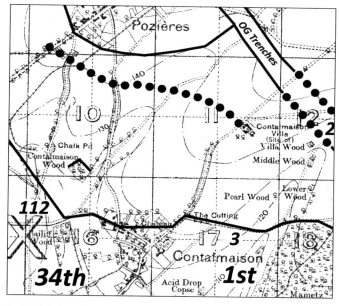

15 July, III Corps: 34th Division made good progress towards Pozières but 1st Division faced a long struggle to clear the OG Trenches.

1st Division, Bazentin-le-Petit Wood

Overnight 1st Division had relieved 21st Division along the west edge of Bazentin-le-Petit Wood. It was astride the German Second Line and Major General Peter Strickland put plans into place to advance along the two trenches[96] which ran north-east of Pozières. At 9am the following morning, the 1st Loyal North Lancashires[97] cleared 400 metres of OG1 and 200 metres of OG2.[98] British artillery forced the Loyals to withdraw from part of the trenches while the 2nd Welsh[99] were unable get any further during

---

95 From 112 Brigade.
96 Called OG1 and OG2; Original German 1 and Original German 2.
97 2 Brigade
98 OG stands for Original German, as in the Original German Second Line.
99 3 Brigade.

the afternoon. However, 3 Brigade was able to link up with 34th Division after dusk.

Early the following morning, the 2nd Welsh failed to advance along a communications trench towards the German Second Line west of Bazentin-le-Petit Wood, because the rain had turned it into a muddy ditch. After the field artillery spent all day cutting the German wire, it was 3 Brigade's turn and at 11.50pm the 2nd Royal Munster Fusiliers and 1st Gloucesters overran the German Second Line; they pursued the fleeing Germans until the protective barrage stopped them. Their officers made the men withdraw to the objective where every man donned a German greatcoat to protect themselves from the pouring rain. Lieutenant Colonel Lyons's request to push the Munsters into Pozières was denied. At the same time the 1st South Wales Borderers occupied Black Watch Alley on the left while 2nd Welsh carried out a bombing raid on the right.

Summary
The Germans resorted to shelling III Corps' new line on 17 July but Pulteney was still looking to improve its position. The 12th Durhams[100] relieved 112 Brigade[101] during the afternoon and they advanced at 8pm; the German machine-gun teams in Pozières Trench were waiting for them. General Ingouville-Williams cancelled an attack planned against Pozières at 3.30am.

XV Corps, 15 July

33rd Division, the Switch Line
The 33rd Division faced the Switch Line west of High Wood and General Landon's plan was to capture Martinpuich while III Corps attacked Pozières. On the evening of 14 July, 98 Brigade and 100 Brigade occupied the space between Bazentin-le-Petit and High Wood. However, there was no co-ordination with 7th Division in Bazentin-le-Petit while the 1/9th Highland Light Infantry could not find 91 Brigade in High Wood.

The two brigades advanced towards the Switch Line at 9am the following morning. The 1st Middlesex advanced from Bazentin-le-Petit only to be pinned down by shell and machine-gun fire. The 1st Queen's discovered two new belts of wire in the long grass and Major Palmer's men were shot down by the machine-guns in the Switch Line as they tried to cut through. The Highlanders' platoons failed to clear the west edge of High Wood, leaving the rest of Lieutenant Colonel Stormonth-Darling's men at the mercy of a strongpoint near the northern corner.

All three battalions were pinned down in front of the Switch Line and

---

100 68 Brigade.
101 From 34th Division.

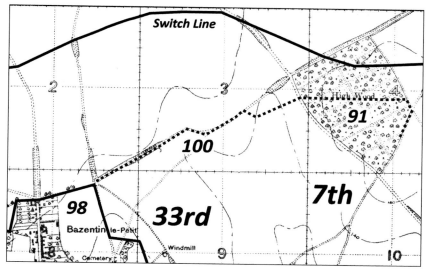

15 July, XV Corps: The opportunity had passed by the time 33rd Division advanced towards the Switch Line and 7th Division moved into High Wood.

the 2nd Worcesters and 16th KRRC were hit by cross-fire as they reinforced the line. Lieutenant Colonel Pardoe managed to get some of the Worcesters into High Wood, but the cost had been high. The survivors of the attack fell back during the afternoon and withdrew during the night.

7th Division, High Wood

While High Wood was divided by a number of rides there was plenty of undergrowth to scramble through. The crest of a ridge ran through the centre of the wood and the Switch Line was on the reverse slope, making it impossible to target. The west corner had a commanding view across to Bazentin-le-Petit and the east corner could see across to Longueval. Squadrons of the 20th Deccan Horse and 7th Dragoon Guards had already withdrawn from the area east of the wood during the early hours.

The fight for High Wood by 91 Brigade continued throughout the day and General Minshull-Ford had sent the 21st Manchesters forward to reinforce the 1st South Staffords and 2nd Queen's. Their 9am attack on the Switch Line was stopped by machine-gun fire. At 2.30pm a German barrage heralded a counter-attack and 91 Brigade's reserve battalion had to be sent forward to recapture the lost ground. Then 91 Brigade made a new attack at 4.45pm but it also failed. Shelling had cut all communications and General Watts did not know what 91 Brigade's situation was in High Wood.

Around 11.20pm General Horne obtained General Rawlinson's permission to withdraw 91 Brigade so the corps artillery could shell the wood. If 7th Division could not take it, he was determined the Germans were going to suffer. During the early hours the Staffords' rear guard 'listened to their comrades withdrawing and wondered if they would get back' as they fought off the Germans. Lieutenant English Murphy was the last to leave.

XIII Corps, 15 July
9th Division, Longueval and Delville Wood
General Furse's men were in an awkward salient with Longueval and Delville Wood at its apex. Delville Wood was thick with undergrowth and smashed trees; it was also cut by rides. It was situated on the crest of a low ridge and Rawlinson was worried the Germans would reinforce the wood, infiltrate Longueval and threaten Caterpillar Valley and Fourth Army's rear. The 9th Division had to secure its position and the plan was for 27 Brigade to advance through Longueval, while the South African Brigade attacked Delville Wood and Waterlot Farm at dawn on 15 July.

In Longueval, the 12th Royal Scots advanced astride North Street but Company Sergeant Major Geddes' men could not cross the square because the Germans had turned it into a killing zone. They could not advance to the west either, where the garden hedges had been interlaced with barbed

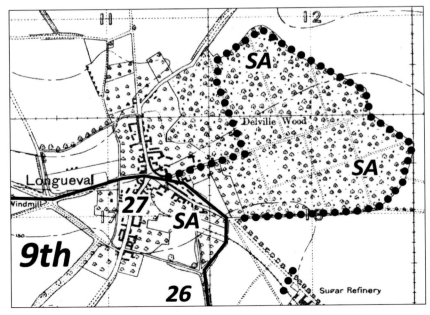

15 July, XIII Corps: 9th Division could not clear Longueval but its South African Brigade captured most of Delville Wood.

wire. A second attempt to clear Longueval by Lieutenants Noble and Armit at 7.30pm also failed.

Brigadier General Lukin was given orders to capture Delville Wood 'at all costs' and over half the South African Brigade assembled under Lieutenant Colonel Tanner of the 2nd South African Regiment. At 6.15am the South Africans advanced astride the chateau driveway into the south-west corner of the wood and had soon cleared the 'profligate undergrowth and the tangle of trees and branches' south of Prince's Street. After regrouping and turning to face north, the South Africans cleared all but the north-west corner of the wood, all 159 acres of it, taking 140 prisoners. The German artillery retaliated by targeting the wood while the South Africans struggled to dig through the tree roots. And then the counter-attacks started; they lasted all afternoon. But Tanner's men held on with the help of the 1st South African Regiment while a company the 9th Seaforths erected barbed wire fences.[102]

On 9th Division's right flank, a 5th Camerons'[103] company and two 4th South African companies rushed Waterlot Farm and 'slaughtered the garrison and consolidated the buildings'. Unfortunately, the sugar refinery was an exposed position and artillery fire forced them to withdraw.

The German bombardment and counter-attacks on 9th Division's line continued throughout the night and the following morning General Furse ordered a new attack. After trench mortars had shelled the ruins, Second Lieutenant Turner led the 11th Royal Scots[104] forward at 10am but the wired hedges again stopped them advancing through the orchards west of North Street. Colonel Dawson's 1st South African Regiment advanced through Delville Wood at the same time, only to find the Germans had reinforced the wood.

General Furse ordered everyone to regroup ready to attack again the following morning but Rawlinson had other ideas. He instructed Congreve to secure the village and the wood before dawn. General Furse did not learn of the change of plan until 8.40pm and it took several hours to get the message to the front line because the signal wires had been cut by shell-fire. Meanwhile, the South Africans were busy fending off a counter-attack and could not withdraw to a safe distance until 12.30am.

An hour-long barrage culminated in two minutes intense shelling but it was unobserved fire which failed to supress the Germans. At 2am the 12th Royal Scots and the 6th KOSBs advanced astride North Street through heavy rain. They missed many of the dug-outs in the darkness and the Germans emerged to open fire when illumination flares lit up the sky; Captain Whitley was killed and Lieutenant Turner had to organise the

---

102 9th Division's pioneers.
103 26 Brigade.
104 27 Brigade.

withdrawal. The South Africans were also unable to make converging attacks west from the Strand and north from Prince's Street.

General Furse's men spent a difficult night withdrawing to their trenches under heavy fire. The only good news came at 9am when the 9th Seaforths and two companies of the 4th South African Infantry secured Waterlot Farm.

FOURTH ARMY, 18 AND 19 JULY

At midnight on 15 July General Rawlinson issued orders for an attack on 17 July. III Corps would advance towards Pozières in co-operation with the Reserve Army. XV Corps had to capture the Switch Line south of Martinpuich and secure High Wood. XIII Corps had to seize Delville Wood and advance towards Ginchy and Guillemont, alongside the French Sixth Army. Three cavalry divisions would be on standby to exploit any breakthrough.

But when Pulteney, Horne and their artillery officers gathered at Fourth Army headquarters at 9.30am the following morning, they were told the attack had been postponed by 24 hours. They also learned Fourth Army had to send some of its heavy artillery north to Third Army ready to exploit the anticipated breakthrough.

Fourth Army issued its orders on 16 July and artillery registration began at once, even though poor weather prevented aerial observation. Rawlinson was unhappy about the situation around Longueval and Delville Wood and Horne reluctantly agreed to attack alongside XIII Corps even though XV Corps' guns would not have time to register their targets.

Rawlinson also told Foch that XIII Corps would attack Ginchy and Guillemont on 19 July. The following day it would capture Falfemont Farm, while the French attacked from Hardecourt. But there was plenty of work to be done before Fourth Army could attack and at 7pm on 17 July the three corps commanders were told the attack had been postponed.

Rawlinson was also aware that First Army would attack at Fromelles, fifty miles to the north, on 19 July. IX Corps attacked with two divisions and although the 5th Australian Division held a foothold in the German trenches until the following morning, 61st Division could not cross no man's land.

III CORPS, 18 JULY

1st Division, Munster Alley

The 2nd Royal Munster Fusiliers[105] captured the junction of Munster Alley and OG2 but they could not hold it. Two more attempts early on 20 July also failed. In the meantime, the division concentrated on digging outposts and strongpoints across the gap between Bazentin-le-Petit Wood and High Wood.

---

105 3 Brigade.

XV Corps, 18 July

3rd Division, Longueval

General Congreve had told General Haldane that 3rd Division had to capture its objectives 'at all costs'. The first attempt was made by 76 Brigade at 3.45am and the 1st Gordons and two 8th King's Own companies left their trenches west of the village, wheeled right and attacked the west side of Longueval.

The advance took the wired hedges in the flank and Brigadier General Kentish was pleased to hear progress was being made. Although the orchards north of the village had to be abandoned, the ruins along North Street were cleared. Some of the Gordons and the King's Own dug in along Duke Street while others entered Delville Wood and met the South Africans. But the Germans were not going to give up Longueval and Delville Wood without a fight and 76 Brigade later had to withdraw in heavy rain to escape the artillery fire.

9th Division Delville Wood

The German artillery shelled Delville Wood all day until 'nothing could live outside the dug-outs' and all communications had been cut. The outposts had to be abandoned and then at 3.30pm the German infantry attacked the east side. The South Africans stopped the first counter-attack but a second one pushed them back to Lieutenant Colonel Thackeray's headquarters on Prince's Street. A third attack around 6pm pushed 27

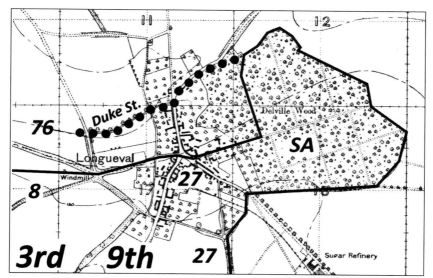

18 July, XIII Corps: 9th Division eventually secured the north end of Longueval and the north-west corner of Delville Wood.

Brigade back to the south edge of Longueval and for a time it looked as if the village was lost.

At 6pm 26 Brigade counter-attacked and Lieutenant Colonel Gordon's 8th Black Watch and Lieutenant Colonel Kennedy's 7th Seaforths drove the Germans back through Longueval. Lieutenant Colonel Duff's 5th Camerons also charged from Buchanan Street and into the square to cries of 'Come on boys!' The front line was once again back in the centre of the village and as the infantry reorganised, the artillery resumed shelling.

General Congreve wanted to expand the foothold in Delville Wood and he issued orders to attack the following morning. But 9th Division was too weak so 18th Division sent 53 Brigade forward to make the attack while the 19th Durham Light Infantry helped secure Longueval. The plan was for the 8th Norfolks to set zero hour when they were ready but their deployment was delayed by machine-guns firing along Prince's Street. Lieutenant Colonel Ferguson's message did not get to the artillery in time so the attack had to go ahead without a covering barrage.

The 8th Suffolks were unable to advance into the north half of Longueval. Lieutenants MacNichol and Benn were killed leading the Norfolks' left company and it could not advance past the chateau at the south-west corner of the wood. But Lieutenants Hughes and Gundry-White led the right company through the southern side of the wood and Colonel Scott ordered the 10th Essex forward to follow them. The 6th Berkshires also ran the gauntlet of fire in Longueval square but Captain Hudson 'did not see a single man falter'. A new barrage was organised so the Essex and Berkshires could advance north of Princes Street but many shells fell short and neither were able to advance far so they dug in south of the ride.

During the night 3rd Division relieved 9th Division but it was too difficult to extricate 53 Brigade and the South Africans from Delville Wood and they both suffered badly from artillery fire. On 17 and 19 July Private William Faulds, from the 1st South African Battalion, ran out into no man's land to rescue injured men; he was awarded the Victoria Cross. Captain Ackroyd also risked his life many times to evacuate the Berkshires' wounded.[106]

FOURTH ARMY, 20 JULY

XV Corps would advance towards High Wood and the ground to the east. General Congreve's XIII Corps had to finish clearing Longueval and Delville Wood, but it also had to attack the Guillemont area to the east. The shelling went on through the hours of darkness, intensifying at 2.55am and lifting thirty minutes later.

---

106 Captain Harold Ackroyd would be awarded the Victoria Cross for a similar deed in the Ypres Salient on 6 September.

XV Corps, 20 July

While 33rd Division cleared High Wood, 7th Division and 5th Division would capture Black Road and Wood Lane between High Wood and Longueval.

33rd Division, High Wood

Brigadier General Baird's 100 Brigade was still fighting inside High Wood and at dusk on 19 July the 2nd Worcesters established a line between Bazentin-le-Petit and the wood, to protect its flank. 19 Brigade was given the difficult task but Brigadier General Mayne did not receive the order to advance until 10pm. His men faced a three-mile march to their jumping off position and then had to cross 1,200 metres of open ground before the fight for High Wood began; and they had to do it all on a misty night.

Scouts led the 5th/6th and 1st Scottish Rifles forward and they crawled the final 100 metres while the British artillery shelled High Wood. When the guns lifted, the Scots charged through the trees, coming under fire from the Switch Line, while a strongpoint at the west corner caused many casualties. As the two battalions fought to capture the Switch Line, the 20th Royal Fusiliers occupied the south half of the wood.

At 8am a counter-attack overwhelmed the 5/6th Scottish Rifles and over 200 of Colonel Kennedy's men were never seen again. General Mayne ordered the 2nd Royal Welsh Fusiliers forward and Lieutenant Colonel Crawshay's men were shelled as they crossed no man's land around midday. They joined the 'hopeless mix-up of bush fighting' and eventually captured the Switch Line. While Colonel Crawshay's men dug a new trench through the centre of the wood, General Mayne asked for help to fend off the inevitable counter-attack.

General Landon sent the 16th KRRC and 1st Queen's of 100 Brigade forward but they did not reach High Wood until dusk, by which time the Welsh had lost the Switch Line. The 33rd Division faced an anxious night as 100 Brigade relieved 19 Brigade. The 2nd Worcesters also withdrew from the open ground west of High Wood.

7th Division, Wood Lane

General Deverell's 20 Brigade had a long way to go to get to Black Road. Two companies each of the 2nd Gordons and the 8th Devons began crawling through the mist twenty minutes before zero hour and rushed the German trench as the barrage lifted. Ten minutes later they advanced over the crest, only to be pinned down by machine-gun teams hiding in the long grass in front of Wood Lane. The strongpoint in High Wood also fired into

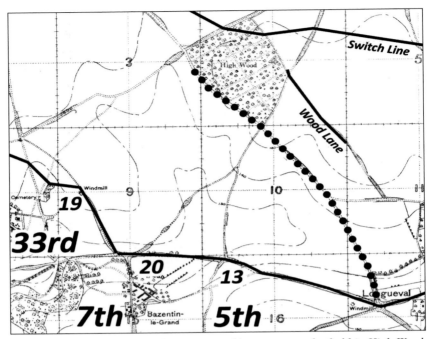

20 July, XV Corps: While 33rd Division could not secure a foothold in High Wood, neither 7th Division nor 5th Division could reach Wood Lane.

the Gordons' flank causing many casualties, including Captain Heywood and Lieutenant Savill of the Devons.

Sergeant Potter's and Lance Corporal Forrester's Lewis gun teams of the Devons covered 20 Brigade as it crawled back to Black Road and then it had to stop a counter-attack. Private Theodore Veale returned to find the wounded Lieutenant Savill but he could not rescue him because of heavy fire. He would return when it was dark, using a Lewis gun to keep a German patrol at bay while his comrades carried the officer to safety. Private Veale was awarded the Victoria Cross.

General Deverell believed High Wood had been captured and the Switch Line had to be shelled before his men could take Wood Lane. His advice was heeded and a second attempt was called off.

5th Division, Black Road

Brigadier General Jones's 13 Brigade also moved up on 7th Division's right, finding few Germans in the area. Later that night it relieved 7th Division along Black Road.

XIII Corps, 20 July

3rd Division, Longueval and Delville Wood

The second attempt by 76 Brigade to capture Longueval and Delville Wood started badly when the 10th Royal Welsh Fusiliers' guide lost his way in the mist. At 3.35am the 2nd Suffolks attacked Longueval from the west alone and Major Catchpole's and Captain Wood's companies 'pressed on with great resolution and were almost entirely lost' in the mist. The Germans were waiting for Lieutenant Colonel Long's Fusiliers when they advanced towards Delville Wood ten minutes later and as flares lit up the sky, machine-guns covered the village square and the chateau driveway. But the main problem was that the 11th Essex had not been told about the Welsh attack and thought they were Germans in the darkness; many Fusiliers were hit by 'friendly fire' before the mistake was discovered.

With so many problems, the Welsh advance was bound to fail but while some fell back, others remained in the wood all day. Corporal Joseph Davies gathered eight men into a shell hole when they were surrounded during a counter-attack. They drove off the Germans with rapid fire and grenades and then chased after them when they fell back; Davis was awarded the Victoria Cross.

Private Albert Hill also found himself surrounded by over twenty Germans and he used two hand grenades to drive them away before fighting his way back to his company with his sergeant. He then went into no man's land to rescue his mortally wounded company commander, Captain Scales. Hill also captured two prisoners; he was awarded the Victoria Cross.

On 20 July 3rd Division's chances of success had been compromised by two factors. Firstly, mist had prevented artillery registration, so the guns were firing blind. Secondly, General Kentish's troops were exhausted before zero hour. Later that evening 76 Brigade relieved Colonel Thackeray's group in the south part of Delville Wood, where they had held out under artillery fire and attacks since 15 July.

There is one final casualty to mention: Major Billy Congreve, Brigade Major with 76 Brigade. Congreve had helped to guide battalions into line and attended the wounded during the fighting around Longueval. He was killed on 20 July while gathering information on a failed attack. Congreve was awarded the Victoria Cross.

35th Division, Guillemont

Major General Reginald Pinney's 35th Division was holding Trônes Wood on XIII Corps' right flank. It had to capture a trench between Arrow Head Copse and Maltz Horn Farm before it could attack Guillemont and the

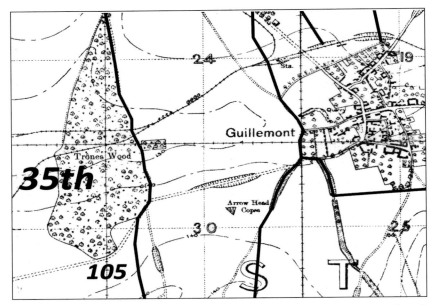

20 July, XIII Corps: 35th Division's scaled down attack failed to gain any ground south of Guillemont.

German Second Line. Zero hour was 5am but the French cancelled their infantry assault around Hardecourt because the thick mist prevented artillery registration. XIII Corps persisted and its guns fired blind for thirty minutes before zero hour.

In 105 Brigade's sector, Colonel Gordon's 15th Sherwood Foresters were hit by gas shells all night and only two companies were fit to attack by morning so one was tasked with seizing the trenches south of Arrow Head Copse and the other with taking Maltz Horn Farm. But while the artillery barrage had been unobserved, the sun had risen by the time the Foresters advanced and they were hit by artillery and machine-gun fire in no man's land; those who made it to the German trenches were soon forced to withdraw. Brigadier General Marindin organised a second attempt at 11.35am[107] by two 23rd Manchester companies. Although they reached their objective south of Arrow Head Copse, the trench had been obliterated and they had to withdraw.

RESERVE ARMY

The Reserve Army carried out subsidiary operations between 14 and 20 July to draw attention from Fourth Army's attack.

---

107 Or 10.45am, sources differ.

X Corps

Leipzig Salient

On 14 July X Corps fired gas and lachrymatory shells on the Thiepval heights, on the east bank of the Ancre, but 49th Division could not capture any more trenches around the Leipzig Salient. It was forced to fend off bombing and flame-thrower attacks on 15 July.

The Battle for Ovillers

On 14 July 32nd Division's 96 Brigade and the 1st Dorsets[108] cleared more trenches west of the village while the 8th Borders[109] gained ground to the south. In 7 Brigade's sector the 3rd Worcesters took all day to capture a trench north-east of Ovillers as did the 1/7th Warwicks[110] and 10th Cheshires to the south-east. Captain Lowry's company of Cheshires suffered heavy casualties and had to withdraw.

At 2am on 15 July, 32nd Division attacked the south-west side of Ovillers while 25th Division attacked the south side and tried to work around the east side. No one got very far. Later that night, Major General Robert Fanshawe's 48th Division relieved 32nd Division and 143 Brigade planned a surprise attack to isolate the Ovillers garrison. At 1am on 16 July Captain Castle's and Lieutenant Fisher's companies of the 1/4th Gloucesters captured trenches on the west side of village while the 1/7th Worcesters did the same to the south. The 1/5th Royal Warwicks advanced along a trench to the north-east, cutting off the village, and the 130-strong garrison surrendered to Second Lieutenant Callaghan's bombers of the 11th Lancashire Fusiliers. After two long weeks, the village was finally clear.

The following morning, the 1/4th Gloucesters cleared 300 metres of the trench north of Ovillers and cleared nearby communication trenches during the night of 18/19 July. The 1/5th and 1/6th Gloucesters then advanced north of the village.

Brigadier General Done's 145 Brigade relieved 25th Division on the north side of the Bapaume road ready to advance towards Pozières during the early hours of 21 July. But the barrage started two minutes early, alerting the Germans opposite 144 and 145 Brigades and their machine-guns mowed down the Gloucesters and Worcesters when they advanced at 2.45am; the two brigades withdrew after a three-hour battle.

---

108 14 Brigade.
109 75 Brigade.
110 143 Brigade.

Chapter 5

The Trouble with Villages and Woods – 21 to 31 July

RESERVE ARMY, 23 JULY

It was clear resistance was stiffening on Fourth Army's front so GHQ planned to transfer Pozières to the Reserve Army's sector. On the morning of 18 July Kiggell met Gough and Pulteney while Rawlinson's chief of staff and artillery officer represented Fourth Army.[111] Arrangements were made for I Anzac Corps to relieve III Corps' left on the night of 19 July. General Gough had orders to 'carry out methodical operations against Pozières with a view to capturing that important position with as little delay as possible'. But there was insufficient artillery to hit all the targets and the Reserve Army could not attack the same day as Fourth Army.

Gough's plan was for Major General Robert Fanshawe's 48th Division to advance between Ovillers and Pozières while Major General Harold Walker's 1st Australian Division captured Pozières Trench and the village beyond. It also had to bomb along the OG trenches on the right to the windmill on the Bapaume road. But the Australians' right was cramped and the digging of new assembly trenches delayed zero hour until the early hours of 23 July. In the meantime, 9th Battalion's[112] attempt to clear the OG trenches at 2.30am on 22 July failed.

The bombardment increased at dusk on 22 July, then five minutes before zero hour it intensified on the western side of Pozières, to make the Germans think the assault would come from that direction. The ruse did not work because the counter-barrage hit all the trenches around the village with equal ferocity.

X Corps, 23 July

48th Division, Schwarzband Graben

The German bombardment forced many of General Fanshawe's men out of

---

111 Major-General Archibald Montgomery and Major-General Charles Budworth.
112 From 3 Brigade.

their assembly trenches and when they advanced at 12.30am they found their own artillery had failed to silence the German machine-guns. In 144 Brigade's sector, Lieutenant Paramore was killed leading the 1/6th Gloucesters forward 'as if on the barrack square'; they were shot down in no man's land. The 1/4th Gloucesters' bombers had to be recalled on the left while 1/6th Gloucesters' bombers on the right were overrun.

While 145 Brigade faced Black Belt Trench (Schwarzband Graben) west of Pozières and the 1/5th Gloucesters were mown down on the left, the 1/4th Ox and Bucks had mixed fortunes. Captain Viney's company was hit by their own barrage, leaving Captain Birchall's company to capture the German front trench. Captain Aldworth brought two 1/4th Berkshires' companies forward and they helped seize 500 metres of trench and 150 prisoners. At dawn a new barrage hit the German trenches and an attack at 6.30am by the 1/1st Bucks extended 145 Brigade's hold on Schwarzband Graben. Although 143 Brigade relieved 145 Brigade, the 1/5th Warwicks were unable to bomb their way through to the Australians in Pozières on their right.

I ANZAC Corps, 23 July

1st Australian Division, Pozières

The German bombardment also forced the Australians to leave their assembly trench. As they crept towards the German front line, Lieutenant Thurnhill moved his field gun onto the Bapaume road and fired through the centre of Pozières village. At zero hour 2nd Battalion and 1st Battalion led Brigadier General Smyth's 1 Brigade while 11th Battalion and 9th Battalion led Brigadier General Sinclair-MacLagan's 3 Brigade. Only 9th Battalion were spotted crawling forward and machine-gun fire caused some casualties.

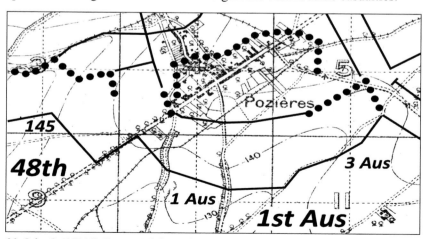

23 July, I ANZAC Corps: While 48th Division advanced west of Pozières, the 1st Australian Division cleared the village.

All four battalions overran a battered Pozières Trench and they moved towards the village as flares lit the night sky. Then the second wave advanced through the gardens and towards the ruins lining the Bapaume road. When thirty Germans made a run for it on the right, 140 men of the 11th and 9th Battalions took up the chase, passing through their covering barrage to kill them. They ignored their NCOs' calls to stop and went as far as Pozières windmill before heading back to their battalions believing they could have 'walked to Berlin'.

The toughest fight was faced by 9th Battalion's right flank in the battered OG trenches. Lieutenant Armstrong's party could not clear OG2 but Lieutenant Monteath's company advanced along OG1 until hidden machine-guns forced them to find cover. During the bombing fight, Private John Leak jumped out of the trench and ran forward under heavy machine-gun fire to attack a group of German bombers. Around 2.30am, 9th Battalion saw the 1st Loyal North Lancashires stopped by machine-gun fire in front of Munster Alley on their right;[113] the same guns then returned to firing at the Australians.

With the help of Captain McCann's men from 10th Battalion, 9th Battalion reached the junction with Pozières Trench by dawn. Second Lieutenant Arthur Blackburn joined them and his 10th Battalion bombers cleared another 250 metres of the OG Trenches. Blackburn crawled forward to reconnoitre the rest of the trench before leading his men forward; he was awarded the Victoria Cross for securing the division's right flank.

There was still a 300 yard gap on 3 Brigade's right where the Germans held OG1 south of the Bapaume Road and they counter-attacked here at 5.30am. Private Leak was always the last man to withdraw, throwing bombs to stop the Germans from exploiting the gap; he was awarded the Victoria Cross.

While 4th and 3rd Battalions of 1 Brigade only had about 400 metres to cover on the left, 12th and 10th Battalions of 3 Brigade had twice that distance to cover on the right. At 1am they advanced to the Bapaume road. As they dug in and checked the cellars,[114] patrols crossed the road and captured 100 prisoners and half a dozen artillery pieces along the road to Mouquet Farm. The Germans withdrew after their dawn counter-attack through the north-west side of Pozières failed.

Artillery observers and contact aeroplanes watched the Germans withdraw from Pozières and Gough ordered Walker to send patrols forward to investigate. At 4pm the order was given to clear the rest of Pozières but it was issued too late to act on. So the artillery continued shelling the north-west side of the village until 5pm and the infantry advanced as soon as they received their orders.

---

113 2 Brigade, 1st Division in III Corps sector, Fourth Army.
114 The Australians called the searching of dug-outs and cellars 'ratting'.

The Germans could not stop Lieutenant Waterhouse of 2nd Battalion occupying Cement House observation point at the south-west corner of the village.[115] Then 2 Brigade sent up two 8th Battalion companies and Captain James' men secured the ruins along the road running north towards Mouquet Farm. Lieutenant Colonel Elliott's 12th Battalion moved up on the right and Lieutenant Laing's patrols cleared the ruins along the northern side of the Bapaume road. Machine-gun fire stopped 3 Brigade clearing the rest of the OG trenches on the division's right flank.

While the Australians had a strong hold on Pozières, their flanks were in the air. Artillery had cut all signal wires and the front line units relied on runners. Although contact aeroplanes flew overhead at dawn, low cloud obscured the observers' view.

RESERVE ARMY, 25 JULY

Gough wanted the Australians and III Corps to work together to clear the OG trenches south-east of the Bapaume road and Rawlinson told Pulteney to attack Munster Alley 'either simultaneously with I Anzac Corps or later. Zero hour was to be before daybreak on the 24th July'. But the Australians needed time to reorganise and Gough's instruction to attack on the night of 24/25 July was too optimistic so he asked Walker to determine zero hour; 48th Division would secure the Australian's left flank at the same time.

Haig visited Gough on 24 July to discuss how to exploit the capture of Pozières. The problem was the Australians were under fire from every German battery in range and their observers were using the ruins to range their guns in.

I ANZAC Corps, 25 July

1st Australian Division, Pozières

Brigadier General Smythe's 3 Brigade[116] had two objectives on 25 July. The attack against the OG trenches to the east would begin at 2am while the advance north, astride the Mouquet Farm road would begin ninety minutes later. As the sun set, II Corps artillery began shelling OG1 while III Corps' guns hit OG2. The divisional artillery fired an intense barrage on OG1 for two minutes before zero hour.

After leaving Pozières Trench 3 Brigade had to wheel ninety degrees to face OG1. But the two left-hand companies lost their way and missed zero hour, returning to Pozières Trench later. Meanwhile, Lieutenant Colonel Le Maistre's 5th Battalion rushed OG1 and Captains Leadbeater and Lillie led the charge towards OG2, only to find it had been obliterated. Captain Lillie rallied the survivors in OG1 but they were soon bombed out and forced to

---

115 Better known as Gibraltar today, where you will find 1st Australian Division's memorial
116 5th, 7th and 8th Battalions of the 2 (Victoria) Brigade had been attached to 3 Brigade for the attack.

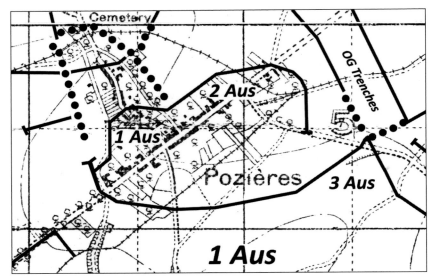

25 July, I ANZAC Corps: 1st Australian Division cleared the ruins along the Mouquet Farm Road.

withdraw. The 10th and 9th Battalions[117] connected the OG lines on the division's right flank but the Germans stopped Lieutenants Melville and Hillier capturing the junction of OG2 and Munster Alley.

In 3 Brigade's second attack, 4th Battalion was supposed to bomb north at 3.45am but the wrong date had been put on the orders. While the mistake was clarified, Lieutenant Fay's company of the 8th Battalion advanced astride the Thiepval road, outflanking the German position. Major Brown's bombers advanced ten minutes late, encountered little resistance and the companies advanced 700 metres, digging in near the cemetery. Private Thomas Cooke was ordered to take his Lewis gun team forward to a key position when a gun jammed. They came under heavy fire and were all killed but Cooke fought on until he too was killed; he was posthumously awarded the Victoria Cross.

When 11th Battalion advanced to the light railway north of the village, it came under fire from 8th Battalion to their left; Lieutenant Le Nay was one of those who stopped the 'friendly fire'. Heavy artillery fire forced 11th Battalion to withdraw at first light. Meanwhile, 12th Battalion was hit by enfilade machine-gun fire from OG1 Trench and could make no progress north of the Bapaume Road. Finally, 6th Battalion helped to consolidate its position while 3rd Battalion formed a link between 2 and 3 Brigade.

---

117 Assisted by two companies of the 7th Battalion.

By the morning of 25 July, 1st Australian Division held all of Pozières. While the only counter-attack at 8.30am from the direction of the windmill was stopped, the German artillery shelled the Australian positions all day.

During the night 2 Brigade took over the western half of the village while 5 Brigade took over the eastern half; it was the start of Major-General James Legge's 2nd Australian Division takeover of Pozières. During the early hours of 26 July, Major Hanson's company of the 1/7th Royal Warwicks[118] finally contacted the Australians' left flank north-west of Pozières.[119] Around the same time a 20th Battalion company raided OG1 Trench near the Bapaume road on the right flank. Meanwhile, 17th Battalion and 18th Battalion bombers joined 23rd Division's fight for Munster Alley.

The 2nd Australian Division took over the whole Pozières front when 6 Brigade took charge of the western side of the village during the night. The German artillery continued to shell Pozières mercilessly and it took until the following day to locate the batteries around Le Sars and Courcelette. Then one by one they were silenced, making General Legge's preparations easier.

Gough was anxious to keep the pressure on but Legge wanted time to prepare and he chose to attack the OG trenches astride the Bapaume road 12.15am on 29 July. The final stage of the bombardment of OG1 was only going to be one minute before lifting to OG2, so as not to alert the Germans.

2nd Australian Division, North of Pozières
The plan was for 6 and 7 Brigades to capture the OG1 lines north of the village while 5 Brigade did the same on the right flank. The 11th Middlesex[120] were due to cover the Australian's flank west of Pozières but they were unable to reach Western Trench. There had been no time to dig assembly trenches and the 23rd, 26th, 25th and 28th Battalions assembled in the open before creeping towards the OG trenches at midnight. The artillery only fired at a normal rate but the Germans soon spotted the advancing troops and as flares lit up no man's land, the assault troops were forced to run forward from shell hole to shell hole. The barrage intensified at 12.14am, lifted one minute later and then the Australians overran the German outposts. However, 23rd Battalion failed to notice their objective and the first two waves kept going until they ran into their own barrage; most were never seen again. Captain Maberley Smith made sure the support waves consolidated a shallow trench along the Ovillers road.

Three battalions of 7 Brigade cleared OG1 trench but barbed wire stopped most of the men reaching the OG2 trench, 200 metres beyond. While fog, dust and smoke obscured their signal lamps, shellfire had cut

---

118 143 Brigade.
119 The 1/8th Royal Warwicks bombed forward again the following morning.
120 36 Brigade, 12th Division.

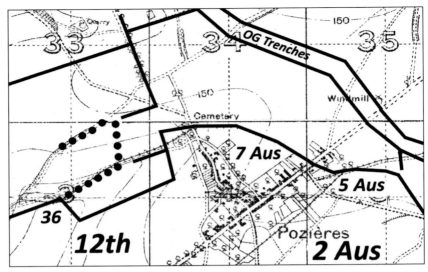

29 July, I ANZAC Corps: While 12th Division made progress west of Pozières, 2nd Australian Division could not capture the OG Trenches north of the village.

the signal wires so there was no way of asking for help. Pinned down and with casualties rising, all three battalions fell back to the OG1 trench. Then they withdrew all the way to their start line, leaving 23rd Battalion in a precarious salient north of the cemetery.

South of the Bapaume road, 5 Brigade's line ran obliquely to the objective, too close for artillery support. The trench mortar barrage had failed to silence the machine-guns and neither 20th nor 17th Battalions reached the OG1 trenches when they advanced four minutes after zero. Many wounded were left in no man's land following the attack and Sergeant Claud Castleton[121] was determined to rescue some. He was making his third trip with a wounded man on his back when he was shot and killed. Sergeant Castleton was posthumously awarded the Victoria Cross.

Legge was anxious to fulfil Gough's wish to press on and the decision was taken to attack on the night of 30 July at the same time as III Corps and XV Corps. The 2nd Australian Division had lost nearly 3,500 officers and men but Legge was confident it could attack again.

FOURTH ARMY, 23 JULY

Rawlinson met his corps commanders and their artillery officers on 18 July to discuss reorganising their frontages. III Corps would shift its right flank

---

121 Serving with the 5th Machine Gun Company.

north of Bazentin-le-Petit, while XV Corps took over High Wood and moved its right flank towards Longueval.

Although the forward movement of guns and ammunition began immediately, the lack of roads meant it took longer than expected to prepare. Heavy rain on 18 July prevented aerial observation and artillery registration so Rawlinson asked for a further postponement. Fourth Army would attack on 22 July while XIII Corps and the French XX Corps would make a second attack the following day.

Haig visited Fourth Army headquarters on 19 July and two things came from the discussion with Rawlinson's Chief of Staff. General Montgomery was still concerned the Germans could recapture Longueval and reach the head of Caterpillar Valley, threatening many British batteries. XV Corps also had to clear High Wood, to strengthen its position. After advising General Horne 'to relieve pressure on XIII Corps', Haig visited Rawlinson and agreed XV Corps would attack High Wood. Congreve also had to secure Longueval and Delville Wood the following morning.

Montgomery suggested the best way to capture Guillemont and Falfemont Farm was by co-operating with the French. But he also thought XIII Corps had to secure Guillemont as a preliminary operation and Congreve was told to attack it the following morning.

Rawlinson visited Fayolle to discuss the details and then Foch visited Rawlinson to make the final arrangements. The attack would stretch from Waterlot Farm, south of Delville Wood, to the River Somme and zero hour was set for the night of 22 July.

The three corps commanders and their artillery officers met at Fourth Army headquarters on 21 July. III Corps had to capture the trenches south of Martinpuich and XV Corps had to secure High Wood and Longueval. XIII Corps needed to clear Delville Wood and the line in front of Guillemont before taking the village.

Fourth Army wanted to attack after dusk and the main zero hour was fixed for 9.50pm on 22 July while III Corps would advance at 11.30pm. This was subsequently changed so III and XV Corps could attack at 12.30am on 23 July, at the same time as the Reserve Army's attack on Pozières. Although the artillery had begun registration work on 21 July, haze and cloud interfered with air observation at times. The bombardment started at 7pm on 22 July and the plan was for only five minutes of intense fire before zero hour.

Then on 22 July the French announced they would not be ready, so XIII Corps' right had to limit its operations to the capture of Guillemont. Zero hour in 30th Division sector was also changed to 3.40am, the original

French time, because their artillery would supplement the British barrage. XIII Corps' attack against Delville Wood was also moved to the same time.

On the night of 21/22 July the area east of Bazentin-le-Petit was handed over to III Corps and 19th Division while Major-General George Harper's 51st Division took over High Wood. But the troops were new to the ground and the two divisions did not have time to establish contact. A new trench had been spotted west of the wood and a plane confirmed Intermediate Trench had been dug in the middle of no man's land. It meant 19th Division had a new first objective. Later that evening General Horne got permission to change zero hour to 1.30am, so the advance to the main objective would be at the same time. Something was bound to go wrong with all the time changes on what would be a dark moonless night.

III Corps, 23 July

Zero hour for the attack towards Martinpuich had been changed to 12.30am on 23 July. While 1st Division's objective was the Switch Line south of the village, 19th Division had to capture the Intermediate Trench and Switch Line west of High Wood.

1st Division, Switch Line

The Germans spotted the assault troops assembling before zero hour and they lit up no man's land with flares; then their machine-guns opened fire. In 2 Brigade's sector, the 2nd Royal Sussex and the 2nd KRRC came under heavy cross fire as they were funnelled into the re-entrant between Munster Alley and the Switch Line. Brigadier General Hubback reported the Sussex

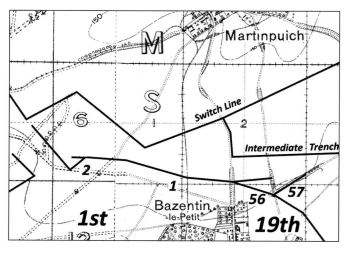

23 July, III Corps: Neither 1st Division nor 19th Division could advance towards Martinpuich.

had been unable to get into Munster Trench while the few riflemen who entered the Switch Line were forced to withdraw. In 1 Brigade's sector, the 10th Gloucesters and 1st Camerons were surprised by machine-gun teams hidden in long grass in front of the Switch Line. They too had to withdraw to their trenches.

19th Division, Intermediate Trench

German artillery fire delayed the issuing of General Bridges' orders, disrupting 19th Division's assembly north of Bazentin-le-Petit. Although 56 Brigade was only a short distance from Intermediate Trench both the 7th South Lancashires and Captain Thompson and Lieutenant Porter's companies of the 7th Loyal North Lancashires were stopped by machine-gun fire.

The 10th Worcesters had spent the evening trying to silence the machine-gun posts in Intermediate Trench; they had failed. The British trench bent away from the German line so Brigadier General Jeffreys ordered the assault troops to creep as close as they could. Unfortunately, the 10th Royal Warwicks did not relieve the Worcesters on the brigade right in time, so the 8th Gloucesters advanced alone. They were stopped by crossfire from Intermediate Trench and High Wood and the survivors were back in their own trenches before dawn.

XV Corps, 23 July

While the barrage started at 7pm on 22 July, the divisions had different distances to travel and the timings had been set so they all reached their objectives at 1.30am. While 51st Division would advance through High Wood, 5th Division's left would capture Wood Lane and its right would attack the orchards west of Longueval.

5th Division, Wood Lane

Zero hour was timed for 10pm and 5th Division's left had the furthest to go. Flares lit up the sky as 13 Brigade crossed the crest and approached Wood Lane. The 1st Queen's Own and 14th Royal Warwicks came under crossfire from Wood Lane to their front and from the east corner of High Wood to their left, where a platoon of the 1/4th Gordon's[122] had failed to silence the strongpoint. Lieutenant Scott's platoon of the Queen's Own captured fifty metres of Wood Lane while Lieutenant Dando's platoon went further but the Warwicks were pinned down in front of it. While Lieutenant Bartlett reinforced Scott's group, the Queen's Own soon had to withdraw.

---

122 154 Brigade, 51st Division.

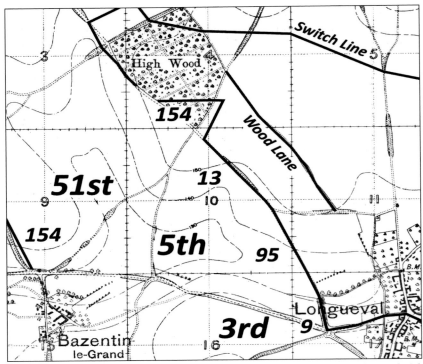

23 July, XV Corps: While 51st Division established a foothold in High Wood, 5th Division could not clear Wood Lane and 3rd Division could not capture the northern half of Longueval.

Major General Stephens was determined to clear Wood Lane but a second attack by the 15th Royal Warwicks and Major Anderson's 2nd KOSBs also failed so 13 Brigade withdrew to its start line before dawn.

51st Division, High Wood
The attack by 13 Brigade had alerted the Germans in High Wood and they were ready for 154 Brigade when it advanced at 12.45am. While the 1/9th Royal Scots and 1/4th Gordons were new to the area, the Germans knew the ground well. The Royal Scots came under artillery fire as they approached the south-west corner of the wood and then flares lit up the area. Machine-guns at the east end of Intermediate Trench made short work of Major Ferguson's and Major Moncreiff's men. The Gordons advanced through High Wood only to be shot down cutting through the wire in front of the Switch Line. Brigadier General Stewart's men were back in their trenches by 3am.

5th Division, Longueval

With only a short distance to travel, 95 Brigade attacked Longueval's orchards from the west at 3.20am. While the 1st East Surreys advanced past the north end of the village, a counter-attack stopped them turning the German flank and they were forced to withdraw to Pont Street. The 1st Duke of Cornwalls advanced into Longueval but the failure on their flanks forced Brigadier General Lord Gordon-Lennox's men to withdraw from their awkward salient.

XIII Corps, 23 July

XIII Corps made two attempts to capture the ground in front of Guillemont. The 17th Lancashire Fusiliers from 35th Division were ordered to clear the wire between Arrow Head Copse and Maltz Horn Farm because the artillery observers could not see it. Lieutenant Colonel Mills did not have enough time to prepare for the 1.30am zero hour and while the left column was pinned down, Lieutenant Wood's column spent five hours clearing the wire as Lewis guns kept the Germans at bay.

3rd Division, Delville Wood

General Haldane's 3rd Division held an awkward salient through Longueval, Delville Wood and Waterlot Farm. General Potter's 9 Brigade assembled late in Pont Street, west of Longueval, having only just arrived in the area. The 1st Northumberland Fusiliers were delayed because there was no last-minute intense barrage as promised and the minutes passed before Lieutenant Colonel Wild confirmed Lieutenant Cooper could advance. The Fusiliers were then hit by crossfire from the orchards to the left and Piccadilly to the front.

The 13th King's and 12th West Yorkshires did not have time to reconnoitre the ground either and they lost contact with the Northumberland Fusiliers. They were then hit by heavy fire along Piccadilly inside the wood and all three battalions eventually retired to their start line. Brigadier General Potter wanted to attack again but changed his mind after a visit to the front; he was later wounded by shell-fire.

While 8 Brigade was detailed to clear the ground south of Delville Wood, 30th Division attacked Guillemont. The 2nd Royal Scots found troops in their assembly trenches, delaying its advance, and it lost the barrage. Captain Cochrane was among the many casualties when they eventually advanced from Waterlot Farm towards Guillemont station. An 8th East Yorkshires' company, supported by bombers of the 7th Shropshires, failed to clear the area south of the railway. General Williams' men fell back to the Waterlot Farm area and then had to stop a German counter-attack.

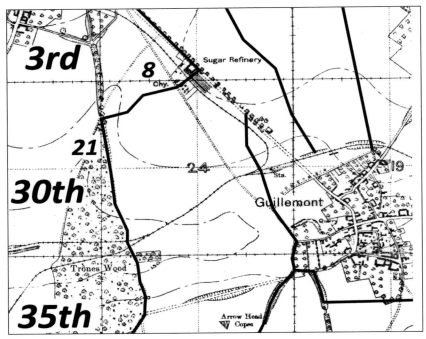

23 July, XIII Corps: No ground was gained west of Guillemont.

30th Division, Guillemont

Brigadier General Sackville-West's 21 Brigade held the trenches north-west of Guillemont. Smoke bombs exploded in the 2nd Green Howards' assembly trenches before zero hour, causing confusion and delay, and then wind blew the smoke across their front. Major Richard's men lost direction and while some mingled with the 8th East Yorkshires on the left and ended up withdrawing with them to Waterlot Farm, others mixed with the Manchesters on the right.

The 19th Manchesters suffered heavy casualties cutting through the wire covering Guillemont. German artillery stopped the runners getting through and no reinforcements were sent forward, leaving the Manchesters isolated and outnumbered. Only the left company was able to withdraw, taking the Green Howards with them; the remaining two companies were cut off and never seen again.

Summary

It was soon clear the attack had been a failure. While the Reserve Army had secured Pozières, Fourth Army had only secured a couple of footholds between Bazentin-le-Petit and Longueval. It left Fourth Army holding an uneven line of salients and re-entrants, making it difficult to register its artillery or stage attacks.

Rawlinson's headquarters had a lot of issues to address, particularly the problem of communications during an attack. A night assault had its advantages but it was difficult to keep track of the assault. The alterations to timings meant some units received their orders late while the different zero hours alerted the Germans.

Fourth Army also faced the problem of attrition. Many divisions were being engaged for the second time and some had absorbed several thousand replacements, many who had recovered from injuries. Most were drafted to battalions who needed reinforcements, rather than back to their old units and they were meeting strangers rather than re-joining old friends; the experience had an adverse impact on morale and efficiency.

FOURTH ARMY, 27 JULY

Haig's first visit on 23 July was to Reserve Army headquarters. He approved Gough's plan to advance beyond Pozières because it would outflank Thiepval and improve observation over Grandcourt and Courcelette. Haig then told Pulteney to cover the Reserve Army's right flank. Finally, Haig told Rawlinson to straighten Fourth Army's line ready for the next general attack. He believed it was taking too long to prepare for each attack, giving the Germans time to dig in; the attacks were also costing too many casualties. The only positive aspect was that the artillery, infantry, mortars and machine-guns were learning new lessons each time; the question was, were the lessons being exchanged between the armies, corps and divisions?

Rawlinson then assigned preliminary tasks to each corps. III Corps had to secure the re-entrant between Munster Alley and the Switch Line re-entrant on its left and Intermediate Trench on its right. XV Corps still had to capture High Wood, Wood Lane and the area north of Longueval. XIII Corps had to clear Longueval and Delville Wood on its left and capture Guillemont and Falfemont Farm on its right.

The German artillery was active on XV and XIII Corps fronts on 24 July but two counter-attacks were stopped by the British artillery. Rawlinson met Foch during the afternoon and they agreed to postpone their attacks for forty-eight hours because bad weather had disrupted counter-battery work. The German artillery had also upset the French preparations.

Rawlinson and Foch then met Haig and while he approved the postponement, he insisted on consolidating the captured line in depth. Rawlinson met his three corps commanders and their artillery officers the following morning and discussed Haig's concerns about a counter-attack through Longueval and Delville Wood. He wanted XV and XIII Corps to concentrate all their heavy artillery on the village and the wood while III Corps' heavy guns targeted distant villages; the French heavy artillery would shell the trenches around Flers, Ginchy and Guillemont. Zero hour was set for 7.10am on 27 July, and it would follow a one-hour barrage.

III Corps, 25 to 29 July

1st Division, Munster Alley
In 3 Brigade's sector, machine-guns around Pozières windmill stopped Captain Walshe's company of 1st South Wales Borderers first attempt to take Munster Alley at 2am on 25 July. At 3am the following morning the 2nd Welsh advanced without a covering barrage and took the Germans by surprise. They also linked up with the Australians at the junction of Munster Alley and OG2.

23rd Division, Munster Alley
General Babington's 23rd Division relieved 1st Division the following morning but two of the 2nd Welsh companies stayed behind and their bombers were advancing along Munster Trench when the Germans counter-attacked. The Welsh later gained some ground with Australian help. Although 68 Brigade took over the fight, the stalemate lasted well into the night.

On the night of 28/29 July the 10th Duke's bombed along Munster Trench and advanced over the top, while Australian troops filled sand bags and passed up ammunition. By dawn they had nearly reached the Switch Line.

XV Corps, 27 July

5th Division, Longueval
A German counter-barrage hit 15 Brigade, burying the 1st Norfolks left company, including Captain Francis and Lieutenant Ham, and their Stokes mortar teams in Longueval. But the rest of the Norfolks and the 1st Bedfords advanced through Longueval and the west side of Delville Wood. Second Lieutenant Hewitt was killed leading the Norfolk bombers through the village but the machine-guns in the orchards stopped them going too far while German artillery fire cut all communications to Brigadier General Turner's headquarters. As the Norfolks linked with 99 Brigade in the centre of wood, Captain O'Connor was killed trying to silence a strongpoint which had been overlooked during the advance. Part of the 16th Warwicks consolidated the west side of the wood but yet again the exposed north-west corner could not be held.

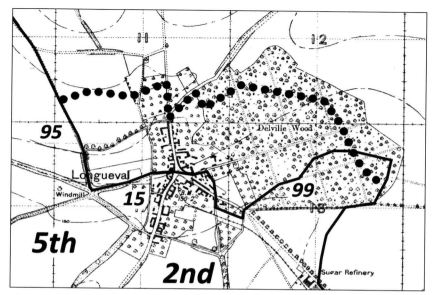

27 July, XV Corps: 5th Division was able to recapture the northern end of Longueval while 2nd Division cleared Delville Wood again.

2nd Division, Delville Wood

Major General William Walker's 2nd Division had just relieved 3rd Division. Brigadier General Kellett's 99 Brigade held the line through the south half of Delville Wood and the surrender of sixty Germans before zero hour was a good omen. The 23rd Royal Fusiliers and 1st KRRC found the artillery had done its work as they advanced through the wood and they found many dead and injured along Prince's Street, while those who could ran for their lives. The rear companies then advanced to a line fifty metres inside the north edge of the wood.

Although Delville Wood was clear, trouble was brewing while the 1st Berkshires mopped up. Around 9am the German machine-gun teams in Longueval spotted the 23rd Fusiliers in the north-west corner. Although the Fusiliers moved forward to escape their attention, they were forced to return to their exposed objective before the Germans exploited the gap.

There was also trouble on the east side of the wood where German artillery was firing straight down Prince's Street, making life difficult for the men in the support trench. Second Lieutenant Childs' Berkshire company helped to steady the 1st KRRC. But the German artillery often cut communications and General Kellett's message that 99 Brigade had cleared the wood was one of the few to reach divisional headquarters. He was correct but not for long.

The British artillery stopped reinforcements approaching from the Flers direction but a bombing attack around 9.30am against the east side of Delville Wood overran several outposts, capturing six heavy machine-guns. The bombers then infiltrated behind Prince's Street, forcing the 1st KRRC's right company to form a new line. But Sergeant Albert Gill rallied his platoon and made sure his men used a grenade store when the bombers were killed. As the Germans closed in, Gill stood up and pointed out the snipers until he was shot dead. Sergeant Gill was posthumously awarded the Victoria Cross.

So began a long stalemate of sniping and bombing with the British holding the centre of the wood and the Germans holding the east side. During the long and difficult night 95 Brigade relieved 15 Brigade in Longueval and occupied an abandoned Duke Street on the west side of the village. The 2nd South Staffords and 17th Middlesex of 6 Brigade relieved 99 Brigade in Delville Wood and after dusk it was their turn to endure the bombardments and counter-attacks.

At 3.30pm on 29 July, 95 Brigade attacked Longueval following a thirty-minute bombardment. While the 12th Gloucesters advanced 500 metres north of Duke Street, north-west of the village, the 1st East Surreys cleared the northern half of the ruins.

FOURTH ARMY, 30 JULY

On the afternoon of 26 July Rawlinson and Fayolle discussed details for the next combined attack. Rawlinson and Haig then heard that Foch and Fayolle planned to extend their next attack south of the Somme. While the French only required one day of good weather for their artillery observers north of the river, they needed three days to the south.[123] Haig told Foch XIII Corps could attack Guillemont without French assistance but the attack against Falfemont Farm had to be a combined effort.

The following day Rawlinson and Foch agreed to make the attack on 30 July on condition that the British captured Guillemont before the French advanced into Combles. Rawlinson also promised to extend Fourth Army's attack as far west as possible to stretch the German resources.

On 28 July the corps commanders gathered at Fourth Army headquarters to receive their orders. It was known that I ANZAC Corps would capture the high ground around Pozières windmill and III Corps would clear the re-entrant between Munster Alley and the Switch Line while improving its position north of Bazentin-le-Grand. XV Corps would advance between

---

123 Because there had been a lull in their operations south of the river.

High Wood and Delville Wood while its artillery hit the German batteries facing XIII Corps. Zero hour was set for 4.45am, but XV and III Corps' zero hour was delayed to 6.10am, to give them more time to prepare.

Fourth Army's barrage started on 29 July and although the fine weather helped the artillery observers correct their guns, it also aided the German observers. They realised something was afoot and their artillery disrupted XIII Corps preparations.

The bombardment along XV and XIII Corps' fronts increased at 3.45am but a morning mist blanketed the battlefield at zero hour, reducing visibility to less than fifty metres.[124] As the assault troops went over the top at 6.10am, the question being asked was would it help them or hinder them?

III Corps, 30 July

19th Division, Intermediate Trench

The 23rd Division fired Stokes mortars on the left flank while a smoke screen covered the west edge of High Wood. The mist delayed the 10th Worcesters and 8th Gloucesters getting into position on 57 Brigade's left and they missed the covering barrage. They were soon pinned down and had to withdraw later on. The 7th King's Own[125] and 10th Warwicks followed the barrage closely on the right and they captured their half of Intermediate Trench.

The two battalions stopped a counter-attack but the heavy shell-fire made it difficult to consolidate the trench until Captain Rose's 5th South Wales Borderers' company arrived. Private James Miller was shot as he ran back with an important message for the King's Own. Pressing his hand to his abdominal wound, he kept going until he delivered the note; he then collapsed and died. Private Miller was awarded the Victoria Cross.

XV Corps, 30 July

51st Division, High Wood

The 51st Division had been digging every night to finish a trench across the gap between Bazentin-le-Petit and High Wood but it was only a shallow affair suitable for defence. It was also over 1,000 metres away from the Switch Line, too far to be used as a jumping off trench, so there would be no attack west of the wood.

The first attempt by 154 Brigade to capture the strongpoint at the eastern corner of High Wood was made at 9.20pm on 29 July but the party of 1/4th Seaforths was stopped by machine-gun fire. Trench mortars were supposed to suppress the strongpoint the following morning but German artillery fire

---

124 It would last for the first two hours of the battle.
125 Attached from 56 Brigade.

forced the mortar teams to withdraw and the 1/7th Black Watch had to advance unsupported at 6.10am; they could not reach the strongpoint.

Brigadier Campbell's 153 Brigade advanced east of High Wood but the 1/6th Black Watch and 1/5th Gordons came under heavy fire from Wood Lane. Captain Innes' and Hally's Black Watch companies were stopped after only 200 metres but some of the Gordons kept going until they ran into a hidden belt of wire; few returned.

When Horne learnt of 51st Division's failure he wanted to make a second attack at 9.45pm but Harper told him there was insufficient time to reorganise his men. Instead he asked if the corps artillery could shell High Wood's garrison into submission.

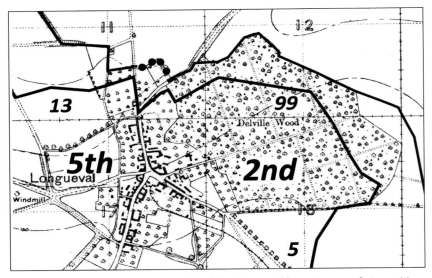

30 July, XV Corps: 5th Division and 2nd Division could not improve their positions around Longueval and Delville Wood.

5th Division, Longueval

Brigadier General Jones's 13 Brigade faced the area north of Longueval. The 14th Warwicks crawled forward on the left only to be hit fire from the south-east end of Wood Lane when they charged at 6.10am. The 2nd KOSBs cleared strongpoints at the north end of Longueval but Captain Paterson's men came under heavy shellfire as they moved into the north-west corner of Delville Wood; they were eventually forced to dig in north of the treeline. The 1st Queen's Own were supposed to reinforce the attack but the shelling stopped Lieutenant Colonel Dunlop's men getting forward.

Meanwhile 13 Brigade held onto its exposed trenches until the 16th Warwicks and the 1st Bedfords[126] took over Longueval and Delville Wood respectively.

Horne ordered 5th Division to secure the area north of Longueval the following day but General Stephens told him the brigades were too exhausted. So General Robertson's 17th Division relieved 5th Division the following night.

XIII Corps, 30 July

Delville Wood was held by 99 Brigade and 5 Brigade held the Waterlot Farm area to the south. While General Pinney's 35th Division held Trônes Wood, General Shea's 30th Division would move through its lines and make the attack.

2nd Division, Delville Wood

General Walker had orders to support XIII Corps' attack and 5 Brigade had to capture the trenches north-west of Guillemont. The early morning mist stopped the machine-guns and trench mortars in Delville Wood giving support fire while machine-gun fire stopped the 24th Royal Fusiliers and 2nd Ox and Bucks in no man's land. A few Ox and Bucks reached the railway station on the right, but they were surrounded and none returned; the rest withdrew later.

30th Division, Guillemont

Guillemont had to be taken by 90 Brigade while 89 Brigade captured the German trenches of Guillemont in co-operation with the French.

But the two 16th Manchester companies had to make a difficult manoeuvre before they could attack. They left their assembly trenches east of Trônes Wood and moved south to make way for 5 Brigade before wheeling ninety degrees to face Guillemont. The mist delayed the deployment and the Manchesters were then stopped by a belt of wire between the station and the quarry. The failure by 5 Brigade meant the Manchesters came under enfilade fire and were forced to regroup in the German front line.

The 18th Manchesters stormed the German front trench west of Guillemont, taking a large number of prisoners, but they were stopped by crossfire from machine-guns around the quarry and the station. Although they were reinforced by two companies each from the 16th and 17th Manchesters as they regrouped, a second attack also failed.

The 2nd Royal Scots Fusiliers advanced astride the road into the south-

---

126 Both from 15 Brigade.

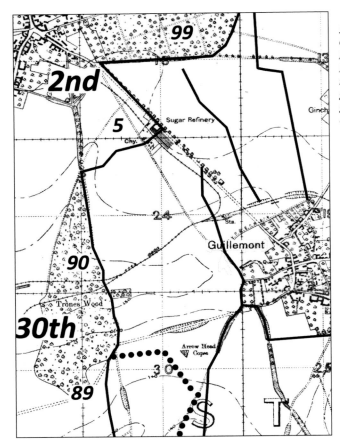

30 July, XIII Corps: While 2nd Division and 30th Division could not reach Guillemont, ground was gained south-west of the village.

west side of Guillemont, capturing fifty prisoners. Lieutenant Colonel Walsh's men then followed the barrage through the ruins, digging in alongside some of the 18th Manchesters on the north-east side of the village.

When the fog lifted around 9am, General Shea did not know only the 2nd Royal Scots Fusiliers were in Guillemont and that Lieutenant Murray's company was under attack. Signal wires had been cut, mist prevented visual signalling and carrier pigeons could only fly one way. Only one runner had made it through and his name was Company Sergeant Major Evans. He volunteered to take a message to brigade headquarters after five runners had been killed trying to take back news of the 18th Manchesters' attack. Running from shell-hole to shell-hole, he crossed 700 metres of bullet and shrapnel swept ground. Although he was wounded, he refused to go to the dressing station, choosing to run back across no man's land to his company.

In 89 Brigade's sector, Lieutenant Colonel Rollo's 19th King's were disorganised by the German counter-barrage as they groped forward through the mist. Some made it to the sunken Hardecourt road while Captains Dodd and Nicholson led their men to the orchards on the south-east edge of Guillemont 300 metres beyond. The 20th King's on the right were more successful, and two groups led by Second Lieutenants Moore and Musker reached the Hardecourt road despite heavy machine-gun fire. Colonel Fairfax's 17th King's then crossed no man's land in small columns to support their sister battalions. On the brigade's right, a 2nd Bedfords' company attacked Maltz Horn Farm alongside the French and they captured sixty Germans.

General Shea also heard no news from 89 Brigade but he believed it had taken its objective and wanted Brigadier General Stanley to hold onto the Hardecourt road. However, the 19th King's were concerned about their isolated position and they withdrew early in the afternoon; some of the men holding the sunken road followed. The rest dug in while Lieutenant Colonel Poyntz brought the 2nd Bedfords forward to extend 89 Brigade's line from Arrow Head Copse to Maltz Horn Farm.

While XIII Corps' new line was being consolidated, its artillery put down protective barrages in front of Ginchy, Guillemont and Leuze Wood to stop German counter-attacks. It did not shell Guillemont because the Royal Scots Fusiliers were still holding the south-east part; they did not hold it for long as 89 Brigade had no reserves left and the second counter-attack overran the Fusiliers.

Both 30th and 35th Divisions were exhausted by their efforts to take Guillemont and they had to be relieved by Major General Hugh Jeudwine's 55th Division.

Summary

Fourth Army's attack on 30 July had little to show for all the ammunition expended and the casualties suffered. The artillery had been given too much to do in a short time, and most of the barbed wire and machine-gun posts had been untouched. The infantry then paid the price, although much less than they might have done due to the mist.

The Germans were using small garrisons to hold their front trenches and placing their machine-guns in their second position. The tactic saved reserves and counter-attacks could be made once their counter-barrage had targeted no man's land, cutting off the British assault troops. By giving up a small area, the Germans were able to limit the number and size of penetrations, isolating them and overrunning them in turn.

Chapter 6

Facing a Wearing Out Battle –
1 to 17 August

RESERVE ARMY, 4 TO 17 AUGUST

Haig wanted the Reserve Army to stop the Germans moving reinforcements to Fourth Army's front and on 30 July Gough was ordered to attack. While the final objective was to reach the high ground between Pozières and Grandcourt, Haig's order on 2 August instructed the Reserve Army's right to capture the trenches running between Thiepval, Mouquet Farm and Pozières Mill on the Bapaume road. The problem was Reserve Army only had two divisions[127] to advance out of the salient.

XIV Corps would fire shell, smoke and tear gas north of the river Ancre while 49th Division would shell targets around Thiepval. It would also release smoke in the Ancre and Nab valleys to create diversions.

II Corps, 4 August

Lieutenant General Claud Jacob had to consider how to get out onto the Thiepval heights on his left, where the troops in the Leipzig Salient had to link up with those advancing north from Ovillers. His right had to take the trenches protecting the crest of Skyline Ridge.

12th Division, west of Pozières

At 11.15pm on 3 August, the 8th Royal Fusiliers[128] and 6th Buffs[129] cleared the south-west half of Fourth Avenue while Lieutenant Hammer's bombers took Ration Trench, removing an awkward salient on the division's left flank. The following morning patrols led by Lieutenant Rolfe of the 7th Sussex and Second Lieutenant Routley of the Buffs discovered there was no one left alive in Sixth Avenue. But machine-gun fire stopped them exploiting the gap and they withdrew when they saw 300 Germans heading their way.

---

127 One from II Corps on the left and one from ANZAC Corps on the right.
128 36 Brigade.
129 37 Brigade.

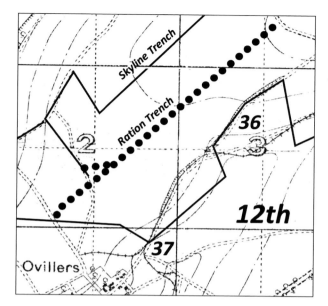

*4 August, II Corps:
12th Division
eventually captured
Ration Trench.*

The 12th Division attacked Ration Trench between the Nordwerk and West Trench at 9.15 pm on 4 August.

In 37 Brigade's sector, the 6th Queen's and 6th Queen's Own spent the night clearing the west end of Ration Trench and Brigadier General Cator's men had taken 115 prisoners by dawn. In 36 Brigade's sector the 9th Royal Fusiliers and 7th Sussex advanced over the top while the 8th Royal Fusiliers bombed along the trenches. Brigadier General Boyd Moss's men took most of their objective but the Sussex could not advance astride West Trench on the right. By morning, 12th Division was holding 1,200 metres of Ration Trench and Lance Corporal Camping crept out during the afternoon and spoke German to convince 115 men holding the rest of the trench to surrender.

During the early hours of 6 August counter-attacks with eight flame-throwers[130] forced the 9th Royal Fusiliers to evacuate Ration Trench but Captain Cazelet and Second Lieutenant Fifoot organised counter-attacks to recapture the two ends. Then 35 Brigade relieved a tired 36 Brigade and Lieutenant Edwards and Company Sergeant Major Waite made sure the German flame-thrower teams did not retake the ends of Ration Trench during the early hours of 8 August. The east end of the trench was taken from the 5th Berkshires after sunrise.

At 9.20pm the 7th Suffolks tried to recapture Ration Trench, but while wire stopped the bombers moving along the trench, machine-gun fire

---

130 The crews were dressed in black oilskins for protection.

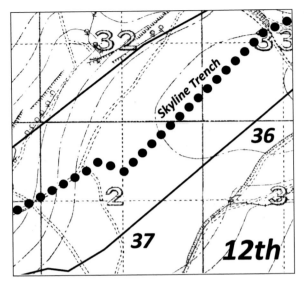

12 August, II Corps: While 12th Division could take Skyline Trench, it could not advance beyond the crest.

stopped Captain Isham's company working their way up West Trench. An attack planned for 10 August was cancelled when a trench mortar bomb destroyed the 6th Buffs' grenade store, injuring Captain Ward and Lieutenant Onslow.

Gough ordered Jacob to recapture the east end of Skyline Trench at 10.30pm on 12 August but the German barrage on Ration Trench was so heavy the troops had to assemble in the open. In 37 Brigade's sector the 7th East Surreys struggled to cross a crater field while the 6th Queen's Own were stopped by artillery and machine-gun fire. Meanwhile, the 9th Essex and 7th Norfolk found few Germans holding Skyline Trench in 35 Brigade's sector. But while Skyline Trench had commanding views across Nab Valley, the Germans knew exactly where it was and began shelling it. Brigadier General Solly Flood told each battalion to establish two strongpoints and withdraw as many men as possible, to avoid overcrowding; patrols sent into Nab Valley also had to withdraw.

I ANZAC Corps, 4 August

The 2nd Australian Division had a lot of preparations to do and on the evening of 31 July the infantry dug assembly trenches while the field artillery and mortars hit the German wire. The rest of the heavy artillery fired a fake barrage every day. But there was too much to do and the German artillery fire was too heavy so Gough postponed the attack to 4 August.

2nd Australian Division, the OG Trenches

The German barrage hit the assembly trenches and many companies moved out into no man's land to avoid it. All three brigades were in line and while 6 Brigade was to form the northern flank, 7 and 5 Brigades would capture the OG Trenches north and south of the Bapaume road.

Wind interfered with the smoke on 6 Brigade's left and machine-guns stopped 23rd Battalion blocking the OG Trenches on the Courcelette track. The 22nd Battalion[131] advanced alongside 26th, 25th and 27th battalions[132] from the north-east side of Pozières. The first two waves found the wire had been cut and they overran the OG1 and OG2 Trenches, catching many Germans in their dug-outs. The support waves were hit by the German barrage, but they reached the OG2 Trench. The trench was consolidated on the left and centre[133] but it had been obliterated around Pozières windmill, so Captain Fosse made the 27th Battalion dig in beyond it.

In 5 Brigade's sector, 18th and 20th Battalions overran OG1 south of the Bapaume road. But OG2 trench had been so badly damaged that some Australians failed to notice it and advanced into their protective barrage. They quickly withdrew to the OG2 Trench and set up their Lewis guns. Meanwhile, 20th Battalion had blocked Torr Trench on the right where Fourth Army troops had failed to advance.[134]

4 August, I ANZAC Corps: 2nd Australian Division captured the OG Trenches at their second attempt.

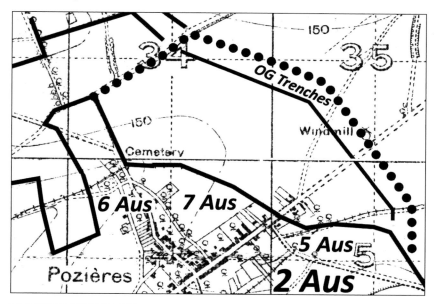

---

131 6 Brigade.
132 All 7 Brigade.
133 Either side of a kink in the OG Trenches called the Elbow.
134 68 Brigade, 23rd Division.

In less than an hour 1,500 metres of the OG Trenches had been captured along with over 500 prisoners. The plan was to set up machine-gun posts along OG2 and withdraw the infantry but the Germans intervened before the Australians were ready. At 4am they counter-attacked from Courcelette only to be shot to pieces and while some surrendered the rest withdrew. An hour later another group were stopped north of the Elbow.

RESERVE ARMY, 6 TO 17 AUGUST

While Gough wanted to keep advancing towards Courcelette, the Reserve Army needed fresh troops and 4th Australian Division was moved forward. The 12th Division and the Australians consolidated on 5 August but the German artillery fired relentlessly and there were signs that their infantry were preparing to counter-attack.

But II Corps' right could not go beyond Skyline Ridge until Nab Valley had been cleared. Meanwhile, I ANZAC Corps had to capture Mouquet Farm and Fabeck Graben, north of Pozières as well as secure the OG trenches north-east of the village. The narrative follows the order of the attacks.

I ANZAC Corps, 6 to 14 August

4th Australian Division, Mouquet Farm to Pozières Mill

During the early hours of 6 August, 12 Brigade took over part of the OG Trenches. The 48th and 45th Battalions were ready astride the Bapaume road when the Germans made a dawn attack. The German attack overran part of 48th Battalion, taking fifty prisoners. While flares brought down a SOS barrage, the infantry had to round them up.

The Germans also overran part of 14th Battalion and Lieutenant Albert Jacka[135] learnt about the attack when a grenade exploded inside his dug-out in OG1. He emerged with his remaining men and came upon many Germans rounding up Australian prisoners. Jacka then shot at the prisoners' guards, allowing them to break free. South of the Bapaume road 45th Battalion stopped another counter-attack. The following night 4 Brigade took over the rest of 2nd Australian Division's positions, with 15th Battalion on the left flank and 14th Battalion around the Elbow.

At 9.20pm on 8 August 15th Battalion advanced from the trenches north of Pozières cemetery, capturing fifty prisoners in Park Lane. The Australians also captured some of the OG trenches near the Courcelette road but the position was exposed and they had to withdraw from the west end of Park Lane. Early the following morning 16th Battalion renewed the attack and Lieutenant Colonel Brockman's men soon held all of Park Lane. With fresh troops on hand, 4 Brigade was able to extend its sector as far as the Thiepval road west later that evening.

---

135 Lieutenant Jacka had been awarded the Victoria Cross while a private in Gallipoli, the first Australian to receive the award.

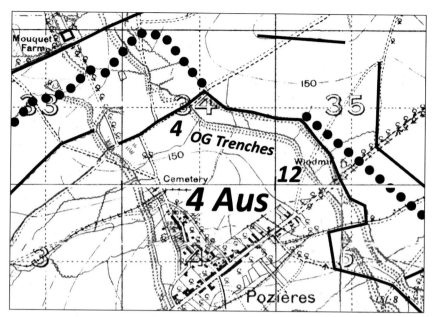

8 August, I ANZAC Corps: 4th Australian Division struggled to expand the Pozières salient.

Although Gough issued orders for a new attack on Mouquet Farm and Fabeck Graben at 10.30pm on 12 August, Major General Sir Herbert Cox kept pushing forward. At 1am on 9 August 4 Brigade advanced from Park Lane and while 16th Battalion got close to a quarry, 13th Battalion established posts in the OG Trenches south-east of Mouquet Farm. The German artillery caused so many casualties 4 Brigade could not attack again but it was able to stop all counter-attacks.

Between 9 and 12 August, Private Martin O'Meara rescued many of 16th Battalion's wounded men from no man's land south-west of Mouquet Farm. He also carried ammunition and bombs through the German bombardment many times. He was awarded the Victoria Cross.

The 50th Battalion[136] later relieved 16th Battalion and advanced towards Mouquet Farm at 10.30pm on 12 August. While the covering barrage was good, some of 50th Battalion's platoons did not receive the order to advance from Ration Trench and Park Lane, resulting in a disorganised attack. The left flank advanced along the Thiepval road, next to 12th Division, but the centre headed towards Mouquet Farm; the few who made it to the farm were later forced to withdraw and dig in.

---

136 13 Brigade.

Haig visited Gough on 13 August to discuss a new attack on the night of 14 August but the loss of Skyline Trench at midnight meant the objective had to be reduced on the left flank. During the evening 13 Brigade relieved 4 Brigade ready to make the attack but the Germans suspected something because their artillery hit the assembly areas.

Zero hour was at 10pm but 50th Battalion was not fit to advance and the few men who made it beyond the quarry had to withdraw. Swerving right to avoid Mouquet Farm, 13th Battalion ended up in Fabeck Graben where they were joined by 49th Battalion.[137] The 51st Battalion was stopped by machine-gun fire leaving Captain Murray's men in an isolated position; they withdrew before dawn.

II Corps, 14 to 16 August
48th Division, Skyline Ridge
At midnight on 13/14 August the Germans drove the two 1/4th Ox and Bucks companies from Skyline Trench but 145 Brigade held onto Ration Trench. A counter-attack failed and the 1/4th Berkshires were also unable to capture the lost ground at 5.15am. General Fanshawe could not leave Skyline Trench in German hands because it threatened I ANZAC Corps' left flank and the 1/1st Ox and Bucks' bombers cleared it the following night.

The German artillery once again fired on the exposed trench and by 3pm the Ox and Bucks had been forced out of it. They established posts 100 metres ahead of Skyline Trench during the night to stop the Germans reoccupying it. They were able to occupy it after the shelling died down and a counter-attack the following day was stopped by artillery fire.

With Skyline Trench secure, it was time to capture Pole Street to the south-west but attacks by the 1/6th Gloucesters[138] on the evening of 14 August and by the 1/5th Gloucesters, 1/1st Ox and Bucks[139] and 1/4th Gloucesters[140] the following afternoon failed. An early morning counter-attack through the mist failed to dislodge the 1/6th Gloucesters in Nab Valley and another attack during the evening was stopped. The 1/4th Gloucesters also stopped several attacks during the night.

FOURTH ARMY, 1 TO 17 AUGUST
Rawlinson met his corps commanders and their artillery officers on the morning of 31 July. While Pulteney and Horne were ordered to capture the Switch Line, Congreve was instructed to take Guillemont first and then Ginchy and Leuze Wood, alongside the French.

---

137 13 Brigade.
138 144 Brigade.
139 Both from 145 Brigade.
140 144 Brigade.

Fourth Army's artillery commander, General Budworth, believed XIII Corps' artillery could only deal with one target at a time, either Ginchy or Guillemont, so arrangements were made for XV Corps' artillery to help; III Corps' heavy artillery would in turn shell High Wood. Counter-battery work was also divided up with III Corps covering Flers and Ginchy while XV Corps shelled Morval and Lesboeufs.

While the shift in artillery distributed the weight of fire across Fourth Army's front, it complicated communications. Divisions would have to rely on batteries in different corps sectors, increasing the response time between targets being reported and being shelled.

Foch visited Haig on 1 August to tell him the French Sixth Army would be attacking north of the Somme and they agreed to make a combined attack six days later. Two days later Haig told his army commanders they had to capture the ridge which arced from Thiepval on the left to Morval on the right. But he thought the Germans had dug in and were moving more men and guns into the area ready for a long fight and they faced a 'wearing out battle', or a battle of attrition. So they had to economise on men and material ready to defeat the Germans when the anticipated climax of the battle came during the second half of September.

III Corps and XV Corps had to dig new trenches close to the Switch Line while XIII Corps still had to capture Ginchy, Guillemont and Falfemont Farm. Haig's final instruction to Congreve was to make sure the attacks were only made when 'the responsible commanders on the spot are satisfied everything possible has been done to ensure success'. On 5 August Rawlinson and Fayolle agreed the British would attack Guillemont while the French advanced north of Hem on 7 August. Four days later XIII Corps would capture Falfemont Farm when the French advanced again.

Rawlinson then met Foch but Congreve telephoned during the meeting to say he had to delay his attack until 8 August because heavy artillery fire was disrupting XIII Corps' preparations. After Rawlinson called GHQ to inform them of the delay, Haig joined them and they agreed the French would still attack on 7 August.

III Corps, 8 August

III Corps had two trenches to clear south of Martinpuich, Munster Alley and Intermediate Trench.

23rd Division, Munster Alley
The first attempt was made by 68 Brigade on the night of 4/5th August. The 13th Durham Light Infantry came under machine-gun fire from Torr Trench

and Munster Trench while smoke and dust from the Australian bombardment of Pozières drifted across their front and many men lost sight of their officers. Captain Austin led the second wave into Torr Trench but they were never seen again. The battalion bombers eventually cleared fifty metres of Munster Alley.

On the afternoon of 6 August 69 Brigade tried again and Major Western led the 8th Green Howards' bombers along 150 metres of Munster Alley. Private William Short was wounded in his foot but he refused to go back and continued to throw bombs until a shell shattered his leg; he lay on the trench floor, preparing bombs for his comrades until he died. Private Short was posthumously awarded the Victoria Cross. The Green Howards also bombed along the east part of Torr Trench while Australian troops supplied them with bombs. The 11th West Yorkshires then took over the trench and the fighting lasted all night.

34th Division, Intermediate Trench
The task facing 101 Brigade was to clear Intermediate Trench and while the 16th Royal Scots failed to bomb along the trench on the night of 1/2 August they cleared 100 metres the following night; Captain Hendry was mortally wounded leading the bombing party. The plan to advance over the top at 2.30am on 4 August failed when only Captain Brown's 11th Suffolk company made it on time; while it reached the objective, it had to withdraw before dawn. The three missing companies had to attack in daylight and they suffered dearly. Later that evening the 15th Royal Scots bombers cleared another fifty metres and the following night Lieutenant Tempest stopped a German counter-attack.

On the night of 6 August 112 Brigade moved into line but the 8th East Lancashires bombers failed to make progress the following morning. The 10th Loyal North Lancashires both bombed and attacked over the top at 2am on 11 August and eventually captured 200 metres. Two nights later the 11th Royal Warwicks failed to take any more of the trench.

1st Division, Intermediate Trench
On 15 August 1st Division relieved 34th Division and the following evening it made a Chinese Attack[141] to keep the Germans on their toes. The 1st Black Watch[142] made the first attempt to take Intermediate Trench but a bombing attack led by Lieutenants Urquhart and Templeton failed. An attack over the top at 4.15am on the 17th captured part of the trench but the Black Watch had to withdraw. They then discovered the map was wrong because the trench was 250 metres longer and hidden by the contours of the ground; they had failed because the artillery had not shelled the whole length.

---

141 A Chinese Attack was a simulated assault used to confuse the enemy. It could involve an artillery barrage, smoke, cheering and the waving of bayonets above the parapet to simulate an attack.
142 1 Brigade.

At 10pm on 16 August 2 Brigade attacked the new trench running across no man's land west of High Wood. Two companies of the 1st Northants and three of 2nd Sussex captured most of it and then barricaded the ends. A counter-attack from High Wood recovered 100 metres of the trench a few hours later.

15th Division, the Switch Line

On the morning of 8 August 15th Division relieved 23rd Division and Major General Frederick McCracken's objective was to clear the west end of the Switch Line. The attack was timed for 10.30pm on 12 August and the intense bombardment was followed by fifteen minutes of normal artillery fire to make the Germans think it was a Chinese Attack. In 45 Brigade's sector the 6th Cameron Highlanders cleared the trench on the left and they met the Australians at the top of Munster Alley. The 12th Highland Light Infantry were stopped by machine-gun fire in the centre but the 6/7th Royal Scots Fusiliers captured part of the trench on the right. Pipe pushers were then detonated across no man's land to make it easier to dig communication trenches.[143]

The bombing never ceased in the Switch Line and many Germans surrendered when the 7th Cameron Highlanders[144] advanced over the top on the morning of 17 August. Captain MacRae and Lieutenant Orr stopped bombing attacks from the Elbow until the 8th Seaforths could reinforce them. The 10/11th Highland Light Infantry[145] then extended their hold east of the Elbow.

XV Corps, 8 August

XV Corps had lodgements in High Wood and Delville Wood while the centre faced Wood Lane.

33rd Division, High Wood

XV Corps' front was quiet between High Wood and Delville Wood when 33rd Division took over during the night of 6/7 August. Their engineers set up two flame-throwers and drums to fire burning oil while pipe pushers were drilled under no man's land.

17th Division, Longueval and Delville Wood

On 1 August 17th Division took over from 5th Division in Longueval and the west side of Delville Wood. It took forty-eight hours to clear up the situation, particularly in the wood where there were several gaps in the line. At 12.40am on 4 August 52 Brigade planned to attack Orchard Trench, north

---

143 The Bartlett Forcing Jack had driven iron pipes filled with tin cans containing ammonal under no man's land.
144 44 Brigade.
145 46 Brigade.

of the village, but the 9th Northumberland Fusiliers and 12th Manchesters were disorganised by gas and artillery fire before zero hour. They were stopped by machine-gun fire despite the efforts of Captain Benton to renew the Manchesters' attack. Later that night 17th Division took over the rest of Delville Wood.

On 5 August 51 Brigade took over Delville Wood and Brigadier General Trotter was ordered to attack at 4.30pm on 7 August. The 8th South Staffords and the 7th Border Regiment were hit by machine-gun fire as they emerged from the tree line because the Germans had dug a trench in an arc around the perimeter of the wood. The British artillery was finding it difficult to target the trench while the German artillery was having no such difficulty hitting the wood. Attempts were made to establish observation posts later that night but only the 10th Sherwood Foresters captured useful positions north of Longueval.

Major General Victor Couper's 14th Division took over the wood on the night of 12 August and General Clarke summed up the situation in the wood:

> 'Conditions were appalling. It was full of gas and corpses; no regular line could be discerned, and the men fought in small groups, mostly in shell holes hastily improvised into fire trenches.'

No wonder the men called it Devil's Wood.

XIII Corps, 8 August

Congreve had limited objectives for 8 August and while 2nd Division had to seize the trenches north-west of Guillemont, 55th Division had to capture the trenches south-west of the village; they would then move through the village. Six fake artillery barrages were used on 7 August with the barrage intensifying as if zero hour was approaching, and then creeping forward to encourage the Germans to leave their dug outs; it then dropped back to catch them manning their parapet. Only time would tell if the Germans had been fooled

The assault plan was the same as the one tried on 30 July but zero hour was set for 4.20am. After the lack of information on 30 July, many steps were taken to improve communications and Congreve made sure conferences were held from battalion commander level down to sergeant level.

2nd Division, North-west Guillemont

The assault troops left their trenches at 4.20am and headed through the mist as the German barrage threw up clouds of dust and smoke. While 6 Brigade attacked the north side of Guillemont station, the 17th Middlesex entered

ZZ Trench astride the Longueval road and the 1st King's advanced over the German trenches around Guillemont station. An injured Captain Last crawled back to report High Holborn had been taken and Lieutenant Colonel Charles Goff sent a pigeon message reporting the news to Brigadier General Daly's headquarters. However, the men had been unable to mop up the dug-outs in the mist and the Germans reoccupied their front trench in time to stop the fourth company crossing no man's land. It left the King's isolated while a Middlesex company was wiped out trying to bomb across.

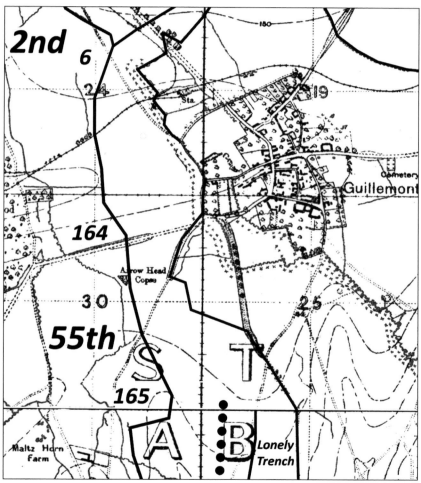

8 August, XIII Corps: Although 2nd Division and 55th Division could not capture Guillemont, some ground was gained on the ridge to the south.

55th Division, South-west Guillemont

From 164 Brigade's line astride the Montauban road, the 1/8th King's[146] crossed the trenches west of Guillemont, by-passed the quarry and entered the village. Major Parker's company of the 1/4th Loyal North Lancashires followed and encountered many Germans in the trenches. The 1/4th King's Own were spotted creeping towards the trench next to the Hardecourt road and they then encountered belts of barbed wire blocking their way.

Once again the mist prevented visual signalling while many runners were shot down in no man's land and by the time Brigadier General Edwards found out what had happened it was too late to help. The King's Own withdrew when the mist cleared and the Loyals were then bombed out of the trench in front of the quarry. Although Captain Murphy withdrew the King's from their isolated position in the village, many were captured.

Second Lieutenant Gabriel Coury was supervising the digging of a communications trench near Arrow Head Copse for the 1/4th South Lancashires, the divisional pioneer battalion, when he heard his commanding officer, Major Swainson, had been wounded. Lieutenant Coury left his work to rescue his officer from no man's land; he was awarded the Victoria Cross.

Elements of 165 Brigade advanced alongside the French. The 1/5th King's crossed the Hardecourt road south of Guillemont only for machine-gun fire to force them to take cover in shell holes. Colonel Shute arranged to send a plane over to locate the King's position and Major Keet waved his helmet on a rifle to get the observer's attention. Shute could then adjust the artillery range to give them protection. The 1/6th King's bombers worked their way along Cochrane Alley until the Germans blew up the trench in front of Lieutenant Blackledge's men.

Neither corps nor divisional headquarters knew what was going on because the aerial observers could see little, and while the initial messages were confusing, they soon stopped. The King's had missed many dug-outs in the mist and the Germans had cut them off. While General Congreve wanted to reinforce the troops in Guillemont, the division's assembly trenches were under shell-fire, making it impossible to organise anything. All General Edwards could do was to send fighting patrols into the village after dusk.

XIII Corps, 9 August

Congreve was determined to take Guillemont and, after getting Fourth Army's permission, he ordered Generals Walker and Jeudwine to make

---

146 The Liverpool Irish.

another attack at 4.20am the following morning. But the German shelling delayed the reliefs and few battalions were ready by zero hour. The artillery preparation was also hurried and German machine-gun teams were waiting.

2nd Division, North-west Guillemont
Again 6 Brigade attacked and while the 17th Middlesex were unable to bomb south from Waterlot Farm, the 13th Essex could not reach the German line north-west of Guillemont and they fell back to their start line.

55th Division, South-west Guillemont
The attack orders for 166 Brigade were delayed. The 1/5th Loyal North Lancashires struggled to get through the congested trenches and advanced late; the German machine-gun teams were waiting for them. The 1/10th King's[147] only reached their trenches a few minutes before zero and advanced unaware they were heading for a belt of wire; machine-guns stopped them cutting through. Lieutenant Colonel Davidson rallied his men three times but they could not get into Guillemont. Meanwhile, the 1/5th King's failed to improve their position in Cochrane Alley.

The 1/10th King's medical officer, Captain Noel Chavasse, spent the day attending to the wounded and was himself wounded while carrying an injured man to the dressing station. Later that night he took twenty volunteers forward to search for the wounded and bury the dead in no man's land. Captain Chavasse was awarded the Victoria Cross.[148]

Summary
Neither 2nd Division nor 55th Division could reinforce the isolated pockets of men in the enemy trenches but the Germans could. While local reserves pressurised the King's, two battalions counter-attacked Guillemont during the afternoon overrunning some groups while the men around the station and the quarry surrendered after running out of ammunition. By the evening of 9 August the fight was over.

XIII Corps, 12 August
55th Division, Lonely Trench
Lonely Trench, on the spur south of Guillemont, was held by a strong garrison, protected by wire and difficult to observe; no man's land was also so narrow that the British trench had to be evacuated before the heavy artillery could shell it.

The attack by 165 Brigade was set for 11 August but the warm weather turned to mist and rain, delaying it for twenty-four hours. The bombardment

---

147 The Liverpool Scottish.
148 Captain Chavasse was awarded a second Victoria Cross for similar activities in the Ypres Salient the following year, only this time he succumbed to his wounds.

started at 3.30pm and at 5.15pm two 1/9th King's companies advanced over the top while the battalion bombers advanced down Cochrane Alley on the right. The French failed to advance into Maurepas ravine and Captain Fulton's men withdrew from their isolated position after dusk.

3rd Division, South of Guillemont

Major General Cyril Deverell's 3rd Division relieved 55th Division[149] on the night of the 14/15 August and prepared to attack again. The troops evacuated their trenches at dusk while the heavy artillery shelled Lonely Trench and when the barrage stopped at 8pm, the 12th West Yorkshires[150] and 10th Royal Welsh Fusiliers[151] crept back into their trenches. But there was a mix up over zero hour and the Fusiliers advanced at what they thought was the correct time, 10pm. Major Thomson's West Yorkshires scrambled out of their trench when they saw the Welsh moving and they set off 100 metres behind. The Germans were waiting for them and only a few reached Lonely Trench. The two battalions repeated the attack at 4am the following morning; it also failed.

FOURTH ARMY, 16 AUGUST

On 13 August, Rawlinson and Foch agreed a combined plan, starting with the French capturing Angle Wood and Maurepas Ravine on 16 August. XIII Corps would clear the spur south of Guillemont in two stages before capturing the village on the 18th; it would then follow up with attacks on Wedge Wood and Falfemont Farm the following morning. The final assault on 22 August involved XIII Corps taking Ginchy and Leuze Wood while the French attacked south of Combles.

Later on 16 August, Haig gave Rawlinson new instructions based on Joffre's promises for greater co-operation. XIII Corps had to capture Angle Wood first and then secure Guillemont and Falfemont Farm forty-eight hours later. The combined attacks planned for 22 August had not changed. Kiggell joined the meeting to pass on Haig's views on XIII Corps' recent operations. Firstly, he wanted to know if sufficient troops had been used; secondly, had gas and smoke been used and finally, had incendiary shells been used on the German positions. Congreve explained how the Germans were using small garrisons to hold their front trench while the machine-gun teams hid in shell holes, battered trenches and dug-outs. They were hard to spot in the mist and they opened fire when the barrage lifted, stopping reinforcements crossing no man's land.

---

149 The division had dug 13,000 metres of new trench and improved 3,000 metres of existing trench in two weeks.
150 9 Brigade.
151 76 Brigade.

XIII Corps, 16 August

Congreve abandoned any ideas of attacking Guillemont from the north-west to focus on seizing the spur south of the village alongside the French. The artillery made a special effort to silence the German batteries on 16 August and their observers made the most of the sunny weather. However, the guns targeting Lonely Trench fired short because there had not been enough time to register the guns properly and 3rd Division suffered casualties. The barrage intensified at 5.37pm and three minutes later the infantry went over the top.

24th Division, Arrowhead Copse

Strongpoints south of Guillemont road were to have been cleared by 72 Brigade. Rifle fire to the front and machine-gun fire to the flanks hit the 9th East Surreys as soon as they left Lamb and New Trenches around Arrowhead Copse; a shower of grenades stopped them before they reached the German trench.

3rd Division, Lonely Trench

As 9 Brigade advanced across the spur the 4th Royal Fusiliers and 13th King's came under fire and neither could reach Lonely Trench. Meanwhile, 76 Brigade faced a bigger problem because the Stokes mortars had not silenced the machine-guns. While the 8th King's Own attack failed, the 2nd Suffolks cleared the trench along the Hardecourt road and Cochrane Alley on the right. The Suffolks had to withdraw from the exposed position as soon as it was dark. The French 153rd Division had also been unable to capture Angle Wood.

Summary
Later that afternoon, Rawlinson met Fayolle to discuss details for a new advance in which XIII Corps secured the spur south of Guillemont while the French attacked either side of Maurepas. They would advance together towards Guillemont and Maurepas when they were ready.

When Congreve was given the order, he reported XIII Corps could be ready to attack Guillemont on 17 August. However, he would not be there to see it take place. The question of XIII Corps' ability to continue in command had been discussed during the 16 August meeting. While Congreve had been ill for some time, Kiggell wondered if his staff also needed a rest. XIII Corps handed over its sector to Lieutenant General Rudolph Lambart, 10th Earl of Cavan, and XIV Corps staff at midnight on 16/17 August.

Chapter 7

Straightening the Line – 18 to 31 August

RESERVE ARMY

On 15 August Haig ordered Gough to scale down attacks around the Ancre for the time being. But then two days later he told him to prepare the Reserve Army for a two-division attack astride the river on 30 August; the order was eventually issued on 24 August.

II Corps, 18 to 28 August
48th Division, Nab Valley
On 18 August heavy artillery fire isolated the Leipzig Salient while 49th Division fired its machine-guns at Thiepval. Smoke released to cover the north flank was blown across 143 Brigade's front, blinding the artillery observers and the Germans alike. But the 1/5th and 1/6th Warwicks overran the German trenches and the 1/7th Warwicks bombers set about clearing the dug-outs; more ground was captured the following morning.

The rest of 19 August was spent handing the Leipzig Salient over to General Bainbridge's 25th Division. Two days later Gough told General Jacob that II Corps had to take Pole Trench and the Wonder Work. In fact 144 Brigade had already started, with the 1/6th Gloucesters bombing towards Pole Trench, but the main attack was made at 6pm on 21 August. The 1/4th Gloucesters surprised the Germans holding the south-east side of Leipzig Salient and then the two Gloucester battalions cleared Hindenburg Trench, taking 200 prisoners.

An attempt by the 1/4th Ox and Bucks to advance along the east side of Nab valley at 3pm on 23 August failed because the barrage stopped a couple of minutes early. The Germans had time to man their trench and shoot down Second Lieutenants Bates' and Heath's companies.

The situation remained unchanged until the 48th Division attacked at 7pm on 27 August. In 145 Brigade's sector the 1/5th Gloucesters and 1/4th

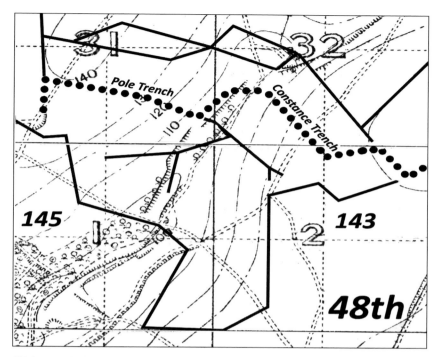

27 August, II Corps: 48th Division cleared Pole Trench and Constance Trench to get out of Nab Valley.

Berkshires cleared the trench in front of Pole Trench as Captain Aldworth drove many Germans into the hands of the Warwicks. Lieutenant Ridley's bombers moved forward on the flank and Lance Corporal Rixon climbed on the parapet to direct the party after his officer was killed. In 143 Brigade's sector, the 1/8th Warwicks swerved to the flanks to avoid its own barrage and only a few reached Constance Trench on the right; they were soon driven out. The following morning, 25th Division relieved 48th Division.

25th Division, Leipzig Salient
On 25 August smoke blinded the Germans in Thiepval while a heavy bombardment hit Hindenburg Trench. As 7 Brigade advanced at 4.10pm the 1st Wiltshires and 3rd Worcesters took the Germans by surprise and captured around 150; another 100 were killed by their own artillery fire as they headed into captivity. But the Wiltshire bombers could not advance fast enough through the crater field surrounding the original

German front trench and Second Lieutenant Ross had to withdraw his men.

At 7pm on 26 August, Captain Cash led the 8th Loyal North Lancashires[152] into the west end of Hindenburg Trench but the garrison was larger than expected and they had to withdraw. The 8th South Lancashires[153] tried and failed in the same place at 4pm on 28 August.

I ANZAC Corps, 16 to 31 August
1st Australian Division, North of Pozières
The 1st Australian Division relieved 4th Australian Division at 5pm on 16 August and 2 Brigade dug new trenches in front of OG2. At 9pm on 18 August, 7th Battalion came under fire from a machine-gun filled strongpoint as it advanced south of the Bapaume road; the few who reached the strongpoint were killed.

The 8th Battalion had not been told the barrage timetable, so the officers told their men to watch for when the barrage started moving. They advanced three times to the crest only for the machine-gun teams on the reverse slope to stop them. Before dawn 2 Brigade was back in its assembly trenches. The following day 6th Battalion dug a trench from the Elbow obliquely across no man's land to join 7th Battalion's advanced trench.

North of Pozières, 1 Brigade's preparations were interrupted by night attacks from Fabeck Graben. When the barrage began, the gun batteries had no idea where the German trenches were and the barrage fell short on Brigadier General Smyth's assembled troops hitting the Australians rather then the Germans. At 9pm, 4th Battalion captured posts in Quarry Trench and they held a line around the quarry in spite of several counter-attacks. But 3rd Battalion's bombers were unable to capture a new trench in front of Fabeck Graben, east of the OG lines. The following day 3 Australian Brigade took over the trenches facing Mouquet Farm.

On 21 August, Gough made it clear I ANZAC Corps had four days to advance beyond Mouquet Farm. The 1st Australian Division planned to start at 6pm the same day, but a German aircraft spotted the troops assembling and called down a heavy bombardment on 3 Brigade. Only a few men of 12th Battalion reached Mouquet Farm and they were forced to withdraw when the garrison emerged from the cellars; only the battalion bombers held onto a strongpoint east of the farm. As 10th Battalion entered Fabeck Graben enfilade machine-gun fire forced them to withdraw and they dug in across no man's land. Raiding parties from 11th Battalion set off late in the centre of the attack but they eventually linked up the two battalions. Bombing continued throughout the following day and 6 Brigade[154] took over the front later that night.

---

152 From 7 Brigade.
153 From 75 Brigade.
154 From 2nd Australian Division.

2nd Australian Division, North of Pozieres

The 2nd Australian Division completed the relief of 1st Australian Division on the morning of 23 August. While 6 Brigade could not establish if the Germans held Mouquet Farm, 5 Brigade knew they were holding Fabeck Graben and wasted no time securing a footing in the trench.

After two days of probing, 2nd Australian Division was ready to attack and it attacked at 4.45am on 26 August following a short bombardment. A company of 22nd Battalion was disorientated and they stopped in the wrong trench on the left flank where they were surrounded and forced to surrender. The 21st Battalion also lost their sense of direction and, while some occupied a trench south-west of Mouquet Farm, some pressed on to Zig Zag Trench where there was a fight to hold the strongpoint at the end of the Mouquet Farm track. On the right 24th Battalion's bombers, led by Lieutenant Jones, were unable to take Fabeck Graben. The situation was still confused at dawn but while a few Australians were fighting in Zig Zag Trench most of 6 Brigade's men were scattered across the trenches south-west of Mouquet Farm.

4th Australian Division, North of Pozières

Later that evening, 4 Brigade relieved 6 Brigade, signalling the return of the 4th Australian Division. The following night, two 14th Battalion bombing parties went out at midnight and captured the strongpoints at each end of the Mouquet Farm track. But the German garrison again clambered out of the farm cellars to cut off the bombers; few returned.

At noon on 28 August 4th Australian Division took over but the rain slowly turned the ground into a quagmire. At 11pm on 29 August 4 Brigade attacked and while 16th Battalion's left could not take Zig-Zag Trench, the right entered Mouquet Farm only to be forced out later. The 13th Battalion's left company was unable to capture the west part of Fabeck Graben but the right company captured 150 metres of the trench east of OG1.

Although 12 Brigade relieved 4 Brigade, the arrival of the 1st Canadian Division at Pozières marked the start of the Canadian Corps' replacement of I ANZAC Corps. The 1st Canadian Brigade started by taking over the Pozières mill sector.

FOURTH ARMY

Joffre had written to Haig on 11 August, to express his dissatisfaction at the localised attacks which were getting nowhere. He wanted combined attacks along a broad front, starting with the capture of Thiepval, High Wood, Ginchy and Combles on 22 August. A second attack around 1 September would capture Grandcourt, Courcelette, Martinpuich, Flers, Morval, Rancourt and Bouchavesnes. The following day Haig and Joffre agreed to make a start by advancing between High Wood and the River Somme on 18 August.

III Corps, 18 August

1st Division, Intermediate Trench

In 1 Brigade's sector the 1st Black Watch left their trench at 4.15am. The covering barrage fell short, disorganising the advance, and then the German artillery joined in. Only a few men reached Intermediate Trench in the thick fog and they soon had to withdraw. General Strickland wanted to make another attempt at 2.45pm but a British heavy gun fired short and an exploding shell blocked the assembly trench. The 8th Berkshires reached Lancashire Sap, west of High Wood, as the smoke covering their left flank drifted across their front. They were then stopped by artillery and machine-gun fire.

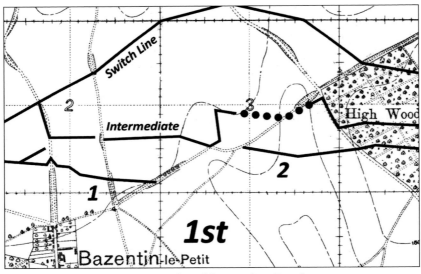

18 August, III Corps: 1st Division cleared Intermediate Trench.

In 2 Brigade's sector, the 1st Loyal North Lancashires attacked the trench at the north-west corner of High Wood. The right company left their trenches early and ran into their protective barrage. The left company advanced alone and captured its half of the trench before spreading out to occupy the whole trench. The 1st Northants later bombed east and helped the Loyals get closer to High Wood.

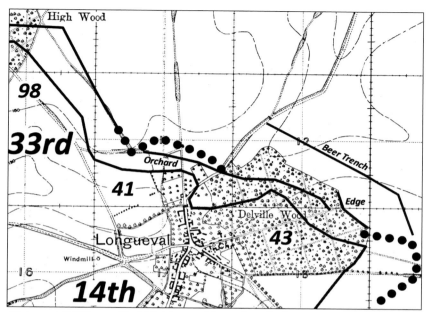

18 August, XV Corps: 33rd Division could not clear High Wood or Wood Lane to the east, 14th Division struggled to extend its hold on Longueval and Delville Wood.

XV Corps, 18 August

General Landon's 33rd Division had to clear High Wood while Major General Victor Couper's 14th Division had to advance out of Delville Wood.

33rd Division, High Wood

Major Sim and his Royal Engineers had been preparing for 98 Brigade's attack. Flame-throwers were set up to spray the Switch Line while thirty oil drums were prepped to cover it with burning oil; pipe-pushers loaded with explosives had also been burrowed beneath the trench.

But the British artillery fired short and destroyed the flame-throwers. The pipe pushers had also failed to burrow through the tree roots and one exploded under the 2nd Argylls at zero hour. While the drums worked, the burning oil did no harm to the infantry hiding in their dug outs and Captain Mackay's men were shot down when they advanced towards the Switch Line at 2.45pm.

Smoke bombs were fired late and they failed to create a screen but Second Lieutenant Bedwell led the 1/4th Suffolks as far as Wood Lane despite the enfilade fire from High Wood. The 4th King's advanced into their own covering barrage while machine-gun teams sheltering in shell-holes in front of Wood Lane stopped them going any further. Lieutenant Colonel Beall was ordered to make another attempt with the King's but he did not have enough men. It left the Suffolks holding an isolated section of Wood Lane and the death of Lieutenant Bedwell forced them to retire in the face of bombing attacks.

Later that evening Brigadier General Heriot-Maitland asked for reinforcements but General Landon chose to relieve 98 Brigade with 19 Brigade.

14th Division, Wood Lane and Delville Wood

On the left 41 Brigade faced the south end of Wood Lane and Orchard Trench. The attack against Wood Lane by 33rd Division had failed early on and the machine-guns swung round to pin down 7th Rifle Brigade's left flank. The rest of the battalion cleared the south end of Wood Lane alongside the 7th KRRC. The KRRC found that Orchard Trench had been obliterated so they dug in 200 metres beyond.

On the right 43 Brigade had to clear Edge Trench on the east side of Delville Wood and Beer Trench and ZZ Trench to the south-east. The 6th Duke of Cornwalls were hit by German artillery fire and by British trench mortars before zero hour and then machine-gun fire disorganised Colonel Stokie's men as they advanced towards Edge Trench. Second Lieutenant Jessup's bombers captured a small section of the trench leading to Hop Alley. The 6th Somersets overran Beer Trench and ZZ Trench as many Germans surrendered; they also cleared Hop Alley as far as Beer Trench.

XIV Corps, 18 August

The failure to advance south of Guillemont on 16 August upset Fourth Army's plan for a co-ordinated attack with the French on 18 August. So Rawlinson and Fayolle reaffirmed their commitment to capture Guillemont and Angle Wood on 17 August. But Cavan had fallen ill and General Morland commanded XIV Corps until he recovered. His plan was to capture the German front trench on 18 August and the village the following day while the French captured Angle Wood ready for their main attack on 22 August.

Major General John Capper's 24th Division faced the trenches covering Guillemont while General Deverell's 3rd Division faced the spur to the south, next to the French. Zero hour was set for 2.45pm on 18 August and Morland gave orders not to increase the intensity of the bombardment before zero, to catch the Germans out. While the assault troops would follow the 'field artillery curtain' as close possible, Morland did not want them to move too fast and the timetable allowed two hours to clear and consolidate Guillemont.

The firing of the mine under Hawthorn Ridge on 1 July compromised VIII Corps' attack. (IWM Q754)

7th Division advance across the chalk lines marking the trenches east of Mametz on 1 July. (IWM Q87)

A howitzer crew waits beneath camouflage netting for the barrage to start. (IWM Q6460)

An 18-pounder crew in the Carnoy Valley fire a protective barrage for an attack on High Wood on 30 July. (IWM Q4063)

A Vickers machine-gun team keep firing at targets near Ovillers during a gas attack. (IWM Q3996)

A Canadian officer explains the planned attack north of Courcelette to his platoon. (IWM CO957)

An Australian battalion assembles before heading to Pozières. (IWM Q1559)

The 1st Wiltshires make the long walk across no man's land during 25th Division's advance from the Leipzig Salient (IWM Q1142)

5th Division's support waves move forward during the advance on Morval on 25 September (IWM Q1312)

A fatigue party carries bombs forward during 18th Division's attack on Trônes Wood in July (IWM 4052)

This tank was ditched near Flers on 15 September and two days later a company headquarters has taken it over. (IWM Q5577)

A machine-gun team in action near Mouquet Farm in September; they have dug a shelter and covered it with logs. (IWM Q1419)

Artillery signallers use a lamp to relay a message to their battery near Fricourt Wood. (IWM Q4131)

Dirty and tired, 4th Worcesters assemble after a spell in the trenches near Gueudecourt in September (IWM Q1455)

Canadian medics carry out emergency first aid during the battle for Courcelette in September (IWM CO756)

An armoured car stops next to a Guards Division dressing station on the road to Guillemont. (IWM Q1222)

24th Division, Guillemont

In 17 Brigade's sector, on the north-west side of Guillemont, Captain Gullick was injured leading the 8th Buffs during the capture of Machine-Gun House and part of ZZ Trench. The 3th Rifle Brigade did not notice the barrage moving for several minutes, but when they did they captured the German front trench and Guillemont station, taking many prisoners. They also met the Buffs bombing down the Longueval Road. The Buffs had also bombed north-east, meeting soldiers from 14th Division in ZZ Trench; altogether the battalion had taken around 100 prisoners.

At zero hour 73 Brigade advanced astride the Trônes Wood road. The 7th Northants reached the German front line north of the road but they were hit by machine-guns hidden in Guillemont's ruins. It made consolidation difficult, particularly on the left flank where there was a fierce fight around the quarry. The 12th Middlesex faced the same problem south of the road and it too struggled to hold the German front line. In both cases the German barrage pinned down the support waves in no man's land, but the Northants held on and later that evening they met the 3rd Rifle Brigade in front of Guillemont, with the help of a 9th Royal Sussex company.

3rd Division, Lonely Trench

In 9 Brigade's sector crossfire stopped the 8th East Yorkshires[155] reaching the trenches south-east of Arrow Head Copse while the 1st Northumberland Fusiliers were unable to capture the north half of Lonely Trench. But in 76 Brigade's sector the 10th Royal Welsh Fusiliers overran the south part of Lonely Trench and some even reached the road beyond alongside the 1st Gordons. The failure of the Northumberlands meant the Germans were able to force the Welsh Fusiliers to withdraw. But the Gordons held on, in touch with the French in Maurepas Ravine. The German artillery concentrated on the ravine, driving the Gordons and the French back during the evening.

During the early hours of 19 August a senior staff officer discovered that the Germans had evacuated Lonely Trench and Angle Wood. So the Welsh Fusiliers and the Gordons advanced beyond Lonely Trench and the road beyond, alongside the French. Later that night Major General Reginald Pinney's 35th Division relieved 3rd Division.

Summary

Despite the difficulties, XIV Corps' robust communication arrangements held up. The limited objectives meant the artillery could give covering fire during the advance through Guillemont so the German reinforcements faced well-organised troops protected by a wall of shrapnel and high explosive.

---

155 Attached from 8 Brigade.

FOURTH ARMY, 19 TO 21 AUGUST

On 17 August Rawlinson received an intriguing letter from GHQ regarding a new weapon called the 'tank'. Two days later he received a GHQ memorandum detailing a big offensive in which the tanks would secure 'the enemy's last line of prepared defences between Morval and Le Sars with a view to opening the way for cavalry' and it was timed to take place in the middle of September.

But Haig wanted to secure the best possible jumping off line first. He wanted the Reserve Army to start from the ridge north of Thiepval and north-east of Pozières and Fourth Army to start from a line running from High Wood, north of Delville Wood to Ginchy and Leuze Wood. Both Gough and Rawlinson had similar thoughts but they only had limited resources. On 20 August Rawlinson told his corps commanders they had three weeks to secure the line but they could not afford to wear out too many divisions because he needed six for the September offensive.

Haig and Foch met on 19 August and they agreed ambitious plans for the next attack on 24 August. While XV Corps would clear the east edge of Delville Wood ready to attack Ginchy, XIV Corps would capture Guillemont and the ridge to the south; the French would take Maurepas. Two or three days later, Fourth Army would attack the German Second Line, east of Guillemont while the French cleared the Le Forest-Cléry line.

III Corps, 19 to 21 August

15th Division, South of Martinpuich

The 15th Division released smoke, drawing German artillery fire away from the attack. Patrols then discovered the Switch Line south of Martinpuich had been abandoned. By occupying it, the Scots outflanked the German advanced position in Intermediate Trench.

1st Division, the Switch Line

During the afternoon of 19 August there were signs that the Germans were withdrawing from the High Wood area when patrols from the 1st Northants[156] occupied part of the Switch Line, west of the wood; they had to stop a counter-attack during the early hours. The 2nd KRRC relieved the 1st Loyal North Lancashires on the Northants' right after dusk. Both battalions then established an outpost line, reducing no man's land in front of the Switch Line to 200 metres.

A second counter-attack the following morning forced the Northants to withdraw while cross-fire from High Wood and the Switch Line stopped them retaking the trench. Meanwhile, the 2nd KRRC held onto its position.

---

156 2 Brigade.

An attempt by two companies each from the Northants and 2nd Sussex failed to retake the Switch Line west of the wood at 2.15pm.

XV Corps, 19 to 21 August

33rd Division, Longueval

During the night of 19/20 August, 100 Brigade took over the line north of Longueval from 14th Division.[157] The following night the 1/9th Highland Light Infantry[158] occupied part of Wood Lane east of High Wood, after it was abandoned by the Germans. But the 2nd Royal Welsh Fusiliers[159] were unable to clear the trench on the west side of Delville Wood.

On 21 August the 8th KRRC[160] failed to drive the Germans out of Delville Wood although smoke was used to cover their flanks. General Landon wanted 100 Brigade to capture Orchard Trench at midnight but the decision was taken late and the 2nd Worcesters could not get into position in time. The 1/9th Highland Light Infantry had to advance alone and it was stopped by machine-gun fire.

XIV Corps, 19 to 21 August

During the night of 20/21 August General Pinney's 35th Division took over the trenches between Arrowhead Copse and Maltzhorn Farm. The French occupied Angle Wood the following day.

24th Division, Guillemont

The day started badly when a pre-dawn attack failed to capture the strongpoint opposite Arrow Head Copse. But when patrols from the 8th Buffs and the 3rd Rifle Brigade discovered that ZZ Trench had been abandoned, plans were put into place to attack Guillemont at 4.30pm. In 17 Brigade's sector one company each from the 3rd Rifle Brigade and 1st Royal Fusiliers failed to advance south-east from Guillemont station. The 8th Queen's reached the quarry in 72 Brigade's sector but they had to withdraw after a bombing fight.

35th Division, Arrow Head Copse

An attack by the 16th Cheshires at 10pm failed for several reasons. The heavy artillery barrage damaged the assembly trenches and then continued firing after zero hour so the troops could not follow the creeping barrage. It did not help that many of the replacements for the original Bantam soldiers were 'either half grown lads or degenerates' and their first experience of battle had been a disaster.

---

157 14th Division's 43 Brigade still held the line through the wood.
158 100 Brigade.
159 19 Brigade.
160 41 Brigade, 14th Division.

FOURTH ARMY, 24 TO 31 AUGUST

Rawlinson issued Fourth Army's instructions for the next attack on 22 August. III Corps would capture Intermediate Trench, XV Corps had to break free of Delville Wood and XIV Corps' left had to clear the area between Ginchy and Guillemont. But then the objective on XIV Corps' right had to be altered to co-operate with the French.

Three days later Rawlinson explained GHQ's revised objectives to his corps commanders. III Corps had to clear the High Wood area while XV Corps had to capture Beer Trench, east of Delville Wood and Ginchy; XIV Corps still had to take Guillemont and the trenches to the south. Haig then visited Rawlinson to discuss the plan. While Haig believed the artillery and troops were good enough to capture their objectives, he wanted the division commanders to pay attention to detail when planning their attacks. His main concern was about the Germans using dug-outs and cellars to avoid the bombardment. Gas could not be used because there were insufficient troops to carry the cylinders forward so the artillery would use lachrymatory shells[161] to force them out into the open.

Later that evening Rawlinson set 29 August as the date to co-operate with the French. But the rain which started on the afternoon of 25 August delayed the preparations and the artillery registration and the date was changed first to 30 August, then 1 September and finally to 3 September.

III Corps, 24 to 31 August

15th and 1st Divisions, Intermediate Trench

Following a trench mortar barrage on 24 August the 6th Camerons[162] failed to clear the west end of Intermediate Trench while Captains Kennedy and Jordeson's companies of the 2nd Munsters[163] could not clear the east end. Captain Inglis's company of the 1st South Wales Borderers[164] and the Munsters eventually cleared the east end of Intermediate Trench during the night of 26/27 August.

The following night 15th Division took over the area and the Scots had established a ring of outposts around Intermediate Trench by 30 August. While two companies of the 12th Highland Light Infantry were taken prisoner, the Germans holding Intermediate Trench were eventually forced to surrender.

XV Corps, 24 July

33rd Division, Longueval

General Landon planned to capture Tea Trench, a new trench connecting

---

161 Shells filled with tear gas.
162 45 Brigade, 15th Division.
163 3 Brigade, 1st Division.
164 3 Brigade.

Wood Lane to the Flers road. Although 100 Brigade was heavily shelled before zero hour, the British barrage was equally effective and a smoke screen blinded the Germans as the 1st Queen's bombed along Wood Lane. The 2nd Worcesters and the 16th KRRC reached their objective[165] with Captain Henderson leading his men forward shouting 'Come on the Worcestershires!'

14th Division, Delville Wood

The task for 42 Brigade was to establish a new line outside the perimeter of Delville Wood. At 5.45pm the 5th Ox and Bucks captured the west part of Beer Trench, linking up with 33rd Division on its left. The 5th Shropshires and 9th KRRCs cleared the centre part of Beer Trench but the machine-guns in Ale Alley stopped the 8th KRRC capturing the east end. The Germans then drove the 9th KRRC back into wood and the 5th Shropshires followed. Although only part of the objective had been taken, Brigadier General Dudgeon reported his men had captured over 200 prisoners and a dozen machine-guns. The following morning, the 9th Rifle Brigade[166] cleared Edge Trench on the east side of Delville Wood.

XV Corps Summary

General Horne wanted to capture the rest of Beer Trench but 33rd and 14th Divisions were exhausted. On the afternoon of the 27th the 10th Durhams[167] made 14th Division's last attack, capturing Edge Trench. The final part of Delville Wood's 159 acres had been cleared after six weeks of fighting.

Between 27 and 28 August 1st Division took over High Wood and Wood Lane. 7th Division also moved into Delville Wood and the 1st Royal Welsh Fusiliers[168] and the 10th Durhams cleared part of Ale Alley, east of the wood.

XIV Corps, 23 to 31 August
20th Division, Guillemont

Major General Douglas-Smith's 20th Division had to work through heavy shelling and bad weather to prepare for the attack on Guillemont. By the evening of 23 August, the Germans knew something was afoot because their artillery began shelling the British trenches and then their infantry counter-attacked the 11th KRRC near the quarry.[169]

35th Division, Falfemont Farm

The shelling continued throughout the night and by the morning Major General Reginald Pinney reported most of the troops were still not ready to advance. So Rawlinson cancelled most of 35th Division's attack, leaving

---

165 Some accounts have the 9th Highland Light Infantry in the centre of the attack.
166 42 Brigade.
167 43 Brigade.
168 22 Brigade.
169 59 Brigade.

only the right flank battalion to advance to appease the French. But Major Crook of the 17th Lancashire Fusiliers protested because he had not had time to prepare, there were no assembly trenches and his left flank would be exposed. Although he was overruled the plan of attack was changed so the Fusiliers would advance in echelon with the French flank.

The attack began well with the French entering the trenches south-east of Falfemont Farm as the Fusiliers advanced alongside. But they were soon driven from the farm ruins by enfilade fire and the Fusiliers withdrew at the same time.

24th Division, Counter-attack on Delville Wood

General Capper's 24th Division took over Longueval and Delville Wood in pouring rain on the night of 30/31 August. The weather cleared up at dawn but the shelling did not stop. While the 9th Rifle Brigade[170] reported Beer Trench had been abandoned, their outposts could see infantry assembling, ready to attack. German planes also flew low over the Delville Wood area, an unusual sight because the Royal Flying Corps normally dominated the skies. Something was afoot and then the bombardment intensified, caused many casualties, particularly in 73 Brigade's sector north of Longueval.

31 August, XV Corps: While 24th Division held onto Longueval, 7th Division held most of Delville Wood during the German counter-attack.

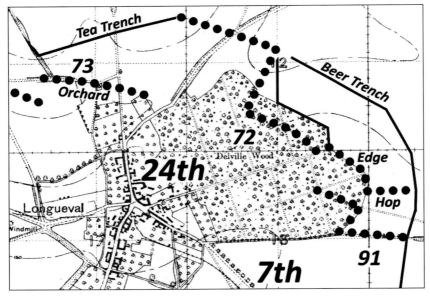

---

170 42 Brigade.

The German attack drove the 13th Middlesex out of the west ends of Tea Trench and Orchard Trench and while the 9th Sussex held onto Tea Trench, the 2nd Leinsters held onto Orchard Trench. In 72 Brigade's sector north of the wood, the 1st North Staffords dug pits in front of Tea Trench to escape the bombardment but they were not attacked. Meanwhile, Major Whitty's 8th Queen's Own had to withdraw its right flank to Inner Trench inside the wood to avoid the worst of the bombardment.

7th Division, Counter-attack on Delville Wood

Lieutenant Colonel Ovens' 1st South Staffords bore the brunt of the attack in 7th Division's sector and his men noticed that the Germans wore khaki uniforms and were only carrying rifles, bombs and flares. They may have been trying to fool the British troops but Lieutenant Henderson's men stopped the bombing attacks along Ale Alley while Captain Jones's and Lieutenant Jones-Mitton's men stopped later attacks against Hop Alley.

Another fly-over by the German spotter planes was followed by a second bombardment. And then a new attack at 7pm forced most of the Staffords from the east corner of the wood. An unknown machine-gun sergeant stayed at his gun until he was killed, giving Captain Burt and Lieutenant Jones-Mitton time to rally their men in Edge Trench.

The German bombardment had cut all XV Corps communications and it was late in the night before Horne learnt what had happened. He immediately made plans to recover the lost ground the following morning, but for now the troops around Longueval and Delville Wood fought to recapture their trenches.

In 24th Division's sector, the 2nd Leinsters[171] twice tried to bomb along Orchard Trench. The 3rd Rifle Brigade[172] then moved forward and at 6.30pm they cleared Orchard Trench and Wood Lane. In 7th Division's sector two 2nd Queen's[173] platoons failed to clear the Germans from the eastern edge of the wood, near Hop Alley, while the 1st North Staffords only managed to clear twenty metres of Edge Trench in the afternoon. Another attempt by the Queen's at noon the following day also failed.

Plans for a Mid-September Offensive

On 1 August Haig had written a report to Robertson, Chief of the Imperial General Staff, for presentation to the War Committee. He was satisfied with the results of the Somme campaign so far and while the Verdun crisis had passed, his army had to fight on 'without prejudicing, probably fatally, the offensive of our Allies and their hopes of victory'.

---

171 73 Brigade.
172 17 Brigade.
173 91 Brigade.

Haig hoped the Russian offensive would continue on the Eastern Front[174] while his own army had to keep the pressure on, 'giving the enemy no rest and no respite from anxiety'. Although casualties had been high, he expected to inflict more on the Germans to compensate for them. 'It would not be justifiable to calculate on the enemy's resistance being completely broken by these means without another campaign next year. But, even if another campaign proves to be necessary, the enemy will certainly enter the coming winter with little hope left of being able to continue his resistance successfully through next spring and summer. I am confident it will prove beyond his power to do so, provided the Allies maintain their determination to fight on together, vigorously, to a successful conclusion.' In other words Haig wanted to continue the war of attrition.

Haig was also anxious to use the few tanks available as soon as possible because they might prove to be decisive. He had been kept up to date on their progress and had suggested halting production in July so twenty could be tested on the battlefield to discover what faults they had. But the element of surprise would be lost if only a few were deployed. While 150 tanks would be ready by September, 350 could be ready by January 1917, giving an offensive a much greater punch and more time to train crews.

Haig then discovered the first batch would be worn out by training and trials and on 29 July said while he appreciated seeing what a few tanks would do it was not his 'intention to employ tanks in small numbers, unless and until I am convinced the advantages to be gained by doing so are great enough to outweigh the disadvantages of making known to the enemy the existence of these new engines of war'.

While Haig believed German morale was falling, he knew his own army could only continue its offensive until the autumn 'if the enemy is not forced from his entrenched positions – as there is good hope he will be – before the autumn; it is unlikely to be possible to arrange for another simultaneous effort on a large scale before next spring...' On 11 August Haig learnt the tanks would not arrive until 1 September; four days later he was told the first six were on their way.

On 16 August Haig told Rawlinson and Gough there would be a mid-September offensive. But the tanks were not the catalyst. GHQ believed German morale had been falling since the beginning of the month and the time was approaching for a breakthrough battle.

On 22 August Haig told Robertson that he was counting on tanks for the big attack. 'Even if I do not get so many as I hope, I shall use what I have got, as I cannot wait any longer for them and it would be folly not to use every means at my disposal in what is likely to be our crowning effort for

---

174 The Brusilov Offensive had begun on 4 June but it had petered out by mid-June. Offensive operations had resumed on 28 July.

this year.' The British attacks were also wearing out the Empire's resources and some in the government were querying Haig's strategy. Robertson noted that, 'while certain Ministers thought Haig was doing too much fighting, the French military authorities complained he was doing too little'.

On 25 August, Joffre suggested attacking on 5 September but Haig wanted Fourth Army to have taken Ginchy and Guillemont first and he told Joffre so two days later; Fourth Army also needed to relieve divisions and move artillery. But bad weather postponed the preliminary operation to 3 September, pushing back the main offensive to the middle of September. Joffre agreed to the revised timetable the following day.

GHQ issued instructions to Gough and Rawlinson on 16 August, stating fifty or sixty Heavy Section armoured cars (the name used for tanks at this time) would reach France in mid-September. The plan was for the Reserve Army to use six divisions and between eighteen and twenty-four tanks to advance towards Pys and Le Sars. Meanwhile, Fourth Army would use eight divisions and between thirty-six and forty-two tanks to break through the German Third Line.

GHQ's memorandum on 19 August stated Fourth Army would make the main attack, securing 'the enemy's last line of prepared defences between Morval and Le Sars with a view to opening the way for the cavalry'. After forming a defensive flank between Bapaume, Le Transloy and Morval, there would be an attack north-west in co-ordination with a frontal offensive. Both Rawlinson and Gough were told to submit plans for the offensive and explain how they proposed to use tanks by 28 August.

Planning for Tanks
Winston Churchill had submitted his memoranda on the capabilities of Caterpillars to the War Committee on 3 December 1915.[175] He stated: 'The cutting of the enemy's wire and the general domination of his firing line can be effected by engines of this character. About seventy are now nearing completion in England and should be inspected. None should be used until all can be used at once. They should be disposed secretly along the whole attacking front, 200 or 300 metres apart. Above all surprise.' The paper was shown to Field Marshal Sir John French but he was about to resign and the paper was not shown to his successor, Sir Douglas Haig.

In February 1916 Lieutenant Colonel Sir Ernest Swinton, Assistant-Secretary of the War Committee, wrote a paper on the use of the tank and Haig later approved of his tactical principles: 'The chance of success of the new arm lies in its ability to effect a complete surprise and machines should not be used in driblets. Their existence should be kept secret until the whole

---

175 Just before he was sacked as First Lord of the Admiralty as a result of the failed Gallipoli operation.

are ready to be launched together with the infantry assault in one great combined operation.' Swinton wanted to deploy them 100 metres apart, or eighteen on every mile of front.

The Mark I tank was 6.73 metres long, 3.50 metres wide and 1.90 metres high and weighed 28 tons. While the six-cylinder, 105-horsepower Daimler engine gave it a maximum speed of 3.7 miles an hour, it was reduced to ½ a mile an hour on rough terrain. It carried enough petrol to travel through the German defensive zone and back without refuelling. Two trailing wheels helped the officer and seven crewmen steer the machine and it had been designed to cross a trench 3.5 metres wide. The Male version was armed with two six-pounder guns and four Hotchkiss machine-guns while the Female version was armed with five Vickers and one Hotchkiss machine-guns.

'Preliminary notes on tactical employment of tanks' issued to Fourth and Reserve Armies on 16 August said: 'Its safety lies in surprise, in rapid movement, and in getting to close quarters. It must emerge from cover (either material cover or the cover of smoke or darkness), and it must return to cover or find other concealment or safety when its task is done.' They would start in camouflaged assembly positions and move forward in the dark, ready for a pre-dawn assault when it was light enough for the crews to navigate but dark enough to blind the German artillery spotters. The tanks would move ahead of the infantry to draw the German rifle and machine-gun fire and the ideal was for them to be astride the first trench, shooting along it, when the infantry made their final charge. The tanks would continue, preferably driving alongside communication trenches so the Germans could not use them, as soon as the infantry had taken control of the fire trench.

While Swinton wanted the tanks under infantry command and supporting them, GHQ had its own ideas. The tanks would advance ahead of the infantry in small groups of two or three, supressing villages, woods and strongpoints; they would also deal with machine-guns as soon as they were spotted.

The limited number of tanks meant a large breakthrough could not be made, so new ideas had to be discussed. Rawlinson wanted to break through the German lines over three successive nights. All the tanks would contribute to a wide breakthrough on the first night while twelve would make a lodgement in the second line of trenches near Lesboeufs on the second night. All the surviving tanks would drive north through the lodgement towards the Bapaume road on the third night.

Haig disagreed and issued his instructions on 31 August. Most of the tanks would be given to XV and XIV Corps so they could create a gap between Gueudecourt and Morval on the first day. The cavalry would establish a flank between Bapaume, Le Transloy and Morval and then help Fourth Army to roll up the German defences while the Reserve Army made frontal attacks. Kiggell told Rawlinson and he in turn advised his corps commanders to prepare to be 'forcing the battle to a decision at the earliest possible moment'. He also asked Haig to deploy the five cavalry divisions, one behind the other.

On 1 September, the day of the assault was set for 15 September, giving the tank crews no time for training in France; they would have to go straight into action. Five days later General Allenby was told to prepare Third Army for an attack on Gommecourt around 20 September. General Sir Charles Monro was also told to prepare First Army for an attack against Vimy Ridge ten days later. Although GHQ plans were set, on 9 September Joffre urged Haig to attack sooner; Haig refused. Three days later Joffre promised Sixth Army would attack Frégicourt, to protect Fourth Army's right flank.

Chapter 8

Preparing for Another Big Push – 1 to 14 September

The Reserve Army's preparations to advance either side of the River Ancre went ahead in spite of the bad weather. Major-General Gerald Cuthbert's 39th Division, on V Corps' right, would capture three trenches on the west bank, south-east of Beaumont Hamel, at 5.10am. Major General Edward Perceval's 49th Division, on II Corps' left, would capture two trenches on the east bank, starting three minutes later. It would also take a third trench the following day, opening the way for an attack against Schwaben Redoubt and Thiepval.

39th Division, West Bank of the Ancre
Major General Gerald Cuthbert's battalions were weak in numbers but the preliminary barrage had cut the wire while the creeping barrage and the brigade machine-guns provided good support. Unfortunately, the width of no man's land had been underestimated and the men had not crossed it by the time the creeping barrage moved off. It also landed behind a salient in 117 Brigade's sector and several machine-guns stopped all but Major Stollard's company of the 17th Sherwood Foresters crossing no man's land. The 16th Rifle Brigade became disorientated in the mist and only a few entered the German trenches with the help of the 17th KRRC.

In 116 Brigade's sector, Second Lieutenant Leach led the 14th Hampshires across no man's land but Captain Skinner's men were stopped by wire. The 11th Sussex crossed the badly damaged front trench and continued to the support trench; some even made it to the final objective. But Captain Rettie's and Cunningham's companies of the 4/5th Black Watch[176] could not hold the German support line in the Ancre valley and had to withdraw.

---

176 Attached from 188 Brigade.

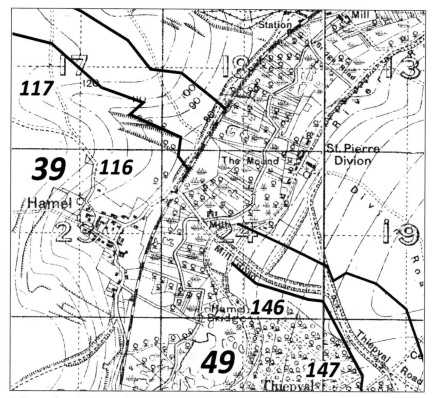

3 September, II Corps: Neither 39th Division nor 49th Division could advance along the banks of the River Ancre.

49th Division, East Bank of the Ancre

While the heavy artillery shelled Schwaben Redoubt and Thiepval was hit by gas and ammonal, 49th Division advanced behind an excellent creeping barrage. In 146 Brigade's sector, the 1/8th West Yorkshires crossed no man's land next to the river but only a few men reached the support line. The 1/6th West Yorkshires were stopped by enfilade machine-gun fire because 147 Brigade had not captured the Pope's Nose salient.

The problem was the 1/5th Duke's had been stopped by wire and, while some followed the 1/4th Duke's through a gap, the Pope's Nose garrison continued firing. The front line and parts of the support trench were taken but the Germans still held the trenches around the Pope's Nose. The machine-guns in the Strasburg Line took their toll on the Duke's as did counter-attacks by bombers.

The Withdrawal

The mist prevented visual signalling and many runners had been hit running through the German barrage hitting no man's land. The German gunners also targeted the British rear and Captain William Allen attended to the wounded after a shell hit on one of 246 Brigade's ammunition wagons. Despite being injured four times he continued with his work before having his wounds dressed; Captain Allen was awarded the Victoria Cross.

With casualties mounting and ammunition dwindling, the troops could not hold on. It was 146 Brigade which fell back from the St Pierre area first and it was back in the British trenches by 7.30am, leaving 116 Brigade under fire across the river. Brigadier General Goring-Jones wanted 146 Brigade to try again but 147 Brigade had withdrawn by 10am and his orders were cancelled. Once 49th Division's failure was known V Corps decided not to send forward 39th Division's reserves. Most of General Cuthbert's men withdrew when their bombs ran out but some of the Sussex and Black Watch waited until nightfall before pulling back.

II Corps, 3 to 14 September

25th Division, The Wonder Work

At 5.13am Lieutenant Colonel Cotton's 1st Wiltshires[177] entered the German line west of the Wonder Work while Colonel Gibb's 3rd Worcesters[178] entered the trenches south-west of the redoubt. Regimental Sergeant Major Nicholson led the 2nd South Lancashires[179] into the trench to the south. But no one entered the Wonder Work and artillery and machine-gun fire forced the Wiltshires to withdraw. General Bainbridge's men had not cleared the way to Thiepval.

11th Division, Skyline Ridge

On 7 September General Sir Charles Woollcombe's 11th Division took over Skyline Ridge. The Reserve Army had been told to limit attacks to no more than two battalions but General Jacob wanted 11th Division to advance on to the Thiepval spur.

At 6.30pm on 14 September, 32 Brigade advanced from Hindenburg Trench with two companies each from the 6th Green Howards, 9th West Yorkshires and the 8th Duke's. The artillery missed Turk Trench and the Green Howards suffered heavy casualties, including Lieutenant Colonel Forsyth who went forward after Captain Earle was wounded. But Captain Goy and Second Lieutenant Hartley led the West Yorkshires into the Wonder Work. While an important position had been taken, the German barrage which followed caused 700 casualties.

---

177 7 Brigade.
178 Attached to 75 Brigade from 7 Brigade.
179 75 Brigade.

I ANZAC Corps, 3 September
4th Australian Division, Fabeck Graben

At 5.10am 13 Brigade advanced close behind the barrage and while the 51st Battalion reached Mouquet Farm, some went beyond the objective. In the centre 52nd Battalion captured part of Fabeck Graben as did 49th Battalion on the right. The Australians had taken 100 prisoners but they had suffered heavy casualties taking the three isolated footholds. The Germans emerged from tunnels to surround Lieutenant Clifford's men north of Mouquet Farm; they were never seen again. In the centre 52nd Battalion was driven back but 49th Battalion held onto 300 metres of trench while 50th Battalion protected its left flank; the Germans eventually pushed back 49th Battalion's right.

Canadian Corps, 3 to 10 September
1st Canadian Division, Pozières

Lieutenant General Sir Julian Byng's Canadian Corps took over the Pozières sector on the afternoon of 3 September and the fighting around Mouquet Farm and Fabeck Graben continued as General Arthur Currie's 1st Canadian Division settled in. Early on 8 September the Germans sensed a relief was underway and they rushed Fabeck Graben, recapturing everything the Australians had taken. Two further German attacks from Mouquet Farm failed to recover any more ground.

At 4.45pm on 9 September 1st Canadian Division struck back when 2nd Canadian Battalion captured 500 metres of trench and sixty prisoners east of Pozières. Corporal Leo Clarke's section fought to secure the battalion's left flank until only Clarke was left standing. He then fought off twenty Germans with a revolver and captured rifles, killing all but one of them, whom he took prisoner; Corporal Clark was awarded the Victoria Cross.

On the night of 11/12 September Major-General Richard Turner's 2nd Canadian Division took over the OG Trenches north-east of Pozières. The following night Major-General Louis Lipsett's 3rd Canadian Division took over Mouquet Farm sector from 1st Canadian Division. In five days Currie's division had suffered over 2,800 casualties from shell fire; the equivalent to 560 a day or one every three minutes.

FOURTH ARMY, 3 SEPTEMBER

The plan was for Fourth Army to attack at noon on 3 September. III Corps would capture High Wood and Wood Lane while XV Corps extended its hold on Delville Wood. XIV Corps would take Ginchy, Guillemont, Leuze

Wood and the Combles spur. It would also link with the French advance near Savernake Wood.

The bombardment started at 8am on 2 September and the German artillery retaliated, shelling Delville Wood and the assembly trenches facing Ginchy. III and XV Corps' heavy artillery would not change their rate of fire before zero, to try and fool the Germans, but XIV Corps' heavy artillery would intensify theirs as usual.

III Corps
1st Division, High Wood and Wood Lane
It was 1 Brigade's task to clear High Wood and capture Wood Lane. The 1st Black Watch planned to use flame-throwers, blazing oil drums and pipe-pushers inside the wood again. A mine had also been set and it destroyed the strongpoint at the east corner of High Wood thirty seconds before zero. While the Black Watch's right company captured the crater the rest of the battalion had no such luck; the pipe-pushers blew back[180] while the Stokes mortars fired short and ignited the oil drums. The problems delayed Lieutenant Colonel Hamilton's men and they were then stopped by machine-gun and rifle fire. Meanwhile, the 1st Camerons captured Wood Lane to the south-east but a detachment of the 8th Berkshires could not cross no man's land on the right.

Three hours later Germans counter-attacked through High Wood, driving the Black Watch from the crater. They then fired on the Camerons' flank until the nearest company withdrew; by 3.30pm the rest of the battalion had pulled back.

XV Corps
General Capper's 24th Division held Orchard Trench and part of Tea Trench, north of Longueval; it also held the northeast side of Delville Wood. General Watts' 7th Division held the east corner of the wood and Pilsen Lane; it also held Porter Trench facing Ginchy.

24th Division, Longueval and Delville Wood
The 8th Buffs[181] were supposed to attack at midday but the runners sent to synchronize the time were killed en route to brigade headquarters. While the bombers cleared Sap A, the riflemen were stopped by machine-gun fire when they advanced late over the top. A second attack led by Major Hamilton at 4pm did not get far because the covering artillery barrage did not creep forward at the appointed hour. The only consolation was that the 7th Northants[182] had captured the part of Tea Lane west of North Street.

---

180 The thick tree roots meant the pipes had not penetrated far into no man's land.
181 17 Brigade.
182 Lent from 73 Brigade to 17 Brigade.

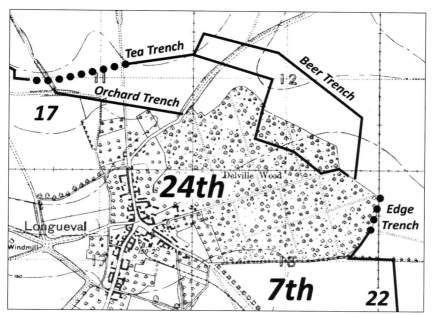

3 September, XV Corps: 24th Division struggled to improve its position north of Longueval and 7th Division did the same around Delville Wood.

7th Division, Ginchy

The east corner of Delville Wood had to be cleared of Germans by 22nd Brigade. The barrage began at 10.25am and at midday the 2nd Queen's advanced along the south-east edge of Delville Wood towards Hop Alley. Unfortunately, smoke from fumite grenades[183] revealed their position and they were stopped by machine-gun fire and snipers. An attack towards Ale Alley by a 9th East Surrey's detachment failed to materialise due to a mix-up over orders.

Meanwhile, the rest of 7th Division's attack was underway. Before zero hour 22 Brigade left its trenches and crept across the 400 metres of no man's land. But smoke from the fumite bombs raised the alarm and the 1st Royal Welsh Fusiliers were hit by enfilade fire from Ale Alley when the barrage lifted. While Captain Dadd's company captured the south end of Beer Trench, Captain Peter's company was pinned down in shell-holes south of Hop Alley. Lieutenant Davies's company entered the north part of Ginchy but *'nothing was ever heard of them'*. Only a few men of the Fusiliers' support company reached the orchards north-west of the village. The 2nd Warwicks were sent up to occupy Ale Alley but most were pinned down

---

183 Burning fumite is used to kill insects. Fumite grenades were used to smoke the Germans out of their dug-outs.

amongst the Welsh Fusiliers. Only the 20th Manchesters reached their first objective in the southern half of the village, having cleared Waterlot Farm.

At 2.15pm General Steele ordered Captain Moore-Brabazon's company of the 2nd Royal Irish forward to clear the left flank but it was a case of too little too late; Lieutenant Harrison discovered the Germans had already secured the area. The Manchesters reported they were digging in on the east side of Ginchy at 3.50pm under Lieutenant Ryall of the Royal Irish because most of their officers had been hit. But then the Germans infiltrated the north side of Ginchy and by 4.15pm Major Hutching's Manchesters had retired across no man's land to Porter Trench, taking most of the Royal Irish and some of the Warwicks with them; Lieutenants Harrowing and Sulman used the Warwicks Lewis guns to keep the Germans at bay. Captain Williams-Freeman's and Lieutenant Willis's groups of Warwicks held onto the south-west corner of the village, alongside 20th Division.

Meanwhile, the Royal Irish were ordered to capture Hop Alley and re-occupy Ginchy but artillery and machine-gun fire stopped them before they could reach their own front line. At 5pm the Irish bombers moved along the perimeter of the wood but Captain Considine's company was stopped by machine-gun fire as soon as they advanced. Major Roche-Kelly joined the survivors sheltering in the shell holes alongside the Welsh Fusiliers, Warwicks and Manchesters.

Later on contact aeroplanes saw flares fired in Ginchy but there were no other messages. General Watts wanted to attack again until Colonel Seymour of the 20th Manchesters reported there were no more troops to make it. Instead Watts asked corps headquarters to arrange a new artillery barrage so 20 Brigade could take Ginchy. But when a patrol reported the Germans had re-entered Ginchy, the attack was postponed until the following morning.

XIV Corps

While 20th Division held the trenches facing Guillemont, it was too weak to carry out the attack and 47 Brigade had been sent up from 16th Division. The brigade was also low in numbers and it had been reinforced by two battalions from 61 Brigade.

Major General Reginald Stephens' 5th Division held XIV Corps' right flank and 13 Brigade made an early attack on Falfemont Farm in co-operation with the French. But neither the promised French barrage nor the infantry attack materialised at 8.50am, leaving the 2nd KOSBs to face 'the old story of the murderous efficiency of the German machine-gun'. Nearly 300 men were hit as they climbed the slope and it looked as if 'they had been mown down on parade'.

20th Division, Guillemont

The day started with the barrage creeping forward at 8.15am, the same time as the 5th Division advanced to the south-east. The real attack was at noon and both the 6th Connaughts and the 10th KRRCs charged through their own the barrage into the village, suffering heavy casualties. Lieutenant Colonel Lenox-Conyngham's last words were 'that, Connaught Rangers, is what you have to take' as he pointed his cane towards Ginchy.

The 7th Leinsters advanced past Guillemont station and entered the village where they 'bombed, captured, bayoneted or brained with the butts of their rifles all the Germans'. Lieutenant John Holland led twenty-six men through the covering barrage to clear a large part of the ruins, taking fifty prisoners. Only five men returned but they had played an important part in capturing Guillemont; Holland was awarded the Victoria Cross for leading them.

While the 6th Connaughts moved into quickly into Guillemont, they forgot to leave men behind to clear out the quarry and were soon under fire from behind. Although wounded, Private Thomas Hughes returned to the

3 September, XIV Corps: While 20th Division cleared Guillemont, 5th Division crossed the valley to the south.

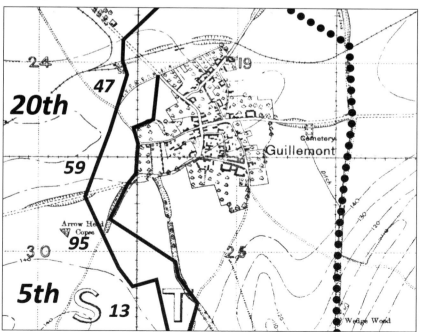

Connaughts' front line and captured the machine-gun shooting up his company. Though wounded again, he returned with three or four prisoners; Hughes was awarded the Victoria Cross.

The 10th KRRC were left in a difficult position by the quarry situation and Lieutenant Colonel Blacklock sent his reserve company forward to clear it. The rest of the battalion soon joined the 10th and 11th Rifle Brigade along the Hardecourt road, south-west of the village.

At 12.30pm a contact plane reported the first objective had been taken and twenty minutes later the 8th Munsters took over the advance, reaching North Street on the east side of Guillemont. The 6th Ox and Bucks and 7th Somersets also overran the trench along South Street before the Germans could man the parapet.[184]

The advance beyond Guillemont began at 2.50pm and neither brigade met any opposition. After 59 Brigade reported 'nothing in front' the 6th Royal Irish and a few of the Munsters joined them, led by the Royal Irish pipers. Two 12th King's companies joined the Connaughts in Guillemont, while Captain Mitchell's Somerset company reinforced the south side of the village. The 7th Duke of Cornwall's[185] also moved into Guillemont to help the divisional pioneers and engineers secure the ruins.

To the south-east many prisoners had been taken and the area in front of Leuze Wood appeared to be clear of German troops but General Smith stopped General Shute pushing 59 Brigade forward. Instead his troops linked up with 5th Division on the slopes of Wedge Wood Ravine.

But while there was no opposition in front of the division, two events changed everything. By 5.30pm General Smith knew 7th Division had lost Ginchy, on his left flank, and 5th Division had failed to capture Leuze Wood on his right flank.

Captain Cleminson had the foresight to get the 12th King's[186] to dig in on the north side of Guillemont, while a barrage helped stop several counter-attacks. When a Royal Irish platoon lost its lieutenant en route to the King's, Sergeant David Jones of the King's led the survivors to a critical position where they fought off counter-attacks for two days without food or water. Sergeant Jones was awarded the Victoria Cross.

General Smith sent out patrols to check the south flank and Lieutenant Hill of the Somersets confirmed his worse fears. German infantry were gathering for a counter-attack inside Leuze Wood; two were stopped before nightfall. German planes also flew over 20th Division's new line and the artillery bombardment followed. Later on the 7th Somersets' patrols discovered Leuze Wood had been abandoned.

---

184 6th Ox and Bucks from 60 Brigade and 7th Somersets from 61 Brigade.
185 61 Brigade.
186 61 Brigade.

5th Division, Wedge Wood and Falfemont Farm

While 95 Brigade faced the ravine south-east of Guillemont, 13 Brigade faced Wedge Wood and Falfemont Farm. Zero was timed for noon.

The 1st Duke of Cornwall's and 12th Gloucesters captured the battered German trenches on the spur south of Guillemont, finding them full of dead and wounded men. Fifty minutes later the Cornwall and Gloucester support companies advanced to the trenches south-east of Guillemont under heavy fire from Falfemont Farm. At 2.50pm 95 Brigade continued the advance to the sunken track which ran into Wedge Wood ravine, capturing 150 prisoners.

In 13 Brigade's sector the guns supporting the 14th and 15th Warwicks fired so short their shells landed behind the assault troops. While the Warwicks cleared the rest of the German trenches in Wedge Wood ravine, they could not reach Falfemont Farm on the spur on their right flank. The artillery starting shelling Leuze Wood spur at 2.45pm but it took until 6.30pm before 15 Brigade relieved an exhausted 13 Brigade. The 1st Bedfords were able to clear Wedge Wood but the 1st Cheshires could not capture Falfemont Farm.

While it was clear there were no Germans on the Leuze Wood spur, neither Brigadier General Gordon-Lennox nor Brigadier General Turner were authorised to advance towards the wood because it would create an exposed salient. Instead 15 Brigade was warned it would have to attack Falfemont Farm again the following afternoon.

FOURTH ARMY, 4 TO 8 SEPTEMBER

III Corps

Rawlinson gave Pulteney orders to clear the area west of High Wood, starting at 6pm on the 8th.

15th Division, Intermediate Trench

Captains Stirling and Binnie's 9th Black Watch[187] companies captured and held Intermediate Trench until the 1st Gloucesters fell back from the eastern half of the trench; they too then had to pull back.

1st Division, High Wood

The High Wood area was held by 3 Brigade but the British barrage hit the 1st Gloucesters' assembly trenches west of the wood, killing Lieutenant Peate and Sergeant Major Hird. Lieutenant Colonel Pagan's men still advanced along the west side of the wood but artillery and machine-gun fire stopped the Gloucesters' support companies and neither the infantry

---

187 From 44 Brigade.

nor the artillery could do any more. The 2nd Welsh struggled to advance through the wood but while the left company could not clear the western perimeter, the right company reached the Switch Line. Although the Gloucesters stopped a counter-attack at 8pm, they had to pull back to New Trench before midnight.

XV Corps

General Horne had three objectives; secure Longueval, push out from Delville Wood and capture Ginchy.

55th Division, Delville Wood

On the night of 4/5 September Major-General Hugh Jeudwine's 55th Division relieved 24th Division and 165 Brigade took over the trenches north of Longueval. The following evening Lieutenant Blackledge and the 1/6th King's bombers failed to advance along Wood Lane but the 1/7th King's discovered the Germans were abandoning Tea Trench and they occupied it as far west as Wood Lane. They then dug posts between Tea Lane and the Flers road. The 1/5th South Lancashires and the 1/10th King's also dug a new trench, extending 165 Brigade's line.

On the evening of 7 September 1/5th King's patrols discovered the Germans had abandoned part of Wood Lane and they occupied the south end. The following night the 1/5th and 1/9th King's linked up but they had to re-dig Tea Trench because it had been obliterated.

During the night 166 Brigade took over the north side of Delville Wood while 164 Brigade took over the east side, leaving General Jeudwine holding all of XV Corps' front.

7th Division, Ginchy

Horne's late night order on 3 September instructed General Watts to secure Ginchy if he had troops in the village. If he did not 7th Division was to capture it the following afternoon. Watts did neither; he waited until 20 Brigade was ready in Stout and Porter Trenches.

The 9th Devons had a difficult time reaching the assembly trenches and they then learnt Ginchy would not be shelled because troops might still be holding the ruins. Major Green's men advanced at 8am the following morning, only to be hit by artillery and machine-gun fire; the survivors were back in their trenches within the hour. Watts reported 20 Brigade would be unable to join the noon attack but he obtained Horne's permission to make a surprise attack at 3.30am the following morning, believing some of the Devons were still in the village.

Meanwhile, the 21st Manchesters' attack at 2pm failed to capture Ale Alley or Hop Alley. At 5.30pm two 2nd Queen's[188] companies advanced towards the east corner of Delville Wood only to discover the trench mortars had failed to knock out the machine-gun teams. They had to be content with holding the edge of the wood while the Germans held the junction of Ale Alley and Beer Trench.

Watts' plan for surprise night attack against Ginchy never got off the ground. Colonel James reported the 8th Devons would be late while the 2nd Gordons lost all their officers to artillery fire before they reached Porter Trench. Watts postponed the attack until the following afternoon.

The trench mortar barrage on Ale Alley had been unobserved and machine-gun fire stopped the 2nd Queen's reaching the east edge of Delville Wood but they did take the south-east corner and Lieutenant Lock brought forward the 8th Devons to help.

The Gordons left their trenches at 5am on 6 September but they went in the wrong direction and Major Oxley had to lead his men back to the start line so they could advance the right way. They were pinned down 100 metres in front of Ginchy. Captain Hearse and Lieutenant Underhill moved up two 9th Devons companies on their right flank and the attack was tried again at 2pm. Captain Turnbull led the Gordons into Ginchy but the German barrage made it impossible bring up reinforcements and a counter-attack forced them back at 4.30pm. It was 7th Division's final attempt; 55th Division and 16th Division relieved 7th Division the following evening.

XIV Corps

Rawlinson wanted Leuze Wood and Borleaux Wood captured to close the trap around Combles. Late on 3 September General Cavan ordered 20th Division and 5th Division to attack at 3.10pm the following afternoon but high winds and heavy showers interfered with the artillery bombardment. On the morning of 5 September General Rawlinson told General Cavan he had to capture Combles with the men he had, to free up his right flank 'as soon as possible'.

20th Division, Leuze Wood

On 4 September 20th Division was to check the area north of Leuze Wood but General Smith still did not know if 7th Division had secured Ginchy. He did not know the situation around the Quadrilateral, east of the village, either so he asked for a protective barrage to cover his left flank. The patrols detailed to cover the left of the advance were late but the 7th Somersets still established posts between the Guillemont Road and the west corner of Leuze Wood.

---

188 91 Brigade.

16th Division, Bouleaux Wood

While 49 Brigade took over the north edge of Leuze Wood early on 5 September, 48 Brigade did not reach the left sector until dusk because its guides got lost. Both brigades dug in along the Combles road and linked up with 5th Division in Leuze Wood.

The following morning 48 Brigade's patrols came under fire from the Quadrilateral while 49 Brigade entered Bouleaux Wood. Then at 3pm Major General William Hickie ordered the brigades to push their inner flanks forward to straighten their line; the Quadrilateral again stopped 48 Brigade advancing.

5th Division, Falfemont Farm and Leuze Wood

At 3.10pm on 4 September 15 Brigade attacked Falfemont Farm. The 1st Bedfords had to withdraw from their trenches before zero to avoid casualties from their own barrage but they still managed to bomb from Wedge Wood to the north-west corner of the farm, taking 130 prisoners. The 1st Norfolks crawled across a crater field towards the opposite corner of the farm, only to find the French had not moved forward; they were pinned down by the machine-guns in Combles ravine. Captain Francis led a few men to the south-west corner of the farm but they were forced to retire. At the same time Captain White's 1st Cheshire company reached the far side of the spur and they were reinforced by the 16th Royal Warwicks. A second attempt by the Norfolks failed to capture the farm but the 16th Warwicks spent a rainy night digging in close to the ruins.

At 6.30pm on 4 September 95 Brigade advanced towards Leuze Wood and the 1st East Surreys occupied Valley Trench, only suffering casualties from their covering barrage. The creeping barrage stopped the 1st Devons entering the wood until the artillery observers spotted the problem and lengthened the range; the Devons found few Germans inside.

Captain Brown was killed leading the 1st Norfolks as they captured Falfemont Farm at 3am on 5 September. Then Lieutenant Brown took his Lewis guns south-east to capture Point 48. At 8.30am 15 Brigade sent forward two 16th Warwicks' companies and they dug in along the slope, meeting 95 Brigade in Leuze Wood. The British protective barrage stopped them advancing further. At 4pm the 1st Devons moved through the rest of Leuze Wood, finding it clear of Germans.

When Rawlinson visited XIV Corps headquarters at 11.45am, he learnt the Germans were disorganised on 5th Division's front. Both the Bedfords and the Norfolks were asking for fresh troops and Rawlinson instructed Cavan to seize Leuze Wood and the high ground to the north-east, starting at 4pm.

The 7th Royal Irish Fusiliers[189] were ordered to relieve the Warwicks, but belts of wire hidden in the corn in front of Combles Trench stopped them and machine-gun fire forced them to withdraw. A second attempt at 7.30pm also failed. The 1st Devons[190] managed to occupy a trench in the middle of Leuze Wood.

56th Division, Leuze Wood[191]

Major General Charles Hull's 56th Division took over from 5th Division and 168 Brigade was the first to enter the front line on the evening of 7 September. The Germans spotted the relief taking place and they drove the 13th and 14th London back into Leuze Wood; the Londoners recovered the lost ground before nightfall. The 1/5th London spent the afternoon bombing along Combles Trench; a counter-attack the following morning forced them to withdraw. Then 169 Brigade took over the area south of Leuze Wood but its first attempt to clear Combles Trench failed.

FOURTH ARMY, 9 SEPTEMBER

On 6 September Rawlinson issued orders for an attack on 9 September. While III Corps had to clear High Wood and High Wood, XV Corps would clear Beer Trench and Ale Alley on the east side of Delville Wood. XIV Corps still had to take Ginchy, the Quadrilateral and get to the Combles road alongside the French. The barrage would start at 7am and there would be no increase in fire before zero hour at 4.45pm.

III Corps

1st Division, High Wood and Wood Lane

The west side of High Wood was held by 1 Brigade. Although the 10th Gloucesters advanced through the north-west corner, bombing and machine-gun fire from the Switch Line forced them to retire. The rest of the wood was held by 3 Brigade and a second mine was blown under the strongpoint at the eastern corner of the wood thirty seconds before zero. The 1st Northants captured the crater but neither the 2nd Munsters nor the rest of the Northants could capture the Switch Line. The mine explosion helped 2 Brigade and both the 2nd Sussex and 2nd KRRC captured Wood Lane; the Sussex dug a trench connecting the east side of the wood to Wood Lane.

XV Corps

55th Division, Wood Lane

In 165 Brigade's sector the 1/5th and 1/6th King's bombed from Orchard

---

189 Attached from 49 Brigade to 15 Brigade.
190 95 Brigade.
191 Called Lousy Wood by the men.

Trench into Wood Lane. In 164 Brigade's sector the 1/4th Loyal North Lancashires captured the trenches east of Delville Wood and then 2/5th Lancashire Fusiliers tried to reach Hop Alley only to capture an unknown trench later called the Haymarket. The 1/5th King's[192] also bombed along Ale Alley at the northeast corner of the wood. Two days later the 1/4th King's Own tried and failed to capture Hop Alley.

XIV Corps

16th Division, Ginchy

While 48 Brigade advanced north through Ginchy, 47 Brigade would capture the ground to the east, including the Quadrilateral. The oblique angle of the front line meant 47 Brigade moved first at 4.45pm while 48 Brigade wheeled its right forward two minutes later, and then the whole line advanced together. But while 47 Brigade had dug new assembly trenches 200 metres closer to the German front line to narrow no man's land, the British artillery had not been told and the 8th Munsters and 7th Royal Irish Rifles were hit by friendly fire.

In 48 Brigade's sector, the 7th Royal Irish Fusiliers and 7th Royal Irish Rifles[193] advanced astride Hans Crescent into the south-west corner of Ginchy.[194] At 5.25pm the 9th and 8th Royal Dublin Fusiliers passed through

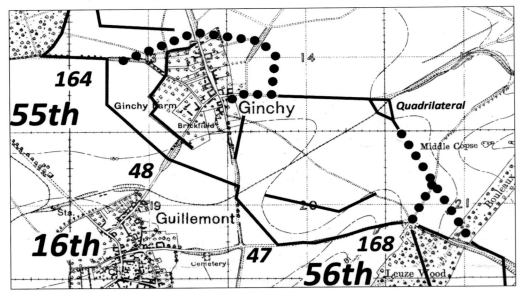

9 September, XIV Corps: 16th Division captured Ginchy and 56th Division advanced north of Leuze Wood but neither could reach the Quadrilateral.

---

192 166 Brigade.
193 Attached from 49 Brigade.
194 The name for the Delville Wood road.

their lines and began clearing the north and east sides of the village while the Fusiliers and Rifles mopped up the west side. By dusk Ginchy was secure and Lieutenant Colonel Bellingham organised the 8th Dublins as they dug trenches around the village; all the German counter-attacks failed.

But while there was success on the left, there was failure in 47 Brigade's sector on the right. Machine-gun fire stopped the 8th Munsters and the 6th Royal Irish advancing south-east of Ginchy. Meanwhile, the 6th Connaught Rangers became disorientated and its right moved into 56th Division's sector, behind the 1/4th London, rather than towards the Quadrilateral.

The Guards Division relieved 16th Division during the night only to discover Ginchy was in a salient which attracted artillery fire and counter-attacks from all sides.

56th Division, the Quadrilateral

On the left flank, 168 Brigade had to wheel right so it could advance north-east towards the trench between the Quadrilateral and Leuze Wood. Meanwhile, 169 Brigade had to establish a defensive flank overlooking Combles Ravine. Zero hour was set for 4.45pm.

In 168 Brigade's sector, the 1/12th London set off late, missed the barrage and then came under fire from the Quadrilateral as they breasted the low ridge. The 1/4th London advanced on time and Lieutenant Colonel Duncan-Teape's men reached the trench between the Quadrilateral and Bouleaux Wood, despite heavy losses. Lieutenant Colonel Bayliffe reorganised the 1/12th London but their second advance was in the wrong direction and they ended up reinforcing the 1/4th London. The 1/13th London moved up in support and Major Dickens tried to establish contact with the Irish on the left.[195] Brigadier General Loch had no idea what was happening because the aerial observers could not see through the evening mist while the German barrage had stopped runners crossing no man's land.

The attack by 169 Brigade got off to a bad start. While the heavy artillery barrage hit the assault troops, the creeping barrage was 'practically non-existent'. Captains Davies' and Woods' companies of the 1/9th London captured a trench inside Bouleaux Wood, bringing them closer to the Quadrilateral. But neither Captains Noble's nor Captain Mathews' companies of the 1/5th London could capture Loop Trench, despite help from the 1/2nd London. Brigadier General Coke ordered the 1/16th London forward after hearing the Germans had entered Leuze Wood. But Lieutenant Colonel Shoolbred's men became lost in the mist and they did not arrive until 11pm, too late to make a counter-attack.

---

195 Major Cedric Dickens was grandson of the author Charles Dickens. A cross still stands close to where he was killed.

The 1/16th London advanced out of Leuze Wood through a thick mist at 7am the following morning. There was no barrage on the left flank because the telephone line to the batteries had been cut. It meant the machine-gun teams in Loop Trench and along the Combles road were free to shoot at Captains Green and Grizelle's men. A second attack was planned for 3pm but the Stokes mortar bombardment failed to knock out the machine-guns in the Quadrilateral and they shot down Captain Long's company of the 1/2nd London. The division's bombers could not get any closer to the Quadrilateral either.

The 1/14th London was supposed to capture the trenches west of the Quadrilateral at 12.15am and link up with 16th Division. But they lost direction in the darkness and found themselves in the trench south-east of the Quadrilateral, alongside the 1/4th London and 1/12th London. Despite 56th Division's efforts, the Quadrilateral still dominated a 1,000 metre sweep of XIV Corps' centre.

XIV Corps, 10 to 13 September

With plans afoot for the main attack with tanks on 15 September, the divisions allocated for the assault began to take over XIV Corps' line. The Guards Division started to take over the Ginchy sector late on 9 September. Then 6th Division relieved the Guards' right and 56th Division's right on 12 and 13 September, so it faced the Quadrilateral. But General Cavan still wanted to clear the low ridge east of Ginchy and the Quadrilateral before the offensive.

Guards Division, Ginchy

The Guards Division had taken over the Ginchy sector on 10 September and the Germans attacked before they had settled in. They advanced through the mist and forced a way through the Welsh Guards and into the north-east side of Ginchy; they were soon forced out. Further attacks were stopped with the help of the 1st Grenadier Guards, who reinforced the Welsh Guards and the 4th Grenadier Guards.

Once the line had been stabilised, 3rd Guards Brigade was ordered to clear the re-entrant facing the Quadrilateral. The 1st Grenadiers pushed east of Ginchy[196] on 12 September and later that evening they cleared the re-entrant with the 2nd Scots Guards and captured 116 prisoners. The following evening the 2nd Grenadiers[197] straightened out the line north of Ginchy but the 2nd Irish Guards[198] were unable to silence the machine-guns north of the Quadrilateral.

---

196 Towards a point known as Ginchy Telegraph.
197 1 Guards Brigade.
198 2 Guards Brigade.

6th Division, Quadrilateral

On 13 September 6th Division took over XIV Corps' centre and Major General Charles Ross had orders to capture the Quadrilateral. At 6am 71 Brigade advanced but machine-gun fire stopped the 2nd Sherwood Foresters and the 9th Suffolks. Lieutenant Macdonald of the Suffolks advanced 400 metres to get close enough to throw bombs into the German trench before he was wounded. Captain Ensor made several attempts to rescue the injured officer. Another attempt at 6pm also failed and Cavan eventually conceded that the 'situation must be accepted'; XIV Corps would have to capture the Quadrilateral on 15 September.

56th Division, Bouleaux Wood

On 11 September Rawlinson suggested 56th Division captured Loop Trench the following day, at the same time as the French attacked. General Hull disagreed because his troops could already see over Combles Ravine and his right flank was secure in Leuze Wood. He also wanted to save his men for the main offensive; Rawlinson agreed.

The 1/8th Middlesex[199] stopped a German counter-attack from Bouleaux Wood on 11 September and then Captains White and Tremlett's companies advanced towards the south-east side of the Quadrilateral. They were later forced to withdraw from their isolated position.

---

199 167 Brigade.

Chapter 9

Armoured Creepers Join the Fray – 15 to 24 September

FOURTH ARMY

Planning and Preparation

After two weeks of army and corps conferences, orders were issued on 11 September for a major attack four days later. The first objective was the Switch Line, code-named the Green Line, which ran from Martinpuich through High Wood and north of Delville Wood before it turned south to the high ground north-west of Combles. The second objective was the German Third Line, code-named the Brown Line, and it ran through Martinpuich, Flers and Morval before turning south towards Combles. XIV Corps would not advance into Combles Ravine because it was hoped the French advance to the east would force the Germans to abandon the village.

The third objective, code-named the Blue Line, involved III Corps outflanking Martinpuich, XV Corps capturing Flers village and XIV Corps clearing the Morval and Lesboeufs defences. The fourth objective, code-named the Red Line, involved XV Corps taking Gueudecourt village while XIV Corps cleared Morval and Lesboeufs villages.

If all went to plan, the three corps would advance three miles on a four-mile wide front and the breach would be extended by another two miles if the Germans abandoned Combles. III Corps would link up with the Reserve Army at Martinpuich, XV Corps would have a flank facing north-west towards Le Sars while XIV Corps would have a flank facing south-east of Morval.

The advance would be complete by midday, leaving eight hours of daylight for the cavalry divisions to seize the high ground south of Bapaume and clear the batteries around Le Sars, Warlencourt and Thilloy. Fourth

Army would then be ready to advance north behind the German lines facing Third Army.

But Fourth Army's firepower had only been increased by two 9.2-inch howitzer batteries, one 6-inch howitzer battery and five 60-pdr batteries. Many batteries had moved as far forward as possible so they could fire deep into the German rear but they would still have to move quickly once the advance started. Fourth Army instructions laid down the principles of the follow up; the artillery would move first, then the cavalry and finally the ammunition wagons.

The inclusion of tanks called for several modifications to the fire plan and there had been a special emphasis on counter-battery work to reduce the amount of enemy artillery fire. The tanks would lead the infantry but there could not be a large gap between the barrage and the infantry because the Germans would emerge from their dug-outs once the tanks had gone past. Instead, 100 metre wide lanes would be left in the stationary and creeping barrages as far as the first objective. While this compromise worked if a battery was firing straight across no man's land, it was impossible to create narrow gaps if a battery was firing from the flanks and some artillery commanders had to widen the 'tank lanes' to make their barrage work. All the divisional commanders made contingency plans to close the tank lanes with artillery fire if the tanks failed to advance for any reason.

While the field batteries would cut the wire in front of the first two objectives, they could not reach the entanglements covering the third and fourth. The plan was for the tanks to crush gaps in the wire, and for the first time, the long-standing problem of cutting wire at long range had a possible solution.

At night the field batteries turned to harassment barrages and targeted the enemy batteries with gas shells while the howitzers targeted Bapaume and other villages in range. While Fourth Army's barrage was nothing new, it would be far more controlled and intense that previous ones.

The gunners just needed good weather but low cloud and showers on 13 September made aerial observation difficult. The skies brightened the following day, allowing the observers to pick out their targets and German artillery fire noticeably reduced. Meanwhile, fresh divisions were relieving battle weary units all along the line. In III Corps area 50th Division faced Martinpuich while 47th Division took over High Wood. In XV Corps sector 55th Division had dug assembly trenches north of Delville Wood and the New Zealand and 41st Divisions took over the line just before the battle.

At the same time the 14th Division and the Guards Division had failed to clear the awkward re-entrant on the east side of Delville Wood. Instead Rawlinson gave permission to carry out a preliminary operation, starting at 5.30am on 15 September. Three tanks would clear the area before the main attack began.

On 13 September, GHQ reminded Gough and Rawlinson that they outnumbered the enemy four to one in infantry; they also had more guns than the Germans and they had air supremacy. The tanks would be leading the attack while the cavalry was waiting to exploit the breakthrough. Meanwhile, the Germans were under pressure and they only had weak reserves. Their trenches had saved them so far but this time the tanks would make the difference they had been looking for. Haig also expected both armies to be bold and vigorous.

RESERVE ARMY

On 12 September, Gough was ordered to support Fourth Army's attack. II Corps would clear the spur south of Thiepval, while the Canadian Corps advanced onto the high ground between Pozières and Courcelette. Gough allocated three groups of heavy artillery and as much field artillery as possible to the Canadian Corps.

The following day Rawlinson told Gough that III Corps would advance towards Le Sars as soon as XV and XIV Corps had broken through, taking Martinpuich in the flank. Gough in turn told his corps commanders that the Canadian Corps would capture Courcelette on the morning of 16 September and II Corps would advance towards Mouquet Farm if all went well.

On 14 September Haig made it clear III Corps had to take Martinpuich as soon as XV Corps had captured Flers so the Reserve Army could advance. He then left a message for Gough to capture Courcelette on the afternoon of 15 September. The two armies could advance side by side once the two villages were clear. Gough had anticipated Haig's order and was in the process of planning the accelerated attack.

Finally, the assembly points for the tanks following the capture of the fourth objective were issued on the night of 14 September. XV Corps' tanks would rally west of Gueudecourt while XIV Corps tanks would gather north of Bouleaux Wood ready to join the cavalry advance.

The Assembly
The tanks had left their depot at the Loop, near Bray-sur-Somme, during the night of 13 September and they moved to their assembly points while the tank commanders checked the routes to the front line at dawn. Meanwhile the Cavalry Corps had been riding across country, so as not to

block roads, and they were in their assembly positions by 14 September. 1st Cavalry Division was north of Carnoy; 2nd Indian Cavalry Division was south of Mametz; 2nd Cavalry Division was north of Bray; 1st Indian Cavalry Division was south of Dernancourt and 3rd Cavalry Division was south-west of Albert.

As it grew dark on 14 September, the assault troops left their bivouacs and made their way into the assembly trenches. The tanks were also led forward to their starting positions but some developed mechanical problems while a few ditched when old dug-outs collapsed. While only thirty out of forty-two tanks made it to the front in Fourth Army, all six allocated to the Canadian Corps made it to their assembly points. But the tanks drew attention everywhere they went because few men had heard about them and even fewer had seen them before.

The weather stayed dry and while light winds had dried open areas, the trenches and depressions were still muddy. Even the forecast was promising with an early mist turning into a fine day with cloudy skies.

RESERVE ARMY

Canadian Corps, 15 September

General Byng's Canadian Corps was poised to attack on 15 September. Major General Louis Lipsett's 3rd Canadian Division held a salient north of Pozières while Major General Richard Turner's 2nd Canadian Division was astride the Bapaume Road, north-east of Pozières.

3rd Canadian Division, Mouquet Farm

The 1st Canadian Mounted Rifles made two raids in 8 Brigade's sector. While Lieutenant French's party raided Mouquet Farm under cover of a smoke barrage, Captain Caswell's party was unable to reach the trenches leading to Zollern Redoubt. The Rifles managed to establish posts close to the farm the following morning. In 7 Brigade's sector, the 5th Canadian Mounted Rifles secured the left of the main attack and blocked the trench linked to Fabeck Graben.

2nd Canadian Division, Courcelette

A German barrage at 3.10am signalled the first of two bombing raids against 4 Brigade but the raiders were forced to withdraw before the Canadians attacked at 6.20am. The infantry and tanks were to advance together at zero hour but the infantry had orders to keep moving if the tanks slowed down or stopped. The Canadians advanced across no man's land under a machine-gun barrage to begin with, while the creeping barrage started only fifty

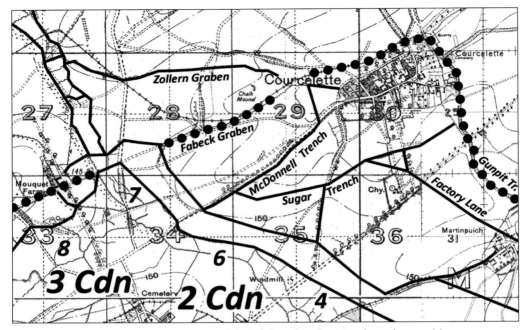

15 September, Canadian Corps: While 3rd Canadian Division drew closer to Mouquet Farm, tanks helped 2nd Canadian Division capture Courcelette.

metres in front of the German trench. It took the garrison by surprise and both brigades captured the front line in less than fifteen minutes.

While 6 Brigade advanced slowly towards the first objective, 28th Battalion took time to clear a strongpoint on the Ovillers – Courcelette road. It then cleared McDonnell Trench, where machine-guns firing in support allowed 27th Battalion to advance. One tank had track trouble before it started while the other two drove along McDonnell Trench until they ditched. Soon after 7.30am 28th Battalion reached their objective and 31st Battalion mopped up and bought supplies forward.

Although one tank ditched early on as 4 Brigade advanced astride the Bapaume Road, two helped 21st Battalion capture the Sugar Factory, a large building surrounded by pits for fermenting sugar beet. Captain Miller led the assault and his men captured 125 prisoners. Meanwhile, Captain Heron led 20th Battalion as far as Gun Pit Trench on the outskirts of Courcelette, before pulling back to his objective. The 18th Battalion came under sniper and machine-gun fire from Factory Lane about 7am and although the tanks were supposed to help they had both headed back.

Reserve Army Summary

General Byng thought 'tanks are a useful accessory to the infantry, but nothing more' but they had given his troops 'a feeling of superiority and security'. One had also used a drum on its tail to lay 400 metres of telephone cable along the road to the Sugar Factory, demonstrating how tanks could carry heavy items.

The Canadians had advanced 1,200 metres on a 1,500 metre wide front. Patrols kept probing the German positions and three from 28th Battalion entered Courcelette on the left flank before withdrawing when the British barrage lifted. Lewis guns were also set up in the sunken road next to Gun Pit Trench, covering the ground between Courcelette and Martinpuich.

When Major General Turner learned the attack had been a success, he issued instructions to push forward at 9.20am and 21st and 20th Battalions advanced to the edge of Courcelette before they came under fire. They then stopped counter-attacks in the afternoon. Meanwhile, 18th Battalion established outposts in the sunken road next to Gun Pit Trench, linking up with 15th Division.

FOURTH ARMY

III Corps, 15 September

The 15th, 50th and 47th Divisions had limited objectives because the Switch Line would give them observation towards Bapaume. The first objective for 15th Division was the south edge of Martinpuich while 50th and 47th Divisions' second and third objectives were the trenches between Martinpuich and Flers. If XV Corps' advance went to plan, 15th Division would advance through Martinpuich while 50th Division advanced to meet the 2nd Canadian Division north of the village.

15th Division, Martinpuich

Major General Frederick McCracken's 15th Division faced Martinpuich; 46 Brigade had the 10th/11th Highland Light Infantry, 7th/8th KOSBs and 10th Scottish Rifles leading.[200] While one tank was disabled before zero hour, the second followed the infantry across no man's land, causing the Germans to run from Bottom Trench.

The 10th/11th Highland Light Infantry initially wheeled left to clear dug-outs along the Pozières – Martinpuich road, with the help of the tank.[201] The battalion then wheeled right and advanced north-east across Factory Lane, reaching the Courcelette road around 7am; the Scots then dug in alongside the Canadians.

The KOSBs advanced along the west side of Martinpuich while the 10th

---

200 The 12th Highland Light Infantry in support and the 9th York and Lancasters (attached from 23rd Division) in reserve.
201 The tank had to return for fuel after helping clear the road.

182 The Somme Campaign

Scottish Rifles prepared to search the ruins. Patrols explored them when the covering barrage lifted at 9.20am and the 10th Scottish Rifles then dug in through the village. When the signalling sergeant called, Lieutenant Colonel Deans replied: 'I am in Martinpuich smoking a fine Boche cigar, can you smell it over the line?'

In 45 Brigade's sector, many Germans surrendered as the 13th Royal Scots and 11th Argylls entered Tangle Trench.[202] The Royal Scots then approached Martinpuich while the Argylls bombed Tangle South and the sunken Longueval road to the south-east.

Although 15th Division had taken all its objectives, there were delays across the rest of III Corps, making it unwise to go beyond Martinpuich. At 10.30am Pulteney ordered General McCracken to dig in around the perimeter of the village and await further instructions. The Scots then spent the afternoon clearing the village, taking many prisoners.

50th Division, the Starfish Line
The 50th Division held a 200 metre deep salient south-east of Martinpuich and no man's land was much narrower than it was on its flanks. Rather than waiting for the divisions either side to catch up, Major General Percival Wilkinson's men would advance at zero hour 'to envelop the enemy in Martinpuich and High Wood'.

The 1/5th and 1/4th Green Howards and 1/4th East Yorkshires[203] of 150 Brigade were in the lead and they overran Hook Trench with the help of two tanks. One enfiladed the trench until it was disabled and the crew then clambered out and deployed their Lewis guns.

The infantry advanced across Martin Trench and they reached the Starfish Line by 10am, while the second tank knocked out three machine-guns on the east side of Martinpuich. But while Brigadier General Price's men had taken their objectives, the 1/4th East Yorkshires had an exposed right flank in the Starfish Line because 149 Brigade was nowhere to be seen.

The 1/7th and 1/4th Northumberland Fusiliers had led 149 Brigade[204] across Hook Trench but they came under enfilade fire from High Wood as they advanced towards the second objective. Meanwhile 47th Division was fighting for its life inside High Wood, leaving the machine-guns on its north-west side free to engage the Fusiliers.

The advance was already an hour behind schedule when Brigadier General Ovens learnt of the problem. He ordered the 1/4th Northumberland Fusiliers to bomb along the Switch Line towards the machine-guns while the rest of the brigade supported their attack. However, all the officers were soon hit and a corporal led the survivors forward.

---

202 The 6th Cameron Highlanders in support with the 8th York and Lancaster (attached from 23rd Division) and the 6th/7th Royal Scots Fusiliers were in reserve.
203 They were supported by the 1/5th Durhams.
204 The 1/6th and 1/5th Northumberland Fusiliers were in support and reserve.

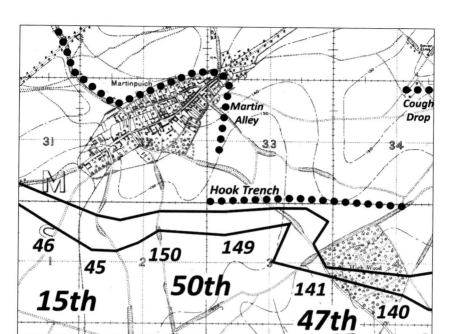

15 September, III Corps: 15th Division was able to capture Martinpuich but 50th Division's advance was compromised by 47th Division's failure to clear High Wood.

The 1/7th Northumberland Fusiliers reached the sunken Martinpuich – Flers road by 10am, taking more prisoners than there were Fusiliers; it would push onto the Starfish Line by noon. At the same time the 1/6th Northumberland Fusiliers organised a defensive flank facing High Wood as the fighting in the Switch Line intensified. The delay at High Wood had compromised III Corps' advance and Pulteney obtained Fourth Army's permission to dig in along the final objective.

47th Division, High Wood
Major General Sir Charles Barter's 47th Division had the most difficult task on 15 September: it had to clear High Wood. No man's land was narrow and it had always been difficult to hit the Switch Line with an accurate barrage. Despite the rough terrain inside the wood, two tanks had been allocated to each of the brigades against General Barter's advice, and that meant gaps in the covering barrage. To make matters worse, even the Stokes mortars would stay silent.

General McDouall's 141 Brigade faced the west side of the wood but as 1/18th and 1/17th London Regiment[205] advanced, one tank ditched in no

---

205 1/19th and 1/20th London Regiment would advance to the Starfish Line north of the wood.

man's land. Both battalions faced a tough fight for the German front trench and the support battalions became involved in it. While Lieutenant Colonel Matthews led the 1/20th London Regiment through the west side of the wood, Lieutenant Colonel Hamilton was killed rallying the 1/19th London Regiment in the centre. The remaining tank ditched close to the Switch Line at the north end of the wood, but it gave supporting fire until it was disabled.

The two tanks allocated to 140 Brigade were unable to get into the south end of the wood so they drove across the open ground to the east, where one ditched in a shell hole. The lack of tanks and the absence of a barrage left the German machine-gunners free to shoot up the 1/15th London Regiment as they advanced through the east side of the wood and the 1/7th London Regiment as they approached Crest Trench.[206]

Three of the 1/15th London Regiment companies were hit badly as they assembled; Captains Davies and Roberts were killed and Captain Gaze had been wounded. Only Second Lieutenant Burtt's company moved forward with Colonel Faux's 1/7th London Regiment as they advanced across Wood Lane and over the crest. They crossed the Switch Line, capturing over 100 Germans, and then dug in beyond the trench, avoiding most of the German artillery fire.

Then the remaining tank appeared. It shot up the 1/6th London Regiment, nearly ran over 1/15th London Regiment's battalion headquarters, 'got stuck in a communications trench and materially interfered with the wounded'. There was then a 'heated altercation when the tank commander asked Lieutenant Colonel Warrender where High Wood was'.[207]

The 1/8th London Regiment passed through the 1/7th London Regiment in the Switch Line and advanced to Flag Lane. So while High Wood was a no-go area, the area to the east was clear. At 8.20am the 1/6th London Regiment advanced towards Flers only to come under fire from the Cough Drop so Captain MacDonald's company charged the strongpoint. Captain Brooke's company joined them but there were still only forty men able to hold the Cough Drop and establish contact with the New Zealanders to the east.

When General McDouall learnt of the problem in High Wood, he withdrew his troops so they could reorganise and asked General Barter for a second bombardment of the wood. Following a fifteen-minute trench mortar barrage on the Switch Wood, McDouall's men attacked at 11.40am while bombers moved around the flanks. This time the Germans had had enough and several hundred surrendered; six machine-guns and two 105mm howitzers were also captured. But while High Wood had been cleared, 141 Brigade was finished and Lieutenant Colonel Norman of 1/17th London

---

206 1/8th London Regiment would take Flag Lane while the 1/6th London would capture Prue Trench.
207 One account reports the tank crew refused to go any further.

Regiment organised the survivors into a composite battalion while Captain Read consolidated the Switch Line.

Lieutenant Colonel Kennedy led an attack on the Starfish Line at 6pm and while 1/24th London Regiment could not advance north of the wood, 1/21st London Regiment reached Starfish Redoubt on the right; it could not reach the Cough Drop.

XV Corps, 15 September

Horne's XV Corps had three divisions holding an arc of trenches around the north and east side of Delville Wood. The New Zealand Division was north of Longueval and 41st Division was north of Delville Wood. Meanwhile, 14th Division had to clear a pocket of German troops between the wood and Ginchy as a preliminary operation. Eighteen tanks had been allotted to XV Corps, and the majority would advance on Flers and Gueudecourt; only fourteen reached their starting points.

New Zealand Division, Flers

Major General Sir Andrew Russell's New Zealand Division held the line with 2 Brigade. All four tanks allocated to the New Zealanders drove north along the track out of Longueval and then fanned out to deal with strongpoints. Russell made sure they followed the infantry, doing away with the gaps in the artillery barrage.

The 2nd Otago Battalion left their trenches thirty seconds early and moved so fast they ran into their own creeping barrage. Although they came under enfilading fire from High Wood, where the Londoners were struggling, they overran Crest Trench. The Auckland Battalion did not give the Germans time to man their trenches and they overran Coffee Lane and the Switch Line. They then dug in sixty metres north of the Switch Line to avoid the German counter-barrage. Sergeant Donald Brown dealt with two machine-gun posts on the exposed flank as the Otagos chased the Germans to the Switch Line; he then organised his men to defend their trenches. Sergeant Brown was awarded the Victoria Cross.

Fifteen minutes later the 4th New Zealand Rifles moved forward 'in high spirits, some of them singing' and they lay down close to the protective bombardment. Although the tanks were lagging behind, the Rifles advanced at 7.20am to Flag Lane and Fat Trench. The 3rd and 2nd NZ Rifles then passed through at 8.20am but the tanks were behind schedule and the wire in front of Flers Trench still had to be cut.

The 3rd NZ Rifles lay down and waited two hours for the tanks to drive through it and while one was disabled crossing Fat Trench, the other three eventually crushed the wire. They then shot up the German machine-guns and helped the Rifles round up 100 prisoners in Flers Trench.

The 2nd NZ Rifles found a way through the wire and after taking eighty-five prisoners in Flers Trench, they entered an abandoned Flers Support. But there were more Germans waiting for them and they came under machine-gun fire from Abbey Road and from the ruins at the north-west corner of the village. They were clearing the dug-outs along the road when the 3rd NZ Rifles moved up on the left and the 1st NZ Rifles joined them from support.

41st Division, Flers
Major General Sydney Lawford's 41st Division was to advance from the trenches north of Delville Wood, north-east through Flers. Six tanks started from the north end of Longueval and four tanks started on the Flers road 250 metres to the east; the New Zealand Division tanks would join the division on the way to its fourth objective. But three tanks broke down on their way to the start line and few, if any, moved ahead of the infantry.

In 122 Brigade's sector, the 18th KRRC and 15th Hampshires[208] advanced behind a barrage which was 'excellent; just what the men had been trained to expect' as the tanks followed. Tea Support and Flers Trench were taken with many prisoners while the tanks used their machine-guns to shoot down those who ran towards Flers. But one tank was disabled in front of the Switch Line, one ditched south of Flers and one was damaged crossing the Flers Trench.

In 124 Brigade's sector the 21st KRRC and 10th Queen's crept into no man's land before zero hour and some advanced too soon, running into the creeping barrage. But their haste meant both Tea Support and the Switch Line were taken by 7am. The 26th and 32nd Royal Fusiliers then passed through, heading towards Flers Trench.

Brigadier General Clemson's men continued towards Flers with all four tanks and around 8.20am Lieutenant Hastie's tank crawled along the main street while 300 cheering infantry walked alongside. There were some of the 18/KRRC led by Captain Baskett, some of the 8th East Surreys led by Lieutenant Stadden and some of the 11th Queen's Own led by Second Lieutenant Cooksey. While the other three tanks cleared strongpoints along the east side of the village, most of the garrison ran towards Gueudecourt, abandoning their officers, and the ruins were clear by 10am.

Most of 124 Brigade withdrew from the ruins to avoid the German barrage and they rallied under Colonel Townsend of the Queen's Own in Flers Trench, south of the village. Only a few of General Towsey's men

---

208 The 12th East Surreys and 11th Queen's Own were following, ready to continue to the fourth objective.

15 September, XV Corps: All three divisions advanced alongside the tanks to Flers but the advance was compromised due to failures on the flanks.

assembled north of the village and they were in no fit state to advance when the corps barrage lifted from the Gird Trenches at 10.50am. Meanwhile, the withdrawal from Flers had a knock-on effect on 122 Brigade and General Towsey hesitated sending his men forward until he knew what was happening.

14th Division, Gueudecourt

General Couper's 14th Division had to advance from the east side of Delville Wood to Gueudecourt. But first the re-entrant east of Delville Wood had to be cleared. The plan was for two 6th KOYLI companies[209] to take them with three tanks but one tank broke down and a second ditched.

---

209 43rd Brigade.

Captain Mortimer's machine left Pilsen Lane at 5.15am[210] and the Germans ran until it was disabled as it crossed Hop Alley. Fifteen minutes later Lieutenant Colonel Charlesworth's bombers followed and, although they lost all their officers, their NCOs made sure they cleared Ale Alley and Hop Alley.

Although 41 Brigade was supported by three tanks, one ditched in Delville Wood and one was late. The third led the infantry towards Cocoa Lane on the left. The 8th KRRC and 8th Rifle Brigade ran into their own creeping barrage, were hit by the machine-guns in Pint Trench and then overran the Germans who had been hiding in shell holes in no man's land to escape the bombardment. Although the remaining tank was disabled, 41 Brigade overran Tea Support and Pint Trench.

Brigadier General Skinner's men also captured the Switch Line, only to crowd inside to escape the German bombardment, making it difficult to consolidate the trench. The 8th KRRC formed a defensive flank on the left while the KOYLIs were in touch with Guards to the right.

Artillery fire on no man's land disorganised and delayed the 7th KRRC and 7th Rifle Brigade so they missed their creeping barrage but there were few Germans in Gap Trench. Although the 7th KRRC had still not seen 41st Division on the left, the 7th Rifle Brigade encountered Guardsmen on the right.

The barrage moved forward on time but 42 Brigade was thirty minutes late and there were no tanks to cut the wire either.

The 5th Shropshires were pinned down in front of Bulls Road by machine-gun fire from the Hog's Head on the left where 124 Brigade should have been. The 9th Rifle Brigade was pinned down in front of Bulls Road by enfilade machine-gun fire from the right, where the Guards should have been. The 5th Ox and Bucks and the 9th KRRC advanced across the Bulls Road when the barrage lifted, only to be stopped by the machine-guns in Gird Trench.

Brigadier General Dudgeon only had 350 men left and he deployed them between the Ox and Bucks on the Bulls Road, east of Flers, and the 1st Guards Brigade in Gas Alley to secure his exposed position. Patrols discovered the wire was passable and few Germans could be seen in the Gird trenches beyond, so Dudgeon called for reinforcements.

XIV Corps, 15 September

General Lord Cavan's XIV Corps held a line between Ginchy and Leuze Wood and it was to advance north-east across the ridge to Morval and Lesboeufs.

---

210 The first tank to go into action.

Guards Division, Lesboeufs

Major General Geoffrey Feilding's Guards Division held a line around the north-east side of Ginchy. The ruins were an easy target for the German batteries so the assault troops deployed in shell craters beyond the village. In some cases the trenches were too narrow to sit in so the men had to stand shoulder to shoulder, while shells were landing every second around them. Tight discipline made sure everyone was ready to move off on time.

Ten tanks, or 'Armoured Creepers', had been allotted to the Guards Division but one was disabled before it could help 14th Division clear the east side of Delville Wood. The rest were organised into three groups of three. In the left group, one ditched, one returned low on petrol, the third broke down, started late and then got lost. In the centre group, one broke down, while the other two ditched around Ginchy. In the right group, one broke down while the other two headed into 6th Division's sector.

The tanks had done nothing to help the Guards Division and Feilding later reported they had 'lost all sense of direction and wandered around aimlessly'. The Guardsmen had to go it alone and at 6.20am they advanced close behind the creeping barrage. The problem was the artillery had left gaps in the barrage to accommodate the tanks and there were none.

On the north side of Ginchy 1 Guards Brigade held an awkward salient with its left flank bent back opposite Hop Alley. The early attack by 14th Division was supposed to have allowed the Guardsmen to deploy in no man's land. The 3rd and 2nd Coldstream Guards could then clear the trenches covering Lesboeufs while the 1st Irish Guards captured the village.[211]

Even though 14th Division had not cleared Hop Alley, the 3rd Coldstream Guards wheeled into line and after seeing the first two waves cut down by machine-gun fire, Lieutenant Colonel John Campbell led the third line wave forward. The machine-guns in Pint Trench and the sunken Flers road enfiladed the two Coldstream battalions as they advanced 'as steadily as though they were walking down the Mall'. Most of the Germans ran at the last moment leaving four machine-gun teams to fight to the last man.

This early action and the cramped deployment resulted in the 1st Irish Guards becoming mixed with the Coldstream battalions as they advanced through a 'haze of flying dirt'. To complicate matters the 1st Coldstream Guards began moving into their sector from the right[212], encouraging 1 Guards Brigade to advance in a northerly direction rather than north-east.

The mixed group of Guardsmen captured what they thought was their first objective a little behind schedule but the trench was north of the corps

---

211 The 2nd Grenadier Guards would give support and protect the left flank.
212 Left of 2 Guards Brigade, shifting left to avoid fire from Straight Trench and the Quadrilateral.

boundary; the Germans still held Serpentine Trench. As the Guards reorganised, the three surviving three battalion commanders believed they had reached their third objective; only it was another 1,300 metres ahead. The change in direction from north-east to north meant they had taken much longer to cross no man's land while the mist and lack of landmarks confused their sense of direction and time. The low mist blinded the contact aeroplanes while the German barrage interfered with communications by telephone and runners. So the three commanders resorted to using a pigeon to report they had reached the third objective.

The 2nd Grenadier Guards advanced in the correct direction in artillery order, believing they were in support. They suffered heavy losses approaching Serpentine Trench but they captured it, filling the gap between the two Guards Brigades.

Lieutenant Colonel Campbell soon realised 1 Guards Brigade was in the wrong place and passed on the message to his subordinates to keep going. The 2nd and 3rd Coldstream Guards advanced to the sound of Campbell's hunting horn as he 'led his men everywhere like a tiger'. They reached the third objective at the north end of the division's boundary around 11.15am and they 'went for the Boche like tigers, got into them with the bayonet and killed every man of them'. Some 1st Irish Guards even met troops from 14th Division. Yet again messages were sent back reporting the third objective had been taken. Colonel Campbell would be awarded the Victoria Cross.

On the east side of Ginchy 2 Guards Brigade assembled with only ten metres between each of the nine waves. The 1st Coldstream Guards and 3rd Grenadier Guards led with the 2nd Irish Guards and 1st Scots Guards in support. The Grenadier Guards and Coldstream Guards advanced over the crest of the ridge towards the Triangle only to come under fire from Straight Trench and the Quadrilateral in 6th Division's sector. They drifted left to avoid the enfilade fire, overran the German outposts sheltering in shell-holes and then negotiated three belts of smashed barbed wire.

Although the four battalions became mixed, the Guardsmen overran part of Serpentine Trench and the north end of the Triangle; the Triangle would eventually be cleared by noon. Around 100 Guardsmen advanced another 800 metres, south of Lesboeufs, but they had to withdraw later.

When Lance-Sergeant Frederick McNess reached the German front line he spotted bombers preparing to attack the 1st Scots Guards' flank. Despite a severe facial wound he organised a group to counter the attack and then helped build a trench block. Sergeant McNess was awarded the Victoria Cross.

6th Division, the Quadrilateral

The 6th Division faced the Quadrilateral but the position was out of sight behind a low rise and General Ross and his brigade commanders did not believe the bombardment had subdued the position. When General Ross heard two of the tanks had broken down, he instructed the artillery to close up the creeping barrage but the gunners failed to do so, leaving a gap in front of the Quadrilateral. It did not help that many batteries had only just arrived in the sector and they had not had time to register targets.

The third tank advanced on time but it fired on the Norfolks assembly trenches until Captain Crosse stopped it and pointed out where the enemy trenches were. The tank then turned north and crawled parallel to Straight Trench rather than advancing towards the Quadrilateral.

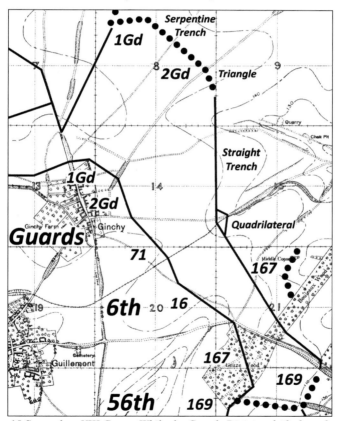

15 September, XIII Corps: While the Guards Division drifted north and 6th Division failed to capture the Quadrilateral, 56th Division made progress around Leuze Wood.

In 71 Brigade's sector the 1st Leicesters and 9th Norfolks advanced over the crest towards Straight Trench. While Lieutenant Colonel Gillespie's Leicesters overran a forward position amongst shell holes, both battalions were stopped by wire hidden in the long grass. The gap left in the barrage meant the Germans were waiting for them and Major Bradshaw and the Norfolks were left scattered in shell holes near the wire as the tank withdrew. Private Parry ran back and forth four times to keep General Edwards informed about the Leicesters' position and eventually had to be detained to stop him making another journey.

In 16 Brigade's sector, the 8th Bedfords were stopped by the Quadrilateral's machine-guns while their bombers could not advance along a trench to the south-east. The 1st Buffs advanced fifteen minutes later on the right only to be stopped by machine-gun fire from the Quadrilateral and Leuze Wood.

At 8.20am 6th Division made a second attempt and the 1st Sherwood Foresters and 9th Suffolks advanced through the Norfolks and Leicesters only to be stopped by the Quadrilateral and Straight Trench. It left all four of 71 Brigade's battalions pinned down in no man's land. Meanwhile, part of 16 Brigade was holding a trench south-east of the Quadrilateral with part of 1/7th Middlesex.[213]

56th Division, Bouleaux Wood

The 56th Division faced Combles and while 167 Brigade was to capture Bouleaux Wood and link up with 6th Division, 169 Brigade was to advance into Combles ravine and clear Loop Trench alongside the French.

One of the tanks detailed to assist 167 Brigade broke a track while the other advanced towards Middle Copse, on the west side of Bouleaux Wood, twenty minutes ahead of the infantry. The creeping barrage was poor and the German machine-guns hit the 1/1st London Regiment as they cut through the barbed wire. Only a few of Lieutenant Colonel Smith's men entered Beef Trench and they bombed towards Middle Copse while the tank crawled around until it ditched. Meanwhile, the battalion bombers were unable to advance towards the Loop on the right.

At 8.20am two 1/7th Middlesex companies advanced towards the north end of Bouleaux Wood. Lieutenant Colonel King's men came under fire from the wood and they sought cover alongside the 1/1st London Regiment in a trench west of the tree line.

In 169 Brigade's sector the solitary tank also advanced twenty minutes early and 'thoroughly frightened the foe'. Although shellfire disabled the tank close to the Loop, the crew continued to fire their machine-guns until

---

213 From 56th Division.

it was knocked out. At zero hour Captain Jephson's and Lieutenant Clive's companies of the 1/2nd London Regiment were hit by crossfire as they wheeled across no man's land ready to advance. They bombed along Loop Trench and Combles Trench with the help of the 1/5th London Regiment's bombers; Captain Kellett then organised the defence.

RESERVE ARMY
Canadian Corps, 15 September Afternoon
Before midday Gough heard that III Corps was preparing to occupy Martinpuich in the afternoon. General Byng was informed and at 11.10am he issued orders to the 3rd Canadian Division to capture Fabeck Graben on the left.

2nd Canadian Division, Courcelette
The advance would start with 7 Brigade probing Courcelette and then 5 Brigade would advance into the village. Zero hour was set for 6pm and when Byng learnt Martinpuich was taken at 5.30pm the attack was on. The destructive barrage overshot Fabeck Graben but the creeping barrage was on target when it lifted thirty minutes later.

On 7 Brigade's left, Lieutenant Colonel Cantie led 42nd Battalion to Fabeck Graben where the barrage had 'completely demoralised the garrison, many of whom could be seen running from the trench'. Major Stewart led Princess Patricia's Canadian Light Infantry from Sugar Trench but they advanced in the wrong direction because they had not had time to carry out any reconnaissance. They had captured seventy prisoners in McDonnell Trench before realising their error and corrected their direction under fire from machine-gun teams sheltering in shell craters. They then captured the east half of Fabeck Graben, linking up with 5 Brigade west of Courcelette. However, the early loss of direction meant the Germans still held 200 metres of Fabeck Graben, around the junction with Zollern Graben.

In 8 Brigade's sector, the 4th Canadian Mounted Rifles advanced at 6.30pm but this time the German barrage caught them in no man's land. The Rifles pushed on and they cleared the west end of Fabeck Graben and dug in beyond it, securing the division's left flank.

At 8.15pm 49th Battalion advanced through the darkness, intending to establish a forward line close to Zollern Graben, ready to attack the following day. But half of the battalion went no further than the existing line while the two companies on the right seized some chalk pits in front of Zollern Graben.

After ten minutes of 'smart bayonet fighting', 5 Brigade pushed on into Courcelette and while Majors Brooks and Tupper led 25th Battalion through the north side, 22nd Battalion reached the cemetery on the east side. The 26th Battalion followed, rounding up prisoners in the cellars while the ones who tried to escape were shot down as they ran. The Canadians stopped several German counter-attacks during the night and Lieutenant Colonel Tremblay of 22nd Battalion wrote: 'If hell is as bad as what I have seen at Courcelette, I would not wish my worst enemy to go there'.

III Corps, 15 September Afternoon

15th Division, Martinpuich

Later that evening the 12th Highland Light Infantry and the 9th York and Lancasters took over the front line around Martinpuich, maintaining contact with the Canadians in Gun Pit Trench on the left. At the same time the 6th Camerons discovered the Germans had abandoned Prue Trench on their right flank and they linked up with the 1/5th Green Howards of 50th Division in Martin Alley.

50th Division, the Starfish Line

While 50th Division held most of its final objective, they were in an exposed position because the Starfish Line was in full view of the German artillery. Many of the British field batteries were moving forward, leaving General Wilkinson's men under heavy shellfire and in need of help. At 1pm he ordered Lieutenant Colonel Bradford's 1/9th Durhams[214] forward to reinforce 149 Brigade but they failed to alter the outcome and by mid-afternoon men were withdrawing behind the crest. While 150 Brigade pulled back to Martin Alley and Martin Trench, 149 Brigade fell back even further to Hook Trench; only a few stopped in the sunken road south of the Bow.

Wilkinson learnt of the withdrawal at 7.30pm and took steps to retake the lost ground. He ordered 150 Brigade to retake the west half of Prue Trench and re-establish its link with 15th Division in Martinpuich while 151 Brigade was also released from reserve with orders to capture the east half of Prue Trench.

But the new advance did not go to plan. In 151 Brigade's sector, the 1/9th and 1/6th Durhams assembled in Hook Trench on time but the guides for Lieutenant Colonel Hedley's 1/5th Borders got lost. After three postponements the Durhams moved forward at 9.40pm but the advance was a disaster. They were shot down as they advanced over the ridge and the few Durhams who made it as far as Prue Trench were killed or wounded.

---

214 151 Brigade.

Those who took shelter in the Starfish Line were later forced to withdraw. The Borders eventually reached the jumping off line and advanced at 11pm; they too were cut down by machine-gun fire.

47th Division, High Wood

Time was passing and 47th Division still had to take the Starfish Line, 700 metres north of High Wood. General Barter released part of his 142 Brigade from reserve but there was no time to reconnoitre the ground. At 5.30pm one company each of the 1/24th London Regiment and 1/21st London Regiment advanced north-east of High Wood only to be pinned down in front of the Starfish Line. The rest of the 1/24th London Regiment was late moving up and they advanced from the west side of the wood at dusk without the benefit of a protective barrage; they too were shot down in front of the Starfish Line.

General Barter had to report his division had only reached the first objective apart from an isolated outpost holding the Cough Drop on the right. The failure to capture High Wood in the first rush had blunted Fourth Army's attack.

XV Corps, 15 September Afternoon

New Zealand Division, Flers

The delay in front of Flers Trench interrupted the Rifle Brigade's advance while the 1st Rifles had been involved in the fighting along Abbey Road. It was 11.30am before they were on the move again; far too late to take advantage of the barrage. The tanks were also supposed to join 41st Division but one had ditched on the west side of Flers while a second had withdrawn because its observation prisms had been shattered; only one was left to help the Rifles.

Two companies of the 1st Rifles attacked Grove Alley, north-west of Flers and the right flank was wheeling half-left to get to it when it came under machine-gun fire from the ridge. Although a few of General Fulton's men reached the trench, they could see German troops approaching from the north and, being too weak in numbers and unsupported, they eventually withdrew. They had been unable to form a defensive flank and they were still in a weak position. The New Zealanders convinced the tank commander to stay with them in case the Germans attacked and it stopped on the Ligny road near the Box and Cox trenches. The situation left the New Zealanders holding an extended flank on XV Corps left. The 47th Division had still not moved up from High Wood, while 41st Division had not advanced north of Flers.

41st Division, West of Flers

By 1pm General Towsey was still unsure whether to move 124 Brigade forward so he sent Major Gwyn Thomas forward to investigate Flers Trench. Gwyn Thomas encountered Lieutenant Carter of 228th Field Company RE en route and he ordered him to abandon his work and go forward in search of men. While Gwyn Thomas collected men on the east side of Flers, Carter's sappers did the same along the west side of the village; he also contacted the New Zealanders. The two officers met on the third objective before 3pm having stopped many men from withdrawing. While they reorganised 124 Brigade north of Flers, some men were detailed to hold three positions known as Box, Cox and the Hog's Head.

But what about the tanks? One had been disabled on the east side of Flers while three had reached 124 Brigade. However, one turned back to refuel while a second one advanced along Glebe Street with the New Zealanders until it was knocked out. The fourth tank had driven into 14th Division's sector.

General Clemson sent forward the 23rd Middlesex[215] as reinforcements when he heard 124 Brigade had fallen back to Flers Trench and two companies eventually joined it. Clemson then went forward to find out what was happening and at 2.30pm he found his brigade in confusion and the battalion commanders unsure about the situation. It took forty minutes to organise a new advance and even then only 200 men took part.[216] They advanced to the Bulls Road, west of Flers, before coming under machine-gun fire from Gird Trench. The few survivors linked up with 122 Brigade on the left and waited to see what happened next.

14th Division, Bulls Road

The 14th Division was ahead of the divisions on its flanks and under machine-gun fire from both left and right. Meanwhile 42 Brigade only had 350 men along Bulls Road, east of Flers, and General Dudgeon had called for reinforcements to attack the Gird Trenches. But 43 Brigade was still at Montauban, four miles behind the front. Most of the field artillery was moving forward and only Second Lieutenant Legge's tank was still moving. It made a lone crusade towards Gueudecourt where it was knocked out in duel with a field battery. Two counter-attacks later that evening were stopped and 43 Brigade relieved 42 Brigade during the night.

<u>XV Corps Summary</u>

At 2.40pm General Horne told General Lawford of 41st Division and General Couper of 14th Division that the corps artillery was going to shell

---

215 123rd Brigade, in reserve.
216 Most from the 10th Queen's and the 21st KRRC.

the Gird Trenches and Gueudecourt and he wanted them to advance a couple of hours later. He then asked Rawlinson for permission to attack at 5pm and if he could deploy the reserve brigades. But Fourth Army only had one division in reserve and Rawlinson postponed further attacks until the following morning. All Fourth Army divisions were then instructed to consolidate the third objective at 3.45pm.

Meanwhile, the Germans had not been idle. Reinforcements had occupied the Gird Trenches south of Le Transloy while others were moving towards Flers. Three divisions, 41st Division, 14th Division and the Guards Division, all stopped counter-attacks from the vicinity of Gueudecourt.

XIV Corps Afternoon
Guards Division, North of Ginchy
On hearing the Guards Division had reached the third objective in front of Lesboeufs, Cavan told General Feilding to make a flanking movement to help 6th Division 'by cutting in behind the Boche' beyond the Quadrilateral. But when the mist cleared, the contact aeroplanes reported the Guards' true position and Cavan had to cancel the order. General Ponsonby suggested pushing 3 Guards Brigade through to Lesboeufs but Feilding refused because it would create a new salient.

At 3.20pm Feilding sent two of 3 Guards Brigade's battalions forward; he added the remaining two battalions later. After hearing the attack would be resumed the following morning, Feilding told his subordinates to prepare.

6th Division, the Quadrilateral
General Ross was anxious to clear XIV Corps' centre and planned a third attempt to take the Quadrilateral at 1.30pm. Both 16 and 71 Brigades would make converging attacks while 18 Brigade moved through the gap created by the Guards Division on the left and headed for Morval. But when the mist cleared, the contact planes reported the Guards true situation on the ground and Cavan changed Ross's plans; 6th Division was to attack Straight Trench and the Quadrilateral at 7.30pm.

With little time to spare 18 Brigade's battalions reached their assembly positions and while two 2nd Durham companies assembled in the Triangle, ready to bomb the Quadrilateral from the north, two 11th Essex companies assembled in Leuze Wood ready to attack it from the south. Unfortunately, the artillery missed the Quadrilateral, the Durhams cleared a trench which did not lead into the Quadrilateral while the Essex lost direction and came under fire from Bouleaux Wood. The Quadrilateral was becoming a big problem for XIV Corps.

56th Division, Bouleaux Wood

General Hull had agreed to help 6th Division capture the Quadrilateral at 1.40pm but the advance was cancelled. While 6th Division told its troops in time, 56th Division could not and the 1/8th Middlesex advanced alone. The Quadrilateral's machine-guns cut the battalion to pieces and it withdrew to the safety of Leuze Wood; another attempt to take the Quadrilateral by surprise at 11pm also failed.

It was planned that 168 Brigade was to pass through 167 Brigade and secure XIV Corps' right flank by linking up with the French. However, 6th Division's failure around the Quadrilateral meant it was unwise to advance beyond Bouleaux Wood. At 4pm 56th Division was told to consolidate its position and prepare for the following morning.

Summary, 15 September

The Reserve Army had accomplished what Haig wanted by capturing Courcelette and supporting Fourth Army's capture of Martinpuich. However, XV Corps' failure to advance north of High Wood meant there would be no co-ordinated advance north, while the Quadrilateral was stifling XIV Corps' advance.

Gough saw Haig at his Beauquesne headquarters and then visited the Canadian Corps headquarters during the evening. The Canadian Corps occupied Mouquet Farm that night and then advanced where possible during the morning, with particular attention on Zollern Graben and Zollern Redoubt.

While Fourth Army had captured a 4,500 metre wide section of the enemy lines and had inflicted heavy casualties, the results fell far short of expectations. Although Courcelette, Martinpuich, Flers and High Wood had been taken, XV and XIV Corps still faced Gueudecourt, Lesboeufs and Morval. They had to clear the trenches protecting these villages before there was a breakthrough. Failure on the French front did not help the situation.

Fourth Army headquarters started receiving information from contact aeroplanes as soon as the mist cleared. They could see the tanks and the infantry's flares but Rawlinson received conflicting information. He did not learn about the Guards situation until 3.30pm, by which time he knew the advance was over for the day.

Fourth Army's artillery had to re-register targets while its reserve divisions had to deploy before they could attack. Haig approved Rawlinson's wish to cancel further advances until all of the third objective had been taken and orders were issued to clear it to 'enable the Cavalry Corps to push through to its objectives and complete the enemy's defeat'. But hopes for a big breakthrough were fading and at 10pm Fourth Army ordered the Cavalry Corps to send back three divisions, leaving the 1st Indian Cavalry Division and the 2nd Cavalry Division on call.

16 to 22 September
Rain showers during the night made movement difficult but 16 September dawned fine and cloudy. As fresh battalions, supplies and artillery moved forward, tired battalions and their casualties headed to the rear. There was still a lot of work to do as although 142 enemy batteries had been located, there were only enough guns to engage forty-five of them.

RESERVE ARMY
II Corps, 16 September
49th Division, East Bank of the Ancre
Several raids were made on the east bank of the Ancre and in front of Thiepval. The 1/7th Duke's[217] made a little progress along the old German front line towards Thiepval.

11th Division, Thiepval to Mouquet Farm
Brigadier General Erskine's 33 Brigade held an extended front facing Thiepval and Mouquet Farm. The 6th Borders found few Germans during a pre-dawn raid on Danube Trench. Second Lieutenant Donald led the 6th Lincolns bombers along Constance Trench towards Mouquet Farm; the 9th Sherwood Foresters then consolidated the trench.

Canadian Corps, 16 and 17 September
3rd Canadian Division, Zollern Graben and Zollern Redoubt
General Lipsett's men faced Zollern Graben and Zollern Redoubt and the plan was for 7 Brigade to attack first on the right. At 5pm on 16 September the barrage landed beyond Zollern Graben and the 42nd Battalion and the Royal Canadian Regiment were pinned down by machine-gun fire; Private Dunn covered 42nd Battalion's withdrawal with his Lewis gun. But 49th Battalion cleared the east end of Fabeck Graben and most of it was taken by Private John Kerr. After the bomb supply ran out, Private Kerr climbed out of the trench and ran along the parapet, shooting at the Germans until they thought they were surrounded. Despite an injured hand, Kerr escorted sixty-two prisoners back with two other men. He had single-handedly captured 250 metres of trench. Private Kerr was awarded the Victoria Cross. Major Stewart made sure the Princess Patricia's Light Infantry held their position in Fabeck Graben.

---

217 From Brigadier General Lewes's 147 Brigade.

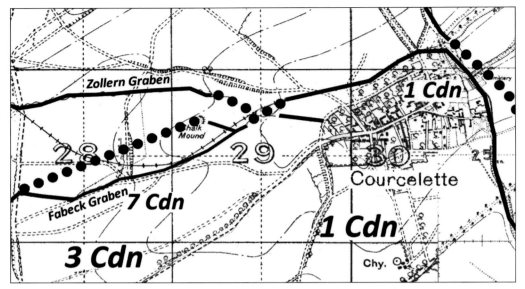

16-22 September, Canadian Corps: As 3rd Canadian Division inched towards Zollern Graben, 2nd Canadian Division improved its position around Courcelette.

Brigadier General Hill's 9 Brigade was due to attack Zollern Redoubt on the left at 6.30pm but it was late reaching the front line and was then hit by German artillery fire so the attack was cancelled. Instead Hill's men spent the evening relieving 7 Brigade.

2nd and 1st Canadian Divisions, Courcelette
At 5pm on 17 September General MacDonnell's 5 Brigade failed to capture the trenches east of Courcelette. Major-General Arthur Currie's 1st Canadian Division took over the sector during the night and the following day it sent patrols out to probe the German trenches. The Germans retaliated during the night but 4th Battalion stopped them entering the north-east corner of Courcelette before occupying a trench east of the village. More trenches were occupied east of Courcelette before dawn.

Reserve Army Summary
The 3rd Canadian Division had three quiet days before it attacked Zollern Graben again at 5am on 20 September. While 58th Battalion[218] bombed from the west end, a company from the 43rd Battalion made a surprise attack over the top while the Germans were distracted, capturing a long section of trench. The Germans retook the trench at the fifth attempt using

---

218 From 9 Brigade.

a smoke screen and a shower of rifle grenades to cover their attack. The attack brought the Canadian Corps' offensive activities to a close.

FOURTH ARMY
III Corps, 16 to 22 September
Pulteney had to clear Starfish and Prue Trenches and 47th Division had the furthest to travel north of High Wood.

23rd Division, Martinpuich
By the morning of 16 September 23rd Division had taken over from 15th Division in Martinpuich. It also took over Starfish and Prue trenches, east of the village, from 50th Division. Twenty-four hours later 69 Brigade attacked from Crescent Alley and extended its hold on the trenches. On the night of 21 September patrols discovered Starfish and Prue Trenches had been abandoned, so 69 Brigade occupied them.

50th Division, Starfish Line and Prue Trench
In 150 Brigade's sector the 1/5th Durhams advanced towards the west end of Prue Trench at 9.25am on 16 September. Heavy fire forced Lieutenant Townsend's men to swerve left and later attempts to bomb from Martin Alley failed. In 151 Brigade's sector the 1/5th Borders and 1/9th Durhams captured the east end of Prue Trench but a counter-attack forced them back, threatening the Starfish Line.

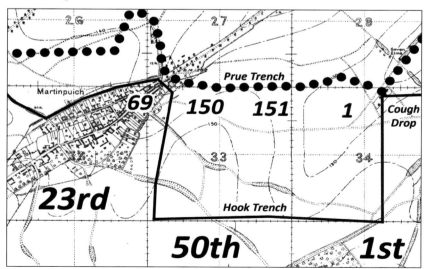

16-22 September, III Corps: As 23rd Division secured Martinpuich, 50th Division and 1st Division occupied an abandoned Prue Trench.

At 4.30pm on 18 September the 1/8th Durhams[219] failed to bomb up Crescent Trench but Lieutenants Jones and Green led the 1/5th Durhams' bombers east along the Starfish Line and Prue Trench towards Crescent Alley. Three nights later patrols discovered the Germans had withdrawn from the two trenches and they were occupied. Further patrols found no Germans south-west of Eaucourt l'Abbaye.

47th Division, Starfish Line and Flers Trench

At 8.55am on 16 September 142 Brigade advanced from Crest Trench. But the 1/23rd London Regiment[220] were shelled and shot at beyond the Switch Line and while only a few of Lieutenant Kemble's men advanced beyond the Cough Drop, none returned;[221] the rest sought cover in the Starfish Line.

The weather was too bad for offensive operations on 17 September but at 5am the following morning Major Whitehead led a charge by 300 men of the 8th and 15th London Regiment against Drop Alley and Flers Trench on the division's right flank. At 4pm companies from the 1/23rd and 1/24th London Regiment tried to expand 142 Brigade's hold on the Starfish Line but Major Hargreaves and Captain Figg could only reinforce the foothold. The Londoners were also engaged in a fierce fight around the Bow. The following day the Germans counter-attacked and by dusk on 19 September the 1/15th London Regiment had been driven out of Drop Alley to Flers Trench and back to the Cough Drop.

1st Division, North of High Wood

General Strickland's 1st Division relieved 47th Division on 20 September. There was no bombardment when the 1st Black Watch[222] advanced at 8.30pm and they took the Germans holding Flers Trenches by surprise in the dark. One of Major Fortune's companies also cleared Drop Alley and linked up with the New Zealand Division. On the night of 21 September patrols discovered the Starfish and Prue trenches had been abandoned and they were occupied.

XV Corps, 16 to 22 September

Air reconnaissance noted no movement in the Gird Trenches in front of Gueudecourt but the attack on 16 September was hampered by many things. The British artillery had not had the time to register targets. Communications were poor because artillery fire killed runners and cut telephone wires. In many cases the tried and tested method of using flares to mark captured trenches failed because they were too damp to light.

---

219 From 151 Brigade.
220 With a company of the 1/22nd London Regiment attached.
221 General Barter was apparently unaware the 1/6th London Regiment were holding the Cough Drop.
222 From 1 Brigade.

New Zealand Division, Flers Trenches

The 1st New Zealand Brigade took over the division's front line early on 16 September and it stopped a counter-attack before zero hour with the help of a tank. The tank was disabled during the 1st Wellington Battalion's 9.25am advance towards Grove Alley. Brigadier General Johnston then learnt 21st Division had been unable to advance on his left so the Wellingtons were told to dig in while the 1st Canterbury Battalion dug back to Box and Cox.

On 18 September the 1st Otago's bombers cleared Flers Support, northwest of Flers, on the division's left flank. The following day the Germans counter-attacked but the 2nd Auckland Battalion[223] bombed along Flers Support as far as Goose Alley on the crest of the ridge.

There was no bombardment for the 8.30pm attack on 20 September. The 2nd Canterbury Battalion crept forward in the dark and took the Germans in Flers Trenches and Goose Alley by surprise. But then the Germans struck back, some advancing over the top to cut in behind the New Zealanders; the Canterbury Battalion stopped them.

21st Division, Flers

The 41st Division was exhausted so 21st Division sent 64 Brigade forward to help. Brigadier General Headlam had a difficult time navigating his way

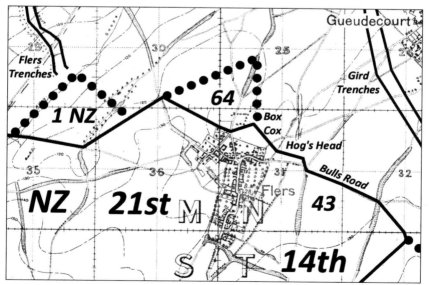

16-22 September, XV Corps: The New Zealand Division advanced along the Flers Trenches and 21st pushed north of Flers village, as 14th Division held its position.

---

223 From 2 New Zealand Brigade.

across the battlefield in the rain and darkness and he was still not sure where he was at zero hour. The 15th Durhams and 9th KOYLIs[224] advanced late even though they were still 1,300 metres short of their jumping off line. The machine-guns and artillery fire intensified as the two battalions advanced through 41st Division's front line north of Flers and they were eventually pinned down in front of Gird Trench. The KOYLI's spirits rose when a tank crawled through their lines but their optimism waned when it was knocked out in front of Gueudecourt. All Headlam could do was wait for his men to rally on Bulls Road. Although Horne issued orders to attack again, a shell had destroyed the brigade signal headquarters in Flers and the message arrived too late to act on it.

On the morning of 17 September Major General David Campbell's 21st Division relieved 14th Division but the Germans were quick to react. They bombed down Gas Alley, driving a wedge between XIV and XV Corps. Later that evening General Jeudwine's 55th Division relieved 41st Division.

14th Division, Gird Trenches

Moving the artillery forward posed many problems and while the heavy guns had not had time to register their targets, the creeping barrage started too far in front of the infantry. South of Gueudecourt 43 Brigade found wire entanglements and machine-gun nests hidden in the crops. The 10th Durhams were hit by the machine-guns in the Gird Trenches and the 6th Somersets were hit by the machine-guns in Gas Alley. While some men occupied a half-dug trench, others sheltered in shell-holes. Brigadier General Wood sent the 6th Duke of Cornwalls and 6th KOYLIs forward to renew the advance but they too ended up pinned down. Captain Macmillan of the 6th DCLI decided against advancing any further because he could see no one on his flanks.

The problem was the half-dug trench was reported as Gird Trench and the encouraging news that the objective had been taken went all the way up to Fourth Army headquarters. It was some time before the truth was known. A late attempt to make 43 Brigade attack again at 6.55pm had no chance of achieving anything.

XIV Corps, 16 to 22 September

Guards Division, North of Lesboeufs

The Guards Division had to continue its advance north of Lesboeufs on 16 September while 6th Division and 56th Division protected its flank with artillery fire. On the left was 3 Guards Brigade but the 1st Welsh Guards and 1st Grenadiers had difficulties assembling and it was nearly 1.30pm

---

224 The 10th KOYLIs and 1st East Yorkshires followed in support.

before they advanced without artillery support. Machine-gun fire, particularly from Lesboeufs church tower, stopped them 1,000 metres short of the village with their left on Punch Trench. But the Welsh Guards dug in facing north rather than north-east, having mistaken Gueudecourt for Lesboeufs.

The Guards were short of troops on their right, so 61 Brigade had been sent up from 20th Division. But the orders were issued late and it was still assembling in shell-holes in front of 2 Guards Brigade at first light. The Germans spotted them and targeted Brigadier General Banbury's men with machine-gun and trench-mortar fire before zero hour.

Even so the 7th Somersets and 7th DCLIs were ready to advance at 9.25am. But the Somersets had lost all their senior officers so Lieutenant Jenne had to lead them forward while Captain Macmillan made sure the DCLI knew where their objective was in front of Lesboeufs. But the delay to the Guards exposed the Duke's left flank so General Banbury sent the rest of the brigade forward and while Lieutenant Colonel Vince's 12th King's covered the left flank, Lieutenant Colonel Robinson's 7th KOYLIs covered the right flank.

20th Division, Lesboeufs

General Smith's 20th Division relieved the Guards Division early on 17 September and prepared to capture the trenches in front of Lesboeufs. But the Germans made the first move against 60 Brigade which was attacked around 1.30pm and while the 12th KRRC were forced back, the 6th Shropshires held their ground.

Then it was 59 Brigade's time to attack north of the Lesboeufs road and the 11th KRRC, the 10th and the 11th Rifle Brigade waited in the rain for zero hour. But there were many problems. Firstly, Brigadier General Shute's men had to advance from old communications trenches at right angles to the German trenches. Secondly, the order was issued late and one company failed to get the message. Thirdly, the late decision to attack meant the artillery did not have time to prepare a barrage plan. Finally, there was not enough time to get enough artillery ammunition forward.

At 6.30pm the understrength battalions left their trenches and deployed. As there were no attacks to the left or right, all the German machine-guns in range turned to shoot at them. A few KRRC men reached the German trench while Captain Ord and the 10th Rifle Brigade were shot down in front of uncut wire. The rest of General Shute's men were pinned down in the mud. General Cavan called off the advance towards the third objective planned for the morning when he heard General Smith's report of the attack.

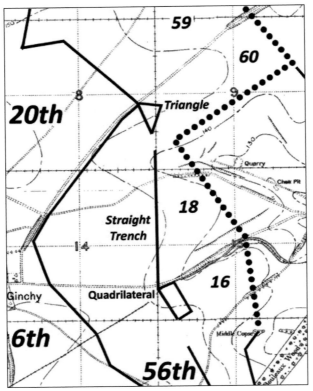

16-22 September, XIII Corps: While 20th Division pushed beyond the Triangle, 6th Division eventually captured Straight Trench and the Quadrilateral.

6th Division, Straight Trench and the Quadrilateral

At 5.50am on 18 September the 1st West Yorkshires attacked in 18 Brigade's sector. Captain Corp's and Captain Trafford Rawson's companies could not reach Straight Trench across the open but Captain Stockdale's bombers were successful. Some entered the north end of the trench while others moved behind it and between them they cleared 600 metres, capturing 140 prisoners and seven machine-guns. They also met the 14th Durhams' bombers heading north from the Quadrilateral. German infantry were seen assembling on the high ground near Morval as they consolidated, so the artillery was called on to disperse them.

An attack on the Quadrilateral from three directions was planned by 16 Brigade. The 1st Shropshires made the main attack from the north-east and Lieutenant Colonel Luard's men overran the Quadrilateral. The 14th

Durhams[225] joined in on the left and they cleared out the dug-outs along the sunken Morval road. The 2nd York and Lancasters moved up on the right, linking up with 56th Division in Middle Copse. Major General Reginald Stephens's 5th Division relieved 6th Division during the night.

56th Division, Bouleaux Wood

Here 168 Brigade needed 'superhuman exertion' to trudge through heavy drizzle across a wasteland of mud and water-filled shell holes. The 1/4th London Regiment did not make it on time and the 1/14th London Regiment only reached the assembly trench with minutes to spare. The Londoners were hit by machine-gun fire from Bouleaux Wood and only eighty men returned to Angle Wood.

While 169 Brigade did advance on time, Captains Green's and Webb's companies of the 1/16th London Regiment were shot down in no man's land and only Second Lieutenant Jones and Sergeant Newnham reached the German trench; only ninety-three men returned. The 1/2nd London Regiment was stopped by machine-gun fire as they approached the sunken Combles road but the 1/5th London Regiment were able to bomb 200 metres towards the road.

Summary
During the afternoon of 18 September Haig told Rawlinson he had four fresh divisions and all he had to do was to exchange them with battle weary divisions. He also learnt that 4th and 30th Divisions would be ready 'to exploit the success' on 21 September.

But the heavy rain on 19 September delayed the French plans to attack and Fayolle told Rawlinson he would not be ready before 21 September. The delay meant XIV Corps had more time to redeploy its artillery and move its ammunition forward. But Rawlinson warned his corps commanders ammunition stocks were still low and they had to conserve what they had.

An Appraisal of the Tank

By the afternoon of 15 September it was clear Fourth Army had broken into the German trench system but it had not broken through. So what had the tanks contributed? Thirty-six tanks had started out but less than a dozen had played a part; the rest had broken down, been knocked out or had been ditched on the rough ground early on. While individual tanks had caused localised panics, German morale had not been broken and they had not fled en masse.

Fourth Army had gambled on the tanks being successful and sent them ahead of the infantry. They were supposed to replace the creeping barrage and

---

225 18 Brigade.

destroy the wire in front of the third objective. But gaps had to be left in the barrage and the gaps remained if the tanks failed to materialise. The bottom line was too few had made it past the first objective, leaving the infantry exposed because the artillery did not have a contingency plan to help them.

The tanks had been deployed in small groups of two or three and limitations on communication meant there was no tactical control. Tank commanders drove to their objective and then returned unless the infantry could persuade them to help. At this stage, combined tactics and co-operation between infantry, artillery and tanks had not been studied. And how could they be? Tanks had been kept under a cloak of secrecy until the last moment.

While the tanks were new to the battlefield, many had been pushed to their limits in trials and it no doubt contributed to the high number of breakdowns. The tanks struggled to cross open ground, but they could move along the remains of an old road and they were useful for clearing villages. They definitely could not drive through shell-shattered woods and it had been a mistake to send them into High Wood.

A lack of spares, tools and workshops made it difficult to keep the tanks running while no dedicated transport had been allocated, so infantry had to be commandeered to carry fuel and ammunition forward.

One thing is definite, many lessons were learnt and 15 September was 'a very valuable try-out' for the tank commanders. A couple of weeks later armies, corps and the Machine Gun Corps' Heavy Section submitted reports to GHQ. Rawlinson thought it was too risky to change 'normal tactical methods' to accommodate the tanks but he did think they were valuable for dealing with strongpoints and villages; Gough sensibly called for 'tactical training' so they could be integrated into the infantry – artillery battle. The consensus of opinion was they needed a more powerful engine, a higher speed, thicker armour and a smaller main gun. They also had to be more reliable and more workshops, mechanics and training had to be made available.

On 5 October Kiggell made it clear tanks were a 'valuable accessory' but they could not interfere with the established tactics of the infantry or the artillery. Starting positions had to be chosen carefully and the area of operations had to be reconnoitred for problems. The ideal was for the tank to reach the German trench just ahead of the infantry but the covering barrage could not be interfered with under any circumstances. The bottom line was the infantry and the artillery continued as before while the infantry had to learn how to co-operate with the tanks and that would take time to master. This supporting role for the tank would not change until the Battle of Cambrai in November 1917.

Chapter 10

Exploiting the Success – 25 to 30 September

GHQ Planning, 25 September

Rawlinson planned to attack again on 18 September but Haig told him to wait until 21 September so Fourth Army could co-ordinate its advance with the French. So the three corps commanders were ordered to clear the third objective and straighten out their line.

But Rawlinson raised two concerns with Haig. Firstly, the attacks were costing too many casualties while the next batch of reinforcements would not arrive until 21 September. Secondly, he was short of ammunition; 600,000 rounds, two-thirds of the reserve, had been fired over the past week and there was a shortage of 18-pounder ammunition. Howitzer ammunition expenditure also had to be 'eased down' to save stocks for the next attack.

The barrage was due to start at 7am on 20 September but the mist restricted what the artillery and air observers could see and the gunners often had to fire at map targets. It then rained, turning the battlefield into a quagmire. There was a shortage of labour and material to repair tracks and thick mud virtually stopped wheeled transport so the artillery had to resort to using pack animals to carry their ammunition forward.

On 20 September Haig and Rawlinson agreed to delay the attack to 23 September. Rawlinson was also told to hand over any spare tanks to the Reserve Army because it was going to attack the Thiepval Ridge, in what would be its biggest assault of the campaign so far.

The following day Foch told Haig that his Sixth Army was running low on ammunition following the recent German counter-attacks and it would take until 25 September to restock. So Fourth Army's assault was put back to 25 September while the Reserve Army would attack the following day.

FOURTH ARMY, 25 SEPTEMBER

Fourth Army had to capture the outstanding objectives which had been set for 15 September. While III Corps had to take Eaucourt l'Abbaye, XV Corps had to clear the Gird Trenches and Gueudecourt and XIV Corps had to take Lesboeufs and Morval.

The plan was for the two corps to advance in three stages. XV Corps would clear the Gird Trenches, and pass through Gueudecourt. XIV Corps would capture Lesboeufs and Morval. XV Corps had the New Zealand, 55th and 21st Divisions in line. XIV Corps had the Guards, 6th, 5th and 56th Divisions in line. This time General Hull had permission to make local arrangements to clear the high ground around the Combles Ravine with the commander of the adjacent French division. It was hoped the Germans would then evacuate the village, extending the breach in their line.

The role of tanks in the attack was discussed on 19 September. GHQ set zero hour at 12.35pm because the French wanted to observe the final stage of the bombardment. But the late start time meant the tanks would have to remain in the open for six hours of daylight before the attack began. Rawlinson wanted to use them during the advance to the final objective, so they could cut through wire beyond field artillery range. But Haig refused because he was worried the German artillery observers would target them.

GHQ moved two brigades of the 1st Indian Cavalry Division to Mametz. But they could only be used if they could deploy beyond Lesboeufs and Gueudecourt before 6.30pm, leaving them only ninety minutes to reconnoitre the enemy rear before nightfall. On 24 September Rawlinson told Pulteney he had to capture Eaucourt l'Abbaye and Horne he had to clear the Gird Trenches, to open the way forward for the cavalry.

Fourth Army had been hoping for fine weather but the bombardment started at 7am on 24 September in a thick autumn mist. Although it cleared later on, a haze persisted all day, curtailing counter-battery work. It did not stop the Royal Flying Corps bombing billets, battery positions and the rail network around Lille and Douai.

There were a few small skirmishes along the front before dawn on 24 September. The 1st Buffs stopped a counter-attack against 6th Division's salient[226] while the 1/9th London Regiment[227] failed to link up with the French in Combles Trench in 56th Division's sector. Around dawn the Germans tried to force the 12th Durhams[228] out of 23rd Division's trenches east of the Bapaume road, on Fourth Army's left flank. The day ended at 8.30pm when the 1st Black Watch[229] failed to bomb along the Flers Trenches in 1st Division's sector.

The postponements did give the divisions extra time to dig better assembly trenches but it was still difficult getting all the troops into position on time. The late zero hour meant the assault troops had to spend over six

---

226 16 Brigade.
227 169 Brigade.
228 68 Brigade, 23rd Division on III Corps' left flank.
229 1 Brigade, 1st Division on III Corps' right flank.

hours waiting in daylight before the attack and the anticipation wore them out.

Despite the morning haze the artillery observers did their work and at zero hour the troops moved close behind the creeping barrage. For once the defensive barrage was too late to catch the troops crossing no man's land and many Germans were trapped in their dug-outs while others ran back to their support trenches.

III Corps, Eaucourt l'Abbaye

III Corps was to improve its position in front of the Flers Trenches around Eaucourt l'Abbaye.

23rd Division, Twenty-Sixth Avenue

The 23rd Division had to capture the western half of Twenty-Sixth Avenue and 68 Brigade held the front line. One tank ditched while the second was hit by artillery fire and had to withdraw. Captain Ellis and Lieutenants Calder, Lock and Noble were killed as the 10th Northumberland Fusiliers were shot down advancing over the crest. Captain Constable's attempt to bomb along Twenty-Sixth Avenue also failed.

50th Division, Crescent Alley

General Price's 150 Brigade had captured its objective the night before, so the 1/5th Durhams established an outpost in Crescent Alley.

1st Division, Flers Trenches

The 1st Black Watch[230] bombed 300 metres along the Flers Trenches.

XV Corps

New Zealand Division, North of Flers

For two hours before zero hour 1 Brigade was heavily shelled in Grove Alley. But the 1st Otago Battalion, the 1st Auckland Battalion and the 1st Canterbury Battalion still advanced in two short stages, finding few Germans apart from a battalion staff who surrendered at Factory Corner. The Otago Battalion then captured the south-west end of Goose Alley, completing the defensive flank facing Eaucourt l'Abbaye. The New Zealanders later linked up with 1st Division in Flers Support and with 55th Division beyond Factory Corner.

55th Division, the Gird Trenches

In 165 Brigade's sector, the 1/9th, 1/6th and 1/7th King's advanced to the

---

230 1 Brigade.

Gird Trenches. The 1/6th King's were inspired by Sergeant Broster who threw off his equipment after being hit in the stomach; he kept walking towards the German trench until he collapsed and died. The 1/9th King's found the bombardment had killed many Germans in Grove Alley and the 1/6th King's blocked the Gird Trenches to stop counter-attacks.

The rest of the 1/6th and the 1/7th King's wheeled their right flank forward to the sunken road in front of Gueudecourt at 2.40pm. They later linked with New Zealanders and 21st Division in the Gird Trenches while Brigadier General Duncan sent the 1/5th King's forward as reinforcements.

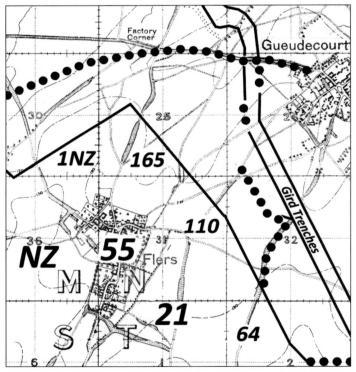

25 September, XV Corps: The New Zealand Division and 55th Division advanced north of Flers, but 21st Division could not clear the Gird Trenches covering Gueudecourt.

21st Division, Gueudecourt

The German artillery hit 110 Brigade as it crossed no man's land but the 8th and 9th Leicesters overran Goat Trench. Enfilade machine-gun fire from the right then stopped them cutting through the wire protecting Gird Trench.

Lieutenant Colonel Haig joined the 9th Leicesters at the front line and reorganised the troops for a second attempt but his runner was wounded en route and the reserve companies never received the message to move forward.

Many of the 8th Leicesters cut through the wire and advanced with 'splendid heroism' but while some may have reached Gueudecourt, they were never seen again. The rest of the battalion stayed in Gird Trench and they linked up with 55th Division. The 9th Leicesters dug in along the sunken road south of Gueudecourt but they did not enter the village.

In 64 Brigade's sector the 1st East Yorkshires and 10th KOYLIs were shot down trying to cut through the wire in front of Gird Trench; the survivors spent the afternoon pinned down in shell holes. The German artillery hit the 1st Lincolns[231] as they moved forward but Captains Edes and Denning led them to the second objective 'as if on parade without in any way having their morale shaken'.

But the attack had disorganised the division and disrupted its communications, leaving General Campbell short of information for some time. Most of the runners were casualties and the disjointed reports later led him to believe his men had taken Gueudecourt. Horne also thought a breakthrough was imminent and at 2.50pm he told the New Zealand and 55th Divisions to prepare to advance to the Gird Trenches, north-west of Gueudecourt. He postponed the move when he heard about 21st Division's difficult situation. Horne even ordered Campbell to use a tank to cut through the barbed wire protecting the Gird Trenches but 21st Division was still in no condition to advance.

XIV Corps

Guards Division, North of Lesboeufs

General Feilding's Guardsmen had to capture the Gird Trenches west of Lesboeufs and then advance north of the village. The 3rd Guards Brigade and the 4th Grenadier Guards suffered many casualties capturing a new trench dug across their front and it delayed them. The barrage had already moved on by the time they had reorganised, leaving them unable to clear the junction of Gas Alley and Gird Trench. But the 2nd Scots Guards found no Germans in their way and they advanced to the final objective.

In 1 Guards Brigade's sector the 1st Irish Guards advanced alongside the Scots Guards to the final objective. The 2nd Grenadiers faced three belts of wire and snipers and bombers gave covering fire while four officers cut through and they then captured the trench beyond. Despite the delays on the flanks one senior Guards officer reported 'the whole show was going like clockwork'.

---

231 62 Brigade.

The Guards resumed their advance at 1.35pm but the 3rd Guards Brigade had an exposed flank where 21st Division had not taken the Gird Trenches. Part of the 4th Grenadier Guards formed a defensive flank while the rest advanced with the Scots Guards to the second objective alongside the 1st Irish Guards and 2nd Grenadier Guards.

The advance continued to the final objective and while the Welsh Guards extended the open flank, the 1st Grenadier Guards advanced north of Lesboeufs, leaving one company to extend the flank astride the sunken Gueudecourt road. Meanwhile, the 2nd Grenadier Guards and the 1st Irish Guards cleared the north half of Lesboeufs as the 2nd and 3rd Coldstream Guards battalions followed in support.

6th Division, Lesboeufs

The advance went even smoother in 6th Division's sector, where General Ross's men already held the Gird Trenches. The 1st Buffs[232] met little resistance as they advanced alongside the 11th Essex and 2nd Durhams.[233] Lieutenant Colonel Lang's 1st West Yorkshires encountered few Germans when they advanced through the southern half of Lesboeufs, and found that most of the cellars had been blown in. The 2nd York and Lancasters and the 1st Shropshires made a 'parade like, steady advance', east of the Lesboeufs – Morval road.

5th Division, Morval

Lieutenant Colonel Stone chose to lead the 1st Norfolk's[234] in person because he was concerned about the large number of replacements in his battalion. He then treated the advance like a pheasant shoot, shooting at the retiring Germans as his servant acted as his loader. The front trench was easily taken because most of the garrison had withdrawn to shell holes behind to avoid the British barrage; 150 prisoners were taken.

The 1st Bedfords and 1st Cheshires then cleared Morval and the 16th Royal Warwicks advanced beyond the ruins. After seeing a friend shot by a sniper, Private Thomas Jones of the Cheshires tracked down and killed him before stalking and killing two more as they fired under a white flag. He then single-handedly disarmed 102 Germans hiding in dug-outs before handing over the trench to the Norfolks. Private Jones was awarded the Victoria Cross.

In 95 Brigade's sector, Captain Halle's company of the 1st Devons side-stepped through 6th Division's sector to avoid a belt of wire and then cleared the Bovril section of Gird Trench. The 1st East Surreys captured the Lemco section of Gird Trench only to come under heavy fire from an embankment

---

232 16 Brigade.
233 18 Brigade.
234 15 Brigade.

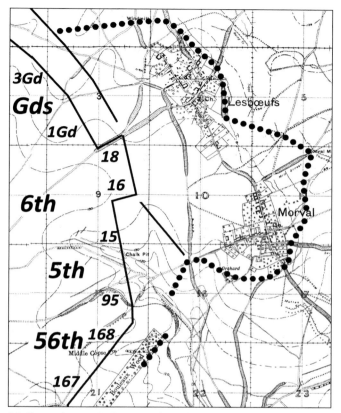

25 September, XIV Corps: While the Guards Division captured Lesboeufs, 6th Division and 5th Division worked together to clear Morval.

beyond. They had to wait for Lieutenant Ross's company of the Devons to clear a strongpoint on the Morval road before they could capture the embankment.

Captain Halle then led the Devons forward with the 1st Bedfords[235] as they advanced to a sunken road while the East Surreys only had a short distance to go on the right. An hour later the 1st Cheshires passed through the Bedfords and cleared the north part of Morval while the 2nd KOSBs and 12th Gloucesters[236] captured the southern half of the village. Lieutenant Colonel Stevenson of the KOSBs reported the Germans 'seemed demoralized and not inclined to show much fight, and nearly every man in the battalion secured a trophy'.

---

235 15 Brigade.
236 Both from 95 Brigade.

The German artillery targeted Morval, forcing the troops to move out as soon as the cellars and dug-outs had been searched. General Stephens gave orders for 5th Division to renew the advance and at 6pm the 16th Warwicks[237] went 200 metres beyond the village. The 2nd York and Lancasters[238] then set up posts between Lesboeufs and Morval mill.

56th Division, Bouleaux Wood
Only 168 Brigade advanced towards Bouleaux Wood and the 1/14th London Regiment left their trench seven minutes after zero hour, so they would be in line with 5th Division's troops. Captain Worlock's company overran the trench north of the wood while Lieutenant Speak's company cleared a strongpoint, taking over fifty prisoners. Worlock's men were then stopped until the Surreys had mopped up an embankment to their left; they could then clear their own part of the embankment, taking eighty prisoners. The Londoners cleared another trench with views over the Combles area but there was no sign of the French advancing through Frégicourt to the east.

25 September Summary
XIV Corps had broken through the main defence line on an 1,800 metre wide front and around 5.30pm contact aeroplanes reported that the German infantry and artillery were withdrawing. Around the same time Rawlinson heard the French Sixth Army had taken Frégicourt but General Cavan contradicted the report thirty minutes later. Battalion commanders had been reporting little opposition but 21st Division's failure to advance and the uncertain situation in the French sector meant the breakthrough was only narrow. So Rawlinson decided to take no further action.

56th Division, Overnight Occupation of Combles
There was a new development. A German officer taken prisoner in 5th Division's area told his captors Combles was about to be evacuated; Cavan's headquarters heard similar news from the French. So it was time to investigate and at 10.40pm a detachment of the 1/14th London Regiment[239] moved towards the north side of Combles. While the 1/4th London Regiment patrolled the northern end of Bouleaux Wood, the 1/1st London Regiment[240] checked the southern end and they saw no one. Then at 2.10am red rockets followed by a green rocket were fired into the sky, telling the German rearguards it was time to leave Combles.

Captain Kellett's patrol of the 1/2nd London Regiment[241] met the French in the middle of Combles around 3.30am and the rest of his battalion

237 15 Brigade.
238 16 Brigade.
239 168 Brigade.
240 167 Brigade.
241 167 Brigade.

26 to 28 September, XIV Corps: 56th Division pushed east of Bouleaux Wood as the Germans withdrew from Combles.

followed down the Ginchy road. The 1/5th London Regiment[242] also met the French in Combles Trench.

The 1/14th London met French patrols on the north-east side of Combles around dawn and they began searching the village, checking all the dug-outs and cellars were empty. At the same time the northern flank of 56th Division moved forward 1,000 metres and dug in between Combles and Morval. The French also captured Frégicourt, east of Combles, and advanced towards Haie Wood during the afternoon.

While 168 Brigade moved along Mutton Trench which connected Morval and Frégicourt, air observers warned 56th Division that the trench was occupied and the 1/12th London's scout, Second Lieutenant Colvin,

---

242 169 Brigade.

confirmed the news. So a hasty plan was put together and two tanks were detailed to lead the 1/12th London Regiment[243] into action. But the tanks floundered in the mud and the attack was called off at dusk as was a second attack the following morning. Captain Copeland registered his disgust with the tanks with the following words:

> 'they would have been capable of putting it across to every qualified Hun in the condemned trench without the aid of any mechanically propelled sardine boxes'.

FOURTH ARMY, 26 AND 27 SEPTEMBER

Preparation and Planning

Foch visited Haig late on 25 September to discuss concerns over the failure of the French advance around Combles. The front facing Sailly-Saillisel was cramped by the huge St Pierre Vaast Wood and Foch wanted to move troops through Morval in the British sector, so they could attack Sailly-Saillisel from the west. They agreed to hand over Lesboeufs and Morval, on Fourth Army's right, to the French and the arrangements were made with Rawlinson the next day.

At 11pm on 25 September Fourth Army issued instructions for the corps to capture the rest of their objectives the following day. III Corps and the left of XV Corps would send patrols ready to advance past Eaucourt l'Abbaye 'at an early date'. The right of XV Corps had to capture the Gird Trenches and clear Gueudecourt while XIV Corps consolidated its position north of Combles alongside the French.

III Corps

23rd Division, Twenty-Sixth Avenue

The plan to occupy Twenty-Sixth Avenue was cancelled because the Canadian Corps had not advanced on the left. The following day Major Shaw, an artillery observer working with the infantry, noticed the Germans had abandoned the trench so he walked all the way along it, meeting Canadian troops on the Bapaume road; 70 Brigade then occupied it. Patrols then discovered the Germans had only withdrawn as far as Destremont Farm.

At dawn on 29 September Captain Barlow's company of the 8th York and Lancasters crept up on the farm in pouring rain and charged into the ruins when the barrage lifted. Lieutenant Searle organised the consolidation and his men found an important ammunition store and engineer dump hidden in the ruins.

---

243 168 Brigade.

50th and 1st Divisions, Crescent Alley and Flers Switch
A new trench connecting Crescent Alley to Flers Trench had to be captured before III Corps could attack Flers Trench. At 11pm 50th and 1st Divisions crept forward without artillery support to surprise the Germans but they were spotted. In 150 Brigade's sector, the 5th and 4th Green Howards entered the west end of the Flers Switch and bombed along Crescent Alley. But 2 Brigade lost their way in the dark and they were stopped by the machine-guns in Flers Switch.

At noon the following day the 5th Durhams bombed along Twenty-Sixth Avenue and Crescent Alley, heading for Eaucourt l'Abbaye. Posts were then established between the two trenches. When 1st Division advanced over the top and bombed towards the Flers Switch it was unable to bomb east along Flers Trench.

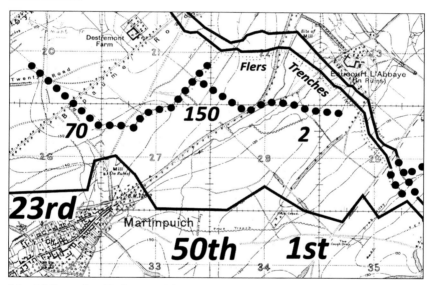

26 to 28 September, III Corps: While 23rd Division advanced astride the Bapaume Road, 50th Division and 1st Division pushed north towards the Flers Trenches.

XV Corps
The 21st Division had to secure Gueudecourt on XV Corps' right before the New Zealand Division and 55th Division could attack the Gird Trenches.

21st Division, the Gird Trenches and Gueudecourt
Rather than make another attack over the top, General Campbell ordered Brigadier General Hessey to make a flank attack on Gird Trenches with 64

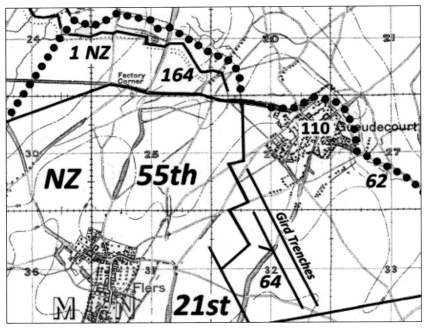

26 to 28 September, XV Corps: The New Zealand Division and 55th Division pushed north, 21st Division captured Gueudecourt and cleared the Gird Trenches.

Brigade. Around dawn a single tank crawled along Pilgrim's Way to join the 7th Leicesters. An aeroplane flying overhead fired a signal flare to tell the artillery to start bombarding the trench and it fired a second flare to stop the guns when the Leicesters had formed up. The plane then flew low, strafing the trench to keep the Germans undercover.

The tank drove alongside Gird Trench and the bombers worked their way down the trenches followed by two Leicester companies. The Germans were taken by surprise and many were caught in their dug-outs. Others were shot down as they ran and 370 prisoners were taken while many more were killed and injured; the Leicesters suffered five casualties. The 15th Durhams then occupied the Gird Trenches on behalf of 64 Brigade so 3 Guards Brigade was able to move forward alongside 1 Guards Brigade. The tank finally made a brief sortie towards Gueudecourt before withdrawing, its work done.

Horne wanted to know if Gueudecourt had been abandoned. At noon the 19th Lancers[244] left Mametz heading for Flers, with instructions to help the South Irish Horse[245] reconnoitre the high ground north of Gueudecourt. They

---

244 Sialkot Cavalry Brigade, 1st Indian Cavalry Division.
245 XV Corps cavalry regiment.

came under machine-gun fire from the Gird Trenches and although one patrol cantered to the far side of the village, it withdrew after coming under artillery fire. The commanders on the spot decided to send their infantry forward to support the cavalry and while a troop of the South Irish entered the ruins from the north-west, a squadron of lancers entered from the south-west.

During the afternoon General Campbell decided 110 Brigade would relieve the cavalry while 64 Brigade investigated the ground south-east of Gueudecourt. As the 6th Leicesters moved forward, they spotted a sizeable force of German troops leaving Thilloy. They went to ground in the long grass when they came under fire from the British artillery and then decided it was safer to remain hidden. The Leicesters continued into Gueudecourt, relieving the cavalry, and by 7pm they had dug in on the east side of the village.

When it became clear Gueudecourt had been occupied, the 15th Durhams[246] advanced towards their final objective and then 62 Brigade took over the advance. The 12th Northumberland Fusiliers moved to the Le Transloy road, south-east of Gueudecourt, meeting the Guards on the Lesboeufs road. The 10th Green Howards joined the Fusiliers after dusk.

XV Corps, 27 September

With Gueudecourt secure, Horne ordered the New Zealand Division and 55th Division to capture the Gird Trenches west of the village, at 2.15pm the following afternoon.

New Zealand Division, Goose Trench

In 1st Brigade's sector one 1st Otago Battalion company bombed along Goose Alley to Abbey Road only to discover the trench had been obliterated by artillery fire, so they established posts in the shell holes. The rest of the Otago Battalion were hit by artillery and machine-gun fire and they were unable to reach Goose Alley. The 1st Auckland Battalion had to cut through wire under fire to capture its part of the Gird Trenches. The 1st Canterbury Battalion secured its objective on the right and then linked up with 1/8th King's on the Thilloy road.

55th Division, the Gird Trenches

The 1/8th King's[247] overran the section of Gird Trenches north-west of Gueudecourt as part of 164 Brigade's attack.

XIV Corps

The German withdrawal from Combles called for a reorganisation of the front. The Guards Division patrols encountered snipers and machine-gun

---

246 With part of the 9th KOYLIs and the 10th KOYLIs.
247 The Liverpool Irish.

posts east of Lesboeufs. The 5th Division captured part of Mutton Trench, south of Morval, and part of Thunder Trench, east of the village. At the same time 6th Division and 20th Division took over 56th Division's front.

Summary
The attack had been Fourth Army's most successful since 14 July and it would have been more so if 21st Division had taken Gueudecourt on the first day. Slow progress by the French had also hindered XIV Corps on the right. The Germans were shaken but they had had time to withdraw their artillery to a safe distance. Despite the promising results, Rawlinson knew he had exhausted all his reserves. All he could do from now on was to probe the German line.

The decision to hand over the Morval sector to the French had been discussed at Fourth Army headquarters on the afternoon of 26 September. The British would continue to hold Lesboeufs with Le Transloy as a XIV Corps objective. XIV Corps handed over a large part of its line to the French, and the reliefs were completed during the early hours of the 29 September. The Germans did not notice any changes.

RESERVE ARMY
Planning and Preparations
While Fourth Army's attack on 15 September had achieved a lot, it had not broken through the German lines. Haig was sure the German reserves were nearly exhausted but Fourth Army's right was dependent on the French advancing and it was moving too slowly. The alternative way forward was for the Reserve Army's right flank to clear Thiepval Ridge, so its left could attack Serre and Beaumont Hamel. Third Army could then extend the action north to Gommecourt. Joffre agreed and he wanted it to happen quickly.

Gough issued operational orders on 22 September to capture 'the ridge which runs from Courcelette to Schwaben Redoubt'; zero hour would be 12.35pm on 26 September. Maxse believed zero hour should be calculated backwards from sunset, allowing no more than three hours of daylight on the objective so his men could consolidate under cover of darkness.

II Corps had to capture Thiepval, Stuff Redoubt and Zollern Redoubt on the left. The Canadian Corps' main objective was Regina Trench. While six tanks were allotted to II Corps and only two to the Canadian Corps, there was plenty of artillery on call: 230 heavy guns, howitzers and mortars and 570 field guns and howitzers. V Corps batteries north of the Ancre would also shell the German lines[248]. The preliminary bombardment started on 23 September and although the morning and evening mists restricted visibility,

---

248 500 lachrymatory shells were fired into Thiepval on the afternoon of 24 September.

the improved day time weather let the observers do their work. Rain soaked the troops the night before the attack but the day of the assault dawned fine.

II Corps, 26 September

General Maxse's 18th Division took over the line south of Thiepval on the night of 24/25 September. He also took command of 146 Brigade,[249] west of the Thiepval salient. Although a 6th York and Lancaster company[250] entered Mouquet Farm in 11th Division's sector on the evening of 24 September; it was later forced out.

The 18th Division had to advance north through Thiepval while General Woollcombe's 11th Division had to clear Midway Trench, Zollern Trench and Zollern Redoubt. II Corps' final objectives were Hessian Trench and Stuff Redoubt on the crest of the ridge; patrols would then investigate Stuff Trench beyond.

18th Division, Thiepval

In 54 Brigade's sector the assault troops were out of their trenches before zero hour and across no man's land before the German artillery could react. Captain Thompson's company of the 11th Royal Fusiliers had a hard fight for Brawn Trench in the original German front line south-west of Thiepval and could not keep up with its barrage; Thompson was killed.

Colonel Maxwell's 12th Middlesex advanced into Thiepval followed by two Fusilier companies. The single tank suppressed machine-gun fire from the chateau but it ditched soon afterwards. The Middlesex right was the first to reach the centre of Thiepval, while the left was close behind and the advance was mainly down to two men. Private Frederick Edwards ran forward to knock out a machine-gun after it hit all his officers and his comrades went to ground. Private Robert Ryder also went forward after all his officers had been hit and cleared a trench with his Lewis gun. Both Edwards and Ryder were awarded the Victoria Cross.

Maxwell reached the chateau around 2.30pm and while his right was on the second objective, north of the village, his left was in difficulties; so he requested reinforcements and a new barrage. A defensive barrage was put down 150 metres beyond the north side of Thiepval and a depleted 6th Northants reached the chateau under heavy fire. The survivors from all three battalions gathered, with Colonel Maxwell in command, on the north-east side of the village while the Germans held the north-west corner. While Captain Johnston's Royal Fusiliers mopped up, Lieutenant Sulman used his Lewis gun to clear a pocket of fifty Germans hiding in the ruins. Lance Corporal Rudy also discovered a hidden underground

---

249 Of 49th Division.
250 32 Brigade.

telephone exchange and he took the garrison prisoner before cutting the wires.

Brigadier General Higginson's 53 Brigade also moved across no man's land before the barrage lifted and Captain Sanctuary led the 8th Suffolks into Joseph Trench with 'great precision' as the Germans ran; Schwaben Trench was taken a few minutes later. On the right Captain Johnston and the 10th Essex found a group of Germans waiting to surrender in the sunken road running through Thiepval. The 8th Norfolks collected many more prisoners as they mopped up. The support battalions waited until the German barrage slackened off and then ran across no man's land in small columns to join the battle for Thiepval.

As the men waited for the barrage to lift, they saw the only tank ditch in Schwaben Trench. Fortunately, German resistance was crumbling and Zollern Trench was cleared by 1.15pm. But the Essex could not reach Midway Trench due to enfilade fire from Martin Trench, Bulgar Trench and the north-west corner of Thiepval. Attempts to bomb up the two trenches failed, leaving the battalion pinned down on the open slope. The Suffolks were also pinned down by fire from Midway Trench but Second Lieutenant Mason held a forward position until he was killed; his men then withdrew.

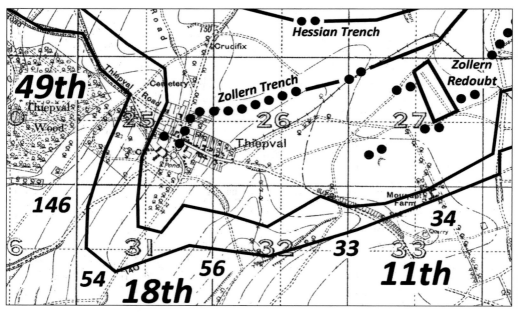

26 September, II Corps: 18th Division cleared all but the north-west corner of Thiepval village but 11th Division struggled to reach Zollern Trench.

11th Division, Zollern and Stuff Redoubts, Mouquet Farm
In 33 Brigade's sector the 6th Border Regiment cleared Joseph Trench on schedule but the 9th Sherwood Foresters moved too fast and ran into the creeping barrage. They then advanced to the first objective, overrunning two machine-gun teams who kept firing until they were killed.

While the Border Regiment cleared Schwartz Trench, taking over 100 prisoners, the Foresters advanced over the crest around 1pm. Zollern Trench and the Midway Line fell next with nearly 200 prisoners and three machine-guns. While the 7th South Staffords mopped up, a combination of runners, visual signalling and runners kept Brigadier General Erskine up to date on progress.

After an hour of reorganising, two Forester companies captured the west end of Hessian Trench and met up with 18th Division. Machine-guns in Zollern Redoubt stopped them taking the east end of the trench and a Stafford's company had to be sent forward to make the link with 34 Brigade.[251]

Lieutenant Harris had led the 9th Lancashire Fusiliers bombers into Mouquet Farm before zero hour and they located the cellar entrances, trapping the garrison underground. The rest of the battalion then crossed High Trench and worked their way through the trenches towards Zollern Redoubt. The 8th Northumberland Fusiliers also crossed High Trench and fought their way through the dug-outs of the old German Second Line.

The barrage plan only allowed 34 Brigade ten minutes to clear their first objective and it was not long enough. The barrage had already moved on before they had finished and the Germans had time to man Hessian Trench; the two tanks allocated to the brigade had also ditched early on. The Lancashire Fusiliers' left company became involved in heavy fighting for the Midway Line while the right company was hit by enfilade fire as it advanced past Zollern Redoubt heading for Zollern Trench. The same happened to the Northumberland Fusiliers and the survivors ended up sheltering in shell-holes, with one group of fifty men facing Zollern Trench on the right. A platoon moving up the sunken Grandcourt road alongside the Canadians was also shot to pieces. The German barrage hit the 5th Dorsets as they crossed no man's land and while some men waited in the German front line, the rest joined the surviving Fusiliers.

By 1.30pm reports stated Zollern Trench had been taken. But when the two Fusilier battalion commanders went forward, they could only find groups of men pinned down in shell holes and trenches. Nobody was moving because machine-gun fire from Mouquet Farm and Zollern Redoubt was sweeping 'an empty battlefield'.

---

251 33 Brigade had suffered less than 600 casualties.

Brigadier General Hill sent the 11th Manchesters[252] forward to clear up Mouquet Farm and they were helped by men from the 5th Dorsets and 6th East Yorkshires[253] while a tank crew gave covering fire with their Lewis guns. After several hours of hand-to-hand fighting, an officer and fifty-five other ranks finally surrendered at 5.30pm.

Although Lieutenant Colonel Hannay was ordered to take Zollern Redoubt and link up with the Canadians on his right, his men were scattered across the battlefield; it would take until midnight to organise them into a coherent unit.

Canadian Corps, 26 September

General Currie's 1st Canadian Division, General Louis Lipsett's 3rd Canadian Division and General Turner's 2nd Canadian Division were in line. The machine-guns opened overhead fire at 12:34pm and a minute later 800 hundred guns, howitzers and mortars opened fire as the infantry climbed out of their trench.

1st Canadian Division, Regina Trench

General Byng made a late modification to 1st Canadian Division's orders because he was concerned his observers could not see all of Regina Trench. Parts of the trench were in dead ground and it was not clear if the wire had been cut, even though the Royal Flying Corps had flown low over no man's land. The plan was to stop the infantry on the second objective while patrols followed the barrage to Regina Trench to investigate. General Currie would make a decision based on what they found.

As 2 Brigade advanced with the Grandcourt road on its left Brigadier General Loomis had to hope 11th Division had cleared Zollern and Stuff Redoubts, because they both overlooked his sector. Major McLeod's company was hit by enfilade fire and pinned down on 8th Battalion's left flank, but the rest of the battalion overran Zollern Trench, trapping 100 Germans in their dug-outs. The delay in the advance meant the German barrage hit the rear waves but a 10th Battalion company was able to mop up the trench, taking 100 prisoners. At 1pm 8th Battalion pushed on to Hessian Trench. While 5th Battalion cleared Zollern Trench, machine-gun fire from Zollern Redoubt wiped out the two 10th Battalion platoons moving up in support. Two platoons then had to block Zollern Trench to stop counter-attacks.

The 8th and 10th Battalions then pushed on into Hessian Trench and the survivors consolidated their position while patrols went forward to investigate. They returned with conflicting reports about the wire and the

252 34 Brigade.
253 The divisional pioneers.

size of the garrison in Regina Trench. But there were problems on the brigade's left flank where 11th Division had failed to capture Zollern Redoubt and Hessian Trench; 2 Brigade's area was swept with machine-gun fire and 8th Battalion eventually had to evacuate Hessian Trench.

At 4pm, General Loomis gave the order to dig a new trench from Hessian Trench back to Zollern Trench, so his troops could get to the front line safely. Twenty minutes later he was told that 11th Division had reached Hessian Trench and he had to retake his section of the trench. But Loomis knew the report was wrong so he ignored the order, leaving 7th Battalion to dig their trench.

As 3 Brigade moved out of their trenches early the German barrage missed the leading waves. But 15th Battalion's right came under fire from machine-gun teams sheltering in shell holes along the Grandcourt road. It took time and casualties to clear them but Lieutenant Colonel Bent's men reached their first objective between Zollern Trench and Sudbury Trench. They then advanced to their second objective under crossfire from machine-guns and snipers in shell holes on the left and Kenora Trench, 'one of the deepest and strongest trenches the men had ever seen'. On the right. Major Girvan and Major Ackland were both hit as 15th Battalion pushed over the crest to Regina Trench so their men withdrew and dug in.

After clearing Sudbury Trench under heavy fire, 14th Battalion continued towards the second objective. At 2.40pm Brigadier General

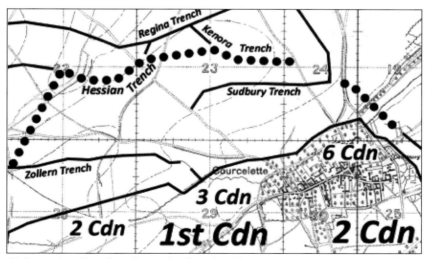

26 September, Canadian Corps: 1st Canadian Division captured Hessian Trench and 2nd Canadian Division improved its position around Courcelette.

Tuxford learnt 14th Battalion had taken the east half of Kenora Trench but the rest of the trench was still in German hands. It left the battalion in an exposed position and while German bombers were soon moving in on their front and flanks, Kenora Trench was held with the help of 16th Battalion.

2nd Canadian Division, Courcelette
Brigadier General Ketchen's 6 Brigade was detailed to clear the German trenches north-east and east of Courcelette. The 31st Battalion was hit by crossfire from Sudbury Trench and only one of Lieutenant Colonel Bell's platoons reached it on the right; 29th Battalion had no such problems and it only took ten minutes to capture the trench. The plan to sweep the trenches east of Courcelette with two tanks fell apart when one ditched and the other was knocked out. The German artillery had the assembly area covered and 28th Battalion could not leave their trenches.

General Turner did not hear that both 31st Battalion and 28th Battalion had failed, leaving 29th Battalion in an exposed position until 2pm. General Ketchen was later told a new bombardment had been arranged and he reported he would be ready for 10.50pm. This time 31st Battalion[254] captured Sudbury Trench and fought off all German counter-attacks.

Summary
At 8.45pm Gough announced that 'all objectives given in today's operations hold good for tomorrow'. General Maxse's plans for a night attack were cancelled at dusk but the battle for Thiepval continued late into the night. At midnight, General Shoubridge learnt 54 Brigade would attack again using battalions from 146 and 55 Brigades.[255] Meanwhile, General Higginson withdrew his men to Zollern Trench while the 8th Norfolks consolidated Schwaben Trench.

General Woollcombe was convinced Hessian Trench had been taken but the truth was only a few men had reached it. While 33 Brigade was holding the second objective on the left, 34 Brigade was scattered between the first and second objectives on the right. Gough wanted to make sure the area was secure so General Jacob was instructed to organise II Corps' front and make contact with the Canadian Corps during the night.

II Corps, 27 to 30 September
18th Division, Thiepval
The 7th Bedfords were to take over 54 Brigade's front ready to attack at 7am but Lieutenant Colonel Price's relief finished earlier than expected. The company commanders had already checked out the ground and the

---

254 With a 27th Battalion company.
255 The three battalions suffered 840 casualties.

decision was taken to attack immediately. At 5.45am Captain Keep led two Bedford companies through the north-west corner of Thiepval without the benefit of a barrage and they took the Germans by surprise. The left company advanced quickly but the right company was pinned down until Second Lieutenant Tom Adlam ran from shell hole to shell hole, collecting men and German grenades. In spite of his injured leg, he relied on his cricketing skills to out throw the Germans and encouraged his men to charge. Thiepval was finally cleared along with seventy prisoners by 11pm. Contact was also made with 53 Brigade in Zollern Trench. The 10th Essex bombers later cleared fifty metres of Bulgar Trench even though the British artillery was shelling the area.

Although 18th Division was in a position to attack Schwaben Redoubt, Maxse wanted to wait until Stuff Redoubt, with its commanding view, had been captured. He believed six hours were required to plan and prepare for an attack to be successful and both II Corps and Fourth Army headquarters approved the postponement.

At 1pm on 28 September 54 Brigade was ordered to capture Schwaben Redoubt. The 7th Bedfords advanced along the German front trench system, parallel to Mill Road, but its right suffered casualties from the machine-guns in Schwaben Redoubt. The 7th Queen's and the 8th Suffolks cleared Bulgar Trench but the machine-guns in Schwaben Redoubt forced them to swerve left and they cleared Martin Trench. They then had a tough time clearing Midway Trench before Captain Sanctuary and Captain Usher led them towards the east end of the redoubt.

The Suffolks had pushed the Bedfords to their left and it took time to re-deploy and renew the advance, but they cleared the original German front line facing Thiepval Wood with the help of Captain Mandeville's 1/5th West Yorkshires. For the second day in a row, Second Lieutenant Adlam inspired the Bedfords to keep going in spite of a serious wound; he was awarded the Victoria Cross.

While progress was being made, General Shoubridge was concerned most of his troops were avoiding Schwaben Redoubt. Captain Longbourne of the Queen's bombed his way along the south side of the redoubt but his men should have cleared the north side. It took time for the Bedfords and West Yorkshires to relieve Longbourne's men, and then Captain Walter's Queen's company could link up with the Suffolks in the Midway Line.

While Brigadier General Higginson ordered his battalions to consolidate their position, the Bedfords and West Yorkshires were gaining the upper hand and by 8pm they had cleared the west side of the redoubt and a trench beyond. With the redoubt secure, 55 Brigade sent the 7th Queen's Own forward to take over. The fighting in the trenches between the German front line and Schwaben Redoubt continued throughout the night. The Queen's Own relieved 54 Brigade's sector before dawn on 29 September, only losing a trench junction in a see-saw battle which lasted well into the night.

It was a day of reliefs on the rest of 18th Division's line and 55 Brigade took over the front during the night. A counter-attack at dawn on 30 September caught the troops in Schwaben Redoubt unawares and while the 7th Queen's Own lost the west side, the 8th East Surreys were forced out of the south side. The Queen's Own could not retake the west face despite help from the 7th Buffs but Lieutenants Barfoot, Milner and Wightman of the Surreys recaptured the south side and the north side. A counter-attack after dusk drove the Surreys from the north face back into Stuff Trench but the men fought true to Wightman's word; 'we shall use the bayonet and no man goes out a prisoner'.

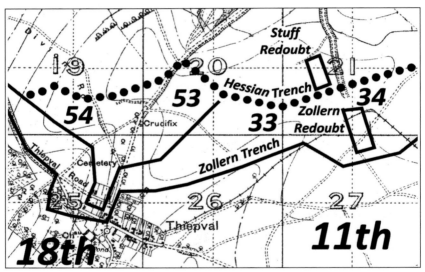

27 to 30 September, II Corps: 18th Division pushed north of Thiepval as 11th Division cleared Zollern Redoubt and captured Hessian Trench.

11th Division, Zollern and Hessian Trenches

General Woollcombe issued orders for a 10am attack but while 33 Brigade was holding a coherent line in Zollern Trench, General Hill only discovered where 34 Brigade's front line was when patrols returned at dawn. They also reported the Germans had withdrawn from Zollern Trench and Zollern Redoubt so the artillery could shell the area in front of Hessian Trench.

It took most of the morning to reorganise 34 Brigade. While Lieutenant Colonel Costa's 9th Lancashire Fusiliers[256] fought for Zollern Trench on the left, the 8th Northumberland Fusiliers tried to clear the redoubt in the centre. The 11th Manchesters reached Zollern Trench on the right, linking with the Canadians.

Then came the news that Stuff Redoubt and Hessian Trench had also been abandoned. But the Manchesters came under fire as they advanced towards Hessian Trench because the report had been wrong. As the Manchesters regrouped in Zollern Trench, General Woollcombe told his three brigadiers they had to attack again at 3pm.

Although 33 Brigade already had a continuous front in Zollern and Hessian Trenches it was a weak one with open flanks. During the early hours, two 6th Border Regiment companies joined the Staffords and Sherwood Foresters. The Staffords bombers also cleared Zollern Trench, meeting 34 Brigade on their right flank. One of the Border companies later cleared the rest of Hessian Trench and linked up with 32 Brigade. The Border Regiment took over the brigade front during the afternoon and patrols went forward as night fell, finding no one.

But 34 Brigade was exhausted after the fighting on 26 September so Woollcombe ordered 32 Brigade to capture Hessian Trench and Stuff Redoubt. When it was clear the 6th Green Howards and 9th West Yorkshires were taking too long to get to the front line, zero hour was delayed an hour. However, the order did not reach the West Yorkshires and they advanced beyond Zollern Trench alone, just after 3pm. The artillery observers saw them advance and called on their guns to move the barrage forward to cover them. But the wire protecting Zollern Redoubt pushed the West Yorkshires east, away from Hessian Trench and into Stuff Redoubt.

There was no artillery barrage when the Green Howards advanced an hour later but they took the Germans by surprise and captured eighty prisoners. By dusk the Howards held Hessian Trench, with 33 Brigade on their left and the West Yorkshires on the right. Captain Archie White of the Green Howards took command of the two depleted Yorkshire battalions and made sure they secured Stuff Redoubt. Later on the 11th Manchesters bombed north-east from Zollern Redoubt, meeting the Canadians on the Grandcourt road. On 28 September 33 Brigade was only troubled by shellfire as it sent out patrols to check out Stuff Trench. They all reported there were plenty of Germans waiting for them.

As 32 Brigade relieved 34 Brigade, the Green Howards and West Yorkshires had to finish clearing Stuff Redoubt. The 8th Duke's were supposed to link with the Canadians in Hessian Trench but congestion in

---

256 With part of the 5th Dorsets.

the trenches meant they were too late to advance at 6pm. Captain White led the two Yorkshire battalions into the north face of Stuff Redoubt but they had to withdraw when their bombs ran out.

Despite three long days of fighting, 18th and 11th Divisions had to keep pushing to fulfil Gough's orders. He wanted Stuff Redoubt and Schwaben Redoubt cleared by 29 September while Stuff Trench beyond the crest of the ridge had to be taken two days later.

At noon on 29 September the 6th York and Lancasters captured the north side of Stuff Redoubt and cleared all but 200 metres of Hessian Trench, linking up with Canadians. But the Germans forced the Yorkshire men out of the north part of the redoubt when their bombs ran out. They then faced losing the south part of the redoubt until the 7th South Staffords[257] reinforced them.

At 4pm on 30 September 11th Division sent three convergent bombing parties against the Stuff Redoubt area. Captain White bombed towards the south-west corner while the 7th South Staffords and 6th York and Lancasters[258] bombed towards the south-east corner. By nightfall they had cleared the southern half of the redoubt. Captain White was awarded the Victoria Cross for his leadership during the fight for Stuff Redoubt.

After three long days it was time for 11th Division to be relieved and General Bainbridge's 25th Division took over Hessian Trench and Stuff Redoubt during the night.

Canadian Corps, 27 to 30 September

Although General Byng was not sure where his front was, he told Gough it was close to Regina Trench. The 1st Canadian Division had suffered casualties, but the Canadian Corps still had plenty of troops available. The main problem was the exposed left flank but General Jacob had promised II Corps would clear it up and Byng told General Currie to co-operate. General Turner was also told 2nd Canadian Division had to take the rest of its objectives north of Courcelette. Only then could the Canadians attack Regina Trench.

1st Canadian Division, Zollern and Hessian Trenches

The 14th Battalion was driven out of Kenora Trench during the night but the Germans abandoned it so their artillery could shell the area. The Canadians returned the following morning and then the German bombers moved in at dusk. Enfilade machine-gun fire increased during the bombing fight and the battalion withdrew back to the support trench after seeing 200 Germans heading their way.

---

257 33 Brigade.
258 32 Brigade.

But General Byng wanted 1st Canadian Division to capture Kenora and Regina Trenches before 2nd Canadian Division took over the sector. General Currie in turn made it clear that Kenora Trench had to be taken 'even if it required the last man in the brigade to do it'. So a weak 14th Battalion prepared to advance on the understanding that 15th Battalion would co-operate on its left; but it could not because it had been relieved. So at 2am on the morning of 28 September, Lieutenant Colonel Clark attacked Kenora Trench with seventy-five men, all that was left of his battalion. The Germans were waiting for them and they illuminated the area with flares before shooting them down.

Early on 27 September 7th Battalion's[259] patrols reported Hessian Trench was empty but by the time a company moved up to occupy it, the Germans had re-entered it. In the bombing battle that followed the Canadians pushed them back towards Stuff Redoubt and Stuff Trench. While 7th Battalion had linked up with 11th Division in Zollern Trench, the machine-guns in Stuff Redoubt swept the area between Zollern and Hessian trenches with bullets.

Later that night, Brigadier General Elmsley's 8 Brigade[260] relieved 2 Brigade in Hessian Trench. Its patrols were soon reporting that parts of Regina Trench were empty.

2nd Canadian Division, Courcelette

By dawn on 27 September, General Byng knew 6 Brigade had cleared more of 2nd Canadian Division's objective. General Turner suggested clearing

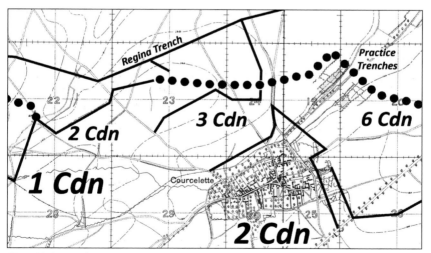

27 to 30 September, Canadian Corps: 1st and 2nd Canadian Divisions pushed north of Courcelette.

259 2 Brigade.
260 3rd Canadian Division.

the rest but 28th Battalion saw the Germans pulling out of the trenches east of the village during the afternoon and 29th Battalion saw more withdrawing on its front a few hours later.

On the left, 31st Battalion occupied the trenches north of Courcelette and it was soon joined by 27th Battalion. They then sent patrols to check out Regina Trench. It allowed 28th Battalion to advance 500 metres north-east of Courcelette while establishing contact with III Corps north of Martinpuich on its right. All the Canadians saw were a few patrols while flares fired above the Le Sars line controlled the withdrawal.

Canadian Corps, 28 September

3rd Canadian Division
Brigadier General Elmsley's 8 Brigade took over the Canadian Corps' left flank, west of the Grandcourt road. General Lipsett's arrangements to attack alongside 11th Division at 6pm were postponed until midday the following day.

2nd Canadian Division, Regina Trench
At 12.15am on 28 September General Turner told General Ketchen to attack at 7am but while 6 Brigade had over six hours to prepare, heavy rain and shelling turned the area into a quagmire. After a difficult night, the day began with an unusual sight when a cavalry patrol rode through 28th Battalion and headed north-east to test the German reaction. It did not go far before machine-gun fire from Destremont Farm sent the cavalrymen heading for the rear.

In 5 Brigade's sector 26th Battalion advanced astride Courcelette Trench only to be stopped by machine-gun fire. General Turner had been told Regina Trench had been abandoned and he told General MacDonnell to occupy it 'if possible'. But the report was incorrect and 24th Battalion's attack over the top was stopped by uncut wire; the bombers could not make any progress along the trenches either; 5 Brigade was 'too exhausted and too few in numbers' to do any more.

Brigadier General Rennie's 4 Brigade relieved 6 Brigade and while 21st Battalion pushed forward a short way, 19th Battalion was pinned by artillery fire in front of Destremont Farm. Further attempts at 3pm and 8.30pm also failed.

Summary
Gough issued instructions for new objectives and dates which coincided with Fourth Army's operations. While the Canadian Corps' left had to hold

what it had, rather than advancing to Regina Trench, the Corps' right had to push north-east towards Le Sars.

Canadian Corps, 29 and 30 September

On the morning of 29 September, General Byng told his divisional commanders they could not pass up any opportunity. But heavy rain turned the trenches into mud-filled ditches and the German artillery never let up. While Fourth Army's left captured Destremont Farm about 6am, 19th and 21st Battalions[261] moved up to extend the line to the north-west.

General Turner then told Brigadier General Macdonnell to capture 1,500 metres of Regina Trench. But 5 Brigade's patrols all came under fire when they left their trenches at 6pm. Later that night 22nd Battalion[262] took over from 26th Battalion.

General Turner persisted but General Macdonnell argued his brigade had less than 1,150 men left while his battalion commanders maintained they were too tired to advance again. There were also complaints that the artillery was 'shooting short' so all fire was stopped until the ranges had been checked out and, if necessary, adjusted. It meant General Turner had to agree to a twenty-four hour postponement on the attack on Regina Trench.

3rd Canadian Division, Hessian Trench

The 2nd Canadian Mounted Rifles[263] attacked at noon on 29 September alongside the 11th Division and captured and held a small part of Hessian Trench. The following day the Mounted Rifles' bombers helped 11th Division capture part of Hessian trench on their left. But the rest of the front line was under a heavy barrage all day, making it impossible to relieve the troops.

---

261 4 Brigade.
262 4 Brigade.
263 8 Brigade.

Chapter 11

The Weather Turns –
1 to 31 October

Haig sent a report to the Chief of the Imperial General Staff on 7 October for the War Committee's information. He estimated the Germans had engaged forty divisions on the Somme battles, the same as the number of British divisions engaged. He also estimated the number of German casualties at 370,000 men.

Haig wanted to continue the offensive but he needed reinforcements and ammunition otherwise all the advantages they had fought for would be lost. Although bad weather would make offensive operations much harder, he did not believe the winter would stop them. While the Germans had built new defence lines they were not as strong nor as deep. He did not know when the enemy would break but when they did, they would reap the 'full compensation for all that has been done to attain it'.

RESERVE ARMY, 1 TO 18 OCTOBER

Haig was hoping to attack around 12 October but Gough had to reorganise the Reserve Army west of the Ancre. Following a series of reliefs, General Congreve's XIII Corps had taken over the front from Hébuterne to Redan Ridge while Lieutenant General Edward Fanshawe's V Corps held a line arcing around Beaumont Hamel and across the River Ancre.

When Gough issued instructions for an attack by XIII and V Corps, he included arrangements for the 1st and 3rd Cavalry Divisions to move forward. But first, II Corps had to capture Schwaben Redoubt and Stuff Redoubt while the Canadian Corps had to take Regina Trench.

Canadian Corps, 1 October

General Byng agreed to delay the attack on Regina Trench until there was 'a reasonable chance of getting in' but 2nd Division had to stay in line until it had taken it. The Canadian Corps was set to attack Regina Trench at 3.15pm and the troops waited in the rain and then sought cover as their own barrage fell short.

3rd Canadian Division, Regina Trench

The protective barrage either overshot or hit 8 Brigade's assembly area and the 4th and 5th Canadian Mounted Rifles (CMR) were hit by the German barrage as they struggled through the mud. Major Parr of the 5th CMR stood on the parapet waving his men forward but they were pinned down in front of the wire. Only two groups could cut a way through and they fought their way into Regina Trench where one group was overwhelmed while the other had to withdraw.

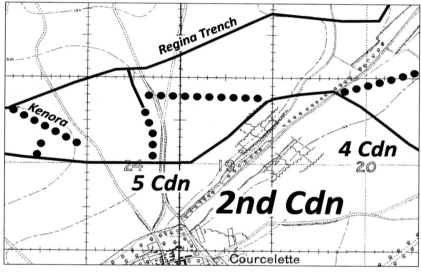

1 October, Canadian Corps: 2nd Canadian Division captured Kenora Trench and advanced towards Regina Trench.

2nd Canadian Division, Regina Trench

In 5 Brigade's sector, two parties of 24th Battalion reached Regina Trench only for one to be annihilated while the other blocked the north end of Kenora Trench. The 25th Battalion only had 200 men and while they reached Kenora Trench only a handful made it to the wire protecting Regina Trench. On the right, machine-gun fire hit the 22nd Battalion's leading waves while artillery fire hit the rear waves. The few men who made it through the wire were overwhelmed in Regina Trench. During the night 6 Brigade took over Kenora Trench and a few other posts.

On the right, 4 Brigade advanced through the mud north of Courcelette only for machine-gun fire to stop both 18th and 20th Battalions 400 metres short of Regina Trench. The Canadians withdrew during the early hours.

II Corps, 1 to 9 October
18th Division, Schwaben Redoubt
Brigadier General Jackson's 55 Brigade spent 1 October fighting for Schwaben Redoubt. Early the following morning, the Germans captured the trenches between the German front line and the east end of the redoubt; Lieutenant Chamberlain's men stopped them taking any more. The fighting died down until the 8th Norfolks[264] tried to bomb the redoubt from two directions on the morning of 5 October but they were beaten by the mud.

39th Division, Schwaben Redoubt
The 39th Division relieved 18th Division on 5 October and there were two relatively quiet days before the Germans attacked 117 Brigade with a flame-thrower; both the 17th and 16th Sherwood Foresters stood their ground. Before dawn on 9 October the 16th Sherwood Foresters made a surprise attack against the north face of the redoubt but they had to go over the top because the trenches were so deep in mud. The Germans spotted them and only the right company reached the trench; it eventually had to withdraw.

RESERVE ARMY, 8 OCTOBER
Poor weather stopped attacks for a week so reliefs were carried out; 3rd Canadian Division took over the left sector while 1st Canadian Division took over the right. The infantry worked on their assembly trenches while the artillery shelled Regina Trench, a difficult task due to the poor visibility and high winds. Patrols also reported the Germans were using concertina wire to repair the wire, a much faster way than the traditional method of wiring which used coils of wire fastened to posts or piquets.

Canadian Corps
The plan was to seize Regina Trench but 1st Canadian Division had further to go to reach the Quadrilateral, at the junction of Regina Trench and the Le Sars trenches. At 4.50am the Canadians clambered out of their trenches and trudged through the mud in pouring rain, looking for the gaps in the wire in the darkness.

---

264 53 Brigade.

3rd Canadian Division, North-west of Courcelette

In 7 Brigade's sector, Lieutenant Colonel Griesbach's 49th Battalion advanced into 'an inferno of shell and machine-gun fire'. While the left company reached Regina Trench the right company swerved towards the north end of Kenora Trench and was never seen again; machine-gun fire prevented the battalion bombers clearing the trench. On the right, the Royal Canadian Regiment had more success when its two right hand companies entered Regina Trench. Captain Spate and Lieutenant Dickson then bombed west before turning on to the West Miraumont road.

In 9 Brigade's sector, 43rd Battalion reached Regina Trench at the junction with Courcelette Trench, but it had to pull back from the isolated position. The left company of 58th Battalion could not get through the wire until Private Simmons found a gap left for German patrols, allowing the right-hand company to enter Regina Trench.

The 3rd Canadian Division's lodgements in Regina Trench were small and easily contained while machine-gun fire stopped reinforcements getting forward. It did not take the Germans long to counter-attack and Major Reid and Lieutenant Howard cheered on 58th Battalion as they fought to escape. The Royal Canadian Regiment withdrew back to its own lines before they too were surrounded.

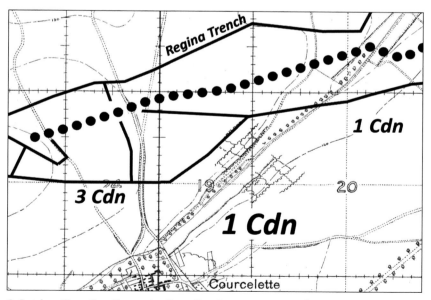

8 October, Canadian Corps: 1st Canadian Division continued to inch towards Regina Trench.

1st Canadian Division, North-east of Courcelette

As 3 Brigade's front was concave the first wave ran into the wire at different times and could not follow the barrage through to Regina Trench. It meant the Germans in the centre had plenty of time to man their parapet and both the 13th and 16th Battalions were pinned down in front of thick wire. After Major Lynch fell, Piper Jimmy Richardson 'strode up and down... playing his pipes with the greatest coolness' while his comrades cut through the barbed wire.

In 1 Brigade's sector, the wire in front of 3rd Battalion had been cut but 4th Battalion ran into intact wire, so it followed the 3rd into the Le Sars Line. After bombing through the west side of the Quadrilateral they captured 400 metres of the Le Sars Line between them.

Contact planes reported 1st Division had taken all its objective when they went airborne at first light but only isolated breakthroughs had been made. The troops in the Quadrilateral found themselves under artillery fire and under attack from the north-west and north-east; they ran out of bombs and withdrew at dusk. It left 16th Battalion in an isolated position and it too fell back. Piper Richardson was escorting prisoners and a wounded comrade back when he remembered he had left his pipes behind. He insisted on going back to look for them and was never seen again; Richardson was posthumously awarded the Victoria Cross. The only permanent gain was made by 4th Battalion on the right flank. It dug a trench close to Le Sars after dark, in touch with 23rd Division across the Bapaume road.

Summary

Gough asked Byng why the Canadians had failed to take Regina Trench and he said he had disagreed with the pre-dawn zero, believing 'If the attack had been delivered any time after midday I believe we would be there yet'. The wire cutting had failed because the artillery had used shrapnel instead of high explosive so no man's land would not be turned into a crater field. It did not help that some patrols had over-emphasised the wire cutting and underestimated the work of the German repair parties. The heavy artillery had not damaged Regina Trench because their fire was unobserved. Lieutenant-Colonel Griesbach of the 49th Battalion said the wire 'was considered to be passable upon the assumption that the enemy trench had been well battered in and the garrison had been severely shocked. With the enemy trench in being and the enemy garrison unshocked, the flimsiest wire constitutes an impassable obstacle'.

II Corps, 9 October
25th Division, Stuff Redoubt

General Bainbridge's men spent a difficult week digging in the mud as they prepared to attack Stuff Redoubt. At 12.35pm on 9 October Second Lieutenants Wilson and Hills led the 10th Cheshires[265] through the north side of Stuff Redoubt while Captain Simmons's men established posts in the old German Second Line. The Germans spent the next three days trying to dislodge the Cheshires and then Captains Atkinson and Underhill of the 8th Loyal North Lancashires held off all their attacks.

The Loyals struck back at 2.45pm on 14 October and Captain Shields' men captured the Mounds, north-west of the redoubt, taking over 100 prisoners. The patch of high ground proved to be an excellent vantage point with views over Grandcourt and the Ancre valley.

II Corps, 14 October
39th Division, Schwaben Redoubt

After a lull in the fighting, 39th Division attempted to clear Schwaben Redoubt at 2.45pm. In 118 Brigade's sector, the 1/6th Cheshires advanced along the German front line while the 4/5th Black Watch and the 1/1st Cambridgeshires bombed along redoubt trenches. Casualties were high and the Germans counter-attacked over the top until Second Lieutenant Cunningham dragged his machine-gun into the open and stopped them.

At the same time the 17th KRRC advanced over the top in 117 Brigade's area. After a battle which lasted into the night, Schwaben Redoubt was captured along with 150 prisoners. Three counter-attacks, two with flame-throwers, were stopped the following day.

FOURTH ARMY, 1 TO 18 OCTOBER

Thiepval ridge was nearly clear and Gueudecourt, Lesboeufs and Morval had been captured so Haig wanted the Third Army to extend the battle northwards. On 29 September the three army commanders were given new objectives with a target date of 12 October. Third Army had to take the spur south-east of Gommecourt to protect the Reserve Army's flank. The Reserve Army's left would advance towards Puisieux while its right would move north towards Miraumont and Irles, pinching out the steep sided Ancre valley. Fourth Army would capture Grévillers, the ridge beyond the Thilloy – Warlencourt valley, Beaulencourt and Le Transloy.

While Haig believed the objectives could be taken in seasonal autumn weather, the question was would it be seasonal? Too much rain and the

---

265 7 Brigade.

ground turned into a quagmire; too much fog or mist and the artillery observers could not work.

III Corps, 1 October

Rawlinson had already issued an order on 28 September calling for III Corps to advance with XV Corps on 1 October. The objective was to clear the Flers line between Le Sars and Eaucourt l'Abbaye so they could advance together towards the Gird Trenches.

At 7am Fourth Army's artillery opened fire all along line, to avoid drawing attention to the Le Sars area. It did not increase the rate of fire until zero hour at 3.15pm, to avoid alerting the Germans.

23rd Division, Le Sars

Major Powell had spent two days hiding in no man's land, correcting the artillery fire on the German wire in the awkward re-entrant facing 70 Brigade. The 8th KOYLIs captured Flers Trench and then, with the help of the 9th York and Lancasters, crossed the Bapaume road to meet the Canadians. However, smoke obscured the Flers Support on the outskirts of Le Sars and the left of the battalion lost direction. Lieutenant Cooke led the 11th Sherwood Foresters over the top while Lieutenant Roddle bombed along Flers Trench. Cooke's men then captured most of Flers Support, linking up with 151 Brigade on their right.

50th Division, South of Le Sars

In 151 Brigade's sector, the 1/5th Northumberland Fusiliers[266] were pinned down in front of Flers Trench but a composite battalion of the 1/5th Borders and the 1/8th Durham Light Infantry captured the first two trenches and formed blocks on its flanks. The 1/6th Durhams suffered a setback when Major Wilkinson was wounded before zero hour and then machine-gun fire hit them as they left their trench. They captured Flers Trench but were bombed out because the Londoners on the right were pinned down. Lieutenant Colonel Roland Bradford[267] reorganised the Durhams and during the night they captured Flers Trench in front of the Tangle and then Flers Support; he was awarded the Victoria Cross.

47th Division, Eaucourt l'Abbaye

While 141 Brigade advanced towards the Flers Trenches in front of Eaucourt l'Abbaye, the 1/17th London Regiment were stopped by thick wire while under machine-gun fire from their left. The 1/20th London Regiment advanced behind two tanks. A group led by Lieutenant Needham

---

266 Attached from 149 Brigade.
267 From the 1/9th Durham Light Infantry in support.

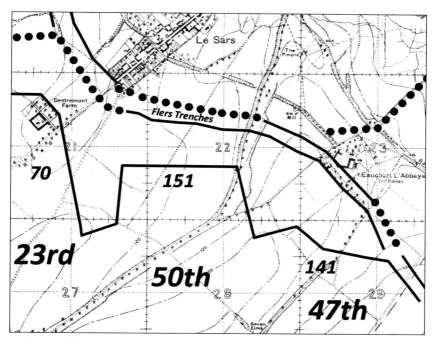

1 October, III Corps: Although 23rd Division and 50th Division cleared the Flers Trenches in front of Le Sars, 47th Division struggled to advance towards Eaucourt l'Abbaye.

captured the Flers trenches and although the tanks crawled through Eaucourt l'Abbaye, the infantry could not clear the ruins.

Machine-gun fire pinned the 1/19th London Regiment down until the tanks drove along the Flers lines, shooting at the Germans as they passed. While the leading companies went beyond Eaucourt l'Abbaye, linking up with the 1/19th London Regiment and the New Zealanders, the rear companies consolidated Flers Support.

The two tanks ditched in the Flers Trenches west of Eaucourt l'Abbaye and the crews set them on fire and withdrew when the Germans counter-attacked.

There was a 500-metre gap in the centre of III Corps line and Major General Sir George Gorringe wanted it clearing. The 1/23rd London Regiment were supposed to advance before dawn but they were delayed moving forward and advanced at 6.45am, by which time it was light; they were stopped by the same machine-guns.

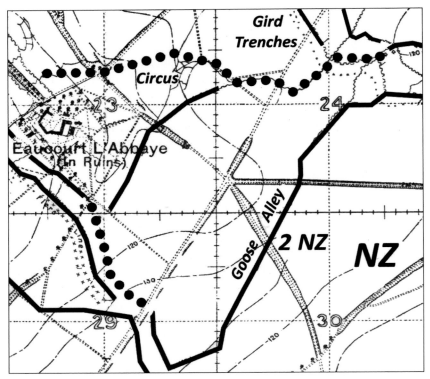

1 October, XV Corps: The New Zealand Division advanced past Eaucourt l'Abbaye.

XV Corps, 1 October
New Zealand Division, Goose Alley

An understrength 2nd Otago Battalion left Goose Alley and passed an abandoned German strongpoint called the Circus. It stopped on the Le Barque road, north-east of Eaucourt l'Abbaye, and linked up with the 1/19th London Regiment to its left. Thirty oil projectors sprayed burning oil over the Gird Trenches one minute before the infantry left their trench. An equally understrength 2nd Canterbury Battalion cleared the east end of Circus Trench, captured the German end of the Gird Trenches and linked up with the Otago men on the left. Despite heavy casualties they had taken their objective along with 250 prisoners.

FOURTH ARMY, 2 TO 6 OCTOBER

The weather turned on 2 October and two days of heavy rain soaked the troops and the battlefield.

23rd Division, Flers Support

At 6pm on 3 October the 10th Duke's tried to advance towards the outskirts of Le Sars but the trenches were close together, making it difficult to shell Flers Support. Lieutenants Stafford and Harris were killed trying to get through the wire and it was down to Second Lieutenant Henry Kelly to continue the fight. Kelly twice rallied his company and then led the three men still standing into the enemy trench. He was eventually forced to retire, carrying his injured company sergeant major; he later rescued three more men. Lieutenant Kelly was awarded the Victoria Cross.

47th Division, Eaucourt l'Abbaye

On 3 October patrols noticed the Germans had abandoned the Flers trenches in front of Eaucourt l'Abbaye and two 1/18th London Regiment companies occupied them, closing the gap on 47th Division's front. The following day the Londoners occupied an empty section of Flers Support, north-west of Eaucourt l'Abbaye; the following evening it captured a ruined mill 200 metres beyond. On 6 October a company of 11th Northumberland Fusiliers[268] entered the Tangle, east of Le Sars, but they had to withdraw under heavy fire.

The weather between 4 and 6 October was windy with rain showers, making life miserable in the trenches, while the low cloud stopped planes flying observation missions making counter-battery fire impossible. Fourth Army's attack was planned for 6 October but the bad weather delayed it until 1.45pm the following day. When the bombardment began at 3.15pm on 6 October, the German batteries retaliated.

III Corps, 7 October

The day dawned fine and zero hour was timed for 1.45pm. Although the southwest half of Le Sars could be taken, the Gird Trenches and the Butte de Warlencourt overlooked the rest of the village, so they had to be cleared first.

23rd Division, Le Sars

The 23rd Division held the arc of the Flers Trench system facing Le Sars. While 69 Brigade held the Flers Line west of Le Sars, 9th Green Howards rushed the Germans holding the south-west corner of the village and Major Barnes supervised the consolidation. Lieutenant Colonel Barker's 11th West Yorkshires advanced on the left towards Flers Support twenty minutes later but the Quadrilateral's machine-guns hit their exposed left flank.

Brigadier General Lambert organised a second attempt, only this time the Germans were attacked from two directions. Bombers worked along the

---

268 68 Brigade, 23rd Division

trench from the direction of Le Sars while the West Yorkshires advanced over the top. Many Germans were shot down as they ran while Lieutenant Hobday forced one German corporal to help him take 100 prisoners to the rear. The 10th Duke's then moved up to secure the left flank and by nightfall 69 Brigade had cleared 300 metres of the Flers Trenches.

Brigadier General Colville's 68 Brigade held the same trench south of the village and the 12th Durhams followed a tank through the Tangle until they were stopped by enfilade fire from Le Sars. The tank was knocked out as it turned towards Le Sars and the Durhams had to dig in to protect the division's right flank.

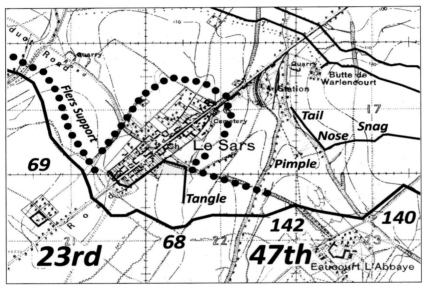

7 October, III Corps: While 23rd Division occupied Le Sars, 47th Division could not capture Snag Trench.

Captain Blake was killed leading the 13th Durhams into Le Sars around 2.30pm, so Captain Clarke led the battalion through the ruins. As the Green Howards entered the sunken lane, the 12th Durhams moved up alongside. They eventually met at the crossroads and after an afternoon of hard fighting they cleared the village between them.

Lieutenant Colonel Lindsey of the Durhams asked Brigadier General Colvile to send two companies and a tank forward to attack the Butte but neither were available. The following morning two 8th York and Lancaster[269] companies cleared more of the Flers Trenches, west of Le Sars.

---

269 70 Brigade.

47th Division, Snag Trench

North of Eaucourt l'Abbaye 140 Brigade held the line and it had to capture Snag Trench, which ran north to the Butte. The 1/8th London Regiment were hit by machine-gun fire as they emerged from the sunken road in no man's land. The 1/7th and 1/15th London Regiments, following in support, could not get any further. While Captain Bates organised the men along the road, Lieutenant Mileman got fifty men of the 1/7th London Regiment to dig a trench for survivors to crawl back to.

Later that night 142 Brigade crawled forward in heavy rain and charged when the barrage lifted at 9pm. While the 1/22nd London captured part of Snag Trench, 1/21st London could not reach a new trench in front of the Gird Trenches.

XV Corps, 7 October

41st Division

Burning oil was sprayed across the Gird Trenches in front of 122 Brigade but it made no difference. The barrage moved too quickly, allowing the German machine-guns to halt the 15th Hampshires and Lieutenant Foster and Sergeant Major Smith had to rally the survivors. The 11th Queen's Own bombers had also been unable to advance far along the two trenches. Reinforcements from 18th KRRC and 12th East Surreys helped stop the German bombers retake the trenches.

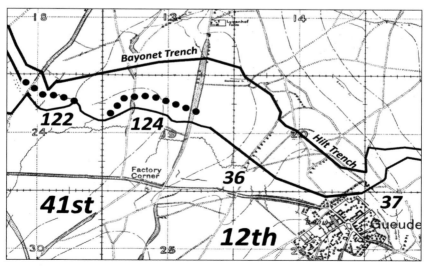

7 October, XV Corps: 41st Division struggled to get closer to Bayonet Trench while 12th Division could not capture Hilt Trench.

Brigadier General Clemson's 124 Brigade was already down to battalion strength and the machine-guns in Bayonet Trench reduced it even more. The 26th Royal Fusiliers and 32nd Royal Fusiliers were soon pinned down in shell holes and neither the 10th Queen's nor the 21st KRRC could help.

12th Division, Hilt Trench

The Germans sensed something was afoot and their artillery hit 36 Brigade's assembly area a few minutes before zero hour; the 8th and 9th Royal Fusiliers were then pinned down by machine-gun fire. Only twenty men of the 8th Battalion entered Bayonet Trench and they soon had to withdraw. The 6th Buffs were also pinned down by heavy fire until Lieutenant Colonel Cope went forward to urge them on. Sergeant Major Maxstead then organised the defence of Rainbow Trench with the sixty men still standing. The 6th Queen's Own were also stopped by the machine-guns in Hilt Trench while the few that reached the German trench had to withdraw when it was dark.

Colonel Cope was injured at the head of his men and five men, including Captain Pagen, Royal Army Medical Corps, were killed trying to rescue him. Corporal Tamblin and Lance Corporal Alexander eventually carried him to safety. Private Brown was the only Queen's Own stretcher bearer still standing but he dragged thirty injured men into shell holes before moving them into dug outs; he then looked after the men until he could escort them to safety.

XIV Corps, 7 October

Machine-gun teams, snipers and infantry platoons were holding gun pits, shell holes and short sections of trench in front of the Le Transloy defences. They were hard to spot and even harder to capture. The poor weather also meant there was no aerial observation and patrols had to be sent out to gather information.

The 6th Division and the Guards Division had occupied empty trenches beyond Gueudecourt and Lesboeufs after the Germans withdrew to a safe distance on 29 September; 20th Division did the same two days later. But following a forty-eight hour delay due to bad weather it was the turn of General Douglas-Smith's 20th Division and General Hull's 56th Division to advance east of the village on 7 October. Their first objectives were new German trenches dug beyond the crest of a ridge. Only time would tell if the wire had been cut and the garrison had been suppressed. Zero hour was at 1.45pm and the troops advanced 'as though on Salisbury Plain'.

20th Division, East of Gueudecourt

In 61 Brigade's sector the 12th King's and 7th KOYLIs were hit by machine-gun fire from their left but many Germans climbed out of Rainbow Trench and surrendered 'in large numbers, holding up their hands'. There was an awkward moment as the two lines of men met, one advancing and one surrendering. But while the prisoners were escorted to the rear, some of their comrades ran. The King's and the KOYLIs advanced to Cloudy Trench only to find it had been obliterated by artillery fire, so they started digging a new one. Captain Milligan made sure the King's threw back a defensive flank on the left where 12th Division had not advanced; Sergeant Parker brought up some of the 7th Somersets to help. Lieutenant Wright had to do the same with the KOYLIs to cover a gap in the centre of the division's front.

In 60 Brigade's sector, the 12th Rifle Brigade and 6th Ox and Bucks found few gaps in the wire and while there were heavy casualties in the first two waves, the third and fourth carried them forward. They too were met by the sight of Germans surrendering or running as they advanced as far as Misty Trench.

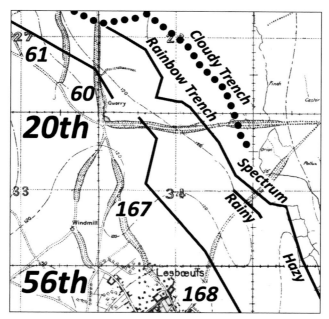

7 October, XIV Corps: Although 20th Division captured Rainbow Trench and Cloudy Trench, 56th Division could not take Rainy Trench or Spectrum Trench.

56th Division, East of Lesboeufs

On 167 Brigade's front, the 1/7th Middlesex captured Rainbow Trench at a heavy loss while the 1/1st London Regiment was pinned down in front of Spectrum Trench. The London bombers managed to find a way forward along battered trenches and shell holes to link up with the 1/7th Middlesex.

With three battalions in line, 168 Brigade staggered their start times to compensate for the different distances to their objectives. The 1/14th London Regiment left their trenches first and after capturing a group of gun-pits they reached the south end of Hazy Trench. The 1/4th London Regiment started two minutes later but were stopped by machine-gun teams hiding in a second group of gun-pits. They then tried to outflank them by moving north through the London Scottish sector. No man's land had been too narrow for the heavy artillery to hit Dewdrop Trench and the trench mortars failed to silence the machine-guns. The 1/12th London Regiment advanced four minutes after zero and were soon pinned down.

The German response was limited. A counter-attack from the direction of Beaulencourt was stopped by 20th Division while the 1/4th London Regiment and 1/14th London Regiment stopped a counter-attack. But a counter-attack from Le Transloy after dusk forced the two London Regiment battalions to withdraw; the French left did the same.

The following day 169 Brigade withdrew from Spectrum Trench and Rainy Trench so the artillery could shell the area. The advance began at 3.30pm but the men were exhausted and they struggled to climb out of the wet, slippery trenches. Once again the machine-gun teams hidden in shell holes stopped the 1/3rd London Regiment[270] reaching Spectrum Trench and the 1/9th London Regiment[271] reaching Dewdrop Trench. The 1/5th London Regiment captured Hazy Trench but counter-attacks during the night forced them to withdraw.

FOURTH ARMY, 12 OCTOBER

Planning and Preparations

On the evening of 8 October, General Rawlinson repeated his orders to secure the same objectives on 12 October. The rain finally stopped on the morning of 9 October but it would take time to dry the ground out and it was difficult to relieve the front line divisions in the mud-filled trenches.

In III Corps' sector, 15th Division replaced 23rd Division at Le Sars while 9th Division replaced 47th Division in around Eaucourt l'Abbaye. In XV Corps' sector, 30th Division replaced 41st Division north of Flers while 88 Brigade[272] was attached to 12th Division. In XIV Corps' sector, 6th

---

270 167 Brigade.
271 169 Brigade.
272 29th Division.

Division replaced 20th Division east of Gueudecourt while 4th Division replaced 56th Division east of Lesboeufs.

The incoming troops were not impressed by the state of the trenches but they did not have time to improve them. There was insufficient time to carry out adequate reconnaissance either and General Furse's request for a forty-eight hour delay, so 9th Division could complete its preparations, was refused.

Dark clouds threatened rain on 11 October but while it stayed dry, poor light reduced the quality of aerial photographs, making it difficult to locate new German trenches and batteries. The weather forecast did not look like changing so Rawlinson set zero hour for 2.05pm on 12 October. A Chinese Attack on the afternoon of the 11th unmasked several machine-guns, so the artillery could shell them.

III Corps, 12 October

III Corps had to capture the Butte de Warlencourt and the Warlencourt Line but 15th Division could not go beyond Le Sars until 9th Division had caught up. Instead it was going to release smoke to blind the Germans in the Gird Trenches and on the Butte.

9th Division, Snag Trench

The barrage was heavy but inaccurate because it had been difficult to identify trenches accurately. The smoke drifted away from 9th Division's front, leaving the 2nd South African Regiment exposed to machine-gun fire

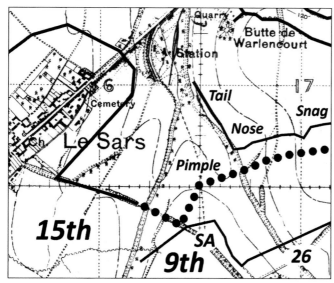

12 October, III Corps: 23rd Division and 47th Division found it difficult to advance towards the Butte de Warlencourt.

from the Butte and they did not get far. The 4th South African Regiment tried to renew the advance but they too were pinned down in front of Snag Trench.

In 26 Brigade's sector the artillery hit the 7th Seaforths in their assembly trenches. They were then stopped by machine-gun fire and the 10th Argylls could only carry them forward another 200 metres. The German artillery had cut all communications and the only reports came from the artillery and aerial spotters. Although there were rumours some men had been seen climbing the Butte, they were false and while a few men dug in in no man's land, most withdrew during the night.

XV Corps, 12 October

29th Division, the Gird Trenches

The Gird Trenches cut obliquely across 89 Brigade's front, making it difficult to plan an attack. The 17th King's were silhouetted as they advanced down the muddy slope, making them easy targets for the machine-gun teams in the shell holes behind Gird Trench; uncut wire stopped them going any further. The 2nd Bedfords captured Bite Trench, a communications trench running back to Bayonet Trench, but they were unable to bomb along the two Gird Trenches.

Although 90 Brigade faced Bayonet Trench only a few of the 17th Manchesters reached it. Machine-gun fire also stopped the 2nd Royal Scots Fusiliers in no man's land. All the survivors eventually had to withdraw.

12th Division, Bayonet Trench

In 35 Brigade's sector, the 7th Norfolks and 7th Suffolks were pinned down in front of the wire protecting Bayonet Trench. Lieutenant Eagle led a few Suffolks through a gap but they were soon forced to withdraw. The rest were unable to cut a way through, even after nightfall, and the survivors crawled back to their own trench.

In 88 Brigade's[273] sector the 1st Essex and the Newfoundland Battalion advanced north of Gueudecourt, capturing 110 prisoners. But the failure of the attacks on each flank forced them to retire to Hilt Trench where Captain Renton organised the Essex to protect their exposed left flank.

At 3.40am the following morning, the 9th Essex were stopped by uncut wire but the 1st Essex and 2nd Hampshires captured Grease Trench with 200 prisoners. The trench was incomplete so Captain Cornish and Lieutenant Harrod led some of the Hampshires as far as Stormy Trench, 200 metres beyond; they later had to withdraw from the isolated position and dig a new trench.

---

273 Attached to 12th Division from 29th Division.

XIV Corps, 12 October
6th Division, Rainbow, Cloudy and Mild Trenches
In 18 Brigade's sector, the 1st West Yorkshires were hit by the British artillery bombardment before zero hour but the 14th Durhams still captured Rainbow Trench, in touch with the Newfoundland Regiment on their left.[274] The 1st West Yorkshires could not capture Cloudy Trench or Mild Trench, either by advancing over the top or by bombing, so the Durhams bombed back along a sunken road to cover the Yorkshires' exposed right flank. The 9th Suffolks[275] did not have to advance from the salient in Cloudy Trench and Misty Trench but the 2nd York and Lancasters[276] did on their right and they tried in vain to enter a new trench called Zenith Trench.

4th Division, Spectrum, Zenith, Dewdrop and Rainy Trenches
Stokes mortars were used to shell Spectrum Trench in 12 Brigade's sector but Lieutenant Colonel Willis's[277] 2nd Lancashire Fusiliers and the 2nd Duke's were surprised by two machine-gun teams who had hidden in no man's land. The survivors tried to advance beyond the crest, only to find more machine-guns waiting for them in the newly dug Zenith Trench.

In 10 Brigade's sector the 1st Royal Irish Fusiliers advanced too fast toward Dewdrop Trench and Rainy Trench and they ran into their own barrage. It took time to reorganise and the Germans were able to man their parapet. The right of the 1st Irish Fusiliers and the left of the 1st Warwicks were shot down by fire from a strongpoint on their boundary but neither had orders to deal with it. Meanwhile, the Warwicks' right advanced 500 metres, next to the French. They then dug Antelope Trench, forming a small salient linking with the French left.

Summary, 12 October
Fourth Army had many problems on 12 October. Many battalions were understrength or relying on inexperienced replacements. Poor visibility had reduced air reconnaissance, leaving many German batteries hidden, while counter-battery work on the rest had been curtailed.

But that was not the whole story. The Germans were now used to the early afternoon attacks favoured by Rawlinson and they were usually ready and waiting. They were also deploying their machine-guns further back, in well hidden positions, opening fire when the British infantry were at their most vulnerable. At times it seemed there were machine-gun teams 'scattered all over the country'. Rawlinson was also convinced the bad weather had given the Germans the opportunity to dig in and he decided longer bombardments would be needed to break them.

---

274 88 Brigade, 29th Division, but attached to 12th Division.
275 71 Brigade.
276 16 Brigade.
277 As a captain, Willis had been awarded the Victoria Cross for leading the 1st Lancashire Fusiliers ashore on W Beach Gallipoli on 25 April 1915. It was one of six awarded to the battalion that day.

FOURTH ARMY, 18 OCTOBER

Haig approved of Rawlinson's desire to attack on 18 October and he issued Fourth Army's orders late on 13 October. After the recent failures, they both emphasized the importance getting it right; jumping off trenches had to be parallel to the objective, adequate assembly trenches had to be dug and while existing communications trenches had to be improved, new ones had to be opened up. Rawlinson was also considering making a night attack supported by tanks; a risky venture. But would the tanks be able to navigate in the dark and would they be able to co-ordinate their movements with the infantry?

Preliminary Operations
But first of all, Fourth Army had to seize new jumping off positions and straighten its line. III Corps had to take Snag Trench and the Gird Trenches while XV Corps had to clear the Gird Trenches cutting across its front. XIV Corps had to take Zenith Trench, Mild Trench and the rest of Cloudy Trench.

III Corps started well on the night of 14 October when Captain Sprenger of the 3rd South African Regiment captured the Pimple but his men were unable to go far along Snag Trench. At the opposite end of Fourth Army's line, 4th Division made several attacks at 6.30pm. The 1st King's Own[278] tried in vain to bomb along Spectrum Trench; a second attempt the following night also failed. In 10 Brigade's sector east of Lesboeufs, the 2nd Dublin Fusiliers failed to take the gun pits in front of Hazy Trench. The 2nd Seaforths also entered Rainy Trench and the nearby gun pits but a counter-attack forced them withdraw.

The following morning, 6th Division tried to improve its position northeast of Gueudecourt. The 11th Essex[279] advanced beyond Mild Trench and bombed along the road to Beaulencourt but they were later forced back. Meanwhile, the 2nd Sherwood Foresters[280] captured a line of gun pits east of Cloudy Trench, taking a number of machine-gun teams prisoner.

A mixture of showers, mist and clear weather meant the artillery and air observers had not been able to work as much as they had liked while a touch of ground frost on the night of 16/17 October showed that winter was on the way.

Zero hour set for 3.40am, two hours before dawn, but as the assault troops moved into line they faced the same old problems. The trenches were full of mud while some had been obliterated by artillery fire and replaced by flooded craters. As officers waded through the mud following compass bearings, their men knew their weapons would soon be jammed with mud and they would have to fight with bomb, bayonet and rifle butt.

---

278 12 Brigade.
279 18 Brigade.
280 71 Brigade.

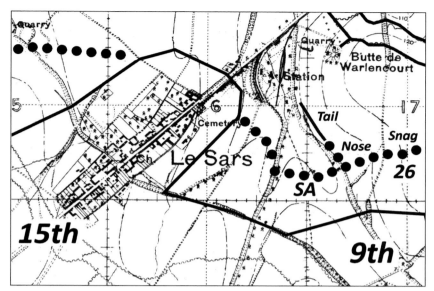

18 October, III Corps: 23rd Division improved its position around Le Sars while 47th Division captured Sang Trench.

III Corps, 18 October

Smoke and lachrymatory bombs were fired from 15th Division's front on to the Butte and the Gird Trenches to cover 9th Division's advance.

9th Division, Snag Trench

The 1st South African Regiment cleared more of Snag Trench but most were shot down as they advanced up the muddy slope towards the Butte; few returned. In 26 Brigade's sector, the 5th Camerons captured their part of Snag Trench and linked up with the South Africans.[281] Lieutenant Colonel Dawson's South Africans bombed in both directions from the Pimple and by nightfall the Germans had been pushed back to the Nose.

The Germans retaliated with a flame-thrower the following morning, driving the South Africans and 8th Black Watch back along Snag Trench until a counter-attack by Captain Taylor's Black Watch company restored the situation. Private Tait knocked out the flame-thrower team with a grenade and then Second Lieutenants Craven and Campsie led the bombers forward. But the counter-attack had exhausted the South African Brigade and 27 Brigade had to take over the maze of water-filled trenches and shell holes.

---

281 They were relieved by the 8th Black Watch later.

Despite the desperate conditions, Brigadier General Scrase-Dickens was ordered to attack at 4pm on 20 October. The appalling ground conditions were described as a 'sea of pewter-grey ooze' and they called for closer co-operation between the infantry and the artillery. The guns lengthened their range by fifty metres every time the 6th KOSBs fired a green flare. Second Lieutenant Johnson's men first captured and then had to evacuate the Nose. Lieutenant Connell sent forward reinforcements and they retook the position before forcing their way along Snag Trench when it was dark. An 11th Royal Scots company also captured 250 metres of the Tail, closing the distance to the Butte.

XV Corps, 18 October
30th Division, Gird Trenches

The assembly trenches were poor and they gave little shelter from the German artillery while the men had to withdraw to a safe distance before the barrage began, increasing their fatigue. The weather did not help either. General Shea had been counting on a moonlit night but clouds filled the sky while rain soaked his men.

In the event 89 Brigade did not attack Rainbow Trench because it faced an area of low ground of no tactical importance astride the Thilloy road. Two tanks had been allocated to 21 Brigade but one ditched in the mud and the other broke down. Captain Clay's company of the 2nd Wiltshires entered Snag Trench but only a few survived long enough to withdraw when the grenades ran out. The 18th King's reached the Nose but for some unexplained reason they did not enter the trench and instead chose to fall back; maybe they were just too tired to go on after all their exertions.

The 2nd Green Howards' attack over the top against Rainbow Trench faltered when most of the officers, including Captain Blackwood, were hit. The German machine-guns stopped reinforcements getting forward through the mud. Meanwhile, Lieutenant Field's bombers found many Germans waiting for them in Bite Trench and he withdrew his men after hearing the main attack had failed.

A tank crossed the British front line around 8am the following morning but it was unable to cross Gird Trench. So it spent the next twenty minutes crawling about in front of it, shooting at the Germans until they ran. Although the tank crew signalled for the infantry to move up, they were too disorganised, so it drove along Gird Trench as far as the Le Barque road and then headed back.

12th Division, Bayonet Trench

In 35 Brigade's sector, the 9th Essex found wire waiting for them but while the left company discovered a gap and entered Bayonet Trench, the right company could not cut a way through. The Germans soon closed in on the isolated group, forcing them to withdraw. In 88 Brigade's sector the 4th Worcesters and 2nd Hampshires[282] found a weak spot in the German defences and they captured Grease Trench with few casualties. They did, however, come under heavy fire when they advanced further. While the Worcesters blocked Hilt Trench, the Hampshires met 6th Division beyond the Beaulencourt road.

XIV Corps, 18 October

6th Division, Mild and Cloudy Trenches

German artillery fire hit 71 Brigade in Shine Trench before zero hour and it took Lieutenant Colonel Prior time to get the 9th Norfolks moving. The men, most of them inexperienced replacements, struggled to clamber over the muddy parapets and many slipped or fell back into the trench. The thick mud delayed them further and they soon lost the barrage. Most of the Norfolks became disorientated in the dark, missed their objective and were never seen again. Lieutenants Cubbit's and Blackwell's platoons reached the north-west part of Mild Trench and had to stop a counter-attack. No one made it to Cloudy Trench.

4th Division, Rainy and Dewdrop Trenches

There was a lengthy bombing fight for Spectrum Trench in 12 Brigade's sector and the 1st King's Own cleared seventy metres of Dewdrop Trench. Concealed machine-guns stopped the 1st East Lancashires advancing across a sea of mud towards Rainy and Dewdrop Trenches while the 1st Rifle Brigade were unable to hold on to the gun pits in front of Hazy Trench. The following evening a platoon of the 1st Somersets[283] occupied and held an abandoned Frosty Trench.

GHQ Planning

The weather conditions were making life hard by mid-October and the soldiers spent most of their time cold, wet and tired. Rain and mist limited aerial reconnaissance while many guns were worn out after weeks of constant use. It meant the artillery barrages were increasingly inaccurate.

On 16 October Joffre told Foch to stop making narrow attacks with shallow objectives and to concentrate on make broad attacks with deep objectives. He also sent Haig a letter on the same subject and urged him to

---

282 Attached from 29th Division.
283 11 Brigade.

plan a big offensive aimed towards Bapaume. Haig knew he was unable to and said his armies would do the best they could under the circumstances. He also knew the moment for widening the attack north of the Ancre had passed and Third Army was stood down on 17 October.

On 19 October Foch, Rawlinson and Gough met Haig at GHQ to agree the timetable for future operations. The Reserve Army would initially capture Regina Trench on Thiepval ridge on 21 October. Four days later it would attack astride Ancre while Fourth Army's left captured the Butte de Warlencourt and the area north of Gueudecourt. Fourth Army's right and French Sixth Army would then advance towards Le Transloy in two stages on 23 and 26 October. The attacks would be made 'weather permitting' but while the heavy rain stopped on 19 October, prolonged wet and stormy weather returned three days later.

RESERVE ARMY, 21 OCTOBER

Gough and Kiggell reviewed the plans for the capture of the Ancre Heights on 14 October. XIII Corps and V Corps would advance west of the Ancre while II Corps attacked to the east. After capturing Serre on the left and Miraumont on the right, they would continue towards Irles and Pys. II Corps was due to capture Regina and Stuff Trenches on 19 October with a follow up attack a few days later.

XIII Corps only had 31st Division to hold its entire front while V Corps had 3rd, 2nd, 51st and 63rd Divisions. II Corps had 39th, 25th and 18th Divisions between the Ancre and Courcelette; it also took over 4th Canadian Division when the Canadian Corps left the line.

Gough asked for extra artillery and while GHQ had transferred twelve siege batteries and the artillery from three divisions to help, the changeable autumn weather made it hard to spot targets. GHQ had added 1st Cavalry Division and tanks to Reserve Army but it was debatable whether they could travel across the muddy ground. It was also intended to detonate a new mine under Hawthorn Ridge by reopening the tunnels used on 1 July. On 19 October the attack on Regina and Stuff trenches was delayed for twenty-four hours.

The dawn of 21 October was cold but fine. II Corps had Major General Gerald Cuthbert's 39th Division facing Schwaben Redoubt on the left, General Bainbridge's 25th Division and General Maxse's 18th Division in the centre and Major General David Watson's 4th Canadian Division on the right. Two hundred heavy guns and howitzers and the field artilleries of seven divisions shelled Regina and Stuff trenches along a frontage of nearly 5,000 metres. Not only did they cut the wire, the first-rate creeping barrage starting moving forward at 12.06pm 'like a wall'.

II Corps

39th Division, Stuff Trench

Before dawn the Germans used flame throwers to establish two footholds in 116 Brigade's sector on the north side of Schwaben Redoubt. The 14th Hampshires and 17th KRRCs[284] fought hard to stop them taking any more trenches. In 117 Brigade's sector, one company each of the 16th Rifle Brigade and 17th Sherwood Foresters captured the Pope's Nose salient. In 116 Brigade's sector Captain Warren's company of the 14th Hampshire joined the 11th Sussex as they entered parts of Stuff Trench, finding it deep in mud. Meanwhile, the 13th Sussex struggled to bomb along the old German Second Line.

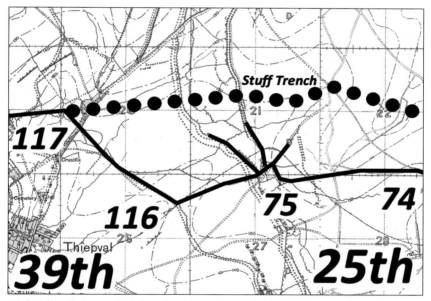

21 October, II Corps: Both 39th Division and 25th Division captured Stuff Trench.

25th Division, Stuff Trench

The barrage fell short in 75 Brigade's sector, stopping the 2nd South Lancashires advancing west of the Pozières – Miraumont road. Sergeant Major Lewis risked the artillery fire to make sure the 8th South Lancashire bombers cleared many dug-outs along Stump Road.

Meanwhile, Second Lieutenant Birnie also risked taking some of the 8th Border Regiment[285] beyond the objective, through their own barrage, to deal with a gun battery. Second Lieutenant Strong could see that a 300-metre

---

284 Attached from 117 Brigade.
285 One 11th Cheshire company attached.

gap had opened between the two brigades, so he recalled Birnie's men and they brought 150 prisoners back.

In 74 Brigade's sector the 13th Cheshires, the 9th Loyal North Lancashires and the 11th Lancashire Fusiliers followed the barrage and then had a tough fight for Stuff Trench. Second Lieutenant Beswick's bombers cleared the Fusiliers section and they linked up with the 8th Norfolks on their right.

18th Division, Stuff Trench

In 53 Brigade's sector, the 8th Norfolks won a bombing fight on the Grandcourt road. Some of the Germans facing the 10th Essex left their trench to surrender but the rest fought on in Regina Trench.

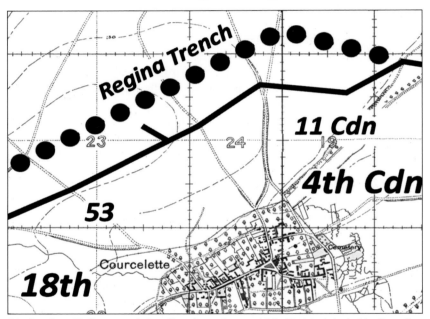

21 October, II Corps and the Canadian Corps: 18th Division and 4th Canadian Divisions worked together to clear Regina Trench.

4th Canadian Division, Regina Trench

In 11 Brigade's sector, 102nd Battalion and 87th Battalion took the Germans by surprise, capturing over 100 prisoners. While 102nd Battalion captured its part of Regina Trench, 87th Battalion formed a defensive flank, east of the Pys road.

Summary
Regina Trench had been captured, along with over 1,050 prisoners, in less than thirty minutes. Although the Germans counter-attacked 102nd Battalion in the Canadian sector several times, no ground was lost. The Germans expected a further advance to the Grandcourt Line so their artillery targeted the ground in front of the trench and they hit no one. The gunners soon realised their mistake and lengthened their range onto Stuff and Regina Trenches.

Although the crest of Thiepval ridge was in British hands, the artillery observers were disappointed with the view. While they could see across the Ancre valley, the convex curve of the hillside meant they could not see the lower slopes or the bottom of the valley.

There was little activity over the next few days, allowing II Corps and the Canadians to carry out reliefs. General Bridges' 19th Division relieved the 25th Division and part of 39th Division on the west side of Schwaben Redoubt on the night of 22/23 October.

After standing in a water-filled trench for twenty-four hours in the pouring rain, 44th Canadian Battalion[286] tried to extend its hold on Regina Trench at 7am on 25 October. But the artillery barrage was 'a flat failure' because it did not cover the Quadrilateral, leaving its machine-guns free to enfilade the attack. Before dawn on 26 October the 7th East Lancashires[287] stopped the Germans retaking Stuff Redoubt. Meanwhile 39th Division tried to improve its position around the Pope's Nose before the weather turned but heavy rain on 30 October put a stop to all attacks.

The 21 October attack was successful, but the poor weather meant the main operation had to be repeatedly postponed. The troops were lashed with rain, frozen by low temperatures, battered by high winds and blanketed by mist as they waited in their water-filled trenches.

V Corps, North of the Ancre

On 28 October steps were taken to make life uncomfortable for the Germans in Beaumont Hamel. Stokes mortars fired 1,126 lachrymatory bombs into the village in two minutes.[288] Later that night mortars fired 135 phosgene bombs at the trenches around Beaumont Hamel.[289] But otherwise the area was quiet as the soldiers struggled on. Patrols and raiding parties often found the Germans had abandoned their front line, preferring to stay in their dug outs further back.

FOURTH ARMY

By the end of October, Fourth Army's attacks were coming to an end as GHQ's focus shifted to the Reserve Army. Fourth Army operations were

286 10th Canadian Brigade.
287 56th Brigade, 19th Division.
288 Lachrymatory bombs gave off a form of tear gas.
289 Phosgene is a gas which attacks the respiratory system.

limited to taking trenches of tactical significance and battalions rarely deployed more than two weak companies, or a couple of hundred men, at a time.

XIV Corps, 23 October

XIV Corps wanted to get closer to Le Transloy but the thick morning mist interfered with the preliminary bombardment. The French insisted on delaying zero hour to 2.30pm so the artillery could have better visibility while the speed of the barrage was reduced to fifty metres per minute because of the muddy ground.

8th Division, Zenith Trench

General Hudson's 8th Division had all three brigades in line east of Gueudecourt. In 24 Brigade's sector the 2nd East Lancashires had a close call because the change in zero hour only reached Colonel Hill at the last moment. But they captured and held Mild Trench, eliminating a re-entrant in the brigade's centre.

The 2nd Rifle Brigade could not capture a strongpoint at the junction of Eclipse and Zenith Trenches in 25 Brigade's sector but they occupied nearby shell holes. The British barrage had stopped the Germans evacuating Zenith Trench in front of the 2nd Lincolns so they had to stand and fight and fight they did. A German officer ran along the parapet encouraging his men to fire and only a few of Captain Burton's and Lieutenant Dysdale's men made it across no man's land.

In 23 Brigade's sector, both the 2nd Middlesex and the 2nd Scottish Rifles stormed the south end of Zenith Trench. Second Lieutenant Ferguson of the Rifles knocked out three machine-guns with the help of Sergeant Hawkins and Private Murray. Although the Middlesex could not bomb the trench in front of the Lincolns, the Rifles also captured Orion Trench; they had to withdraw later on.

At 3.50am 25 Brigade made another attempt to take the north end of Zenith Trench but mud stopped the 1st Irish Rifles and 2nd Berkshire from keeping up with the barrage. The Germans were waiting for them and they were 'simply swept away'. Heavy rain resulted in a final attack on 29 October being cancelled; 8th Division was 'utterly exhausted'.

4th Division, Spectrum and Dewdrop Trenches

General Lambton's 4th Division advanced from the trenches east of Lesboeufs. In 12 Brigade's sector, the 1st King's Own advanced beyond Spectrum Trench as Captain Henniker led the 2nd Duke's bombers along

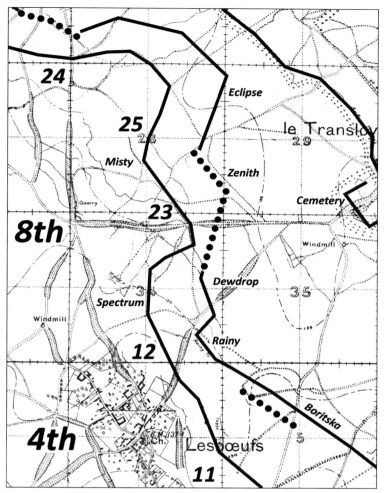

23 October, XIV Corps: Both 8th Division and 4th Division struggled to make progress towards Le Transloy because of the strongpoint in the cemetery.

the Le Transloy road; they later had to withdraw to Spectrum Trench. Meanwhile, the 2nd Essex was stopped by machine-gun fire where Dewdrop Trench crossed the Le Transloy road. The few men who made it to the objective were either killed or captured.

In 11 Brigade's sector the 2nd Dublin Fusiliers secured gun pits and a strongpoint but the advance was delayed when the 1st Warwicks became mixed in with them. Sergeant Robert Downie encouraged his men to keep going with shouts of 'Come on the Dub's'[290] and while they overran the trench beyond, enfilade fire from Boritska Trench stopped them going any further. Although wounded, Downie stayed with his men and he was later awarded the Victoria Cross.

The 1st Hampshires were hit by machine-gun fire from Boritska Trench and Captains Cromie's and Le Marchant's men were pinned down in shell holes. When the 1st Rifle Brigade moved up, some men swerved to the left to avoid the fire from Boritska Trench and they ended up digging in north-west of the objective, alongside the Fusiliers.

XIV Corps, 28 October

The weather deteriorated on 24 October and the attack against Le Transloy was repeatedly postponed. Eventually on 31 October Haig and Foch agreed to delay XIV Corps' attack until 5 November. In the meantime, 17th Division relieved 8th Division while 33rd Division relieved 4th Division.

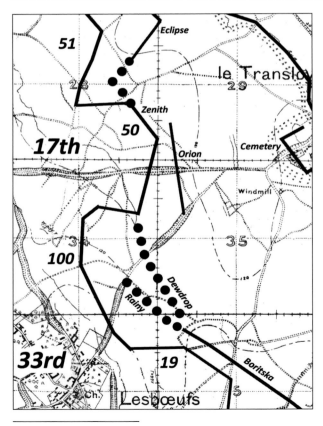

28 October, XIV Corps: Although 17th Division could not get closer to Le Transloy, 33rd Division captured Rainy and Dewdrop Trenches.

---

290 A sporting cry for Dublin often heard during a hurling or Gaelic football match.

17th Division, Eclipse and Zenith Trenches

The plan was for 51 Brigade to clear the salient north-east of Gueudecourt, formed by Eclipse Trench and Zenith Trench and at 5.30pm on 2 November the 7th Borders captured the south side of the salient. The following day the 7th Lincolns stopped German counter-attacks before clearing more of Zenith Trench with the 7th Green Howards' bombers. It was 50 Brigade's turn next but the 7th East Yorkshires and the 7th Green Howards' patrols could not advance far from Zenith Trench on 5 November.

33rd Division, East of Lesboeufs

At 6am on 28 October 98 Brigade attacked and the 4th King's captured Dewdrop Trench along with 150 prisoners. The 1st Middlesex were hit by machine-gun fire but they cleared the rest of Dewdrop Trench and Rainy Trench, taking over sixty prisoners and two machine-guns. Between them the two battalions had removed most of the re-entrant in 33rd Division's line.[291]

The following morning 19 Brigade attacked at 5.45am. While the 5th/6th Scottish Rifles captured the north end of Boritska Trench, the 1st Scottish Rifles were stopped by German machine-gun teams sheltering in nearby shell holes. All the Scottish Rifles withdrew later.

---

291 The divisional history says it was the 2nd Worcesters and 4th Suffolks.

Chapter 12

One Final Push –
1 to 19 November

FIFTH ARMY[292]

On 27 October the provisional date for the next attack was set for 1 November. But the bad weather persisted and on 3 November Haig allowed Gough to postpone the attack indefinitely. All Fifth Army could do was to prepare in case there was a spell of good weather.

On 5 November Haig suggested Fifth Army could make a scaled down attack and Gough thought V Corps could attack Serre and Beaumont Hamel while II Corps advanced on the east bank of the Ancre. After clear weather on 6 November, Gough said he could attack three days later provided the weather stayed dry but Haig wanted the ground to be dry enough to move across. The weather forecast indicated dry days were imminent so the attack was postponed to allow conditions to improve.

On 8 November Kiggell discussed the matter with Gough, who in turn spoke to his corps commanders. The date was set for 13 November, providing there was no more heavy rain. In the meantime, patrols and staff officers would check the ground conditions. As the weather eased on 9 November, the artillery observers could shell targets once again.

4th Canadian Division, Regina Trench
As midnight approached on 10 November, 10 Brigade crept forward under a clear moonlit sky while a 'perfect' artillery barrage hit the east part of Regina Trench. After only eight minutes the guns lifted and 46th and 47th Battalions overran the trench while a company of 102nd Battalion did the same in 11 Brigade's sector. They had taken the Germans by surprise and had captured nearly ninety prisoners.

---

292 The Reserve Army was renamed Fifth Army on 30 October.

XIV Corps, 1 November
17th Division, Zenith Trench and Eclipse Trench

At 5.30pm on 2 November a company of the 7th Border Regiment crept forward from Misty Trench and Gusty Trench in 51 Brigade's sector. There was no preliminary bombardment and the German sentries did not spot them in the winter gloom until the last minute; they ran the final few metres and captured Zenith Trench and Eclipse Trench. The 7th Lincolns relieved the Border Regiment and they had to stop several counter-attacks over the next 24 hours. Second Lieutenant Watts and the 7th Green Howards bombers helped to clear the rest of Zenith Trench during the evening.

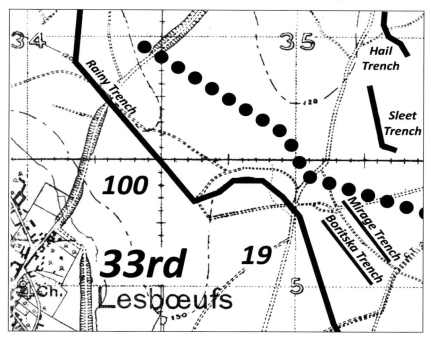

1 November XIV Corps: 33rd Division struggled in awful conditions to advance towards Le Transloy.

33rd Division, Boritska Trench

At 5.45am on 1 November 19 Brigade attacked on the division's right. Some of the 5/6th Scottish Rifles briefly held Boritska Trench but the 1st Scottish Rifles did not make it across no man's land. The next attempt was to be made by 100 Brigade at 3.30pm on 1 November, but both Captain Henderson of the 2nd Worcesters and Lieutenant Colonel Stormonth

Darling of the 1/9th Highland Light Infantry were killed by snipers while out reconnoitring the German trenches. So the officers and men had no idea what to expect as they waited 'up to the waist in slime' for zero hour. Neither battalion could reach Boritska Trench, mainly due to the machine-guns around Le Transloy cemetery. However, the French captured most of their part of Boritska Trench and the Tranchée de Tours, to the south-east.

At 4pm on 3 November the 1st Queen's[293] again tried to capture the troublesome Boritska Trench but the French barrage overshot the target, leaving the Germans free to shoot them down. The following day 98 Brigade was unable to reach the ridge east of Dewdrop Trench.

On 5 November the machine-guns in the cemetery stopped the 2nd Royal Welsh Fusiliers[294] advancing astride the Le Transloy road but 100 Brigade had more success on the right, with the 16th KRRC capturing Hazy Trench[295] while the 2nd Worcesters advanced from French trenches. Lieutenant Eugene Bennett led sixty survivors into Boritska Trench and Mirage Trench after seeing the first wave pinned down. Although wounded, he organised the consolidation of the trenches; finally Boritska Trench was in British hands.

Summary
After four days, XIV Corps had done little to improve its position in front of Lesboeufs. General Robertson of 17th Division summarised the conditions with the following words:

> 'The weather conditions have been simply appalling and the trenches awful; men buried in mud, several deaths from exposure alone, men drowned in mud... I wonder if those behind the lines have the slightest conception of what it is like.'

FOURTH ARMY, 5 November
Fourth Army's left and centre had been on the defensive since 18 October, waiting for Fifth Army to achieve its objectives. General Birdwood's I Anzac Corps relieved XV Corps[296] in the centre of the Fourth Army front during the lull.

On 30 October the decision was taken to straighten the line between the Butte de Warlencourt and Gueudecourt. The date was later set for the 5 November to coincide with the attacks to be made by XIV Corps and the French; but only if the weather permitted.

Over 5,300 casualties had been suffered attacking Le Transloy from the west and on 3 November General Cavan asked if XIV Corps could attack

---

293 From 100 Brigade.
294 19 Brigade.
295 Hazy Trench indeed because there was hardly anything left of it.
296 XV Corps had held Fourth Army's centre since 1 July.

it from the south. The following day Haig told Foch how XIV Corps would only capture the German positions east and north-east of Lesboeufs. Foch intended to attack St Pierre Vaast Wood and Government Farm on 5 November so Haig promised Fourth Army would attack at the same time, pushing the Germans into a salient.

Heavy rain gave way to high winds the following morning and while the open ground dried out, trenches and shell holes were still deep in mud and water. When zero hour came at 11.10am, the troops struggled to pull themselves out of the assembly trenches and then there was another problem. The speed of the barrage had been reduced to twenty-five metres a minute and it was too slow, leaving the Germans time to man their parapets.

III Corps

50th Division, Butte de Warlencourt

It took 151 Brigade too long to get moving and they lost the barrage as they waded through the mud in pouring rain. But the 1/9th Durhams crossed Butte Trench and Butte Alley and Lieutenant Colonel Bradford established a post on top of the Butte. Some men also reached the Warlencourt Line

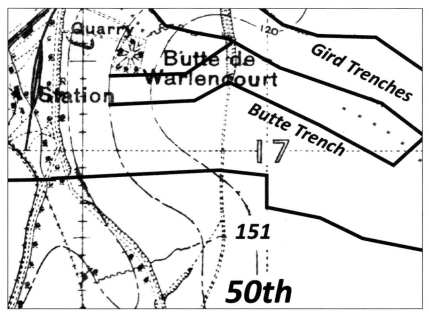

5 November, III Corps: 50th Division faced a series of trenches around the Butte de Warlencourt and the mound could only be held for a few hours.

where it crossed the Bapaume road. A few of the 1/6th Durhams reached the Butte on the left but enfilade fire from Gird Trench pinned the rest down alongside Captain Clark's company of the 1/8th Durhams. The Germans were determined not to give up the Butte and the Durham's advanced posts were forced back during the afternoon. By midnight they had withdrawn from Butte Trench to their own lines.

I ANZAC Corps

Fourth Army's order said the salient north of Gueudecourt would be attacked when the weather permitted. Brigadier General Paton said 7 Brigade was not ready to attack the Maze in 2nd Australian Division's sector but General Legge overruled him. The attack was made at 12.30am in pouring rain.

2nd Australian Division, The Maze

Some companies moved out on time, only for their barrage to land behind them. Some companies advanced three minutes late due to a misunderstanding over times and they could not catch up with the barrage because of the thick mud. The 28th Battalion was pinned down 100 metres in front of the Gird trenches; a second attack also failed. A composite battalion captured the Maze in the centre while 27th Battalion entered Bayonet Trench at several points. But these isolated positions were soon under attack and everyone withdrew after dusk.

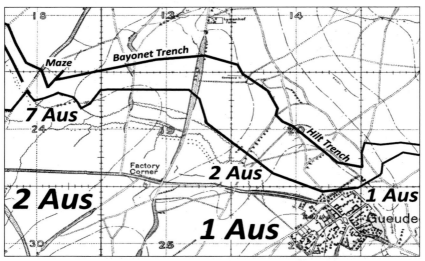

5 November, I ANZAC Corps: While 2nd Australian Division could not capture the Maze, 1st Australian Division was unable to clear Hilt Trench.

1st Australian Division, Hilt Trench

General Smythe's 1 Brigade had to clear a salient north-west of Gueudecourt. However 1st Battalion floundered in the mud, could not keep up with the barrage and was stopped by Hilt Trench's machine-guns; a bombing attack was also stopped. The 3rd Battalion's bombing parties entered Lard Trench on the right and moved both ways around the east side of the salient. The left hand party could not advance along Hilt Trench but the right hand party joined a bombing group moving up the Thilloy road. But 1st Battalion had been unable to get into Hilt Trench and the bombers withdrew when their bombs ran out.

Summary

On 6 November Rawlinson explained Haig's plans to his corps commanders. Allied policy was to keep the pressure on the Germans, stopping divisions moving to other theatres. However, the reality was the French were no longer planning large-scale attacks while the British did not have the manpower to make them. The winter weather was also an important factor. While Fifth Army planned to attack on 9 November, Fourth Army could only repeat its small attacks against tactical points.

The following day, the French Sixth Army announced their objectives were the northern half of St Pierre Vaast Wood and Sailly-Saillisel. While there were negotiations for XIV Corps to take over the line south of Le Transloy, the relief had to wait until the weather improved.

13 to 19 November

Plans and Preparations

The temperature dropped as the skies cleared on 8 November and with the forecast predicting dry weather, Gough set zero hour for 5.45am, 13 November. XIII Corps would establish a defensive flank north of Serre while V Corps made the breakthrough between Redan Ridge and the River Ancre. II Corps would advance along the south bank of the Ancre. Gough also considered how V Corps and II Corps could advance towards Irles and Pys if there was a breakthrough.

On 12 November Kiggell told Gough that Haig 'did not in any way wish to bring on a battle in unfavourable conditions', an unexpected statement considering how many recent attacks had been made in appalling weather. Gough said his divisions had been in the front line for too long and they had to be relieved if they did not attack on 13 November. Haig then visited Gough to tell him he did not want Fifth Army to risk too much but it would help the Russian and Romanian fronts if the attack succeeded.

Fifth Army's heavy guns and howitzers would shell roads, trenches and villages around the objectives while the guns on the flanks shelled distant targets, to make it look like the attack front was wider. False hour-long barrages were fired every morning to get the Germans used to a routine[297] but the start of the intense barrage would signal zero hour on the morning of the attack. While the majority of the guns would shell the German trenches, one in four of the field guns would reduce their range by fifty metres to cover the infantry advance. Then six minutes after zero the barrage would advance at 100 metres every five minutes. The whole idea was to make the Germans think the barrage was still ongoing while the assault troops crossed no man's land. The level of sophistication in the bombardment plan was a complete contrast to the crude jumping barrage used in the same area on 1 July.

Mist and low cloud stopped the artillery spotters doing their work on 11 and 12 November. Mist was also expected at zero hour so innovative sound signals were arranged to let the infantry know what the artillery was doing. The barrage would stop to give the troops a five-minute warning and the first wave would move off when the artillery started again, firing as fast as possible. It both was a clever and dependable way of co-ordinating the infantry advance with the artillery barrage.

One last question was would the tanks cope with the mud? When the first tanks moved forward on the evening of 11 November, the company commander believed the ground was too soft. As many as possible withdrew the following night but some had to stay near the front line.

Then as it grew dark on 12 November, the infantry marched forward under a clear moonlit sky. It did not last for long because a thick fog covered the battlefield, reducing visibility to thirty metres. Fifth Army's troops would have to grope their way through the foggy darkness to reach the German lines.

XIII Corps

31st Division, Serre

The plan was for 92 Brigade to form a defensive flank and 93 Brigade had placed thirty-six machine-guns south-east of Hebuterne to cover its left flank. Snipers and Lewis gun teams were also hiding in shell holes out in no man's land ready to give covering fire.

The 12th and 13th East Yorkshires advanced through the mist and overran the front line, but there was a tough fight for the support trench. Private John Cunningham led a section of 12th East Yorkshire's bombers until he was the only man standing. After collecting all the bombs from the

---

297 At 5am on 12 November 180 lachrymatory bombs hit Beaumont Hamel and at 3.30pm over eighty gas drums hit the village and Y Ravine.

casualties he twice went forward alone, clearing a communications trench and killing ten Germans. Private Cunningham was awarded the Victoria Cross. Only a few of the 13th East Yorkshires reached the reserve line on the right and most were captured or killed. The group detailed to hold an old mine crater opposite John Copse were all killed or injured.

By 8am the Germans were driving the Yorkshiremen back down the communication trenches, while a counter-attack from Star Wood at 9.30am was stopped by machine-gun fire. Artillery fire stopped two 11th East Yorkshire companies and carrying parties crossing no man's land.

By 8am General Wanless O'Gowan knew 3rd Division's attack had failed, leaving 92 Brigade isolated. Although he wanted to arrange a new attack, it took two hours to contact 3rd Division headquarters, by which time the Yorkshiremen were back in the German front trench.[298] 3rd Division was unable to do anything and at 5.30pm V Corps said it could not renew its attack.

At dusk 92 Brigade began sending its wounded back and the last parties made it back to safety at about 9.30pm. While the two battalions had lost nearly 800 officers and men, the Germans had also suffered heavy losses; the Yorkshiremen also took over 130 prisoners.

V Corps

General Deverell's 3rd Division had to cross Serre Trench and capture the ruins of Serre village. Major-General William Walker's[299] 2nd Division was to advance over the Redan Ridge, north of Beaumont Hamel, to Frankfurt Trench. General Harper's 51st Division had to pass through Beaumont Hamel and Y Ravine while the second objective was part of Frankfurt Trench. Major-General Cameron Shute's 63rd (Royal Naval) Division faced the trenches on the west bank of the River Ancre.

3rd Division, Serre

The original plan was for three brigades to advance through the German trenches and then wheel left to form a defensive flank alongside 31st Division. However, thick mud in the trenches meant only two brigades could deploy.

The assault troops lost cohesion in the mist as 76 Brigade advanced from Matthew, Mark and Luke Copses. The first trench was overrun but only a few 2nd Suffolks and 10th Welsh Fusiliers under Captains Rudd and Bishop reached Serre Trench in the gloom; they were never seen again. The 8th King's Own and 1st Gordons became disorganised as they passed through the leading battalions and only a few reached Walter Trench on the right.

---

298 The problem was 31st Division was with XIII Corps and 3rd Division was with V Corps.
299 Walker had been awarded the Victoria Cross during the Third Somaliland Expedition in 1903.

The German barrage stopped the King's Own support companies crossing no man's land.

Then the Germans overwhelmed the men in Serre Trench and recaptured the support trench; by 6.30am exhausted men were withdrawing across no man's land. Some were pinned down and had to wait until dusk before they could escape.

In 8 Brigade's sector the 1st Royal Scots Fusiliers and 2nd Royal Scots lost direction as they advanced astride the Serre road. They also lost the barrage and floundered in the thick mud in no man's land.[300] To make matters worse, the fog was thinner on the low ground, so the Germans around Serre could see the brigade struggling.

Then Captain Strange's men were shot down cutting through the wire. The support waves struggled to find the gaps in the fog and only a few groups made it to the German trenches. Even fewer made it to the support line including one group led by Captain Spafford of the Royal Scots. They were soon forced to withdraw. Some had moved south where 2nd Division was having more success.

Deverell urged his brigades to attack again at 7.30am, to reinforce the isolated parties in the German trenches. While the field artillery barrage shortened their range to Walter Trench, the heavy artillery shelled Serre Trench and Serre.

When General Fanshawe made it clear there had been a breakthrough to the north and south at 10.30am, Deverell sent forward a battalion from 9 Brigade to each brigade.[301] The problem was the telephone wires between 3rd and 2nd Division were cut until 4.30pm.

General Fanshawe's plan was for the 9 Brigade's battalions to make a second attack alongside two 2nd Division battalions. But the German artillery fire did not stop and at 12.45pm General Deverell told General Fanshawe the attack had little chance of succeeding and he wanted to reinforce the men in the German trenches instead. The commander of 31st Division agreed. Although they suggested making an attack at 10pm, General Gough cancelled further operations at 4.30pm.

2nd Division, Frankfurt Trench

On the south side of the Serre Road 6 Brigade faced the Quadrilateral where the mud was thick and the fog was thicker. The 2nd South Staffords took time to cut through the wire, lost the barrage and then came under machine-gun fire from the left flank. Then men from 3rd Division advanced across their front. The Staffords became disorientated, advanced north-east astride the Serre road and the 17th Middlesex followed. Although they captured

---

300 The 7th Shropshires and the 8th East Yorkshires were following in support.
301 There was no breakthrough to the north, 31st Division was fighting to hold a few trenches west of Serre.

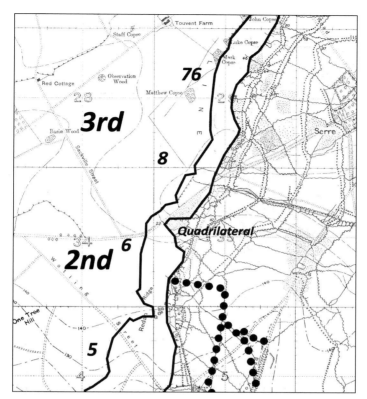

13 November, VIII Corps: 3rd Division failed to advance towards Serre but 2nd Division made progress on Redan Ridge.

several German trenches, they were the wrong ones, leaving Sergeant Major Cox's men isolated. The 13th Essex had the same difficulty fighting their way past the Quadrilateral but a few of Captain Carson's men reached Beaumont Trench and blocked Lager Alley.

In 5 Brigade's sector the 24th Royal Fusiliers and 2nd Highland Light Infantry had to assemble in no man's land because their trenches were deep in mud. Captain Watkyn-Thomas's men captured many Germans in their dug-outs and they kept going as far Beaumont Trench. Meanwhile, the 2nd Ox and Bucks and 17th Royal Fusiliers veered left in the fog and captured Lager Trench which was at right-angles to their objective.

Although Brigadier General Bullen-Smith's flanks were exposed, General Walker's plan was for the support battalions to advance to Frankfurt Trench at 7.30am. But 6 Brigade was too far to the north while 5 Brigade was scattered around the German trenches or pinned down in no man's land. Even so a few isolated groups advanced over the crest to Frankfurt Trench: they were soon making a fighting withdrawal to Munich Trench. Counter-attacks forced them back to Beaumont Trench while some men held on in Crater Lane and the sunken Wagon Road in the centre.

At 9am General Walker instructed Brigadier General Daly to withdraw his men back to the British trenches ready to make a second attack but the reality was 6 Brigade was in no condition to fight. So Walker ordered two 99 Brigade battalions forward to comply with V Corps' order. They would cross no man's land south of the Quadrilateral ready to attack Bow Trench alongside 3rd Division.

However the situation at the front was changing. General Bullen-Smith reported Beaumont Trench was under threat so two of the 23rd Royal Fusiliers companies were sent forward to reinforce 5 Brigade at 9.30am. General Daly then reported 6 Brigade's foothold in Serre Trench was under pressure and the 22nd Royal Fusiliers were ordered forward to establish a line facing towards the Quadrilateral at 2pm.

Fanshawe cancelled the attack after reading Deverell's report on 3rd Division's situation and at 3pm he ordered Brigadier General Kellett to prepare to attack Munich Trench. But the situation was hopeless. No one was sure if 6 Brigade would be able to hold on and it would probably be dark by the time 99 Brigade's three battalions were ready. Fanshawe would have to postpone the attack until the following morning but could 2nd Division hold on that long?

A mixed group of Essex and King's along with some of the Ox and Bucks held onto the junction of Serre Trench and Lager Lane, securing the northern end of Beaumont Trench. They were later joined by the 22nd Royal Fusiliers[302] who secured the division's left flank.

On 5 Brigade's front, the 17th Royal Fusiliers held outposts in Crater Lane and Wagon Road while the 24th Royal Fusiliers and 2nd Highland Light Infantry held the rest of Beaumont Trench. Two 23rd Royal Fusiliers companies[303] reinforced the line later.

51st Division, Beaumont Hamel and Y Ravine
The Scots left their trenches six minutes before zero hour while the barrage started the moment the mine detonated under Hawthorn Crater.

Brigadier General Burn's 152 Brigade faced the west side of Beaumont Hamel. The 1/8th Argylls were hit by machine-gun fire crossing no man's land but they cleared the first two trenches. The 1/5th Seaforths took time to find gaps through the wire in the fog and they then faced a tough fight in

302 From 99 Brigade.
303 From 99 Brigade.

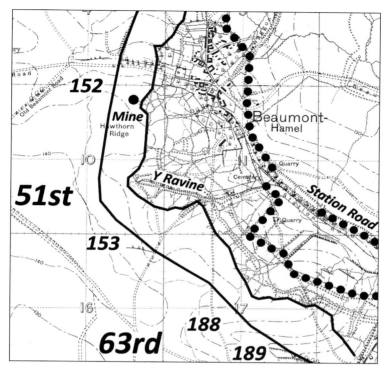

13 November, VIII Corps: As 51st Division cleared Beaumont Hamel, 63rd Division struggled to advance alongside.

the trenches south of Hawthorn Crater. Both battalions soon lost contact with the creeping barrage.

The 1/6th Seaforths helped the 1/5th Seaforths reach the west side of Beaumont Hamel while the 1/6th Gordons sent bombers forward to clear the dug-outs. Two tanks drove forward to support the Scots but one ditched in the German trenches and the other ditched on the north side of the village. General Burn's men carried on mopping up and by mid-afternoon they had reached the east side. At 4pm Lieutenant Colonel Campbell's Argylls were ordered to link up with 2nd Division but the British barrage stopped them advancing north along Wagon Road.

In 153 Brigade's sector, the machine guns at the west end of Y Ravine pinned down most of the 1/6th Black Watch but a few advanced past the northern end and entered Beaumont Hamel. The two left hand companies of the 1/7th Gordons had a tough fight for the middle of Y Ravine and the 1/5th Gordons had to help them but the two right-hand companies crossed the trenches at the eastern end and reached Station Road. Germans could be seen falling back to Beaucourt Trench, so the Gordons went forward and captured forty prisoners before withdrawing back to Station Road.

By 10.30am Brigadier General Campbell knew Y Ravine was holding up his centre so he ordered the 1/4th Gordon Highlanders[304] to surround the gully while Lieutenant Leslie led the Black Watch bombers in from the north side where they took over 100 prisoners. Lieutenant Colonel Booth took another group of forty 1/6th Black Watch to the western end of ravine and started calling for everyone to give up. Private De Reuter of the 1/7th Black Watch could speak German and he convinced another 100 to surrender. By early afternoon Y Ravine was clear and the 1/4th Gordons, the 1/5th Gordons and the 1/6th Black Watch had reached Beaumont Hamel.

By late afternoon 51st Division was dug in along the first objective. The only problem was 63rd Division could not be seen along Station Road to the right, so the 1/5th Gordons established a defensive flank.

63rd (Royal Naval) Division, West Bank of the Ancre

The German barrage caused over seventy casualties while the troops assembled in no man's land on the west bank of the Ancre. As zero hour approached, they crept across the steep slopes through the mist to get close to the German trenches.

Early on 188 Brigade was compromised by the Scots difficulties to their left and Lieutenant Colonel Cartwright's 1st Royal Marines were pinned down after their company commander was killed. Lieutenant Colonel Hutchinson waved his cap and shouted 'Come on Royal Marines' but his 2nd Battalion was also hit by heavy fire from their left flank. Most of the Howe and Anson Battalions were also pinned down in no man's land. Eventually Lieutenant Commander Gilliland[305] rallied 100 men from the Howe, Anson and Nelson battalions and they broke through on the left, heading for Station Road.

Other small groups of Marines kept advancing alongside 51st Division and Captain Gowney's group went as far as the German third trench but there were not enough to mop up the trenches and isolated groups of Germans fought back. Commander Ramsey-Fairfax of the Anson battalion led a bombing attack to silence one troublesome strongpoint which was shooting at anyone who moved in 188 Brigade's area.

On 189 Brigade's left, Lieutenant Colonel Wilson's Hawke Battalion was shot down by a hidden strongpoint and Lieutenant Colonel Burge's Nelson Battalion did not see the disaster unfolding in the mist so it suffered the same fate. On the right, the Hood Battalion and the Drake Battalion

---

304 From 154 Brigade.
305 The Anson Battalion's commanding officer.

came under machine-gun fire from the left, where the Hawke and Nelson battalions were supposed to be. They had a tough fight for the front line trenches but they persevered and captured 300 prisoners.

Lieutenant Colonel Bernard Freyberg of the Hood Battalion rallied everyone he could find and led them forward on a compass bearing when the barrage lifted. The advance involved negotiating water-filled shell craters and mud-filled trenches in the thick mist but they captured 400 prisoners along Station Road and around Beaucourt station next to the river. A company of the 1st Honourable Artillery Company (HAC) captured the Mound and then followed the railway embankment alongside the river, clearing dug-outs along way.

While both brigades had made breakthroughs, 188 Brigade was unable to go any further; 189 Brigade had reached the first objective but it had also suffered heavy casualties. So General Shute ordered Brigadier General Heneker's 190 Brigade forward to continue the advance to the second objective.

The trouble was there were still too many Germans holding out in the front trenches. The 10th Dublin Fusiliers and 4th Bedfords were hit as they crossed no man's land and only a few joined 188 Brigade on the Beaumont Hamel spur. The same happened to the 7th Royal Fusiliers in 189 Brigade's sector and only the HAC reached the German reserve line. General Shute wanted the pockets of resistance cleared up and General Heneker was ordered to exploit the HAC's breakthrough and bomb north-west into the trenches. Unfortunately, everyone was either busy fighting in the German trenches or pinned down in no man's land. The mist stopped aerial reconnaissance so Shute had little idea how far his men had advanced and all he could do was hope they could hold on.

While Commander Gilliland's group of 188 Brigade's men advanced on time to Beaucourt Trench, west of Beaucourt, they were on their own. The rest of the brigade was fully engaged clearing the German front system 1,500 metres behind them. Lieutenant Colonel Freyberg also led around 500 men from the Hood, Drake and HAC Battalions, to Beaucourt Trench, next to the river. A combination of British and German artillery fire stopped them entering the village and Freyberg organised half his men ready to advance when the covering barrage lifted.

But Shute refused to let the barrage lift because he knew the bigger picture. While Gilliland's and Freyberg's two groups had reached the second objective, the rest of the division was scattered between no man's land and the first objective. And he had no reserves left.

Three hours later, the HAC commander was ordered to send two companies forward to Freyberg but he refused because the mist had lifted and the river bank was under machine-gun fire. All the men could do was consolidate their position and make contact with the 1/1st Cambridge across the river by Beaucourt Mill.[306]

At noon Shute had a change of heart and he ordered a bombardment of the German reserve line. But 188 Brigade was not ready when the artillery lifted twenty minutes later. The same happened at 3.45pm because Shute was not giving his infantry time to prepare. By evening he finally knew the situation on his front: 188 Brigade was in touch with 51st Division while 189 Brigade and 190 Brigade were in Station Alley and along the first objective. Gilliland had also joined Colonel Freyberg's mixed force in front of the second objective. But there were still groups of Germans in the trenches behind 63rd Division's front lines.

Shute wanted to press on the following morning and had asked for six tanks to secure a breakthrough. Although 111 Brigade[307] was also sent forward, it took all night for it to move over the rough terrain. There was also confusion over the orders and the 13th KRRC reinforced Freyberg's position rather than deploying ready to attack.

II Corps

Major General Gerald Cuthbert's 39th Division would advance north along the steep slopes overlooking the east bank of the Ancre. The plan was for 117 and 118 Brigades to seize the Hansa Line opposite Beaucourt while General Bridges' 19th Division would advance from Stuff Trench to the Hansa Line.

39th Division, the Hansa Line

The plan was for 117 Brigade to advance later than the brigades either side, giving 63rd Division time to deal with the German machine-guns across the River Ancre. Twelve 18-pounder field guns kept the trenches in front of St Pierre Divion covered until the 16th Sherwood Foresters advanced from Mill Road at 6.15am. Three tanks were due to advance to Strasbourg Trench but one broke down and one ditched. The third lost its infantry escort[308] and then ditched in the German trenches, leaving the Foresters to advance to Strasbourg Trench alone.

Two companies took many Germans by surprise in the dug outs along the river bank and guards waited by the entrances until the moppers-up arrived. A third Sherwood company then advanced across the slope but Captain Plimpton's 4th/5th Black Watch company drifted into its path and joined the attack on St Pierre Divion. St Pierre Divion was cleared by 7.40am with many prisoners, including a battalion headquarters. Brigadier

---

306 From 39th Division, II Corps.
307 From 37th Division.
308 Infantry had been detailed to guide the tanks around shell holes and across trenches.

General Oldman then sent the 17th Sherwood Foresters forward to secure the hamlet and Mill Lane Trench beyond.

All four of 118 Brigade's battalions formed up on the heights above the River Ancre. As we have seen, the 4th/5th Black Watch drifted down the steep slope towards Pierre Divion. The 1/6th Cheshires lost the barrage in the mist and Captain Kirk and Captain Innes were killed. The battalion adjutant, Lieutenant Naden, reorganised the troops but it took a long time to clear the Strasbourg Line. The 1/1st Cambridgeshire's left hand companies also lost their way in the fog and they reorganized before advancing under fire from the Strasbourg Line. They reached Mill Trench by 10am and established an outpost at Beaucourt mill on the river bank.[309] The right hand companies and the 1/1st Hertfords advanced from Schwaben Redoubt and cleared the Hansa Line by 7.30am, capturing 150 prisoners and four machine-guns. The swift advance by 118 Brigade had forced many Germans into the Ancre valley where they were trapped by the flooded river.

While the Cheshires and Cambridgeshires consolidated Mill Lane, Brigadier General Finch-Hatton sent the 7th Loyal North Lancashires forward to help the Hertfords dig a new trench 50 metres in front of the Hansa Line. He also sent the 14th Hampshires[310] forward to mop up and look after the 1,300 prisoners; 'the majority hardly offered any resistance, their tails were right between their legs'. The final attack of the day at 6.45pm captured the strongpoint at the junction of Mill Road and the Hansa Line.

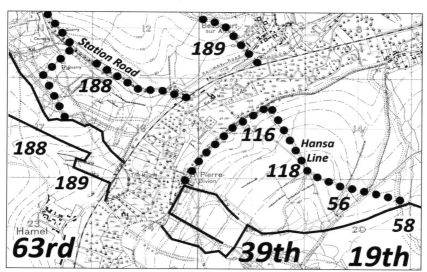

13 November, V Corps: 63rd Division advanced as far as Beaucourt on the west bank of the River Ancre while 39th Division secured the Hansa Line.

309 They met men from the 63rd Division advancing on Beaucourt village later.
310 From 116 Brigade in the Schwaben Redoubt.

19th Division, the Hansa Line

Brigadier General Rowley posted eight machine-gun teams in no man's land to cover 56 Brigade's advance from Stuff Trench. Captain Bennett's company of the Loyals took the Germans by surprise but the rest moved off late and they advanced too far in the mist; they were withdrawn to the correct line by 8.15am. An 18-pounder battery caught the Germans as they emerged from their dug-outs in the sunken road called Lucky Way and then the 7th East Lancashires cleared them out. When the mist cleared around noon, machine-gun fire threatened the North Lancashire's position so a 7th King's Own company was sent forward to reinforce them.

In 58 Brigade's sector the 6th Wiltshires were unable to reach Stump Road but they dug in east of Lucky Way, having captured 150 prisoners. The Germans must have been severely disrupted by 19th Division's attack because the barrage had been erratic and no counter-attacks were made.

Summary

While Gough was only partly satisfied with progress, there was a chance V Corps could take its objectives the following morning. His orders called for 2nd and 51st Divisions to capture Munich Trench and then Frankfurt Trench; 63rd Division would take Beaucourt Trench and then move through Beaucourt village to capture Muck Trench. Zero hour was timed for 6.20am and mist was expected again.

FIFTH ARMY, 14 NOVEMBER

V Corps

2nd Division, Redan Ridge

The covering barrage hit 99 Brigade as it assembled in front of Beaumont Trench and then moved forward through the thick mist. On the left, Second Lieutenants Astley and Stoneham led the 1st Berkshires into Munich Trench but 'hardly enough' men found their way into Lager Alley and Serre Trench. The 1st KRRC drifted right into Leave Avenue but they soon realised their mistake; later attempts to capture Munich Trench failed. Both battalions later fell back to Wagon Road while the 22nd Royal Fusiliers established a flank from the Quadrilateral to Lager Alley.

The 11th Royal Warwicks and 6th Bedfords attacked Frankfurt Trench at 2.45pm only to be stopped by machine-gun fire from Munich Trench; they had to withdraw to Wagon Road.

51st Division, Munich Trench

The orders for 152 Brigade's attack arrived too late for the 1/7th Argylls[311] to

---

311 Attached from 154 Brigade.

take part at 6.20am while the 1/9th Royal Scots' company failed to bomb along Leave Avenue. When the Argylls patrols reported only a few Germans in Munich Trench, a company from each battalion charged the south end at 7.30am. They were later forced out by a combination of British and German artillery fire. The Scots dug a trench overnight called New Munich Trench only to find the Germans had abandoned Munich Trench the following morning.

63rd Division, Beaucourt

The 63rd Division was going to renew its attack along the west bank of the Ancre by making a staggered advance; 111 Brigade[312] would advance from Station Road while 190 Brigade would advance from Beaucourt Trench, 1,000 metres in front.

At 6.20am the 13th Rifle Brigade and part of the 13th Royal Fusiliers advanced while the rest of the 13th Royal Fusiliers extended the line of 13th KRRC.[313] But the men were disorientated by the mist and machine-gun fire stopped them in front of Beaucourt Trench. They eventually cleared it by 7.45am and then the Rifle Brigade bombed west towards Leave Avenue, in search of 51st Division's troops.

Near the river, 400 men of the HAC and eighty men of 7th Royal Fusiliers entered Beaucourt from the south-east while Captain Stocks and Lieutenant Hawkins led the 13th KRRC into the western side of the village. Between them they cleared the ruins by 10.30am, taking around 500 prisoners. Freyberg played a large part in making sure the attack was successful and he was awarded the Victoria Cross.

Three tanks had been sent forward at first light, but one was disabled and a second ditched in no man's land. While the third tank ditched beyond the front trench it continued to fire its 6-pounder guns, inciting 400 prisoners to surrender to the 10th Dublin Fusiliers.[314] They were not the only ones to have success mopping up; the Howe Battalion[315] found 200 Germans hiding in dug-outs along Station Road.

On hearing Beaucourt had been taken, the 13th Rifle Brigade and 13th Royal Fusiliers[316] cleared Beaucourt Trench but the Rifle Brigade still could not contact 51st Division in Leave Avenue. V Corps and II Corps artillery stopped German infantry massing for a counter-attack. Later that evening the 13th KRRC and the HAC secured Beaucourt with the help of the 14th Worcesters.[317]

II Corps

19th Division

Across the river the only activity were two raids made by 19th Division.

---

312 37th Division.
313 111 Brigade.
314 109 Brigade.
315 188 Brigade.
316 Both 111 Brigade
317 The divisional pioneers.

Wire stopped the 7th South Lancashires[318] reaching Lucky Way while the 9th Welsh[319] entered Stump Road. During the night 19th Division relieved 39th Division along the Hansa Line.

15 November
V Corps

The 2nd and 51st Divisions launched a combined attack east of Beaumont Hamel at 9am in appalling conditions as wind drove sleet across the battlefield.

2nd Division, Munich Trench

The 22nd Royal Fusiliers[320] strengthened the Quadrilateral on the left but 112 Brigade from 37th Division made the main attack because 99 Brigade was too weak. The two tanks allocated to the attack ditched in the mud while the 8th East Lancashires and 10th Loyal North Lancashires lost their way in the mist and could not reach Munich Trench.

51st Division, Frankfurt Trench

Two 1/7th Argylls companies were hit by their own covering barrage as they advanced from New Munich Trench. While a few men reached Frankfurt Trench they had to withdraw later.

37th Division, Beaucourt

The 37th Division started relieving 63rd Division and 13th Rifle Brigade[321] bombed along Beaucourt Trench, linking up with 51st Division in Munich Trench around 10am. Meanwhile, 63 Brigade discovered the Germans had abandoned Muck and Railway Trenches north-west of Beaucourt; Muck Trench lived up to its name because deep mud made it impassable.

16 November

The 32nd Division relieved 2nd Division on Redan Ridge and linked up with 51st Division in New Munich Trench. Then 37th Division improved its line north-west of Beaucourt as the 10th Royal Fusiliers and 13th KRRC[322] established a line along Railway Trench and Muck Trench. North-east of the village 21st Division also improved its position when the 8th Somersets[323] advanced along Ancre Trench towards Bois d'Hollande during the night.

II Corps

The Germans made three attempts to retake Schwaben Redoubt on 16 November, two of them with flame-throwers; they were all stopped.

---

318 56 Brigade.
319 58 Brigade.
320 99 Brigade.
321 111 Brigade
322 Both 111 Brigade.
323 63 Brigade.

FIFTH ARMY, 18 AND 19 NOVEMBER

Early on 15 November Kiggell told Gough that Haig did not want any more attacks but when Gough spoke to his two corps commanders, Fanshawe and Jacob, they agreed 'all ranks were keen to attack again', weather permitting. Although Kiggell convinced Haig to let Fifth Army have another go, Gough's outlook changed after hearing 2nd and 51st Divisions had failed to capture Munich and Frankfurt Trenches. V Corps had no men left to attack Redan Ridge. So the new plan was for V Corps to push along the west bank of the Ancre while II Corps advanced towards Grandcourt on 18 November.

The first snow of the winter fell during the night, briefly hiding the horrors of the battlefield. But it had turned to sleet by zero hour, set for 6.10am, and the troops struggled to find their way forward in the poor visibility.

V Corps

32nd Division, Munich Trench

The objective for 14 Brigade was to establish a north-facing flank but the 15th Highland Light Infantry failed to bomb along Ten Tree Alley, only clearing a few trenches around the Quadrilateral. The 2nd Manchesters entered Lager Alley before zero hour and Captain Gwyther's company followed Serre Trench as far as the village. But they had missed a large dug-out in the mist and the Germans emerged, cutting them off. Although surrounded, they refused to surrender and fought to the last man; 'the place was found afterwards with the bodies all grouped together'.

In 97 Brigade's sector, the 2nd KOYLI's left company reached the junction of Lager Alley and Munich Trench and moved down the hill to meet 14 Brigade on its left. But the right company was pinned down in front of Munich Trench and had to wait until dusk before it could withdraw. The 16th Highland Light Infantry's left crossed Munich Trench and reached Frankfurt Trench, near its junction with Lager Alley but the right of the battalion and the 17th Highland Light Infantry were stopped by machine-gun fire. The Highlanders had to abandon their isolated position but few made it back alive.

37th Division, Muck Trench

While there was no formal attack around Beaucourt, 37th Division tried to improve its position. In 110 Brigade's sector the 10th Royal Fusiliers bombed to the junction of Frankfurt Trench and Leave Avenue while the

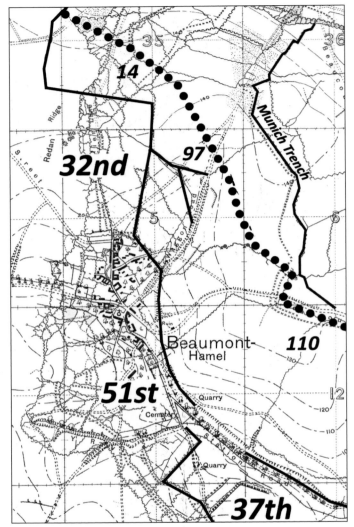

14-18 November, VIII Corps: All three divisions struggled through the mud as they tried to capture Munich Trench.

13th KRRC advanced along Railway Trench. Brigadier General Hill's 63 Brigade also improved its situation around Bois d'Hollande while the 8th Somersets and 4th Middlesex cleared Puisieux Trench, meeting men of 19th Division on the Ancre.

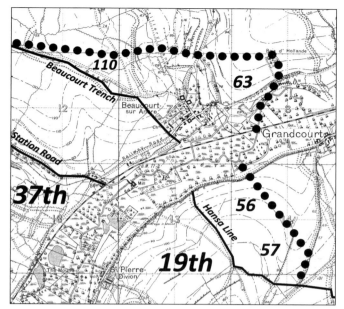

14-19 November, V Corps: While 37th Division was able to advance beyond Beaucourt, 19th Division could not reach Grandcourt.

II Corps

19th Division, Battery Valley

Two 7th South Lancashire companies advanced along the Grandcourt road in 56 Brigade's sector. While one platoon made contact with the troops in Beaucourt across the river, the rest cleared dug-outs lining an embankment on west side of Grandcourt. One 7th East Lancashire company met V Corps troops along the railway line but machine-guns in Grandcourt stopped the other reaching Baillescourt Farm, north of the village.

Meanwhile 57 Brigade advanced across Battery Valley heading for the Grandcourt Line, south of the village. The 8th Gloucesters crossed the Grandcourt Line and entered the western end of the village, meeting up with the South Lancashires. The 10th Royal Warwicks were briefly disorientated in the sleet but while the left company advanced into Grandcourt, the right company was stopped by a wire entanglement. The 8th North Staffords also crossed the Grandcourt Line next to Stump Road and headed into the village where they were cut off; only seventy escaped. A last minute attempt by the 9th Cheshires to capture Desire Trench on the right failed because they had not had time to reconnoitre the ground.

18th Division, Desire Trench

All four of 55 Brigade's battalions were ordered to advance from Regina Trench to Desire Trench. The 7th Queen's and the 7th Buffs disappeared into the blizzard and although seven runners were sent out to find them, it was a long time before anything was heard. The Queen's detachment detailed to clear Stump Road had been annihilated but the rest of the battalion had reached Desire Trench. The Buffs were pinned down in no man's land until the 7th Queen's Own captured their objective. The 8th East Surreys captured their objective, linking with the Canadians to their right.

When General Maxse learnt that 19th Division had failed to clear the ground west of Stump Road, he authorised the 7th Queen's and the 7th Buffs to withdraw to Regina Trench. A trench was dug connecting Desire Trench back to Regina Trench during the night.

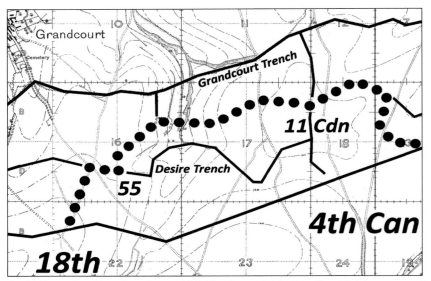

14-19 November, Canadian Corps: 18th Division and 4th Canadian Division captured the Desire Trenches and could have taken Grandcourt Trench.

Canadian Corps

4th Canadian Division, Desire Trench and Desire Support

All four of 11 Brigade's battalions were in Regina Trench; 38th Battalion, 87th Battalion and 54th Battalion all crossed Desire Trench and captured Desire Support beyond. Only the 75th Battalion became disorientated in the sleet and crossed the Pys road by mistake. While 44th and 47th Battalions reinforced the front, patrols pushed forward as far as Grandcourt Trench.

Although the division was in a position to take Grandcourt Trench, it would have left it in an exposed salient so Brigadier General Odlum ordered his patrols to withdraw. They refused and, 'though bothered by the British barrage', they did not leave Grandcourt Trench until the following morning.

General Hughes' 10 Brigade faced Desire Trench and Desire Support Trench east of the Pys road. A smoke barrage on the open right flank spread across the brigade front, further reducing visibility. The 50th Battalion reached Desire Support Trench but the 46th Battalion was stopped by machine-gun fire on the right. The failure of 11 Brigade to clear the trench astride the Pys Road meant 50th Battalion had to withdraw later. Despite varied fortunes, General Watson's men had captured 620 prisoners.

II Corps, 19 November

19th Division, Battery Valley

The 7th South Lancashires stopped a counter-attack at the western end of Grandcourt but the position was difficult to support because it backed onto Battery Valley, so a new trench had to be dug across the valley. The Warwicks, Gloucesters, South Lancashires and East Lancashires later withdrew to the trench but the Germans in the Grandcourt Line still overlooked them. An attempt by the 10th Royal Fusiliers to take the vantage point during the afternoon failed.

FOURTH ARMY, 14 NOVEMBER

XV Corps

Just before dawn on 14 November XV Corps had made one final attack on the Gird Line.

50th Division, Hook Sap

In 149 Brigade's sector 1/7th Northumberland Fusiliers came under fire from Butte Trench as they advanced towards Hook Sap. The assault troops never returned and the rest of the battalion had to fight off counter-attacks. Detachments of 1/4th and 1/5th Northumberland Fusiliers failed to reach Hook Sap at midnight.

2nd Australian Division

In 5 Brigade's sector 19th Battalion found Gird Support was flooded, so they withdrew to Gird Trench. In 7 Brigade's sector, 25th and 26th Battalions were stopped by machine-gun fire as they advanced towards the south side of the Maze. A later attack at 4.45pm by 5 Brigade against the west side of the Maze also failed.

Conclusions

So as the 142-day Somme campaign came to a close, GHQ had to concede it had not been able to break the German line or break German morale. Only time would tell who had suffered the most in the war of attrition adopted later in the campaign. While the British dug in for the winter, the Germans prepared a new line of defence, called the Hindenburg Line. The following spring they withdrew up to fifteen miles along a sixty-mile front to their new position, giving up ground so they could conserve reserves.

The Somme did not end the war, there were many more battles to come; the offensive battles at Arras, Messines and Ypres in 1917 and then the German offensives in the spring of 1918. Finally the British would advance alongside their old ally France and a new one, the United States, in the Hundred Days Campaign which culminated in the Armistice.

But while the Somme campaign did not end in a victory for the Allies, as Haig wanted, it did change the way the British Army waged war. There are major differences between the way offensives were planned and executed on 1 July and on 13 November and all attacks in between. The changes were part of the Army's learning curve; a curve which climbed steeply between the summer of 1916 and the Armistice.

Before 1 July, GHQ had little battle experience to look back on, particularly experience of making successful attacks. Most of the 1914 and the early 1915 campaigns had been defensive battles; the few offensive battles only lasted a few days. While Haig, Gough and Rawlinson had all played a part in the Battle of Loos in the autumn of 1915, the main battle had only lasted three days and there had been many problems. There had also been no chance to test any theories on how to conduct a successful offensive. The Somme changed all that.

The three generals and their subordinates had to understand how to control a battle as part of a sustained campaign, including the control of ammunition supply, the reliance on replacement men and how to co-ordinate offensives with the French.

The generals and their staffs also had to understand command and control as they learned to appreciate time and understand how long everything took. Many mistakes were made in July by underestimating how long it took to move troops. Snap decisions to launch attacks often resulted in failure because the men did not have time to deploy. Ironically launching surprise attacks became acceptable after it was proved attacks made without a barrage, due to failures in timings, could succeed. In September General Maxse of the 18th Division suggested six hours was the minimum amount of time required to organise the infantry and artillery elements of an attack.

The generals also had the opportunity to learn the exacting art of attack, albeit through trial and error. They experimented with many theories on the best time to set zero hour, ranging from the disastrous post dawn attack on 1 July to the successful pre-dawn attack only two weeks later; and all hours in between. Many attacks were carried out at night as the generals became more confident about their men's abilities to deploy and advance in the dark. Maxse preferred late afternoon attacks, leaving only three hours of daylight before dusk. This left the German artillery blind while reinforcements and ammunition were brought forward.

The generals also tried many different types of barrage, ranging from prolonged destructive, to last minute suppressive, to none at all. While they experimented with infantry and artillery co-ordination by using flares and by changing the artillery ammunition, they were often unreliable. They finally chose to use sound during the final battle along the Ancre, so they could co-ordinate the barrage and the advance at night or during poor visibility. It was a simple and reliable system in which the infantry were given a five-minute warning when the guns stopped. They then advanced when the guns fired at twice the normal rate of fire.They occasionally used aerial artillery spotters to help in difficult situations.

The creeping barrage was a major innovation introduced in July and the degree of sophistication increased rapidly during the campaign. The speed of the barrage was altered to suit the terrain and weather conditions through trial and error. Tricks were also introduced into the speed and direction of the creep to catch the Germans out.

One major change to the face of warfare was the introduction of the tank. Some say it was good idea to deploy tanks on 15 September, so problems could be discovered and solutions could be worked out. Others believed it was a bad idea because it exposed the secret weapon to the Germans, giving them the opportunity to devise counter measures. They wanted to wait until the spring when there would have been more tanks available. The problem was it would have been increasingly difficult to keep a growing number of tanks a secret and spies would have eventually leaked information about the new weapon to Germany.

While infantry and tank co-ordination had a shaky start, many problems, both in the workshop and on the battlefield were ironed out either during or as a result of the Somme campaign. By the spring of 1917 tanks were a common sight around Arras and although they struggled in the Flanders mud in the autumn, they proved the effort had been worthwhile during the Battle of Cambrai in November. They also made a valuable contribution to the Hundred Days Offensive.

As a footnote to the argument over whether tanks should or should not have been used on 15 September, the Germans did not think too much about them. If they had had a greater success, surely the German High Command would have called for the deployment of their own tank.[324] Or at least made greater efforts to introduce anti-tank measures.

It became harder to wage war as the campaign went on for several reasons. The artillery, particularly the heavy guns, started to wear out making it difficult to fire accurate barrages to support the infantry. The infantry battalions lost their *esprit de corps* due to the need to replace casualties with new recruits or men who had recovered from injuries. One major mistake made was to send convalesced men to low strength battalions rather than their original units. It meant they were not returning to the friends they had served with and it took time to integrate them into units. Heavy losses amongst the junior officers, the lieutenants and captains who led their men over the top, were the hardest to cover. It took time before an officer gained the battlefield experience required to make him effective and they rarely had time; again and again battalions lost most of their junior officers in their first engagement.

The deteriorating weather in October also introduced many problems which made the planning and execution of attacks harder. Cloud and mist restricted ground observers and grounded air observers, interfering with the artillery bombardments. Prolonged rain created the infamous Somme mud, turning the battlefield into a quagmire which interfered with everything. As autumn turned to winter the drop in temperatures and deteriorating weather made everything more difficult, including just staying alive.

Casualties in any conflict are high. When you engage large armies for prolonged periods of time, like they did in 1916 they will be much higher. The Official History cites 419,654 British and Empire casualties up to the end of November and although this figure is difficult to comprehend, some believe it has been massaged down.

The French records 154,446 casualties for its Sixth Army which fought on the north bank of the Somme, on Fourth Army's right flank. It also records another 48,131 for its Tenth Army which fought south of the river. The German figures are more difficult to estimate. Numbers range from a conservative 400,000 to the 680,000 quoted in the British Official History. Others give different figures and Winston Churchill quotes 513,279

---

324 While the Germans only produced and deployed a few cumbersome A7V tanks in 1918 they did use captured British tanks.

British casualties, although he does include those lost holding the line in other sectors, casualties referred to by the repulsive term 'trench wastage'. Churchill also quotes the German losses as 630,192.

Visitors to the battlefield today will find quiet villages surrounded by fields and farms. There are many cemeteries, some small and personal, others large and imposing. They will also find memorials, ranging from Sir Edwin Lutyen's huge Thiepval Memorial to the missing, down to tiny battalion and individual memorials. But the cemeteries and memorials give us a skewed vision of the battlefield if we use them to guide us round. Most of the smaller ones are close to the early July battles, particularly 1 July, and the traveller is constantly reminded of this fateful day. Yet as the narrative has shown far more activity went on in the later weeks around villages such as Courcelette, Le Sars, Lesboeufs and Gueudecourt. Here there were repeated attacks and, more often than not, successful attacks. Yet the dead from these autumn offensives have been grouped into the huge concentration cemeteries, making it hard to follow the events on the ground.

The bleakness of the undulating terrain in the north-east part of the battlefield, does not help to entice the traveller to this area either. I encourage everyone to spread their wings a little further and use the maps in the book to guide them around the later battles.

Finally, I once had a discussion about how we should remember the men of 1916. Should we pity them for the conditions they endured and the sacrifices they made? Or should we admire them for fighting hard, not giving up and doing the best they could with the tools they had. They were definitely men of their era, tough men who were used to working long hours in factories, down mines and on farms at a time when health and safety was in its infancy. I am sure they complained about their lot, moaned about the food and lack of drink and women, and grumbled about their officers. But they also adapted to the changing face of warfare, adjusting to new tactics and striving to improve how they fought.

They also never gave up. They kept climbing out of their trenches, kept crawling across no man's land in silence in the darkness and kept advancing as close to the creeping barrages as they dared before charging the enemy trench. And they did so because they knew it was the best way to survive. After researching this book I subscribe to the latter view; I admire the men of 1916 and all they achieved. I hope you do too, I believe they would thank you for that.

Andrew Rawson, 2014

Somme Reading List

Command and Tactics on the Somme

Command and Control on the Western Front, Gary Sheffield and Dan Todman, (Spellmount, 2007)

Battle Tactics of the Western Front, Paddy Griffith (Yale University Press, 1996)

The Chief: Douglas Haig and the British Army, Gary Sheffield (Aurum, 2012)

Command on the Western Front: The Military Career of Sir Henry Rawlinson, Robin Prior and Trevor Wilson (Leo Cooper) 2004

Campaign Histories

Somme, Lyn MacDonald (Penguin, 2013)

The First Day on the Somme, Martin Middlebrook, (Penguin, 2006)

Somme Mud, E.P.F Lynch (Bantam, 2008)

Bloody Victory: The Sacrifice on the Somme, William Philpott (Abacus, 2010)

The Somme, Peter Hart (Phoenix, 2008)

The Somme, Robin Prior and T. Wilson (Yale University Press, 2006)

Somme: The Heroism and Horror of War, Martin Gilbert (John Murray, 2006)

The Somme: A New History, Gary Sheffield (Cassell, 2004)

The Battles of the Somme, Martin Marix Evans (W&N, 6 Jul 1998)

The Somme: The Day-by-day Account, Chris McCarthy (Caxton Editions, 2000)

The Somme: France 1916, Chris McNab (Pitkin, 2010)

The Hell They Called High Wood: The Somme 1916, Norman Terry (Pen and Sword, 2009)

Through German Eyes: The British and the Somme 1916, Christopher Duffy (Pen and Sword, 2007)

Pals on the Somme, Roni Wilkinson, (Pen and Sword, 2008)

Transcriptions of War Diaries

Slaughter on the Somme, War Diaries 1 July, John Grehan and Martin Mace, (Pen and Sword, 2013)

Tracing British Battalions on the Somme, Ray Westlake (Pen and Sword, 2009)

Images

The Somme (Panoramas), Peter Barton (Constable, 2011)

Great Push on the Somme, Images of War, William Langford (Pen and Sword, 2009)

The Germans on the Somme, Images of War, David Bilton, (Pen and Sword, 2009)

Visiting the Battlefield

Holt's Pocket Battlefield Guide to the Somme, Tonie Holt and Valmai Holt (Pen and Sword, 2006)

The Somme Battlefields: A Comprehensive Guide from Crecy to the Two World Wars, Martin Middlebrook and Mary Middlebrook (Penguin, 1994)

Pen and Sword Battleground Series

Walking the Somme, Paul Reed

Mametz Wood, Michael Renshaw

Gommecourt, Nigel Cave

Bazentin Ridge, Edward Hancock

Serre, Jack Horsfall and Nigel Cave

Pozières, Graham Keech

Redan Ridge, Michael Renshaw

Guillemont, Michael Stedman

Beaumont Hamel, Nigel Cave

Combles, Paul Reed

Thiepval, Michael Stedman

Courcelette, Paul Reed

La Boiselle and Ovillers, Michael Stedman

Delville Wood, Nigel Cave

Fricourt-Mametz, Michael Stedman

Flers and Gueudecourt, Trevor Pidgeon

Montauban, Graham Maddocks

Fromelles (Third Army, 19/20 July), Peter Pederson

Index